2005-2006 Supplement

National Security Law

Third Edition

Stephen Dycus
Professor of Law
Vermont Law School

Arthur L. Berney
Professor of Law, Emeritus
Boston College

William C. Banks
Laura J. and L. Douglas Meredith Professor
Syracuse University

Peter Raven-Hansen
Glen Earl Weston Research Professor of Law
George Washington University

111 Eighth Avenue, New York, NY 10011
www.aspenpublishers.com

© 2005 Stephen Dycus, William C. Banks, and Peter Raven-Hansen

All rights reserved. No part of this publication may be reproduced or transmitted in any form or by any means, electronic or mechanical, including photocopy, recording, or any information storage and retrieval system, without permission in writing from the publisher. Requests for permission to make copies of any part of this publication should be mailed to:

Aspen Publishers
Attn: Permissions Department
111 Eighth Avenue, 7th Floor
New York, NY 10011-5201

Printed in the United State of America

1 2 3 4 5 6 7 8 9 0

ISBN 0-7355-5861-2

Library of Congress Cataloging-in-Publication Data

National security law / Stephen Dycus . . . [et al.] – 3rd ed.
    p. cm.
    Includes index.
    ISBN 0-7355-2823-3 (casebook)
    ISBN 0-7355-5861-2 (supplement)
    1. National security – Law and legislation – United States.
        1. Dycus, Stephen

KF4651.N377 2002
343.73'01 – dc21   2001058379

EDITORIAL ADVISORS

Erwin Chemerinsky
Alston & Bird Professor of Law
Duke University School of Law

Richard A. Epstein
James Parker Hall Distinguished Service Professor of Law
University of Chicago
Peter and Kirsten Bedford Senior Fellow
The Hoover Institution
Stanford University

Ronald J. Gilson
Charles J. Meyers Professor of Law and Business
Stanford University
Marc and Eva Stern Professor of Law and Business
Columbia University

James E. Krier
Earl Warren DeLano Professor of Law
University of Michigan

Richard K. Neumann, Jr.
Professor of Law
Hofstra University School of Law

Kent D. Syverud
Dean and Garner Anthony Professor
Vanderbilt University Law School

Elizabeth Warren
Leo Gottlieb Professor of Law
Harvard University

EMERITUS EDITORIAL ADVISORS

Geoffrey C. Hazard, Jr.
Trustee Professor of Law
University of Pennsylvania
Distinguished Professor of Law
Hastings College of the Law, University of California

Bernard Wolfman
Fessenden Professor of Law
Harvard University

E. Allan Farnsworth
On January 31, 2005, Aspen Publishers lost a great author, colleague, and friend with the death of E. Allan Farnsworth, the Alfred McCormack Professor of Law at Columbia Law School and author of the seminal student treatise, Contracts, Fourth Edition, by Aspen Publishers.

About Aspen Publishers

Aspen Publishers, headquartered in New York City, is a leading information provider for attorneys, business professionals, and law students. Written by preeminent authorities, our products consist of analytical and practical information covering both U.S. and international topics. We publish in the full range of formats, including updated manuals, books, periodicals, CDs, and online products.

Our proprietary content is complemented by 2,500 legal databases, containing over 11 million documents, available through our Loislaw division. Aspen Publishers also offers a wide range of topical legal and business databases linked to Loislaw's primary material. Our mission is to provide accurate, timely, and authoritative content in easily accessible formats, supported by unmatched customer care.

To order any Aspen Publishers title, go to *www.aspenpublishers.com* or call 1-800-638-8437.

To reinstate your manual update service, call 1-800-638-8437.

For more information on Loislaw products, go to *www.loislaw.com* or call 1-800-364-2512.

For Customer Care issues, e-mail CustomerCare@aspenpublishers.com; call 1-800-234-1660; or fax 1-800-901-9075.

Aspen Publishers
a Wolters Kluwer business

Contents

Preface   *xi*
Table of Cases   *xiii*

Chapter 4. The President's National Security Powers   1

A. Foreign Relations Powers   1
D. Executive Privilege   3

Chapter 7. The Domestic Effect of International Law   5

A. Treaties and Agreements   5
C. The Domestic Legal Effect of Customary International Law and *Jus Cogens*   6

Chapter 8. General War   7

E. War Against Iraq – 2003   7
        Authorization for Use of Military Force Against Iraq Resolution of 2002   7
        Notes and Questions   12

Contents

Chapter 10. Intelligence Operations — 19

C. Problems in the Reform of Intelligence Operations — 19
   2. Executive Branch Reforms — 19
F. The Privatization of Intelligence Operations — 20
   2. Dirty Assets — 20
G. Intelligence Reorganization — 21
   1. An Intelligence Czar? — 22
   2. The New Structure — 24
      Notes and Questions — 26

Chapter 11. Organizing for Counterterrorism: An Overview — 31

A. Countering Terrorism at Home and Abroad — 31
   1. Defining the Terrorist Threat — 31
      a. What Is Terrorism? — 31
         United States v. Yousef — 31
         People's Mojahedin Organization of Iran v. Department of State — 34
         Notes and Questions — 38
   2. Planning for Homeland Security — 38

Chapter 12. Investigating Terrorism and Other National Security Threats — 39

B. The Fourth Amendment Framework — 39
   5. Interrogation and Treatment of Detainees Held Abroad in the "War on Terrorism" — 39
      Application of Treaties and Laws to Al Qaeda and Taliban Detainees — 45
      Decision re Application of the Geneva Convention to the Conflict with Al Qaeda and the Taliban — 52

	Letter of Attorney General John Ashcroft to President George W. Bush	56
	Comments on Your Paper on the Geneva Convention	58
	Working Group Report on Detainee Interrogations	59
	Counter-Resistance Techniques in the War on Terrorism	69
	Notes and Questions	73
6.	Extraordinary Rendition	95
	Arar v. Ashcroft (Complaint)	95
	Notes and Questions	100
C.	Congressional Authority for Surveillance	102
	In re: Sealed Case No. 02-001, 02-002	105
	Notes and Questions	118
	Doe v. Ashcroft	122
	Notes and Questions	143
D.	Executive Authority for National Security Investigations	149
1.	Initiating Investigation	149
	Executive Order No. 12,333	150
	Domestic Security Guidelines	152
	National Security Investigations Guidelines	157
	Notes and Questions	165
4.	Balancing Privacy and Security	172
	Notes and Questions	174
E.	Profiling Suspects for Investigation	175
F.	Preventive Detention	176
	Office of the Inspector General, Department of Justice, The September 11 Detainees	176

Chapter 13. Consequence Management: When the Worst Happens   *185*

B.	Who's in Charge? Taking Command of the Situation	185
1.	Assigning Lead Agency Responsibility	185
	d. The Department of Homeland Security	185
	Notes and Questions	193
2.	Addressing Medical Emergencies	195

Contents

    a. Case Study: A Plague on Your City   195
    b. Statutory and Regulatory Authority   195
    c. Civil Liberties Implications   197
   3. The Role of the Armed Forces   199
    a. The Military in American Society   199
    b. Military Responsibility for "Homeland Security"   202
 C. Wartime Detention and Suspension of the Writ   203
  1. Detention of Non-Combatants Before 9/11   204
    Alien Enemy Act   204
    Korematsu v. United States   205
    Notes and Questions   205
  2. Suspension of the Writ of Habeas Corpus   205
    Ex parte Milligan   206
    Notes and Questions   207
  3. Detention of Combatants Before 9/11   207
    Ex parte Milligan   207
    Ex parte Quirin   207
    Notes and Questions   207
  4. Detention of U.S. Citizens as Enemy Combatants After 9/11   207
    Hamdi v. Rumsfeld   208
    Order by President George W. Bush to the Secretary of Defense   234
    Padilla v. Rumsfeld   235
    Notes and Questions   246
  5. Detention of Alien Enemy Combatants After 9/11   252
    Military Order of November 13, 2001   252
    Rasul v. Bush   252
    Notes and Questions   263
    In re Guantanamo Detainee Cases   265
    Khalid v. Bush   278
    Notes and Questions   286

Chapter 14. Trying International Terrorists   **289**

A. Criminalizing Sedition, Terrorism, and Support for Terrorism   289
    Notes and Questions   289

	United States v. Al-Arian	292
	Notes and Questions	306
C.	Bringing Them Back Alive: Extradition and Other Rendition	313
D.	Trying Terrorists and Other International Criminals	314
	1. Secret Information in Proceedings Against Terrorists	314
	United States v. Moussaoui	315
	Notes and Questions	325
	2. Trial by Military Commission	330
	Hamdan v. Rumsfeld	334
	Notes and Questions	342

Chapter 15. Public Access to National Security Information   *345*

A.	Executive Order No. 12,958 – Classified National Security Information	345
B.	The Freedom of Information Act	346
	1. The Statutory Text	346
	2. Statutory Exemptions and Judicial Review	346
C.	Other Open Government Laws	348
	1. Presidential Records Act	348
	3. Open Meetings Laws	348
D.	Common Law Right to Know	349
E.	Constitutional Right to Know	350
	Detroit Free Press v. Ashcroft	352
	North Jersey Media Group, Inc. v. Ashcroft	368
	Notes and Questions	379
F.	Protecting "State Secrets" in Civil Litigation	382
	Tenet v. Doe	383
	Notes and Questions	387

Preface

Just two summers ago, we wrote in our first annual Supplement to the third edition of our casebook that "the executive branch has predictably become the 'first responder' [to the terrorist threat] at the federal level, . . . Congress has followed at a short distance, . . . and [t]he courts have followed reluctantly at a greater distance, waiting until the cases come to them, but sometimes prolonging the wait by declining on various grounds to become involved."

The wait is over. Congress and the courts are rapidly catching up. This year's Supplement discusses ambitious statutory initiatives in the reorganization of the intelligence community, homeland defense, and surveillance authority, as well as more new national security cases than had been decided in many years preceding 9/11. Indeed, four of the new cases selected for inclusion in this Supplement are presently on appeal, and another was decided literally on the day we finished the manuscript, too late for inclusion. By the time you read this, you will surely have to supplement the Supplement.

Partly as a result, this year's Supplement is approaching book length. We are therefore already preparing a fourth edition of the casebook for publication in 2006. It will not only incorporate updated materials from this Supplement, it will also introduce several brand new chapters and will substantially revise the style and length of the old ones.

These are sure signs of a maturing field of legal study, as well as evidence of its importance and dynamism. They also offer increasing hope of an answer to the National Security Law student's perennial plaint: "What's the black letter?" A black letter outline of National Security Law is still in the far distance, but the outlines of analytic approaches that we have tried to sketch in the first three editions of the casebook and three Supplements are filling in.

In this year's Supplement, we discuss the aftermath of Operation Iraqi Freedom, add a new subchapter on intelligence reorganization, revise and update the rich case study on torture, and add a new section on extraordinary rendition. There are updated materials on surveillance, a new section on investigatory access to electronic communications and transactional records, and updated materials on the Department of

Preface

Homeland Security. We have also included a newly revised subchapter on wartime detention and suspension of the writ (which we hope will make the rapidly evolving and overlapping case law more manageable to teach and understand), the first post-9/11 judicial opinion on trial by military commission, and new materials on the *Totten* doctrine.

One thing has not changed. National Security Law is still the most interesting and exciting course we have ever taught, and it engages students like no other. Whether it is offered as a survey course or as a dedicated Counterterrorism Law course (we and our adapters have used the casebook and Supplement successfully to teach both), it is a daily challenge and a daily connection to the headlines. More fundamentally, it is a unique opportunity to imprint the importance of the rule of law and the applicability of sound legal analysis – even to the life and death decisions that government must make in securing us from terrorists, rogue states, and international criminal gangs.

As always, we are extremely grateful to our adopters, fellow members of the growing National Security Law Section of the Association of American Law Schools, fellow members of the editorial board of the Journal of National Security Law & Policy, fellow casebook authors (our collaborators in building the field), and our many midnight oil-burning friends in the national security community. We also wish to thank our research assistants: Kelly Rich and Stephan Rice at George Washington University Law School; Barbara Anderson and Bill Dorry at Syracuse; and Sara Baynard, Edward Demetriou, Abigail Doolittle, Matthew T. Einstein, Byron W. Kirkpatrick, Robin Longe, Jesse Moorman, Catherine Rawson, Alan Roughton, Sam Schneider, and Emily Wetherell at Vermont Law School. Thanks are due as well to our copy editor, Barbara Rappaport, for her help in preparing this Supplement. Finally, we are grateful to Kathy Yoon, Melody Davies, Peggy Rehberger, and Carol McGeehan of Aspen Publishers for their continued encouragement and support.

Stephen Dycus
William C. Banks
Peter Raven-Hansen

July 31, 2005

Table of Cases

Adebe-Jira v. Negewo, 94
Al-Arian, United States v., 292
All Matters Submitted to the Foreign Intelligence Surveillance Court, In re, 103
Al-Marri v. Hanft, 287, 330
American Civil Liberties Union v. United States, 119
American Historical Assn. v. National Archives and Records Admin., 348
American Insurance Assn. v. Garamendi, 1, 2
Ange v. Bush, 18
Arar v. Ashcroft (Complaint), 95
Awadallah, United States v., 181, 182

Bareford v. General Dynamics Corp., 387
Buckley v. Valeo, 312
Brandenberg v. Ohio, 290
Burnett v. Al Baraka Investment & Development Corp., 388

Center for National Security Studies
 v. United States Dept. of Justice, 184, 347, 349, 380
Chavez v. Martinez, 90
Cheney, In re, 349
Cheney v. United States District Court, 3, 348
Christopher v. Harbury, 20
Clark v. Allen, 5

Dames & Moore v. Regan, 2
Denmore v. Hyung Joon Kim, 179
Dennis v. United States, 289
Detroit Free Press v. Ashcroft, 352
Doe v. Ashcroft, 122
Doe v. Bush, 17
Doe v. Tenet, 388, 389

Edmonds v. United States Dept. of Justice, 388
Ex parte _____. *See* name of party.

Farnsworth Cannon, Inc. v. Grimes, 388
Federal Insurance Co. v. al Qaida, 381
Filartiga v. Peña-Irala, 94

Table of Cases

Fitzgerald v. Penthouse International, Ltd., 388
Flynt v. Rumsfeld, 350

Guantanamo Detainee Cases, In re, 263, **265**, 343
Guong v. United States, 388

Halpern v. United States, 389
Hamdan v. Rumsfeld, 83, 86-87, 286, **334**
Hamdi v. Rumsfeld, 208, 246, 251, 286
Harbury v. Deutch, 20
Herring, In re, 382
Herring v. United States, 383
Humanitarian Law Project v. Ashcroft, 309

In re_____. *See* name of party.
Ingraham v. Wright, 91

Judgment Concerning the Legality of the General Security
  Service's Interrogation Methods, 89

Katz v. United States, 144
Khalid v. Bush, 278, 343
Kielczynski v. U.S. Central Intelligence Agency, 389
Korematsu v. United States, 205, 382

Laird v. Tatum, 200
Lindh, United States v., 309
Loral Corp. v. McDonnell Douglas Corp., 389

M.K.B. v. Warden, 381
Massachusetts v. Laird, 18
McDonnell Douglas Corp. v. United States, 388
Mehinovic v. Vuckovic, 94
Merryman, Ex parte, 205
Miller, United States v., 143
Milligan, Ex parte, 206, 207
Moussaoui, United States v., 315, 381

NAACP v. Alabama ex rel. Patterson, 312
NAACP v. Button, 308
Nixon v. Administrator of General Services, 328
Nixon, United States v., 349
North Jersey Media Group, Inc. v. Ashcroft, 347, **368**

Table of Cases

Odah v. United States, 247

Padilla v. Bush, 248
Padilla v. Hanft, 246
Padilla v. Rumsfeld, 234, 235
Paquete Habana, The, 6
People's Mojahedin Organization of Iran v. Department of State, 34
Prize Cases, 249
Public Citizen v. United States Dept. of Justice, 328

Quirin, Ex parte, 207

Rasul v. Bush, 91, 92, 247, 252
Republic of Ireland v. United Kingdom, 89
Reynolds, United States v., 382
Rumsfeld v. Padilla, 246, 263

Salerno, United States v., 180
Salisbury v. United States, 388
Sattar, United States v., 308, 309, 311
Scales v. United States, 310
Schenck v. United States, 289
Sealed Case No. 02-001, 02-002, In re, 105
Smith v. Maryland, 102, 103, 143
Sosa v. Alvarez-Machain, 6, 94, 313

Tachiaona v. Mugabe, 94
Tenet v. Doe, 383
Tilden v. Tenet, 388
Totten, In re, 387
Trulock v. Lee, 388

Under Seal, In re, 389
United States, In re, 388
United States v. _____. *See* name of party.

Verdugo-Urquidez, United States v., 286
Virginia v. Hicks, 308

Weinberger v. Catholic Action of Hawaii, 388
Willenburg v. Neurauter, 93
Wilson, United States v., 315

Table of Cases

Xuncax v. Gramajo, 94

Yousef, United States v., 31

4

The President's National Security Powers

A. FOREIGN RELATIONS POWERS

Page 70. Add this material after Note 8.

9. *What Counts as Foreign Policy?* In American Insurance Assn. v. Garamendi, 539 U.S. 396 (2003), the Supreme Court struck down a California statute requiring insurance companies to disclose information about insurance policies that they or related companies sold to Europeans during the Holocaust era. There was no federal statute on point. Executive agreements between the United States and Germany, Austria, and France encouraged a voluntary International Commission on Holocaust Era Insurance Claims (ICHEIC) to become the exclusive forum for claims on such policies, but they did not expressly forbid other remedies for claimants. Federal preemption was found on the basis of "interference with the foreign policy those agreements embody." 539 U.S. at 417.

Justice Souter noted for the 5-4 majority that, because of the need for uniformity, state power is preempted by national government policy in the field of foreign relations.

> Nor is there any question generally that there is executive authority to decide what that policy should be. Although the source of the President's power to act in foreign affairs does not enjoy any textual detail, the historical gloss on the "executive Power" vested in Article II of the Constitution has recognized the President's "vast share of responsibility for the conduct of our foreign relations." Youngstown Sheet & Tube Co. v. Sawyer, 343 U.S. 579, 610-611 (1952) (Frankfurter, J., concurring). While Congress holds express authority to regulate public and private dealings with other nations in its war and foreign commerce powers, in

foreign affairs the President has a degree of independent authority to act.

At a more specific level, our cases have recognized that the President has authority to make "executive agreements" with other countries, requiring no ratification by the Senate or approval by Congress, this power having been exercised since the early years of the Republic. . . . Given the fact that the practice goes back over 200 years to the first Presidential administration, and has received congressional acquiescence throughout its history, the conclusion "[t]hat the President's control of foreign relations includes the settlement of claims is indisputable."

Generally, then, valid executive agreements are fit to preempt state law, just as treaties are, and if the agreements here had expressly preempted laws like [the California statute], the issue would be straightforward. But petitioners and the United States as *amicus curiae* both have to acknowledge that the agreements include no preemption clause, and so leave their claim of preemption to rest on asserted interference with the foreign policy those agreements embody. . . .

. . . [However,] the likelihood that state legislation will produce something more than incidental effect in conflict with express foreign policy of the National Government would require preemption of the state law. And . . . it would be reasonable to consider the strength of the state interest, judged by standards of traditional practice, when deciding how serious a conflict must be shown before declaring the state law preempted. Judged by these standards, we think petitioners and the Government have demonstrated a sufficiently clear conflict to require finding preemption here. . . .

. . . [I]t is worth noting that Congress has done nothing to express disapproval of the President's policy. Legislation along the lines of [the California law] has been introduced in Congress repeatedly, but none of the bills has come close to making it into law. In sum, Congress has not acted on the matter addressed here. Given the President's independent authority "in the areas of foreign policy and national security, . . . congressional silence is not to be equated with congressional disapproval." Haig v. Agee, 453 U.S. 280, 291 (1981). [539 U.S. at 414, 420, 430.]

The dissenters complained that no executive agreement mentioned the state's sole concern: public disclosure. *Id.* at 438 (Ginsberg, J., dissenting). They also noted that in cases like Dames & Moore v. Regan, 453 U.S. 654 (1981) (casebook p. 115), the Court gave effect to the express terms of an executive agreement. 539 U.S. at 437-438. Do you think the Court should require a clearer statement of conflicting foreign policy before finding preemption? By relying on inference and implication, has the Court itself effectively become an expositor of foreign policy?

D. EXECUTIVE PRIVILEGE

Page 91. Add the following Note.

5. *Executive Privilege and Discovery Against the Executive.* Does *Nixon* require the executive to make specific claims of executive privilege in order to resist broad-gauged discovery demands in civil litigation? In *Cheney v. United States District Court*, 542 U.S. 367, 124 S. Ct. 2576 (2004), the plaintiffs had made sweeping requests for production of documents reflecting the composition of and communications by the Vice President's National Energy Policy task force. The government resisted these demands as overbroad and unconstitutional, without asserting specific claims of executive privilege. A divided Supreme Court held that it did not have to invoke the privilege, despite *Nixon*. *Nixon*, the Court reasoned, involved criminal, not civil, litigation. "The need for information for use in civil cases, while far from negligible, does not share the urgency or significance of the criminal subpoena requests in *Nixon*." *Id.* at 2589. Withholding the information "does not hamper another branch's ability to perform its 'essential functions' in quite the same way." *Id.* Furthermore, the Court said, in *Nixon* the special prosecutor had already met the exacting standards for a criminal subpoena; a civil litigant has no comparable burden. *Id.* at 2590. "In these circumstances, *Nixon* does not require the Executive Branch to bear the onus of critiquing the unacceptable discovery requests line by line." *Id.* at 2591.

What onus *does* the executive bear in civil discovery after *Cheney*? The Court was vague, admonishing district courts "to explore other avenues, short of forcing the Executive to invoke privilege, when they are asked to enforce against the Executive Branch unnecessarily broad subpoenas." *Id.* at 2592. They could, for example, narrow the scope of the subpoenas on their own or, perhaps, hold the discovering party to some higher relevancy standard than the usual "relevant-to-claim-or-defense" standard of Federal Rule of Civil Procedure 26(b)(1). Does this modification of the civil discovery rules tilt the balance too much in the executive's favor, or is it necessary because the usual checks on civil discovery "have proved insufficient to discourage the filing of meritless claims against the Executive Branch"? *Id.* at 2590.

7

The Domestic Effect of International Law

A. TREATIES AND AGREEMENTS

Page 205. Add the following material to Note 5.

The Supreme Court has also asserted in a dictum that during war "the Chief Executive *or* Congress may have formulated a national policy quite inconsistent with the enforcement of a treaty in whole or in part," Clark v. Allen, 331 U.S. 503, 508-509 (1947) (emphasis added). But the Court relied for this proposition on an earlier state court opinion in which Judge Cardozo asserted that

> the President and Senate may denounce the treaty, and thus terminate its life. Congress may enact an inconsistent rule, which will control the action of the courts. The treaty of peace itself may set up new relations, and terminate earlier compacts, either tacitly or expressly. . . . But until some one of these things is done, until some one of these events occurs, while war is still flagrant, and the will of the political departments of the government unrevealed, the courts, as I view their function, play a humbler and more cautious part. It is not for them to denounce treaties generally, en bloc. Their part it is, as one provision or another is involved in some actual controversy before them, to determine whether, alone, or by force of connection with an inseparable scheme, the provision is inconsistent with the policy or safety of the nation in the emergency of war, and hence presumably intended to be limited to times of peace. [*Id.* at 509, quoting Techt v. Hughes, 229 N.Y. 222, 242-243 (1920).]

In 2002, Attorney General Ashcroft cited *Clark* for the proposition that "when a President *determines* that a treaty does not apply, his determination is fully discretionary and will not be reviewed by the federal courts." See this Supplement p. 56 (emphasis in original). Is this a fair reading of *Clark*?

C. THE DOMESTIC LEGAL EFFECT OF CUSTOMARY INTERNATIONAL LAW AND *JUS COGENS*

Page 235. Add the following material to Note 2.

Those who have argued recently that customary international law is *not* "part of our law" suffered a serious setback with the Supreme Court's decision in Sosa v. Alvarez-Machain, 542 U.S. 692, 124 S. Ct. 2739 (2004). Relying on The Paquete Habana and other cases, the Court declared that while federal courts make it a general practice to look first for legislative guidance, they may enforce "a narrow class of international norms" whose "content and acceptance among civilized nations" are clearly defined. *Id.* at 2764, 2765. In a suit under the Alien Tort Claims Act, 28 U.S.C. §1350 (2000), a Mexican national sought damages for his abduction in Mexico at the behest of the DEA in order to try him on murder charges in the United States. But the Court found that the international law underlying his claim failed to meet the "clear definition" test. An earlier related case may be found at casebook p. 855.

General War

8

Page 333. Add these materials at end of chapter.

E. WAR AGAINST IRAQ – 2003

Authorization for Use of Military Force Against Iraq Resolution of 2002
Pub. L. No. 107-243, 116 Stat. 1498
October 16, 2002

Whereas in 1990 in response to Iraq's war of aggression against and illegal occupation of Kuwait, the United States forged a coalition of nations to liberate Kuwait and its people in order to defend the national security of the United States and enforce United Nations Security Council resolutions relating to Iraq;

Whereas after the liberation of Kuwait in 1991, Iraq entered into a United Nations sponsored cease-fire agreement pursuant to which Iraq unequivocally agreed, among other things, to eliminate its nuclear, biological, and chemical weapons programs and the means to deliver and develop them, and to end its support for international terrorism;

Whereas the efforts of international weapons inspectors, United States intelligence agencies, and Iraqi defectors led to the discovery that Iraq had large stockpiles of chemical weapons and a large scale biological weapons program, and that Iraq had an advanced nuclear weapons development program that was much closer to producing a nuclear weapon than intelligence reporting had previously indicated;

Whereas Iraq, in direct and flagrant violation of the cease-fire, attempted to thwart the efforts of weapons inspectors to identify and destroy Iraq's weapons of mass destruction stockpiles and development capabilities, which finally resulted in the withdrawal of inspectors from Iraq on October 31, 1998;

Whereas in Public Law 105-235 (August 14, 1998), Congress concluded that Iraq's continuing weapons of mass destruction programs threatened vital United States interests and international peace and security, declared Iraq to be in "material and unacceptable breach of its international obligations" and urged the President "to take appropriate action, in accordance with the Constitution and relevant laws of the United States, to bring Iraq into compliance with its international obligations";

Whereas Iraq both poses a continuing threat to the national security of the United States and international peace and security in the Persian Gulf region and remains in material and unacceptable breach of its international obligations by, among other things, continuing to possess and develop a significant chemical and biological weapons capability, actively seeking a nuclear weapons capability, and supporting and harboring terrorist organizations;

Whereas Iraq persists in violating resolution[s] of the United Nations Security Council by continuing to engage in brutal repression of its civilian population thereby threatening international peace and security in the region, by refusing to release, repatriate, or account for non-Iraqi citizens wrongfully detained by Iraq, including an American serviceman, and by failing to return property wrongfully seized by Iraq from Kuwait;

Whereas the current Iraqi regime has demonstrated its capability and willingness to use weapons of mass destruction against other nations and its own people;

Whereas the current Iraqi regime has demonstrated its continuing hostility toward, and willingness to attack, the United States, including by attempting in 1993 to assassinate former President Bush and by firing on many thousands of occasions on United States and Coalition Armed Forces engaged in enforcing the resolutions of the United Nations Security Council;

Whereas members of al Qaida, an organization bearing responsibility for attacks on the United States, its citizens, and interests, including the attacks that occurred on September 11, 2001, are known to be in Iraq;

Whereas Iraq continues to aid and harbor other international terrorist organizations, including organizations that threaten the lives and safety of United States citizens;

Whereas the attacks on the United States of September 11, 2001, underscored the gravity of the threat posed by the acquisition of weapons of mass destruction by international terrorist organizations;

Whereas Iraq's demonstrated capability and willingness to use weapons of mass destruction, the risk that the current Iraqi regime will either employ those weapons to launch a surprise attack against the United States or its

Chapter 8. General War

Armed Forces or provide them to international terrorists who would do so, and the extreme magnitude of harm that would result to the United States and its citizens from such an attack, combine to justify action by the United States to defend itself;

Whereas United Nations Security Council Resolution 678 (1990) authorizes the use of all necessary means to enforce United Nations Security Council Resolution 660 (1990) and subsequent relevant resolutions and to compel Iraq to cease certain activities that threaten international peace and security, including the development of weapons of mass destruction and refusal or obstruction of United Nations weapons inspections in violation of United Nations Security Council Resolution 687 (1991), repression of its civilian population in violation of United Nations Security Council Resolution 688 (1991), and threatening its neighbors or United Nations operations in Iraq in violation of United Nations Security Council Resolution 949 (1994);

Whereas in the Authorization for Use of Military Force Against Iraq Resolution (Public Law 102-1), Congress has authorized the President "to use United States Armed Forces pursuant to United Nations Security Council Resolution 678 (1990) in order to achieve implementation of Security Council Resolutions 660, 661, 662, 664, 665, 666, 667, 669, 670, 674, and 677";

Whereas in December 1991, Congress expressed its sense that it "supports the use of all necessary means to achieve the goals of United Nations Security Council Resolution 687 as being consistent with the Authorization of Use of Military Force Against Iraq Resolution (Public Law 102-1)," that Iraq's repression of its civilian population violates United Nations Security Council Resolution 688 and "constitutes a continuing threat to the peace, security, and stability of the Persian Gulf region," and that Congress "supports the use of all necessary means to achieve the goals of United Nations Security Council Resolution 688";

Whereas the Iraq Liberation Act of 1998 (Public Law 105-338) expressed the sense of Congress that it should be the policy of the United States to support efforts to remove from power the current Iraqi regime and promote the emergence of a democratic government to replace that regime;

Whereas on September 12, 2002, President Bush committed the United States to "work with the United Nations Security Council to meet our common challenge" posed by Iraq and to "work for the necessary resolutions," while also making clear that "the Security Council resolutions will be enforced, and the just demands of peace and security will be met, or action will be unavoidable";

Whereas the United States is determined to prosecute the war on terrorism and Iraq's ongoing support for international terrorist groups combined with its development of weapons of mass destruction in direct violation of its obligations under the 1991 cease-fire and other United Nations Security Council resolutions make clear that it is in the national security interests of the United States and in furtherance of the war on terrorism that all relevant United Nations Security Council resolutions be enforced, including through the use of force if necessary;

Whereas Congress has taken steps to pursue vigorously the war on terrorism through the provision of authorities and funding requested by the President to take the necessary actions against international terrorists and terrorist organizations, including those nations, organizations, or persons who planned, authorized, committed, or aided the terrorist attacks that occurred on September 11, 2001, or harbored such persons or organizations;

Whereas the President and Congress are determined to continue to take all appropriate actions against international terrorists and terrorist organizations, including those nations, organizations, or persons who planned, authorized, committed, or aided the terrorist attacks that occurred on September 11, 2001, or harbored such persons or organizations;

Whereas the President has authority under the Constitution to take action in order to deter and prevent acts of international terrorism against the United States, as Congress recognized in the joint resolution on Authorization for Use of Military Force (Public Law 107-40); and

Whereas it is in the national security interests of the United States to restore international peace and security to the Persian Gulf region: Now, therefore, be it

Resolved by the Senate and House of Representatives of the United States of America in Congress assembled . . .

Sec. 2. Support for United States Diplomatic Efforts

The Congress of the United States supports the efforts by the President to –

(1) strictly enforce through the United Nations Security Council all relevant Security Council resolutions regarding Iraq and encourages him in those efforts; and

(2) obtain prompt and decisive action by the Security Council to ensure that Iraq abandons its strategy of delay, evasion and noncompliance and promptly and strictly complies with all relevant Security Council resolutions regarding Iraq.

Chapter 8. General War

Sec. 3. Authorization for Use of United States Armed Forces

(a) AUTHORIZATION – The President is authorized to use the Armed Forces of the United States as he determines to be necessary and appropriate in order to –

   (1) defend the national security of the United States against the continuing threat posed by Iraq; and
   (2) enforce all relevant United Nations Security Council resolutions regarding Iraq.

(b) PRESIDENTIAL DETERMINATION – In connection with the exercise of the authority granted in subsection (a) to use force the President shall, prior to such exercise or as soon thereafter as may be feasible, but no later than 48 hours after exercising such authority, make available to the Speaker of the House of Representatives and the President pro tempore of the Senate his determination that –

   (1) reliance by the United States on further diplomatic or other peaceful means alone either (A) will not adequately protect the national security of the United States against the continuing threat posed by Iraq or (B) is not likely to lead to enforcement of all relevant United Nations Security Council resolutions regarding Iraq; and
   (2) acting pursuant to this joint resolution is consistent with the United States and other countries continuing to take the necessary actions against international terrorist and terrorist organizations, including those nations, organizations, or persons who planned, authorized, committed or aided the terrorist attacks that occurred on September 11, 2001.

(c) WAR POWERS RESOLUTION REQUIREMENTS –

   (1) SPECIFIC STATUTORY AUTHORIZATION – Consistent with section 8(a)(1) of the War Powers Resolution, the Congress declares that this section is intended to constitute specific statutory authorization within the meaning of section 5(b) of the War Powers Resolution.
   (2) APPLICABILITY OF OTHER REQUIREMENTS – Nothing in this joint resolution supersedes any requirement of the War Powers Resolution. . . .

NOTES AND QUESTIONS

1. *Operation Iraqi Freedom.* On March 18, 2003, President Bush sent the "determination" required by §3(b) of the resolution to congressional leaders, *Presidential Letter*, Mar. 18, 2003, *at http://www.whitehouse.gov/ news/releases/2003/03/20030319-1.html*, and the next day the war began with missile and aircraft attacks on Iraqi targets. The President addressed the nation in these words: "My fellow citizens, at this hour, American and coalition forces are in the early stages of military operations to disarm Iraq, to free its people, and to defend the world from grave danger." *President Bush Addresses the Nation*, Mar. 19, 2003, *at http://www.whitehouse.gov/ news/releases/2003/03/20030319-17.html*. "Our nation enters this conflict reluctantly – yet, our purpose is sure," he declared. "The people of the United States and our friends and allies will not live at the mercy of an outlaw regime that threatens the peace with weapons of mass murder. We will meet that threat now . . . so that we do not have to meet it later with armies of firefighters and police and doctors on the streets of our cities." *Id.*

Less than a month later, with some 135,000 American troops deployed in Iraq, the last stronghold of forces loyal to Saddam Hussein was captured, and on May 1, 2003, President Bush proclaimed that "[m]ajor combat operations in Iraq have ended." *President Bush Announces Major Combat Operations in Iraq Have Ended*, May 1, 2003, *at http://www.whitehouse. gov/news/releases/2003/05/iraq/20030501-15.html*. Day-by-day reports on the progress of the war may be found on the Web site of Global Security.org, *at http://www.globalsecurity.org/military/ops/iraqi_freedom. htm*. For official news releases and press briefings, see the Web site of the Defense Department's Central Command, *at http://www.centcom.mil/*.

Two years later, about 150,000 American forces remained in Iraq to help rebuild the country's infrastructure, restore order, and train Iraqi police and military personnel. Amidst efforts to install a democratic government in Iraq, continuing, organized attacks by "insurgent" forces had taken thousands of lives. By the middle of 2005, more than 1,700 U.S. military personnel had been killed, and a much larger number were wounded. There also had been thousands of Iraqi casualties, most of them civilians.

2. *War Without the 2002 Joint Resolution?* Prior to Congress's approval of the October 16, 2002, joint resolution, some maintained that the President already had the domestic authority needed to send troops into battle. *See* Mike Allen & Juliet Eilperin, *Bush Aides Say Iraq War Needs*

Chapter 8. General War

No Hill Vote; Some See Such Support as Politically Helpful, Wash. Post, Aug. 26, 2002. What theories might support this argument? Are any of these theories suggested by the "whereas" clauses of the resolution?

Did the President already have Congress's approval to go to war? Could he have relied, for example, on the 1991 Authorization for Use of Military Force Against Iraq (casebook pp. 330-331)? Would such reliance have been dependent on the continued viability of United Nations Security Council Resolution 678 (casebook p. 329)? What about the resolution approved by Congress three days after the September 11, 2001, terrorist attack (casebook p. 262)?

Could the President have taken the country to war solely on the strength of his inherent "repel attack" authority, based on the imminence and gravity of an Iraqi threat? If so, what facts would have justified the unilateral use of force? What process, if any, should have been followed before he gave the order to attack?

3. *United Nations Involvement.* Unlike the 1991 Gulf War, the Iraq War that began in 2003 was not conducted with the immediate approval of the United Nations Security Council. But in a resolution passed on November 8, 2002, the Security Council "deplor[ed]" that Iraq had not made full disclosure of or granted the United Nations inspectors unconditional access to its programs and sites for weapons of mass destruction (WMD). It found Iraq to be in "material breach of its obligations under relevant resolutions, including resolution 687," but decided to afford Iraq "a final opportunity to comply." S.C. Res. 1441, U.N. Doc. S/RES/1441 (2002). Perhaps most pertinent, the resolution "recalls . . . that the Council has repeatedly warned Iraq that it will face serious consequences as a result of its continued violations of its obligations," and it pledged to reconvene immediately following any report of future breaches "to consider the situation and the need for full compliance." *Id.*

Iraq's declaration on December 7, 2002, that it had no weapons of mass destruction was deemed inadequate by the head of a new U.N. inspection team, Hans Blix, and others. Meanwhile, U.N. weapons inspectors had resumed their search for WMD in Iraq on November 27, 2002. But aside from some intermediate range missiles, which were destroyed, no such weapons were found before inspectors were forced to leave on March 17, 2002, in the face of the impending invasion. Members of the U.S.-led coalition asserted that even without another meeting of the U.N. Security Council, and without waiting for the inspection process to be completed, Resolution 1441 had cleared the way for coalition forces to "take their own steps" to secure Iraq's disarmament. These developments are traced in UN News Service stories, *at http://www.un.org/news/dh/infocus/iraq/chronology-02-04.htm.*

Do you agree that no subsequent Security Council resolution was necessary to make war with Iraq legal under international law? Relevant provisions of the United Nations Charter are reproduced at pp. 295-297 of the casebook.

The 2002 *National Security Strategy of the United States of America, available at http://www.whitehouse.gov/nsc/nss.html,* embraced for the first time as a public policy "the option of preemptive actions to counter a sufficient threat to our national security. . . . We must be prepared to stop rogue states and their terrorist clients before they are able to threaten or use weapons of mass destruction against the United States and our allies and friends." *Id.* at 9-10. It pointed to international law recognizing that "nations need not suffer an attack before they can lawfully take action to defend themselves against forces that present an imminent danger of attack," *id.* at 9, an apparent reference to Article 51 of the United Nations Charter (casebook p. 297). Do you think this policy is consistent with Article 51? If it is, what factual predicates must be satisfied before it can be invoked? Were those requirements met in the run-up to the invasion of Iraq in March 2003? *See* David M. Ackerman, *International Law and the Preemptive Use of Force Against Iraq* (Cong. Res. Rev. RS21314), Apr. 11, 2003.

4. *Justifications for the War.* Both the October 16 congressional resolution and claims of unilateral presidential authority for the use of force were based on the existence of a serious, continuing threat to the national security of the United States. According to the resolution, the threat was posed, in part, by a "significant" chemical, biological, and nuclear weapons capability, by the risk that the current Iraqi regime would "employ those weapons to launch a surprise attack against the United States or its Armed Forces," and by "the extreme gravity of harm that would result to the United States and its citizens from such an attack." In his 2003 State of the Union message, President Bush described Iraq as "a serious and mounting threat to our country," and he called Saddam Hussein a "dictator who is assembling the world's most dangerous weapons." George W. Bush, *The President's State of the Union Address,* Jan. 28, 2003, *available at http://www.whitehouse.gov/news/releases/2002/01/20020129-11.html.*

More than two years after coalition forces invaded Iraq no chemical, biological, or nuclear weapons had been found. A detailed account of the fruitless search for WMD may be found in *Comprehensive Report of the*

Chapter 8. General War

Special Advisor to the DCI on Iraq's WMD (Duelfer Report), Sept. 30, 2004, *available at http://www.cia.gov/cia/reports/iraq_wmd_2004*. The President continued to insist, however, that the war was justified: "Although we have not found stockpiles of weapons of mass destruction, we were right to go into Iraq. We removed a declared enemy of America who had the capability of producing weapons of mass murder and could have passed that capability to terrorists bent on acquiring them. In the world after September the 11th, that was a risk we could not afford to take." Richard W. Stevenson & Jodi Wilgorin, *Bush Forcefully Defends War, Citing Safety of U.S. and World,* N.Y. Times, July 11, 2004.

Concerning the ongoing threat of terrorism, President Bush asserted before the war that "Saddam Hussein aids and protects terrorists, including members of al Qaeda." *The President's State of the Union Address, supra.* Others in his administration claimed or implied a link between Saddam and the September 11 attacks. National Security Advisor Condoleeza Rice, for example, declared, "Oh, indeed there is a tie between Iraq and what happened on 9/11." Morning Show, CBS, Nov. 28, 2003. She then went on to add, "It's not that Saddam Hussein was somehow himself and his regime involved in 9/11, but, if you think about what caused 9/11, it is the rise of ideologies of hatred that lead people to drive airplanes into buildings in New York. This is a great terrorist, international terrorist network that is determined to defeat freedom. . . . And they're all linked." *Id.* Secretary of State Colin Powell testified to the independent 9/11 Commission that Deputy Defense Secretary Paul Wolfowitz saw the 9/11 attacks as "a way to deal with the Iraq problem." National Commission on Terrorist Attacks Upon the United States, *The 9/11 Commission Report* 335 (July 22, 2004). But the Commission found "no evidence [of] a collaborative operational relationship" between Iraq and al Qaeda, *id.* at 66, while the Senate Select Committee on Intelligence found no "established formal relationship" between the two. *Report on the U.S. Intelligence Community's Prewar Intelligence Assessments on Iraq,* July 9, 2004, at Conclusion 93, *available at http://intelligence.senate.gov/iraqreport2.pdf.* The Committee also cited a CIA assessment that there was "no evidence proving Iraqi complicity or assistance in an Al Qaeda attack." *Id.,* Conclusion 96.

The failure to locate WMD or to uncover clear links to terrorists was blamed in part on bad intelligence. According to the Senate Select Committee on Intelligence, most of the information available in the CIA's October 2002 *National Intelligence Estimate* concerning Iraq's WMD program was either "overstated" or "not supported by" the underlying intelligence reporting. *Id.* at 14. See also Commission on the Intelligence Capabilities of the United States Regarding Weapons of Mass Destruction

(Silberman/Robb Commission), *Report to the President of the United States*, Mar. 31, 2005.

When the Senate Intelligence Committee issued its report in July 2004, it decided to postpone until after the November presidential election a separate report on how the Bush administration used that intelligence to shape policy. *See Transcript: Senate Intelligence Committee Report Released*, Wash. Post, July 9, 2004. But nine months later Committee Chair Pat Roberts said the second report was "on the back burner." Shaun Waterman, *Roberts Calls for Constant Change in Intel*, Wash. Times, Mar. 11, 2005.

Some suggested that the CIA estimate was crafted to support the President's determination to attack Iraq, while others concluded that the Bush administration had simply misled Congress and the American people, as well as the international community, about the existence of WMD. *See, e.g.*, John Prados, *Hoodwinked: The Documents That Reveal How Bush Sold Us a War* (New York: New Press 2004); Joseph Cirincionne, Jessica T. Matthews & George Perkovich, *WMD in Iraq: Evidence and Implications* (Carnegie Endowment for Intl. Peace 2004); Spencer Ackerman & John B. Judis, *The First Casualty*, New Republic, June 30, 2003, at 14. New concerns were raised in 2005 by the report of a meeting of top British officials, including Prime Minister Tony Blair, some three months before Congress voted to authorize the use of force in Iraq. Memorandum from Matthew Rycroft to David Manning, *Iraq: Prime Minister's Meeting, 23 July*, July 23, 2002, reprinted in *The Secret Downing Street Memo*, Sunday Times, May 1, 2005, *available at http://www.timesonline.co.uk/article/0,,2087-1593607,00.html*. The head of MI6, just returned from talks with Director of Central Intelligence George Tenet and other Washington officials, reported that "[m]ilitary action was now seen as inevitable. Bush wanted to remove Saddam, through military action, justified by the conjunction of terrorism and WMD. But the intelligence and facts were being fixed around the policy." *Id. See also* Mark Danner, *The Secret Way to War*, N.Y. Rev. of Books, June 9, 2005, at 70.

Based on the language of the October 16, 2002, joint resolution, how important would you say the perceived WMD threat was in justifying the war? The terrorist connection? If one or both of these factual predicates for the war did not actually exist, would that affect the legal authority conferred by the 2002 joint resolution? Would it have any bearing on the President's exercise of his inherent "repel attack" power? Would it matter how the mistakes arose? Compare the debate about the Tonkin Gulf Resolution (casebook p. 263, Note 8).

In the summer of 2005, faced with declining public support for

Chapter 8. General War

continued U.S. military involvement in Iraq, President Bush described Iraq as the "latest battlefield" in the war on terror. *President Addresses Nation, Discusses Iraq, War on Terror*, June 28, 2005, at http://www.whitehouse.gov/news/releases/2005/06/print/20050628-7.html. "There is only one course of action" against the terrorists, he said: "to defeat them abroad before they attack us at home." *Id.*

> Our mission in Iraq is clear. We're hunting down the terrorists. We're helping Iraqis build a free nation that is an ally in the war on terror. We're advancing freedom in the broader Middle East. We are removing a source of violence and instability, and laying the foundation of peace for our children and our grandchildren. [*Id.*]

How do these reasons compare with the justifications for war set out in the October 16 congressional resolution? Upon what factual assumptions are they based?

Some members of Congress in both parties had begun calling for a withdrawal, or at least a plan for withdrawal, of U.S. troops from Iraq. If the reasons for military action changed over time, was the President's mandate under the October 16 resolution still good? Should the President have sought new authority from Congress? Or was the earlier mandate extended by Congress's recurring vote of appropriations for the war?

Do congressional authorizations for war contribute to political accountability, even if their "whereas" clauses and the attendant debate in Congress carry no direct legal effect? Is it relevant that some members of Congress who voted for the October 16, 2002, resolution may have believed that giving the President the authority he sought made war less likely? That the vote took place just 13 months after the September 11 terrorist attacks and only three weeks before mid-term congressional elections? Would we have had the same debate about WMD or support for al Qaeda if President Bush had taken the country to war against Iraq without congressional authorization?

5. *A Judicial Challenge.* Just days before the war in Iraq began, the First Circuit Court of Appeals affirmed the dismissal of a suit by military personnel, their parents, and several members of the U.S. House of Representatives to enjoin the initiation of hostilities. Doe v. Bush, 323 F.3d 133 (1st Cir. 2003). The plaintiffs had argued that the President was about to violate conditions placed by the October 16, 2002, resolution on his use of force, and that the resolution delegated excessive authority to the President, rendering it constitutionally inadequate as a vehicle for Congress to declare war.

The court based its decision in part on ripeness grounds. It rejected the government's assertion, citing Ange v. Bush, 752 F. Supp. 509 (D.D.C 1990) (casebook p. 159), that no claim could ever be ripe until an attack had actually occurred. 323 F.3d at 138 n.4. Nevertheless, it decided that the case was not fit for review, since either the President, Congress, or the U.N. Security Council might change course, or Saddam might surrender, before the shooting started.

In addition, the court rejected the plaintiffs' nondelegation doctrine arguments, recalling its own Vietnam-era decision in Massachusetts v. Laird, 451 F.2d 26 (1st Cir. 1971) (see casebook p. 271), when it declared that the Constitution overall "envisions the joint participation of the Congress and the executive in determining the scale and duration of hostilities." *Id.* at 32. "An extreme case might arise" said the court in 2003, "if Congress gave absolute discretion to the President to start a war at his or her own will. . . . The mere fact that the October Resolution grants some discretion to the President fails to raise a sufficiently clear constitutional issue." 323 F.3d at 143. Besides, the court observed, "Congress has been deeply involved in significant debate, activity, and authorization connected to our relations with Iraq for over a decade . . . ." *Id.* at 144.

10
Intelligence Operations

C. PROBLEMS IN THE REFORM OF INTELLIGENCE OPERATIONS

2. Executive Branch Reforms

Page 473. Add at the end of Note 5.

The Department of Defense has also developed an Intelligence Support Activity (ISA), created in 1981 to collect intelligence and to conduct covert military operations. Invigorated by Defense Secretary Donald Rumsfeld to participate in the war on terrorism after September 11, the ISA, code-named Gray Fox, now reports to an Under Secretary of Defense for Intelligence. Gray Fox operates independently of the intelligence community. *See* William M. Arkin, *The Secret War: Frustrated by Intelligence Failures, the Defense Department Is Dramatically Expanding Its 'Black World' of Covert Operations*, L.A. Times, Oct. 27, 2002, at M1.

The Department reportedly expanded the ISA role in the war on terrorism to include "special access programs" (SAPs), defined by an Army regulation as "a security program . . . approved by the Deputy Secretary of Defense to apply extraordinary security measures to protect extremely sensitive information." Army Regulation 380-381, *Special Access Programs (SAPs) and Sensitive Activities*, Apr. 21, 2004, at 84, *available at* http://www.fas.org/irp/doddir/army/ar380-381.pdf. One SAP reportedly was diverted from its original purpose of interrogating Taliban and al Qaeda detainees in the war on terrorism to staffing detention and interrogation operations at the Abu Ghraib prison in Iraq. Seymour Hersh, *The Gray Zone: How a Secret Pentagon Program Came to Abu Ghraib*, New Yorker, May 24, 2004. When the prisoner abuse scandal broke in the spring of

2004, the commander of the 800th Military Police Brigade, the unit ostensibly in charge of the Abu Ghraib facility, stated that she could not always be sure who was who among the persons in civilian clothes managing interrogations. *Id.* The interrogation and treatment of detainees for investigative purposes is considered further at pp. 39-94 in this Supplement. Do you think it matters whether those in charge of investigative interrogations are from the Department of Defense or the CIA?

F. THE PRIVATIZATION OF INTELLIGENCE OPERATIONS

2. Dirty Assets

Page 557. Add this new Note.

9. *The Denial-of-Access Claim.* Even though the full D.C. Circuit denied the government's petition for rehearing in *Harbury*, the Supreme Court granted review and unanimously reversed, Christopher v. Harbury, 536 U.S. 403 (2002). In finding that Harbury's complaint did not state a constitutional denial-of-access claim upon which relief could be granted, the Court declared that an access claim is merely ancillary to an underlying claim, without which a plaintiff cannot have suffered injury by being shut out of court. Thus, the underlying claim must be described in the complaint, and the complaint must identify a remedy that could be awarded and that would not be available in some future lawsuit. In this case, because the acts alleged by Harbury "raise concerns for the separation of powers in trenching on matters committed to other branches," the Court said, it was all the more important for the district court to know whether the denial-of-access allegations stated a claim. The best she could offer, accepted by the Court of Appeals as sufficient, was that she would have brought an action for intentional infliction of emotional distress, and that a lawsuit seeking injunctive relief for that wrong might have saved Bamaca's life. The Supreme Court found Harbury's claim inadequate:

> [E]ven on the assumption that Harbury could surmount all difficulties raised by treating the underlying claim as one for intentional infliction of emotional distress, she could not satisfy the requirement that a backward-looking denial-of-access claim provide a remedy that could not be obtained on an existing claim.

Chapter 10. Intelligence Operations

536 U.S. at 420-421.

Harbury's counts naming CIA defendants, including the Guatemalan "asset" who allegedly tortured and killed Bamaca, were among the tort claims that survived the original motion to dismiss in the district court. According to the Supreme Court, Harbury could still seek damages and injunctive relief for emotional distress, although she could not obtain an order that might have saved Bamaca. Her access claim did not support such an order, and it could not compensate her for the loss claimed due to her inability to bring the tort action earlier. What is the likely outcome of the tort claims? What obstacles are most likely to stand in Harbury's way?

Page 557. Add at the end of the Chapter.

G. INTELLIGENCE REORGANIZATION

The September 11, 2001, attacks on the World Trade Center and the Pentagon prompted numerous critiques of what some regarded as massive failures of intelligence. *See, e.g.,* Senate Select Comm. on Intelligence & House Permanent Select Comm. on Intelligence, *Joint Inquiry into Intelligence Community Activities Before and After the Terrorist Attacks of September 11, 2001*, S. Rep. No. 107-351, H.R. Rep. No. 107-792 (2002); *9/11 Commission Report: Final Report of the National Commission on Terrorist Attacks Upon the United States* (2004). How could such a devastating attack have been planned and carried out under our collective noses? Why did our intelligence agencies not know the attack was coming? The two intelligence committees and the 9/11 Commission found that inadequate organization and management of the intelligence community prevented the Director of Central Intelligence (DCI) from ensuring that information about the hijackers' plans was shared with agency analysts, who could have "connected the dots" and uncovered the plot in advance. The 9/11 Commission also noted that limited legal authority forced the DCI to "direct agencies without controlling them." *9/11 Commission Report* at 357. The Commission pointed out that, especially for intelligence elements within DOD, the DCI "does not receive an appropriation for their activities, and therefore does not control their purse strings." *Id.* Similarly, the congressional joint inquiry found that even after DCI Tenet ordered the intelligence community to give the Osama bin Laden network its highest priority, his words had little effect beyond the CIA. *Joint Inquiry* at 236.

Meanwhile, the Bush administration case for the 2003 Iraq war relied heavily on intelligence-based assertions that the Saddam Hussein regime had stockpiles of weapons of mass destruction (WMD) that would imminently be used against the United States and its allies. After President Bush declared an end to major combat operations in Iraq and investigators cleared the battlefield rubble, no WMD were found. In March 2005, a presidentially appointed commission found "that the Intelligence Community was dead wrong in almost all of its pre-war judgments about Iraq's weapons of mass destruction." Commission on the Intelligence Capabilities of the United States Regarding Weapons of Mass Destruction (Silberman/Robb Commission), *Report to the President of the United States* (transmittal letter), Mar. 31, 2005. The Commission found an "inability to collect good information," "serious errors in analyzing" the information collected, and a failure to distinguish assumptions from evidence in its analysis. *Id.*

The intelligence failures of September 11 and Iraq appeared to many observers as symptomatic of a larger struggle by our nation's intelligence agencies to confront the post-Cold War environment. Instead of focusing on the Soviet Union as the dominant threat, as it had since the origins of the CIA in 1947, the intelligence community today faces dozens of high-priority targets that include not only states, but also highly diffuse transnational terrorism, crime, and proliferation networks. Worse yet, advances in technology and potential dual uses of goods have made detection of weapons and facilities harder and their concealment easier.

In its July 2004 report, the 9/11 Commission recommended several changes in the structure of the intelligence community:

- unify strategic intelligence and operational planning against Islamist terrorists across the foreign-domestic divide with a National Counter-terrorism Center;
- unify the intelligence community with a National Intelligence Director;
- unify the many participants in the counterterrorism effort and their knowledge in a network-based information-sharing system that transcends traditional governmental boundaries;
- unify and strengthen congressional oversight to improve quality and accountability; and
- strengthen the FBI and homeland defenders.

See 9/11 Commission Report at 399-400.

1. An Intelligence Czar?

In December 2004, Congress approved the most extensive reorganization of U.S. intelligence in more than half a century. Intelligence

Chapter 10. Intelligence Operations

Reform and Terrorism Prevention Act of 2004, Pub. L. No. 108-458, 118 Stat. 3638 (hereinafter Intelligence Reform Act). (Unless otherwise noted, references in the following description are to sections of the National Security Act of 1947 as amended by the Intelligence Reform Act, and to the Statutes at Large pages where the amendments appear.) The 2004 Act responded – at least in part – to those who sought the creation of a cabinet-level intelligence czar. It created the position of Director of National Intelligence (DNI), appointed by the President and confirmed by the Senate, and subject to the "authority, direction, and control of the President." 50 U.S.C. §102, 118 Stat. 3644. The DNI serves as "head of the intelligence community" and as principal adviser to the President, National Security Council, and Homeland Security Council "for intelligence matters related to the national security." *Id.* §102(b), 118 Stat. 3644. She also oversees and directs implementation of the National Intelligence Program. *Id.* §102(b)(3), 118 Stat. 3644. The DNI cannot simultaneously serve as Director of the CIA or as head of any other component of the intelligence community. *Id.* §102(c), 118 Stat. 3644.

The DNI has direct authority over a Principal Deputy and up to four additional deputy directors, a National Counterterrorism Center, a National Counterproliferation Center, a General Counsel, a Director of Science and Technology, and a National Intelligence Council. *Id.* §§103-103F, 118 Stat. 3655-3660. The former DCI post was eliminated, and the job of running the CIA was given to a Director of the CIA. *Id.* §104A, 118 Stat. 36.

The DNI must "develop and determine" the annual consolidated National Intelligence Program budget. *Id.* §102A(c)(1), 118 Stat. 3645. She is also to direct the allocation of appropriations through the heads of departments containing agencies or organizations within the intelligence community, and through the Director of the CIA. *Id.* §102A(c)(5)(A), 118 Stat. 3645. (Component intelligence agencies and lines of reporting are shown in the chart on page 25.) Although the DNI was thus given considerable new budgetary authority with which to manage the intelligence community, the DNI has no direct prescriptive authority over intelligence support to military operations through the Department of Defense Joint Military Intelligence Program (JMIP) and Tactical Intelligence and Related Activities (TIARA) program. *Id.* §102A(c)(3)(A), 118 Stat. 3645.

After consultation with the Secretary of Defense, the DNI must ensure that National Intelligence Program budgets for components of the intelligence community within DOD are adequate for the intelligence needs of DOD, including the intelligence needs of the service branches. *Id.* §102A(p), 118 Stat. 3654. The DNI, after consulting with the Secretary of Defense and Director of the CIA, must develop joint procedures to "improve the coordination and deconfliction" of operations that involve the Armed Forces and the CIA. Intelligence Reform Act §1013(a), 118 Stat. 3662.

The DNI is responsible for establishing "objectives, priorities, and guidance" for elements of the intelligence community. 50 U.S.C. §102(f)(1)(A), 118 Stat. 3648. She also must "determine requirements and priorities for, and manage and direct the tasking of" intelligence collection, analysis, production, and dissemination by entities of the intelligence community. *Id.* These authorities do not extend to the DNI if the President so directs or if the DNI and Secretary of Defense agree otherwise, or to dissemination of information to state and local governments and the private sector under the Homeland Security Act. *Id.* §102A(f)(1)(B), 118 Stat. 3649.

2. The New Structure

The office of the DNI includes a Senate-confirmed Principal Deputy Director of Intelligence and up to four other deputy directors appointed by the DNI, one of whom may be a commissioned officer of the Armed Forces. 50 U.S.C. §103A, 118 Stat. 3656-3657. A National Intelligence Council (NIC), comprised of senior analysts and other experts appointed by the DNI, is charged to produce national intelligence estimates, evaluate intelligence collection and production performance, and otherwise assist the DNI. *Id.* §103B, 118 Stat. 3657. A Senate-confirmed General Counsel was created, as was a Civil Liberties Protection Officer and a Director of Science and Technology, both appointed by the DNI. *Id.* §§103C-103E, 118 Stat. 3658-3659.

The Director of the CIA reports to the DNI, and she remains responsible for intelligence collection, evaluation, and dissemination by the CIA, as well as for performing "such other functions and duties related to intelligence affecting the national security" as the President or DNI may direct. *Id.* §104A, 118 Stat. 3660.

The DNI oversees the National Counterterrorism Center (NCTC), created by the Act, and any other national intelligence centers determined necessary by the Director. Intelligence Reform Act §1021, 118 Stat. 3672. The Director of the NCTC is a Senate-confirmed presidential appointee who reports to the DNI generally, but to the President on the planning and implementation of joint counterterrorism operations. *Id.*

A Privacy and Civil Liberties Oversight Board, to be appointed by the President, was established within the Executive Office of the President and charged with ensuring that privacy and civil liberties concerns are appropri-

Chapter 10. Intelligence Operations

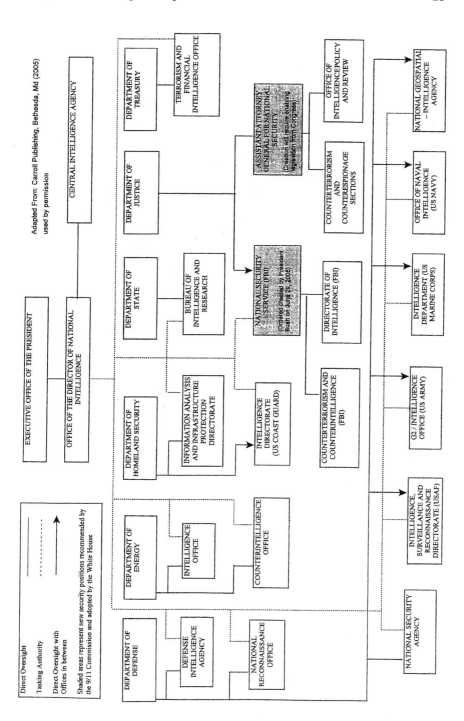

ately considered in the implementation of policies designed to protect against terrorism. The Board will provide oversight of regulations and policies, advise the President and agencies in the executive branch, and report to Congress. The Board has no power to compel production of information, but it may request such assistance from the Attorney General. *Id.* §1061, 118 Stat. 3684-3688.

NOTES AND QUESTIONS

1. *Is the DNI an Intelligence Czar?* The "intelligence community" headed by the DNI consists of all the entities depicted in the chart on p. 25 except the President and the six listed cabinet departments. Intelligence Reform Act §1073, 118 Stat. 3693. The National Intelligence Program directed by the DNI includes "all programs, projects, and activities of the intelligence community," 50 U.S.C. §401a(6), but "does not include programs, projects, or activities of the military departments to acquire intelligence solely for the planning and conduct of tactical military operations of United States Armed Forces." *Id.* In what respects does the DNI constitute a "Secretary of Intelligence," and how specifically does the new post fall short of the Secretary model? Does the Intelligence Reform Act give the DNI the authority he needs to be effective? Can she hire or fire agency heads? Tell an agency what to do?

2. *Defining the Scope of the Mission.* The terms "national intelligence" and "intelligence related to national security" are defined to include "all intelligence, regardless of the source from which derived and including information gathered within or outside the United States, that pertains . . . to more than one . . . agency; and that involves threats to the United States, its people, property, or interests; the development, proliferation, or use of weapons of mass destruction; or any other matter bearing on United States national or homeland security." Intelligence Reform Act §1012, 118 Stat. 3662. Are these definitions useful to the DNI in understanding the scope of her responsibilities? What categories of intelligence are outside the definition? How does this expansive definition affect the geographical boundaries of intelligence activities by the CIA? By the FBI?

3. *Budget Control.* Does the DNI now control the purse strings of the intelligence agencies? Although intelligence budgets will continue to be developed in the agencies, the DNI has discretion under the Act to reject or revise items or programs and to direct that funds be spent or withheld. 50 U.S.C. §102A(c)(5), 118 Stat. 3645. Can you see how this budget and

Chapter 10. Intelligence Operations

spending authority could make the DNI the final decision maker in the agencies of the National Intelligence Program?

4. *The Fifth Function.* Several authorities and responsibilities of the DNI previously belonged to the DCI. For example, the DNI must "ensure compliance with the Constitution and laws of the United States" by the CIA and other elements of the intelligence community. 50 U.S.C. §102A(f)(4), 118 Stat. 3649. The DNI "shall perform such other functions as the President may direct." *Id.* §102A(f)(7), 118 Stat. 3650. The new Director of the CIA continues to "perform such other functions and duties related to intelligence affecting the national security as the President or National Security Council may direct." *Id.* §104A(d)(4), 118 Stat. 3661. Do you suppose the differences in what used to be referred to as the fifth function are purposeful? If so, how do the authorities of the two offices differ in this regard? Parallel authorities for the DNI and Director of the CIA extend to "protect[ing] intelligence sources and methods from unauthorized disclosure." *Id.* §102A(i), 118 Stat. 3651; 50 U.S.C. §403-3(c)(7).

5. *The DNI and Internal Security.* The CIA has since 1947 been forbidden by statute from having an internal security or law enforcement power. Although the CIA proviso remains, 50 U.S.C. §403-3(d)(1) (casebook p. 429), no such constraint was imposed on the DNI in the Intelligence Reform Act. What are the legal and practical implications of omitting the internal security prohibition for the DNI? Does the expanded definition of "national intelligence" noted above undercut the internal security prohibition?

6. *Reforming the FBI.* On March 31, 2005, the Commission on the Intelligence Capabilities of the United States Regarding Weapons of Mass Destruction, co-chaired by Judge Laurence Silberman and former Senator Charles Robb, recommended that the President create a new National Security Service within the FBI under a new Executive Assistant Director. The new service would include the Counterterrorism and Counterintelligence Divisions and the Directorate of Intelligence, and it would be subject to the coordination and budget authorities of the DNI. Appointment of a new Executive Assistant Director would be subject to approval by the DNI. Silberman/Robb Commission (p. 22 *supra*) at 465. The Commission also recommended that the primary Department of Justice national security elements – the Office of Intelligence Policy and Review (OIPR) and the Counterterrorism and Counterespionage Sections – be placed under a new Assistant Attorney General for National Security. On

June 29, 2005, President Bush accepted these recommendations, directed the Attorney General to implement them, and asked Congress to create the new Assistant Attorney General position. Memorandum for the Vice President et al., *Strengthening the Ability of the Department of Justice to Meet Challenges to the Security of the Nation*, available at http://www.whitehouse.gov/news/releases/2005/06/20050629-1.html.

The restructuring was "intended to break down old walls between foreign and domestic intelligence activities." Douglas Jehl, *Bush to Create New Unit in F.B.I. For Intelligence*, N.Y. Times, June 30, 2005, at A1. How do you suppose the new organization will break down walls? Do you see any downside risk in tearing down the wall between foreign and domestic intelligence? In lowering the historic barrier between the FBI and the CIA? To what extent will the FBI now be subject to the authority of the DNI? Whose job is it to determine that the new National Security Service does not undertake activities that violate U.S. laws? The legal consequences of these FBI reforms are considered further in this Supplement, *infra* Chapter 12.

The President also acted to implement other recommendations of the Silberman/Robb Commission by establishing a National Counter Proliferation Center to manage and coordinate Intelligence Community activities related to nuclear, biological, and chemical weapons and delivery systems; by signing an Executive Order to combat trafficking in weapons of mass destruction and related materials by blocking the assets of persons engaged in proliferation activities and their supporters; and by clarifying authorities concerning information-sharing by expanding the authority and control of the DNI. In addition, a new center at the CIA will focus on the collection of open-source intelligence. *See President Bush Administration Actions to Implement WMD Commission Recommendations*, June 29, 2005, at http://www.whitehouse.gov/news/releases/2005/06/20050629-5.html. These reforms are considered further in this Supplement, *infra* Chapter 13.

7. *The NCTC.* The 9/11 Commission proposal to create a National Counterterrorism Center (NCTC) was adopted by President Bush before it was approved by Congress. On August 27, 2004, the President signed Executive Order No. 13,354, *National Counterterrorism Center*, 69 Fed. Reg. 53,589, Sept. 1, 2004. A similar NCTC was provided for in the Intelligence Reform Act a few months later. In the Intelligence Reform Act, the Director of the NCTC reports to the DNI regarding intelligence operations, while she reports to the President regarding the "planning and progress of joint counterterrorism operations (other than intelligence operations)." Intelligence Reform Act §1021, 118 Stat. 3673. What kinds

Chapter 10. Intelligence Operations 29

of operations do you think are included among those that require direct reports to the President by the Director of the NCTC? Why would someone other than the DNI make those reports to the President? (The relationship of the NCTC to other information-sharing and terrorism assessment entities is considered *infra* Chapter 13.)

8. *Conforming Amendments.* In several sections of the National Security Act of 1947, Central Intelligence Agency Act of 1949, Foreign Intelligence Surveillance Act (casebook pp. 666-698), Classified Information Procedures Act (casebook pp. 880-888), and several intelligence authorization acts, DNI is inserted in place of DCI by the Intelligence Reform Act, and similar changes are made to reflect the structure of the new office of the DNI, including the Principal Deputy.

9. *Intelligence and the Department of Homeland Security.* The nascent Department of Homeland Security (DHS) structures were not directly assessed or challenged by the September 11 Commission or by the sponsors of the intelligence reform legislation. As a result, the Intelligence Reform Act simply works around DHS structures, institutions, and processes without considering their utility or the wisdom of overlaying additional new authorities in the homeland security environment. *See infra* pp. 186-189 in this Supplement.

10. *The Other 9/11 Commission Recommendations.* Additional responses by the executive branch and Congress to the 9/11 Commission recommendations for reforms to information-sharing, congressional oversight, and homeland security are considered *infra* Chapter 12 in this Supplement.

11

Organizing for Counterterrorism: An Overview

A. COUNTERING TERRORISM AT HOME AND ABROAD

1. Defining the Terrorist Threat

a. *What Is Terrorism?*

Page 567. Add this material before Notes and Questions.

United States v. Yousef
United States Court of Appeals, Second Circuit, 2003
327 F.3d 56

JOHN M. WALKER, JR., Chief Judge, RALPH K. WINTER and JOSÉ A. CABRANES, Circuit Judges.

[Yousef and others were convicted of conspiracy to bomb United States commercial airliners in Southeast Asia and of involvement in the 1993 bombing of the World Trade Center. They appealed on the ground that the courts lacked extraterritorial jurisdiction over the charged offenses. The District Court had rested jurisdiction in part on the concept of "universal jurisdiction," which "permits a State to prosecute an offender of any nationality for an offense committed outside of that State and without contacts to that State, but only for a few, near-unique offenses uniformly recognized by the 'civilized nations' as an offense against the 'Law of Nations.'" 327 F.3d at 103. See casebook at pp. 840-851. This case presented the question whether "terrorism" is such an offense.]

Unlike those offenses supporting universal jurisdiction under customary international law – that is, piracy, war crimes, and crimes against humanity – that now have fairly precise definitions and that have achieved universal condemnation, "terrorism" is a term as loosely deployed as it is powerfully charged. Judge Harry T. Edwards of the District of Columbia Circuit stated eighteen years ago in *Tel-Oren v. Libyan Arab Republic*, 726 F.2d 774 (D.C. Cir. 1984), that "[w]hile this nation unequivocally condemns all terrorist acts, that sentiment is not universal. Indeed, the nations of the world are so divisively split on the legitimacy of such aggression as to make it impossible to pinpoint an area of harmony or consensus." *Id.* at 795 (Edwards, J., concurring). Similarly, Judge Robert H. Bork stated in his opinion in *Tel-Oren* that the claim that a defendant "violated customary principles of international law against terrorism[ ] concerns an area of international law in which there is little or no consensus and in which the disagreements concern politically sensitive issues . . . . [N]o consensus has developed on how properly to define 'terrorism' generally." *Id.* at 806-07 (Bork, J., concurring).

Finally, in a third concurring opinion, Judge Roger Robb found the question of assigning culpability for terrorist acts to be "non-justiciable" and outside of the competency of the courts as inextricably linked with "political question[s]." *Id.* at 823 (Robb, J., concurring). Judge Robb stated that

> [I]nternational "law", or the absence thereof, renders even the search for the least common denominators of civilized conduct in this area [defining and punishing acts of terrorism] an impossible-to-accomplish judicial task. Courts ought not to engage in it when that search takes us towards a consideration of terrorism's place in the international order. Indeed, when such a review forces us to dignify by judicial notice the most outrageous of the diplomatic charades that attempt to dignify the violence of terrorist atrocities, we corrupt our own understanding of evil.

Id.

We regrettably are no closer now than eighteen years ago to an international consensus on the definition of terrorism or even its proscription;[41] the mere existence of the phrase "state-sponsored terrorism"

---

41. For example, each side of the Israeli-Palestinian conflict charges the other with "terrorism," sentiments echoed by their allies. *See, e.g.*, Todd S. Purdum, *What Do You Mean, "Terrorist"?*, N.Y. Times, Apr. 7, 2002, Week in Review, at 1 ("If Israel sees its military campaign in the West Bank as a justifiable echo of Mr. Bush's assault on Al Qaeda, Palestinians claim affinity with the American colonists' revolt against an occupying power."). The Organization of the Islamic

Chapter 10. Intelligence Operations 33

proves the absence of agreement on basic terms among a large number of States that terrorism violates public international law. Moreover, there continues to be strenuous disagreement among States about what actions do or do not constitute terrorism, nor have we shaken ourselves free of the cliché that "one man's terrorist is another man's freedom fighter."[42] We

---

Conference met in Kuala Lumpur, Malaysia, in April 2002, to define terrorism; the host of the conference, Malaysian Prime Minister Mahathir Mohamad, proposed a definition of terrorism as "all attacks on civilians"; the conference's final declaration, however, stated that terrorism consists only of attacks on civilians perpetrated by non-Palestinians, stating that the Conference "'rejects any attempt to link terrorism to the struggle of the Palestinian people in the exercise of their inalienable right to establish their independent state.'" *Id.* (quoting statements by Mohamad and contained in the conference's final declaration). Sentiments at the conference were far from uniform, however: The deputy foreign minister of Bosnia-Herzegovina stated that "if a person kills or harms a civilian . . . he is a terrorist" irrespective of the "race or religion" of the perpetrator and the victims. *Terrorism Issue Splits Muslim Conferees*, Chi. Trib., April 2, 2002, at 10 (quoting statements of Bosnian-Herzegovinian delegate to conference).

42. Confusion on the definition of "terrorism" abounds. *See, e.g.,* Craig S. Smith, *Debate Over Iraq Raises Fears of a Shrinking Role for NATO*, N.Y. Times, Jan. 26, 2003, at L26 (quoting Celeste A. Wallander, senior fellow at the Center for Strategic and International Studies, as stating that even among members of the North Atlantic Treaty Alliance ("NATO") there is no consensus "on how to define transnational terrorism"). Terrorism is defined variously by the perpetrators' motives, methods, targets, and victims. Motive-based definitions suffer from confusion because of the attempt to carve out an exception for assertedly legitimate armed struggle in pursuit of self-determination. For example, under one of the various United Nations resolutions addressing terrorism, armed and violent acts do not constitute "terrorism" if committed by peoples seeking self-determination in opposition to a violently enforced occupation. *See, e.g.,* Declaration on Principles of International Law Concerning Friendly Relations Among Co-operating States in Accordance with the Charter of the United Nations, Oct. 24, 1970, G.A. Res. 2625, 25 U.N. GAOR Supp. (No. 28) at 21, U.N. Doc. A/8028 (1971), *reprinted in* 9 I.L.M. 1292 (1970). This attempt to distinguish "terrorists" from "freedom fighters" potentially could legitimate as non-terrorist certain groups nearly universally recognized as terrorist, including the Irish Republican Army, Hezbollah, and Hamas. *See Boim v. Quranic Literacy Inst. & Holy Land Found. for Relief & Dev.*, 291 F.3d 1000, 1002 (7th Cir. 2002) (describing Hamas); *Stanford v. Kuwait Airways Corp.*, 89 F.3d 117, 120 (2d Cir. 1996) (describing Hezbollah); *Matter of Requested Extradition of Smyth*, 863 F. Supp. 1137, 1139-1140 (N.D. Cal. 1994) (describing the Irish Republican Army).

By contrast, the European Convention on the Suppression of Terrorism defines terrorism solely based on the methods of violence the perpetrator employs, and explicitly removes political judgment of the acts by defining most violent acts as "non-political" (regardless of the perpetrator's claimed motive). European Convention on the Suppression of Terrorism, Nov. 10, 1976, Europ. T.S. No. 90.

thus conclude that the statements of Judges Edwards, Bork, and Robb remain true today, and that terrorism – unlike piracy, war crimes, and crimes against humanity – does not provide a basis for universal jurisdiction.

Page 569. Add this material after Note 6.

People's Mojahedin Organization of Iran v. Department of State
United States Court of Appeals, District of Columbia Circuit, 2003
327 F.3d 1238

SENTELLE, Circuit Judge. The People's Mojahedin Organization of Iran ("PMOI" or "Petitioner") seeks review of 1999 and 2001 decisions of the Secretary of State . . . designating Petitioner as a foreign terrorist organization. . . .

Thus, in Article I, the Convention defines as terrorism any offenses, *inter alia,* "involving the use of a bomb, grenade, rocket, automatic firearm, or letter or parcel bomb if this use endangers persons," a definition that may fail to circumscribe the offense adequately. The Arab Convention on the Suppression of Terrorism (Cairo, Apr. 22, 1998), *reprinted in* International Instruments Related to the Prevention and Suppression of International Terrorism, 152-73 (United Nations 2001), while condemning terrorism, takes a uniquely restrictive approach to defining it, stating that offenses committed against the interests of Arab states are "terrorist offenses," while offenses committed elsewhere or against other peoples or interests are not. *Id.* at Art. I.3 (defining "terrorist offence" as any of several defined violent actions that occur "in any of the Contracting States, or against their nationals, property or interests"). The Convention further defines as legitimate (non-terrorist) "[a]ll cases of struggle by whatever means, including armed struggle," unless such struggles "prejudic[e] the territorial integrity of any Arab State." *Id.* at Art. II(a).

United States legislation has adopted several approaches to defining terrorism, demonstrating that, even within nations, no single definition of "terrorism" or "terrorist act" prevails. [The court surveyed several of these approaches, some of which are set out at casebook pp. 565-567.]

Still other definitions of "terrorism" may focus on the victims of the attacks or the relationship between the perpetrators and the victims. *See, e.g.,* Alex P. Schmid & Albert J. Jongman, Political Terrorism 1-2 (1988) ("Terrorism is a method of combat in which . . . symbolic victims serve as an instrumental target of violence. These instrumental victims share group or class characteristics which form the basis for their selection for victimization. Through previous use of violence or the credible threat of violence other members of that group or class are put a state of chronic fear (terror).").

I. Background

We note at the outset that this is PMOI's third petition to this court to review designations of the PMOI as a foreign terrorist organization. *See* People's Mojahedin Org. of Iran v. Dep't. of State, 182 F.3d 17 (D.C. Cir. 1999) ("*PMOI*"); Nat'l Council of Resistance of Iran v. Dep't. of State, 251 F.3d 192 (D.C. Cir. 2001) ("*NCOR*"). . . .

II. Analysis

A. Due Process and Sufficiency of Evidence

Petitioner raises several arguments. First, it contends that its redesignation as a terrorist organization under 8 U.S.C. §1189 is unconstitutional under the Due Process Clause of the Fifth Amendment of the Constitution because the statute permitted the Secretary to rely upon secret evidence – the classified information that respondents refused to disclose and against which PMOI could therefore not effectively defend. We reject this contention. . . . [T]hat statute authorizes designation of a foreign terrorist organization when the Secretary finds three elements. As to the first, that is that the organization is a foreign organization, there is not and cannot be any dispute. The People's Mojahedin is so assuredly a foreign organization that until the Secretary's designation of the NCOR as its alias, it could not even establish a presence in the United States. Nothing has changed in that regard since our prior decisions on the subject.

As to the second element, the PMOI advances a colorable argument: that the Secretary was able under §1189(a)(3)(B) to "consider classified information in making [this designation]" and that the classified information was not "subject to disclosure" except to the court ex parte and in camera for purposes of this judicial review. Petitioner contends that this violates the due process standard set forth in Abourezk v. Reagan, 785 F.2d 1043, 1061 (D.C. Cir. 1986), "that a court may not dispose of the merits of a case on the basis of ex parte, in camera submissions." While colorable, this argument will not carry the day.

First, we have already set forth in *NCOR* the due process standards that the Secretary must meet in making designations under the statute. We held that the Constitution requires the Secretary in designating foreign terrorist organizations to provide to the potential designees, "notice that the designation is impending." *NCOR*, 251 F.3d at 208. We further required that the Secretary must afford the potential designee an "opportunity to be heard at a meaningful time and in a meaningful manner." *Id.* at 209. The record reflects that the Secretary complied with our instructions.

Granted, petitioners argue that their opportunity to be heard was not meaningful, given that the Secretary relied on secret information to which they were not afforded access. The response to this is twofold. We already decided in *NCOR* that due process required the disclosure of only the unclassified portions of the administrative record. 251 F.3d at 207-09. We made that determination informed by the historically recognized proposition that under the separation of powers created by the United States Constitution, the Executive Branch has control and responsibility over access to classified information and has "'compelling interest' in withholding national security information from unauthorized persons in the course of executive business." Dep't. of the Navy v. Egan, 484 U.S. 518, 527 (1988) (quoting Snepp v. United States, 444 U.S. 507, 509 n. 3 (1980)). In the context of another statutory scheme involving classified information, we noted the courts are often ill-suited to determine the sensitivity of classified information. United States v. Yunis, 867 F.2d 617, 623 (D.C. Cir. 1989) ("Things that did not make sense to [a judge] would make all too much sense to a foreign counter intelligence specialist. . . ."). The Due Process Clause requires only that process which is due under the circumstances of the case. We have already established in *NCOR* the process which is due under the circumstances of this sensitive matter of classified intelligence in the effort to combat foreign terrorism. The Secretary has complied with the standard we set forth therein, and nothing further is due.

However, even if we err in describing the process due, even had the Petitioner been entitled to have its counsel or itself view the classified information, the breach of that entitlement has caused it no harm. This brings us to Petitioner's statutory objection. Petitioner argues that there is not adequate record support for the Secretary's determination that it is a foreign terrorist organization under the statute. However, on this element, even the unclassified record taken alone is quite adequate to support the Secretary's determination. Indeed, as to this element – that is, that the organization engages in terrorist activities – the People's Mojahedin has effectively admitted not only the adequacy of the unclassified record, but the truth of the allegation. . . .

By its own admission, the PMOI has

> (1) attacked with mortars the Islamic Revolutionary Prosecutor's Office; (2) assassinated a former Iranian prosecutor and killed his security guards; (3) killed the Deputy Chief of the Iranian Joint Staff Command, who was the personal military adviser to Supreme Leader Khamenei; (4) attacked with mortars the Iranian Central Command Headquarters of the Islamic Revolutionary Guard Corps and the Defense Industries Organization in Tehran; (5) attacked and targeted with mortars the offices of the Iranian Supreme Leader Khamenei, and of the head of the State Exigencies Council; (6) attacked with mortars the central headquarters of the Revolutionary Guards; (7) attacked with mortars two Revolutionary Guards Corps headquarters; and (8) attacked the headquarters of the Iranian State Security Forces in Tehran.

Were there no classified information in the file, we could hardly find that the Secretary's determination that the Petitioner engaged in terrorist activities is "lacking substantial support in the administrative record taken as a whole," even without repairing to the "classified information submitted to the court." 8 U.S.C. §1189(b)(3)(D)....

The remaining element under §1189(a)(1) is that "the terrorist activity or terrorism of the organization threatens the security of United States nationals or the national security of the United States." *Id.* §1189(a)(1)(C). The thrust of Petitioner's argument is that its allegedly terrorist acts were not acts of terrorism under the statute, because they do not meet the requirement of subsection (C). Petitioner argues that the attempt to overthrow the despotic government of Iran, which itself remains on the State Department's list of state sponsors of terrorism, is not "terrorist activity," or if it is, that it does not threaten the security of the United States or its nationals. We cannot review that claim. In PMOI we expressly held that that finding "is nonjusticiable." 182 F.3d at 23. As we stated in that decision, "it is beyond the judicial function for a court to review foreign policy decisions of the Executive Branch." *Id.* (citing Chicago & Southern Air Lines v. Waterman Steamship Corp., 333 U.S. 103, 111 (1948)).... In short, we find neither statutory nor due process errors in the Secretary's designation of petitioner as a foreign terrorist organization.

B. Petitioner's Other Claims

Petitioner raises several other arguments to the effect that the designation violates its constitutional rights. Those warranting separate discussion fall under the general heading of First Amendment claims. Petitioner's argument that its First Amendment rights have been violated rests on the consequences of the designation. Petitioner argues that by forbidding all persons within or subject to the jurisdiction of the United States from "knowingly provid[ing] material support or resources," 18 U.S.C. §2339B(a)(1), to it as a designated foreign terrorist organization, the statute violates its rights of free speech and association guaranteed by the First Amendment. We disagree.

As the Ninth Circuit held in Humanitarian Law Project v. Reno, 205 F.3d 1130, 1135 (9th Cir. 2000) [casebook p. 832], the statute "is not aimed at interfering with the expressive component of [the organization's] conduct but at stopping aid to terrorist groups." It is conduct and not communication that the statute controls. We join the Ninth Circuit in observing that "there is no constitutional right to facilitate terrorism by giving terrorists the weapons and explosives with which to carry out their grisly missions. Nor, of course, is there a right to provide resources with which terrorists can buy weapons and explosives." *Id.* at 1133....

III. Conclusion

For the reasons set forth above, we conclude that in the designation and redesignation of the People's Mojahedin of Iran as a foreign terrorist organization, the Secretary of State afforded all the process that the organization was due, and that this designation violated neither statutory nor constitutional rights of the Petitioner. We therefore deny the petitions for review.

So ordered.

EDWARDS, J., concurring [omitted].

NOTES AND QUESTIONS

1. *Process Without Access?* If PMOI is entitled to the protections of the Due Process Clause, how can the process due include denying to PMOI access to the evidence upon which their designation is based? On what basis did the court justify a process that was admittedly not "meaningful"?

2. *Result-Oriented?* The consequences of designation are dire, as the court noted in its 2001 decision, casebook p. 566. Under the circumstances, why do you suppose the process obligations of the government are so scant? Would you say that the outcome in PMOI was determined primarily by the State Department, Congress, or the court?

3. *The Statutory Argument.* Are you persuaded by PMOI's statutory argument? Why should the statutory question be any less amenable to judicial resolution than the constitutional claim?

4. *First Amendment Issues.* The First Amendment consequences of designation are explored at casebook pp. 826-840.

2. Planning for Homeland Security

Page 582. Add this material before the Notes and Questions.

In July 2002, the Office of Homeland Security published the National Strategy for Homeland Security, *available at http://www.whitehouse.gov/homeland*. The document outlined the structure and functions of a proposed Department of Homeland Security (DHS). In November 2002, the new department was authorized in the Homeland Security Act of 2002, Pub. L. No. 107-296, 116 Stat. 2135 (2002). The organization and operation of the new department are described *infra,* pp. 185-194 in this Supplement.

12
Investigating Terrorism and Other National Security Threats

B. THE FOURTH AMENDMENT FRAMEWORK

Page 666. Add this material after Note 10.

5. Interrogation and Treatment of Detainees Held Abroad in the "War on Terrorism"

The question in casebook Note 5, p. 650, about the U.S. government's beating and torturing an "unconnected" alien abroad is no longer merely hypothetical. As early as December 2002, U.S. military and civilian interrogators are reported to have abused those captured and detained in the war on terrorism by beating them and subjecting them to prolonged sleep and sensory deprivation, as well as sexual humiliation, first in Afghanistan, Guantánamo Bay, Cuba, and other offshore U.S. interrogation centers; then later in Iraq.

Our objective here is to introduce the legal regime for U.S. interrogation and treatment of detainees abroad. We will consider both the sources of applicable rules and the limits they impose on interrogation techniques. We will also try to determine whether the President enjoys constitutional or other powers that would excuse him from compliance with these rules. The raw materials for this analysis – recent internal government legal memoranda – provide a remarkable view of the work of lawyers in a wartime executive branch.

In October 1996, Secretary of Defense William Perry spoke at a meeting of Western Hemisphere defense ministers in Argentina. Responding to criticisms of so-called "torture manuals" used to train Latin American intelligence officers at the U.S. Army School of the Americas in the 1980s, and to a 1996 Intelligence Oversight Board report describing intelligence activities in Latin America, Perry said he was shocked when he found out about the manuals. He also declared that the Defense Department would never again advocate torture or other inhumane treatment in its training programs.[1]

Secretary Perry's assertion could not have taken into account September 11 and the war on terrorism. According to Cofer Black, former director of the CIA's counterterrorism unit, "after 9/11, the gloves came off."[2] Beginning with the capture in Afghanistan of senior al Qaeda operatives, the Bush administration had to determine how best to extract intelligence information from individuals detained by U.S. forces. "Setting" the methods and parameters of interrogation thus became an integral part of counter-terrorism planning. Should al Qaeda figures be questioned by the FBI, using traditional methods? By military interrogators, following service branch rules? By the CIA, perhaps using harsher techniques in secret locations?

The Bush administration decided early on to detain indefinitely a number of persons seized in Afghanistan and elsewhere, and to create a new detention facility at the U.S. base at Guantánamo Bay to hold at least some of them. The first detainees taken there in January 2002 were designated "unlawful combatants" by President Bush.

Initially, the Administration contended that Taliban and al Qaeda fighters held at Guantánamo were not eligible for the protections of the Geneva Conventions, the principal set of international legal norms for wartime detainees created by the international community after World War II. The Administration eventually decided that captured Taliban fighters would be protected by the Third Geneva Convention, although not as "prisoners of war." Captured members of al Qaeda would be treated "humanely," although the Geneva Conventions would not apply to them. According to the Justice Department, until December 2002, interrogations at Guantánamo were conducted in accordance with rules set out in Department of the Army, *Intelligence Interrogation* (FM 34-52) (1987).[3]

Nevertheless, in the summer of 2002, the Justice Department was asked to advise what interrogation techniques would violate U.S. or international

---

1. Linda D. Kozaryn, *Perry Bans U.S. Training in Inhumane Techniques*, American Forces Information Serv., Oct. 9, 1996, *available at* http://www.defenselink.mil/news/Oct1996/n10091996_9610095.html.

2. John Barry, Michael Hirsh & Michael Isikoff, *The Roots of Terror*, Newsweek, May 24, 2004.

3. Dept. of Defense News Release, *DoD Provides Details on Interrogation Process*, June 22, 2004, *at* http://www.defenselink.mil/releases/2004/nr20040622-0930.html.

Chapter 12. Investigating Terrorism

law. In August, the Office of Legal Counsel (OLC) opined that

> for an act to constitute torture as defined in [the Torture Statute], it must inflict pain that is difficult to endure. Physical pain amounting to torture must be equivalent in intensity to the pain accompanying serious physical injury, such as organ failure, impairment of bodily function, or even death. For purely mental pain or suffering to amount to torture. . . it must result in significant psychological harm of significant duration, e.g., lasting for months or even years. We conclude that the mental harm also must result from one of the predicate acts listed in the statute, namely: threats of imminent death; threats of the infliction of the kind of pain that would amount to physical torture; infliction of such physical pain as a means of psychological torture; use of drugs or other procedures designed to deeply disrupt the senses, or fundamentally alter an individual's personality; or threatening to do any of these things to a third party.[4]

The OLC memorandum even concluded that torture might be justified in some circumstances. Reacting to what was characterized as "tenacious resistance by some detainees to existing interrogation techniques,"[5] in October 2002 the commander at Guantánamo Bay sought permission to use new interrogation techniques that were more coercive than those authorized in the Army field manual.

By December 2002, the media began reporting that so-called "stress and duress" tactics or "high pressure methods" were being used in secret detention centers overseas by Defense Department and CIA interrogators in pursuit of "actionable intelligence." Those methods included forcing detainees to stand or kneel for hours in black hoods or spray-painted goggles, bombarding the detainees with lights 24 hours a day, withholding painkillers from wounded detainees, confining them in tiny rooms or binding them in painful positions, subjecting them to loud noises, and depriving them of sleep.[6] A June 2004 statement from the Department of Defense confirmed that similarly harsh interrogation techniques were approved by Secretary Donald Rumsfeld on December 2, 2002, for use in

---

4. Office of Legal Counsel, U.S. Dept. of Justice, *Memorandum for Alberto R. Gonzales, Counsel to the President, Re: Standards of Conduct for Interrogation Under 18 U.S.C. §§2340-2340A*, Aug. 1, 2002 (commonly referred to as the Bybee Memo, for its author, Asst. Atty. General Jay S. Bybee), at 1, *available at* http://www.gwu.edu/~nsarchiv/NSAEBB/NSAEBB127/02.08.01.pdf.

5. *Final Report of the Independent Panel to Review DoD Detention Operations* 35, Aug. 24, 2004 [hereinafter *Schlesinger Report*], *at* http://www.dod.gov/news/Aug2004/d20040824finalreport.pdf.

6. *See* Dana Priest & Barton Gellman, *U.S. Decries Abuse But Defends Interrogations*, Wash. Post, Dec. 26, 2002.

Guantánamo, but were rescinded on January 15, 2003.[7] An August 2004 Army report found that interrogators in Afghanistan employed similar techniques beginning in December 2002.[8]

By early 2003, the apparent failure to obtain useful information from certain detainees at Guantánamo led Secretary Rumsfeld to charge an "Interrogation Working Group" of senior Defense Department lawyers to develop guidance on the parameters for interrogation. In April 2003, the working group advised that the President as Commander in Chief could authorize torture despite legal prohibitions. Based at least in part on this advice, Secretary Rumsfeld then approved interrogation techniques that included reversing detainees' sleep patterns, exposing them to heat, cold, loud noise, and bright lights, and extending interrogation sessions to 20 hours or more.[9] The memorandum from Secretary Rumsfeld approving these techniques is reproduced in part below. In June 2004, however, the Defense Department stated that 17 of the 24 techniques approved for use at Guantánamo in 2003 came from FM 34-52, and that four of the remaining seven required notification to the Secretary prior to use. According to the Pentagon,

> It is the policy and practice of the Department of Defense to treat detainees in the War on Terrorism humanely and, to the extent appropriate and consistent with military necessity, in a manner consistent with the principles of the Geneva Convention.
>
> No procedures approved for use ordered, authorized, permitted, or tolerated torture. Individuals who have abused the trust and confidence placed in them will be held accountable.[10]

When the fighting began in Iraq in March 2003, the U.S. command authority there ordered that standard FM 34-52 rules be followed in interrogating detainees. However, a panel headed by former Defense Secretary Schlesinger later found that the actual interrogation practices in Iraq combined FM 34-52 and other techniques that had migrated from

---

7. Dept. of Defense News Release, *DoD Provides Details on Interrogation Process*, June 22, 2004, *available at http://www.defenselink.mil/releases/2004/nr 20040622-0930.html.*

8. Maj. Gen. George R. Fay, *AR 15-6 Investigation of the Abu Ghraib Prison and 205th Military Intelligence Bridgade* 29, Aug. 25, 2004 [hereinafter *Fay Report*], *at http://www.dod.gov/news/Aug2004/d20040825fay.pdf.*

9. *See* Jess Bravin, *Pentagon Report Set Framework for Use of Torture*, Wall St. J., June 7, 2004.

10. *DoD Provides Details on Interrogation Process*, *supra* note 7.

Chapter 12. Investigating Terrorism

Guantánamo and Afghanistan.[11] In August 2003, Secretary Rumsfeld sent the military overseer of interrogation at Guantánamo, Major General Geoffrey Miller, to Iraq, where he "reviewed current Iraqi Theater ability to rapidly exploit internees for actionable intelligence."[12] General Miller brought with him the list of techniques approved by Secretary Rumsfeld for Guantánamo as a potential model, although he noted that the Geneva Conventions were supposed to apply in Iraq.

In September the military commander in Iraq approved the first policy on interrogation for Iraq, including portions of the Guantánamo policy and elements of policies then used by special forces. Central Command disapproved the September policy, and instead approved a new policy in October that mirrored the 1987 iteration of FM 34-52. The outdated field manual permitted interrogators to control "lighting and heating, as well as food, clothing, and shelter given to detainees." Control over such environmental factors was omitted from the 1992 version of the field manual in effect during 2003.[13] The policy on interrogation in Iraq changed again in October, the third change in less than 30 days.[14] Subsequent investigators found confusion about what practices were authorized, and they found migration to Iraq of Guantánamo techniques – such as the use of dogs and forced nudity to intimidate and dehumanize detainees.[15]

In January 2004, Lieutenant General Ricardo S. Sanchez, Commander of Combined Joint Task Force Seven in Iraq, requested that U.S. Central Command appoint an officer to investigate the conduct of operations within the 800th Military Police Brigade in Iraq. His request followed public reports of detainee abuse, particularly at the Abu Ghraib prison near Baghdad. Major General Antonio M. Taguba, who was appointed to conduct the investigation, found "numerous incidents of sadistic, blatant, wanton criminal abuses . . . intentionally perpetrated by several members of the military police guard force" at Abu Ghraib. The abuse included "punching, slapping, and kicking detainees," a litany of sexual and vulgar

---

11. *Schlesinger Report, supra* note 5, at 36.

12. General Antonio M. Taguba, *Article 15-6 Investigation of the 800th Military Police Brigade* [hereinafter *Taguba Report*], Jan. 31, 2004, at 7, *available at* http://news.findlaw.com/hdocs/ docs/iraq/tagubarpt.html.

13. *Schlesinger Report, supra* note 5, at 37-38; *see* Dept. of the Army, *Intelligence Interrogation* (FM 34-52), Sept. 28, 1992, at ch. 3.

14. *Fay Report, supra* note 8, at 28.

15. *Id.* at 10.

insults and attacks, and threats with loaded weapons.[16] In February 2004, the International Committee of the Red Cross (ICRC) issued a report detailing a number of serious human rights abuses by coalition forces in Iraq between March and November 2003.[17] Finally, in May 2004, public attention focused on Abu Ghraib after graphic photos of prisoner abuse were exposed by the media.

A July 2004 Army report found 94 cases of "confirmed or possible abuse of any type."[18] The report determined that the abuses "resulted from the failure of individuals to follow known standards of discipline and Army values and, in some cases, the failure of a few leaders to enforce those standards of discipline."[19] The Army decided not to charge any senior officers with wrongdoing in Iraq. It found that senior military officers were "responsible" for some of the abuse of Iraq detainees, but that the officers were not "culpable."[20] By contrast, the Schlesinger Commission found that the abuses were "more than the failure of a few leaders to enforce proper discipline. There is both institutional and personal responsibility at higher levels."[21]

A March 3, 2005, news release from the Army reported 120 actions taken against 109 soldiers for detainee abuse. Most involved non-judicial sanctions, while 32 courts martial were convened.[22] At this writing, seven soldiers have been convicted for abusing detainees at Abu Ghraib, none higher ranked than staff sergeant, and about one quarter of military sanctions for abuse have involved officers. Four of the five officers

---

16. *Taguba Report, supra* note 11.

17. *Report of the International Committee of the Red Cross (ICRC) on the Treatment by the Coalition Forces of Prisoners of War and Other Protected Persons by the Geneva Conventions in Iraq During Arrest, Internment and Interrogation,* Feb. 2004, *available at http://www.informationclearinghouse.info/pdf/icrc_iraq.pdf.*

18. Inspector General, Dept. of the Army, *Detainees Operation Inspection Report,* July 21, 2004, at foreword, *at http://www4.army.mil/ocpa/reports/ArmyIG DetaineeAbuse/index.html.*

19. *Id.*

20. Josh White & Thomas E. Ricks, *Officers Won't Be Charged in Prison Scandal,* Wash. Post, Aug. 27, 2004, at A17.

21. *Schlesinger Report, supra* note 5, at 5.

22. U.S. Army News Release, *Fact Sheet,* March 3, 2005, *at http://www4.army.mil/ocpa/read.php?story_id_key=6955.*

Chapter 12. Investigating Terrorism

investigated by the Army for their role in the Abu Ghraib abuses were cleared; Brig. Gen. Janis Karpinski, Commander of the 800th Military Police Brigade, was demoted to the rank of colonel.[23] No one has been criminally prosecuted in U.S. civilian courts for detainee abuse.

The following materials trace this tangled history. They include portions of the legal memorandum prepared in early 2002 by Justice Department lawyers that purports to spell out legal requirements for interrogation and treatment of al Qaeda and Taliban detainees. Also included are follow-on correspondence from the White House Counsel, the Attorney General, and General Counsel of the Department of State, along with part of an April 2003 memorandum from the Defense Department "Interrogation Working Group," and portions of another April 2003 memorandum from Defense Secretary Rumsfeld expanding the permissible interrogation techniques at Guantánamo. These materials are followed in turn by extensive notes and questions.

Application of Treaties and Laws to al Qaeda and Taliban Detainees

U.S. Department of Justice, Office of Legal Counsel
January 9, 2002
http://www.gwu.edu/~nsarchiv/NSAEBB/NSAEBB127/02.01.09.pdf

Memorandum for: William J. Haynes II, General Counsel, Department of Defense

**From: John Yoo, Deputy Asst. Attorney General
Robert J. Delahunty, Special Counsel**

You have asked for our Office's views concerning the effect of international treaties and federal laws on the treatment of individuals detained by the U.S. Armed Forces during the conflict in Afghanistan. In particular, you have asked whether the laws of armed conflict apply to the conditions of detention and the procedures for trial of members of al Qaeda and the Taliban militia. We conclude that these treaties do not protect members of the al Qaeda organization, which as a non-State actor cannot be a party to the international agreements governing war. We further conclude that that these treaties do not apply to the Taliban militia. This memorandum expresses no view as to whether the President should decide,

---

23. U.S. Army News Release, *Army Releases Findings in Detainee Abuse Investigations*, May 5, 2005, at http://www4.army.mil/ocpa/read.php?story_id_key =7293.

as a matter of policy, that the U.S. Armed Forces should adhere to the standards of conduct in those treaties with respect to the treatment of prisoners.

We believe it most useful to structure the analysis of these questions by focusing on the War Crimes Act, 18 U.S.C. §2441 (Supp. III 1997) ("WCA"). The WCA directly incorporates several provisions of international treaties governing the laws of war into the federal criminal code. Part I of this memorandum describes the WCA and the most relevant treaties that it incorporates: the four 1949 Geneva Conventions, which generally regulate the treatment of non-combatants, such as prisoners of war ("POWs"), the injured and sick, and civilians.[1]

Part II examines whether al Qaeda detainees can claim the protections of these agreements. Al Qaeda is merely a violent political movement or organization and not a nation-state. As a result, it is ineligible to be a signatory to any treaty. Because of the novel nature of this conflict, moreover, we do not believe that al Qaeda would be included in non-international forms of armed conflict to which some provisions of the Geneva Conventions might apply. Therefore, neither the Geneva Conventions nor the WCA regulate the detention of al Qaeda prisoners captured during the Afghanistan conflict.

Part III discusses whether the same treaty provisions, as incorporated through the WCA, apply to the treatment of captured members of the Taliban militia. We believe that the Geneva Conventions do not apply for several reasons. First, the Taliban was not a government and Afghanistan was not – even prior to the beginning of the present conflict – a functioning State during the period in which they engaged in hostilities against the United States and its allies. Afghanistan's status as a failed state is ground alone to find that members of the Taliban militia are not entitled to enemy POW status under the Geneva Conventions. Further, it is clear that the President has the constitutional authority to suspend our treaties with Afghanistan pending the restoration of a legitimate government capable of performing Afghanistan's treaty obligations. Second, it appears from the public evidence that the Taliban militia may have been so intertwined with al Qaeda as to be functionally indistinguishable from it. To the extent that the Taliban militia was more akin to a non-governmental organization that

---

1. The four Geneva Conventions for the Protection of Victims of War, dated August 12, 1949, were ratified by the United States on July 14, 1955. These are the Convention for the Amelioration of the Condition of the Wounded and Sick in Armed Forces in the Field, 6 U.S.T. 3115 ("Geneva Convention I"); the Convention for the Amelioration of the Condition of Wounded, Sick and Shipwrecked Members of the Armed Forces at Sea, 6 U.S.T. 3219 ("Geneva Convention II"); the Convention Relative to the Treatment of Prisoners of War, 6 U.S.T. 3517 ("Geneva Convention III"); and the Convention Relative to the Protection of Civilian Persons in Time of War, 6 U.S.T. 3317 ("Geneva Convention IV").

Chapter 12. Investigating Terrorism

used military force to pursue its religious and political ideology than a functioning government, its members would be on the same legal footing as al Qaeda.

In Part IV, we address the question whether any customary international law of armed conflict might apply to the al Qaeda or Taliban militia members detained during the course of the Afghanistan conflict. We conclude that customary international law, whatever its source and content, does not bind the President, or restrict the actions of the United States military, because it does not constitute federal law recognized under the Supremacy Clause of the Constitution. The President, however, has the constitutional authority as Commander in Chief to interpret and apply the customary or common laws of war in such a way that they would extend to the conduct of members of both al Qaeda and the Taliban, and also to the conduct of the U.S. Armed Forces towards members of those groups taken as prisoners in Afghanistan.

I. Background and Overview of the War Crimes Act and the Geneva Conventions

. . . We believe that the WCA provides a useful starting point for our analysis of the application of the Geneva Conventions to the treatment of detainees captured in the Afghanistan theater of operations.[4] Section 2441 of Title 18 renders certain acts punishable as "war crimes." The statute's definition of that term incorporates, by reference, certain treaties or treaty provisions relating to the laws of war, including the Geneva Conventions.

A. Section 2441: An Overview

Section 2441 reads in full as follows:

War crimes

(a) Offense. – Whoever, whether inside or outside the United States, commits a war crime, in any of the circumstances described in subsection (b), shall be fined under this title or imprisoned for life or any term of years, or both, and if death results to the victim, shall also be subject to the penalty of death.
(b) Circumstances. – The circumstances referred to in subsection (a)

---

4. The rule of lenity requires that the WCA be read so as to ensure that prospective defendants have adequate notice of the nature of the acts that the statute condemns. See, e.g., Castillo v. United States, 530 U.S. 120, 131 (2000). In those cases in which the application of a treaty incorporated by the WCA is unclear, therefore, the rule of lenity requires that the interpretative issue be resolved in the defendant's favor.

are that the person committing such war crime or the victim of such war crime is a member of the Armed Forces of the United States or a national of the United States . . . .

(c) Definition. – As used in this section the term "war crime" means any conduct –

(1) defined as a grave breach in any of the international conventions signed at Geneva 12 August 1949, or any protocol to such convention to which the United States is a party;

(2) prohibited by Article 23, 25, 27, or 28 of the Annex to the Hague Convention IV, Respecting the Laws and Customs of War on Land, signed 18 October 1907;

(3) which constitutes a violation of common Article 3 of the international conventions signed at Geneva, 12 August 1949, or any protocol to such convention to which the United States is a party and which deals with non-international armed conflict; or

(4) of a person who, in relation to an armed conflict and contrary to the provisions of the Protocol on Prohibitions or Restrictions on the Use of Mines, Booby-Traps and Other Devices as amended at Geneva on 3 May 1996 (Protocol II as amended on 3 May 1996), when the United States is a party to such Protocol, willfully kills or causes serious injury to civilians.

18 U.S.C. §2441.

. . . A House Report states that the original legislation "carries out the international obligations of the United States under the Geneva Conventions of 1949 to provide criminal penalties for certain war crimes." H.R. Rep. No. 104-698 at 1 (1996), *reprinted in* 1996 U.S.C.C.A.N. 2166, 2166. Each of those four conventions includes a clause relating to legislative implementation and to criminal punishment.[5]

In enacting section 2441, Congress also sought to fill certain perceived gaps in the coverage of federal criminal law. The main gaps were thought to be of two kinds: subject matter jurisdiction and personal jurisdiction.

---

5. That common clause reads as follows:

The [signatory Nations] undertake to enact any legislation necessary to provide effective penal sanctions for persons committing, or ordering to be committed, any of the grave breaches of the present Convention. . . . Each [signatory nation] shall be under the obligation to search for persons alleged to have committed, or to have ordered to be committed, such grave breaches, and shall bring such persons, regardless of their nationality, before its own courts. . . . It may also, if it prefers, . . . hand such persons over for trial to another [signatory nation], provided such [nation] has made out a *prima facie* case.

Geneva Convention I, art. 49; Geneva Convention II, art. 50; Geneva Convention III, art. 129; Geneva Convention IV, art. 146.

Chapter 12. Investigating Terrorism

First, Congress found that "[t]here are major gaps in the prosecutability of individuals under federal criminal law for war crimes committed against Americans." H.R. Rep. No. 104-698 at 6, *reprinted in* 1996 U.S.C.C.A.N. at 2171. For example, "the simple killing of a[n American] prisoner of war" was not covered by any existing Federal statute. *Id.* at 5, *reprinted in* 1996 U.S.C.C.A.N. at 2170.[6] Second, Congress found that "[t]he ability to court martial members of our armed services who commit war crimes ends when they leave military service. [Section 2441] would allow for prosecution even after discharge." *Id.* at 7, *reprinted in* 1996 U.S.C.C.A.N. at 2172.[7] Congress considered it important to fill this gap, not only in the interest of the victims of war crimes, but also of the accused. "The Americans prosecuted would have available all the procedural protections of the American justice system. These might be lacking, if the United States extradited the individuals to their victims' home countries for prosecution." *Id.*[8] Accordingly, Section 2441 criminalizes forms of conduct in which a U.S. national or a member of the Armed Forces may be either a victim or a perpetrator.

B. Grave Breaches of the Geneva Conventions . . .

The Geneva Conventions . . . structure legal relationships between Nation States, not between Nation States and private, subnational groups or organizations. All four Conventions share the same Article 2, known as "common Article 2." It states:

> In addition to the provisions which shall be implemented in peacetime, the present Convention shall apply to all cases of declared war or of any other armed conflict *which may arise between two or more of the High Contracting Parties*, even if the state of war is not recognized by one of them.
>
> The Convention shall also apply to all cases of partial or total occupation of the territory of a High Contracting Party, even if the said

---

6. In projecting our criminal law extraterritorially in order to protect victims who are United States nationals, Congress was apparently relying on the international law principle of passive personality. . . .

7. In *United States ex rel. Toth v. Quarles*, 350 U.S. 11 (1955), the Supreme Court had held that a former serviceman could not constitutionally be tried before a court martial under the Uniform Code for Military Justice (the "UCMJ") for crimes he was alleged to have committed while in the armed services.

8. The principle of nationality in international law recognizes that (as Congress did here) a State may criminalize acts performed extraterritorially by its own nationals. *See, e.g, Skiriotes v. Florida*, 313 U.S. 69, 73 (1941); *Steele v. Bulova Watch Co.*, 344 U.S. 280, 282 (1952).

occupation meets with no armed resistance.

Although one of the Powers in conflict may not be a party to the present Convention, the Powers who are parties thereto shall remain bound by it in their mutual relations. They shall furthermore be bound by the Convention in relation to the said Power, if the latter accepts and applies the provisions thereof.

(Emphasis added.)

As incorporated by §2441(c)(1), the four Geneva Conventions similarly define "grave breaches." Geneva Convention III on POWs defines a grave breach as:

> willful killing, torture or inhuman treatment, including biological experiments, willfully causing great suffering or serious injury to body or health, compelling a prisoner of war to serve in the forces of the hostile Power, or willfully depriving a prisoner of war of the rights of fair and regular trial prescribed in this Convention.

Geneva Convention III, art. 130. . . .

Thus, the WCA does not criminalize all breaches of the Geneva Conventions. Failure to follow some of the regulations regarding the treatment of POWs, such as difficulty in meeting all of the conditions set forth for POW camp conditions, does not constitute a grave breach within the meaning of Geneva Convention III, art. 130. Only by causing great suffering or serious bodily injury to POWs, killing or torturing them, depriving them of access to a fair trial, or forcing them to serve in the Armed Forces, could the United States actually commit a grave breach. Similarly, unintentional, isolated collateral damage on civilian targets would not constitute a grave breach within the meaning of Geneva Convention IV, art. 147. Article 147 requires that for a grave breach to have occurred, destruction of property must have been done "wantonly" and without military justification, while the killing or injury of civilians must have been "wilful."

D. Common Article 3 of the Geneva Conventions

Section 2441(c)(3) also defines as a war crime conduct that "constitutes a violation of common Article 3" of the Geneva Conventions. Article 3 is a unique provision that governs the conduct of signatories to the Conventions in a particular kind of conflict that is *not* one between High Contracting Parties to the Conventions. Thus, common Article 3 may require the United States, as a High Contracting Party, to follow certain rules even if other parties to the conflict are not parties to the Conventions. On the other hand, Article 3 requires state parties to follow only certain minimum standards of treatment toward prisoners, civilians, or the sick and wounded, rather than the Conventions as a whole.

Chapter 12. Investigating Terrorism 51

Common Article 3 reads in relevant part as follows:

> In the case of armed conflict not of an international character occurring in the territory of one of the High Contracting Parties, each Party to the conflict shall be bound to apply, as a minimum, the following provisions:
> (1) Persons taking no active part in the hostilities, including members of armed forces who have laid down their arms and those placed *hors de combat* by sickness, wounds, detention, or any other cause, shall in all circumstances, be treated humanely, without any adverse distinction founded on race, color, religion or faith, sex, birth or wealth, or any other similar criteria.
> To this end, the following acts are and shall remain prohibited at any time and in any place whatsoever with respect to the above-mentioned persons:
> (a) violence to life and person, in particular murder of all kinds, mutilation, cruel treatment and torture;
> (b) taking of hostages;
> (c) outrages upon personal dignity, in particular humiliating and degrading treatment;
> (d) the passing of sentences and the carrying out of executions without previous judgment pronounced by a regularly constituted court, affording all the judicial guarantees which are recognized as indispensable by civilized peoples. . . .

The application of the preceding provisions shall not affect the legal status of the Parties to the conflict.

Common Article 3 complements common Article 2. Article 2 applies to cases of declared war or of any other armed conflict that may arise between two or more of the High Contracting Parties, even if the state of war is not recognized by one of them. Common Article 3, however, covers "armed conflict not of an international character" – a war that does not involve cross-border attacks – that occurs within the territory of one of the High Contracting Parties. There is substantial reason to think that this language refers specifically to a condition of civil war, or a large-scale armed conflict between a State and an armed movement within its own territory.

To begin with, Article 3's text strongly supports the interpretation that it applies to large-scale conflicts between a State and an insurgent group. First, the language at the end of Article 3 states that "[t]he application of the preceding provisions shall not affect the legal status of the Parties to the conflict." This provision was designed to ensure that a Party that observed Article 3 during a civil war would not be understood to have granted the "recognition of the insurgents as an adverse party." Frits Kalshoven, *Constraints on the Waging of War* 59 (1987). Second, Article 3 is in terms limited to "armed conflict . . . occurring *in the territory of one of the High*

Contracting Parties" (emphasis added). This limitation makes perfect sense if the Article applies to civil wars, which are fought primarily or solely within the territory of a single state. The limitation makes little sense, however, as applied to a conflict between a State and a transnational terrorist group, which may operate from different territorial bases, some of which might be located in States that are parties to the Conventions and some of which might not be. In such a case, the Conventions would apply to a single armed conflict in some scenes of action but not in others – which seems inexplicable. . . .

Analysis of the background to the adoption of the Geneva Conventions in 1949 confirms our understanding of common Article 3. It appears that the drafters of the Conventions had in mind only the two forms of armed conflict that were regarded as matters of general *international* concern at the time: armed conflict between Nation States (subject to Article 2), and large-scale civil war within a Nation State (subject to Article 3). . . .

Decision re Application of the Geneva Convention on Prisoners of War to the Conflict with Al Qaeda and the Taliban

January 25, 2002
http://www.gwu.edu/~nsarchiv/NSAEBB/NSAEBB127/02.01.25.pdf

Memorandum for: The President

From: Alberto R. Gonzales [Counsel to the President]

Purpose

On January 18, I advised you that the Department of Justice had issued a formal legal opinion concluding that the Geneva Convention III on the Treatment of Prisoners of War (GPW) does not apply to the conflict with al Qaeda. I also advised you that DOJ's opinion concludes that there are reasonable grounds for you to conclude that GPW does not apply with respect to the conflict with the Taliban. I understand that you decided that GPW does not apply and, accordingly, that al Qaeda and Taliban detainees are not prisoners of war under the GPW.

The Secretary of State has requested that you reconsider that decision. Specifically, he has asked that you conclude that GPW does apply to both al Qaeda and the Taliban. I understand, however, that he would agree that al Qaeda and Taliban fighters could be determined not to be prisoners of war (POWs) but only on a case-by-case basis following individual hearings before a military board.

Chapter 12. Investigating Terrorism

This memorandum outlines the ramifications of your decision and the Secretary's request for reconsideration. . . .

Ramifications of Determination that GPW Does Not Apply

The consequences of a decision to adhere to what I understood to be your earlier determination that the GPW does not apply to the Taliban include the following:

Positive:

Preserves flexibility:
- As you have said, the war against terrorism is a new kind of war. It is not the traditional clash between nations adhering to the laws of war that formed the backdrop for GPW. The nature of the new war places a high premium on other factors, such as the ability to quickly obtain information from captured terrorists and their sponsors in order to avoid further atrocities against American civilians, and the need to try terrorists for war crimes such as wantonly killing civilians. In my judgment, this new paradigm renders obsolete Geneva's strict limitations on questioning of enemy prisoners and renders quaint some of its provisions requiring that captured enemy be afforded such things as commissary privileges, scrip (i.e., advances of monthly pay), athletic uniforms, and scientific instruments.
- Although some these provisions do not apply to detainees who are not POWs, a determination that GPW does not apply to al Qaeda and the Taliban eliminates any argument regarding the need for case-by-case determinations of POW status. It also holds open options for the future conflicts in which it may be more difficult to determine whether an enemy force as a whole meets the standard for POW status.
- By concluding that GPW does not apply to al Qaeda and the Taliban, we avoid foreclosing options for the future, particularly against nonstate actors.

Substantially reduces the threat of domestic criminal prosecution under the War Crimes Act (18 U.S.C. 2441).
- . . . A determination that the GPW is not applicable to the Taliban would mean that Section 2441 would not apply to actions taken with respect to the Taliban.
- Adhering to your determination that GPW does not apply would guard effectively against misconstruction or misapplication of Section 2441 for several reasons.
  - First, some of the language of the GPW is undefined (it prohibits, for example, "outrages upon personal dignity" and "inhuman treatment"), and it is difficult to predict with confidence what actions might be deemed to constitute violations of the

relevant provisions of GPW.
- Second, it is difficult to predict the needs and circumstances that could arise in the course of the war on terrorism.
- Third, it is difficult to predict the motives of prosecutors and independent counsels who may in the future decide to pursue unwarranted charges based on Section 2441. Your determination would create a reasonable basis in law that Section 2441 does not apply, which would provide a solid defense to any future prosecution.

Negative:

On the other hand, the following arguments would support reconsideration and reversal of your decision that the GPW does not apply to either al Qaeda or the Taliban:
- Since the Geneva Conventions were concluded in 1949, the United States has never denied their applicability to either U.S. or opposing forces engaged in armed conflict, despite several opportunities to do so. During the last Bush Administration, the United States stated that it "has a policy of applying the Geneva Conventions of 1949 whenever armed hostilities occur with regular foreign armed forces, even if arguments could be made that the threshold standards for the applicability of the Conventions . . . are not met."
- The United States could not invoke the GPW if enemy forces threatened to mistreat or mistreated U.S. or coalition forces captured during operations in Afghanistan, or if they denied Red Cross access or other POW privileges.
- The War Crimes Act could not be used against the enemy, although other criminal statutes and the customary law of war would still be available.
- Our position would likely provoke widespread condemnation among our allies and in some domestic quarters, even if we make clear that we will comply with the core humanitarian principles of the treaty as a matter of policy.
- Concluding that the Geneva Convention does not apply may encourage other countries to look for technical "loopholes" in future conflicts to conclude that they are not bound by GPW either.
- Other countries may be less inclined to turn over terrorists or provide legal assistance to us if we do not recognize a legal obligation to comply with the GPW.
- A determination that GPW does not apply to al Qaeda and the Taliban could undermine U.S. military culture which emphasizes maintaining the highest standards of conduct in combat, and could introduce an element of uncertainty in the status of adversaries.

Chapter 12. Investigating Terrorism

Response to Arguments for Applying GPW to the al Qaeda and the Taliban

On balance, I believe that the arguments for reconsideration and reversal are unpersuasive.

- The argument that the U.S. has never determined that GPW did not apply is incorrect. In at least one case (Panama in 1989) the U.S. determined that GPW did not apply even though it determined for policy reasons to adhere to the convention. More importantly, as noted above, this is a new type of warfare – one not contemplated in 1949 when the GPW was framed – and requires a new approach in our actions towards captured terrorists. Indeed, as the statement quoted from the administration of President George Bush makes clear, the U.S. will apply GPW "whenever hostilities occur *with regular foreign armed forces.*" By its terms, therefore, the policy does not apply to a conflict with terrorists, or with irregular forces, like the Taliban, who are armed militants that oppressed and terrorized the people of Afghanistan.
- In response to the argument that we should decide to apply GPW to the Taliban in order to encourage other countries to treat captured U.S. military personnel in accordance with the GPW, it should be noted that your policy of providing humane treatment to enemy detainees gives us the credibility to insist on like treatment for our soldiers. Moreover, even if GPW is not applicable, we can still bring war crimes charges against anyone who mistreats U.S. personnel. Finally, I note that our adversaries in several recent conflicts have not been deterred by GPW in their mistreatment of captured U.S. personnel, and terrorists will not follow GPW rules in any event.
- The statement that other nations would criticize the U.S. because we have determined that GPW does not apply is undoubtedly true. It is even possible that some nations would point to that determination as a basis for failing to cooperate with us on specific matters in the war against terrorism. On the other hand, some international and domestic criticism is already likely to flow from your previous decision not to treat the detainees as POWs. And we can facilitate cooperation with other nations by reassuring them that we fully support GPW where it is applicable and by acknowledging that in this conflict the U.S. continues to respect other recognized standards.
- In the treatment of detainees, the U.S. will continue to be constrained by (i) its commitment to treat the detainees humanely and, to the extent appropriate and consistent with military necessity, in a manner consistent with the principles of GPW, (ii) its applicable treaty obligations, (iii) minimum standards of treatment universally recognized by the nations of the world, and (iv) applicable military regulations regarding the treatment of detainees.
- Similarly, the argument based on military culture fails to recognize

that our military remain bound to apply the principles of GPW because that is what you have directed them to do.

Letter of Attorney General John Ashcroft to President George W. Bush
February 1, 2002
http://www.gwu.edu/~nsarchiv/NSAEBB/NSAEBB127/020201.pdf

With your permission, I would like to comment on the National Security Council's discussion concerning the status of Taliban detainees. It is my understanding that the determination that al Qaeda and Taliban detainees are not prisoners of war remains firm. However, reconsideration is being given to whether the Geneva Convention III on prisoners of war applies to the conflict in Afghanistan.

There are two basic theories supporting the conclusion that Taliban combatants are not legally entitled to Geneva Convention protections as prisoners of war:

1. During relevant times of the combat, Afghanistan was a failed state. As such it was not a party to the treaty, and the treaty's protections do not apply;
2. During relevant times, Afghanistan *was* a party to a treaty, but Taliban combatants are not entitled to Geneva Convention III prisoner of war status because they acted as unlawful combatants.

If a *determination* is made that Afghanistan was a failed state (Option 1 above) and not a party to the treaty, various legal risks of liability, litigation, and criminal prosecution are minimized. This is a result of the Supreme Court's opinion in *Clark v. Allen*[24] providing that when a President *determines* that a treaty does not apply, his determination is fully discretionary and will not be reviewed by the federal courts.

Thus, a Presidential determination against treaty applicability would provide the highest assurance that no court would subsequently entertain charges that American military officers, intelligence officials, or law enforcement officials violated Geneva Convention rules relating to field conduct, detention conduct or interrogation of detainees. The War Crimes Act of 1996 makes violation of parts of the Geneva Convention a crime in the United States.

In contrast, if a determination is made under Option 2 that the Geneva Convention applies but the Taliban are *interpreted* to be unlawful

---

[24. Noted in this Supplement at p. 5.]

Chapter 12. Investigating Terrorism

combatants not subject to the treaty's protections, *Clark v. Allen* does not accord American officials the same protection from legal consequences. In cases of Presidential *interpretation* of treaties which are confessed to apply, courts occasionally refuse to defer to Presidential interpretation. *Perkins v. Elg* is an example of such a case. If a court chose to review for itself the facts underlying a Presidential interpretation that detainees were unlawful combatants, it could involve substantial criminal liability for involved U.S. officials.

We expect substantial and ongoing legal challenges to follow the Presidential resolution of these issues. These challenges will be resolved more quickly and easily if they are foreclosed from judicial review under the *Clark* case by a Presidential determination that the Geneva Convention III on prisoners of war does not apply based on the failed state theory outlined as Option 1 above.

In sum, Option 1, a determination that the Geneva Convention does not apply, will provide the United States with the highest level of legal certainty available under American law.

It may be argued that adopting Option 1 would encourage the other states to allege that U.S. forces are ineligible for Geneva Convention III protections in future conflicts. From my perspective, it would be far more difficult for a nation to argue falsely that America was a "failed state" than to argue falsely that American forces had, in some way, forfeited their right to protections by becoming unlawful combatants. In fact, the North Vietnamese did exactly that to justify mistreatment of our troops in Vietnam. Therefore, it is my view that Option 2, a determination that the Geneva Convention III applies to the conflict in Afghanistan and that Taliban combatants are not protected because they were unlawful, could well expose our personnel to a greater risk of being treated improperly in the event of detention by a foreign power.

Option 1 is a legal option. It does not foreclose policy and operational considerations regarding actual treatment of Taliban detainees. Option 2, as described above, is also a legal option, but its legal implications carry higher risk of liability, criminal prosecution, and judicially-imposed conditions of detainment – including mandated release of a detainee.

Clearly, considerations beyond the legal ones mentioned in this letter will shape and perhaps control ultimate decision making in the best interests of the United States of America.

Sincerely,
John Ashcroft

Comments on Your Paper on the Geneva Convention
February 2, 2002
http://www.fas.org/sgp/othergov/taft.pdf

Memorandum to: Counsel to the President

From: William H. Taft, IV [Legal Adviser, Department of State]

    The paper should make clear that the issue for decision by the President is whether the Geneva Conventions apply to the conflict in Afghanistan in which U.S. armed forces are engaged. The President should know that a decision that the Conventions do apply is consistent with the plain language of the Conventions and the unvaried practice of the United States in introducing its forces into conflict over fifty years. It is consistent with the advice of DOS lawyers and, as far as is known, the position of every other party to the Conventions. It is consistent with UN Security Council Resolution 1193 affirming that "All parties to the conflict [in Afghanistan] are bound to comply with their obligations under international humanitarian law and in particular the Geneva Conventions. . . ." It is not inconsistent with the DOJ opinion that the Conventions generally do not apply to our world-wide effort to combat terrorism and to bring al Qaeda members to justice.

    From a policy standpoint, a decision that the Conventions apply provides the best legal basis for treating the al Qaeda and Taliban detainees in the way we intend to treat them. It demonstrates that the United States bases its conduct not just on its policy preference but on its international legal obligations. Agreement by all lawyers that the War Crimes Act does not apply to our conduct means that the risk of prosecution under that statute is negligible. Any small benefit from reducing it further will be purchased at the expense of the men and women in our armed forces that we send into combat. A decision that the Conventions do not apply to the conflict in Afghanistan in which our armed forces are engaged deprives our troops there of any claim to the protection of the Convention in the event they are captured and weakens the protections afforded by the Conventions to our troops in future conflicts.

    The structure of the paper suggesting a distinction between our conflict with al Qaeda and our conflict with the Taliban does not conform to the structure of the Conventions. The Conventions call for a decision whether they apply to the conflict in Afghanistan. If they do, their provisions are applicable to all persons involved in that conflict – al Qaeda, Taliban, Northern Alliance, U.S. troops, civilians, etc. If the Conventions do not apply to the conflict, no one involved in it will enjoy the benefit of their protections as a matter of law. . . .

Chapter 12. Investigating Terrorism

Working Group Report On Detainee Interrogations in the Global War on Terrorism[25]

April 4, 2003
http://www.defenselink.mil/news/Jun2004/d20040622doc8.pdf

II. International Law . . .

B. The 1994 Convention Against Torture

(U)[26] The United States' primary obligation concerning torture and related practices derives from the Convention Against Torture and Other Cruel, Inhuman, or Degrading Treatment or Punishment (commonly referred to as "the Torture Convention"). The United States ratified the Convention in 1994, but did so with a variety of Reservations and Understandings.

(U) Article 1 of the Convention defines the term "torture" for purpose of the treaty.³ The United States conditioned its ratification of the treaty on an understanding that:

> . . . in order to constitute torture, an act must be specifically intended to inflict severe physical or mental pain or suffering and that mental pain or suffering refers to prolonged mental harm caused by or resulting from (1) the intentional infliction or threatened infliction of severe physical pain or suffering; (2) the administration or application, or threatened administration or application, of mind altering substances or other procedures calculated to disrupt profoundly the senses or the personality; (3) the threat of imminent death; or (4) the threat that another person will imminently be subjected to death, severe physical pain or suffering, or the

---

[25. The Working Group, consisting of Defense Department officials, was tasked to prepare this report in a January 15, 2003, order from Secretary Donald Rumsfeld.]

[26. The expression "(U)" means that the adjacent material is unclassified.]

3. (U) Article 1 provides: "For the purposes of this Convention, the term 'torture' means any act by which severe pain or suffering, whether physical or mental, is intentionally inflicted on a person for such purposes as obtaining from him or a third person information or a confession, punishing him for an act he or a third person has committed or is suspected of having committed, or intimidating or coercing him or a third person, or for any reason based on discrimination of any kind, when such pain or suffering is inflicted by or at the instigation of or with the consent of acquiescence of a public official acting in an official capacity. It does not include pain or suffering arising only from, inherent in or incidental to lawful sanctions."

administration or application of mind altering substances or other procedures calculated to disrupt profoundly the senses or personality.[4]

(U) Article 2 of the Convention requires the Parties to "take effective legislative, administrative, judicial and other measures to prevent acts of torture in any territory under its jurisdiction." The U.S. Government believed existing state and federal criminal law was adequate to fulfill this obligation, and did not enact implementing legislation. Article 2 also provides that acts of torture cannot be justified on the grounds of exigent circumstances, such as a state of war or public emergency, or on orders from a superior officer or public authority.[5] The United States did not have an Understanding or Reservation relating to this provision (however the U.S. issued a declaration stating that Article 2 is not self-executing).

(U) Article 3 of the Convention contains an obligation not to expel, return, or extradite a person to another state where there are "substantial grounds" for believing that the person would be in danger of being subjected to torture. The U.S. understanding relating to this article is that it only applies "if it is more likely than not" that the person would be tortured.

(U) Under Article 5, the Parties are obligated to establish jurisdiction over acts of torture when committed in any territory under its jurisdiction or on board a ship or aircraft registered in that state, or by its national wherever committed. The U.S. has criminal jurisdiction over territories under U.S. jurisdiction and onboard U.S. registered ships and aircraft by virtue of the special maritime and territorial jurisdiction of the United States (the "SMTJ") established under 18 U.S.C. §7. Acts that would constitute torture are likely to be criminal acts under the SMTJ. . . . Accordingly, the U.S. has satisfied its obligation to establish jurisdiction over such acts in territories under U.S. jurisdiction or on board a U.S. registered ship or aircraft. However, the additional requirement of Article 5 concerning jurisdiction over acts of torture by U.S. nationals "wherever committed" needed legislative implementation. Chapter 113C of Title 18 of the U.S. Code provides federal criminal jurisdiction over an extraterritorial act or attempted act of torture if the offender is a U.S. national. The statute defines "torture" consistent with the U.S. Understanding on Article 1 of the

---

4. 18 U.S.C. §2340 tracks this language. For a further discussion of the U.S. understandings and reservations, see the Initial Report of the U.S. to the U.N. Committee Against Torture, dated October 15, 1999.

5. (U) See discussion to the contrary at the Domestic Law section on the necessity defense.

Chapter 12. Investigating Terrorism

Torture Convention.

(U) The United States is obligated under Article 10 of the Convention to ensure that law enforcement and military personnel involved in interrogations are educated and informed regarding the prohibition against torture. Under Article 11, systematic reviews of interrogation rules, methods, and practices are also required.

(U) In addition to torture, the Convention prohibits cruel, inhuman and degrading treatment or punishment within territories under a Party's jurisdiction (Art 16). Primarily because the meaning of the term "cruel, inhuman and degrading treatment or punishment" was vague and ambiguous, the United States imposed a Reservation on this article to the effect that it is bound only to the extent that such treatment or punishment means the cruel, unusual and inhuman treatment or punishment prohibited by the 5th, 8th, and 14th Amendments to the U.S. Constitution. . . .

(U) An additional treaty to which the United States is a party is the International Covenant on Political and Civil Rights, ratified by the United States in 1992. Article 7 of this treaty provides that "No one shall be subjected to torture or to cruel, inhuman or degrading treatment or punishment." The United States' ratification of the Covenant was subject to a Reservation that "the United States considers itself bound by Article 7 only to the extent that cruel, inhuman, or degrading treatment or punishments means the cruel and unusual treatment or punishment prohibited by the Fifth, Eighth, and/or Fourteenth Amendments to the Constitution of the United States." Under this treaty, a "Human Rights Committee" may, with the consent of the Party in question, consider allegations that such Party is not fulfilling its obligations under the Covenant. The United States has maintained consistently that the Covenant does not apply outside the United States or its special maritime and territorial jurisdiction, and that it does not apply to operations of the military during and international armed conflict. . . .

III. Domestic Law

A. Federal Criminal Law

1. Torture Statute

(U) 18 U.S.C. §2340 defines as torture any *"act committed by a person acting under the color of law specifically intended to inflict severe physical or mental pain. . . ."* The intent required is the intent to inflict severe physical or mental pain. 18 U.S.C. §2340A requires that the offense occur "outside the United States." Jurisdiction over the offense extends to any national of the United States or any alleged offender present in the United States, and could, therefore, reach military members, civilian employees of the United States, or contractor employees.[8] The "United States" is defined to include all areas under the jurisdiction of the United States, including the special maritime and territorial jurisdiction (SMTJ) of the United States. SMTJ is a statutory creation[9] that extends the criminal jurisdiction of the United States for designated crimes to defined areas.[10] The effect is to grant federal court criminal jurisdiction for the specifically identified crimes. . . .

(U) By its terms, the plain language of new subsection 9 includes Guantanamo Bay Naval Station (GTMO) within the definition of the SMTJ, and accordingly makes GTMO within the United States for purposes of §2340. As such, the Torture Statute does not apply to the conduct of U.S. personnel at GTMO. Prior to passage of the Patriot Act in 2001, GTMO was still considered within the SMTJ as manifested by (i) the prosecution of civilian dependents and employees living in GTMO in Federal District Courts based on SMTJ jurisdiction, and (ii) a Department of Justice opinion[11] to that effect. . . .

(U) Although Section 2340 does not apply to interrogations at GTMO, it could apply to U.S. operations outside U.S. jurisdiction, depending on the

---

8. (U) Section 2340A provides *"Whoever outside* the United States commits or attempts to commit torture shall be fined or imprisoned. . . ." (emphasis added).

9. (U) 18 USC §7, "Special maritime and territorial jurisdiction of the United States" includes any lands under the exclusive or concurrent jurisdiction of the United States.

10. (U) Several paragraphs of 18 USC §7 are relevant to the issue at hand. Paragraph 7(3) provides: [SMTJ includes:] "Any lands reserved or acquired for the use of the United States, and under the exclusive or concurrent jurisdiction thereof, or any place. . . ." Paragraph 7(7) provides: [SMTJ includes:] "Any place outside the jurisdiction of any nation to an offense by or against a national of the United States. Similarly, paragraphs 7(1) and 7(5) extend SMTJ jurisdiction to, "the high seas, any other waters within the admiralty and maritime jurisdiction of the United States and out of the jurisdiction of any particular state, and any vessel belonging in whole or in part to the United States . . ." and to "any aircraft belonging in whole or in part to the United States . . . while such aircraft is in flight over the high seas, or over any other waters within the admiralty and maritime jurisdiction of the United States and out of the jurisdiction of any particular State."

11. (U) 6 Op. OLC 236 (1982). The issue was the status of GTMO for purposes of a statute banning slot machines on "any land where the United States government exercises exclusive or concurrent jurisdiction."

Chapter 12. Investigating Terrorism

facts and circumstances of each case involved. The following analysis is relevant to such activities.

(U) To convict a defendant of torture, the prosecution must establish that: (1) the torture occurred outside the United States; (2) the defendant acted under color of law; (3) the victim was within the defendant's custody or physical control; (4) the defendant specifically intended to cause severe physical or mental pain or suffering; and (5) that the act inflicted severe physical or mental pain or suffering. *See also* S. Exec. Rep. No. 101-30, at 6 (1990). . . .

3. **Legal doctrines under the Federal Criminal Law that could render specific conduct, otherwise criminal, *not* unlawful** . . .

   a. **Commander-in-Chief Authority**

(U) As the Supreme Court has recognized, and as we will explain further below, the President enjoys complete discretion in the exercise of his Commander-in-Chief authority including in conducting operations against hostile forces. Because both "[t]he executive power and the command of the military and naval forces [are] vested in the President," the Supreme Court has unanimously stated that it is "*the President alone* who is constitutionally invested with the *entire charge of hostile operations.*" *Hamilton v. Dillin*, 88 U.S. (21 Wall.) 73, 87 (1874) (emphasis added).

(U) In light of the President's complete authority over the conduct of war, without a clear statement otherwise, criminal statutes are not read as infringing on the President's ultimate authority in these areas. The Supreme Court has established a canon of statutory construction that statutes are to be construed in a manner that avoids constitutional difficulties so long as a reasonable alternative construction is available. *See, e.g., Edward J. DeBartolo Corp. v. Florida Gulf Coast Bldg. & Constr. Trades Council*, 485 U.S. 568, 575 (1988) (citing *NLRB v. Catholic Bishop of Chicago*, 440 U.S. 490, 499-501, 504 (1979)) ("[W]here an otherwise acceptable construction of a statute would raise serious constitutional problems, [courts] will construe [a] statute to avoid such problems unless such construction is plainly contrary to the intent of Congress.") This canon of construction applies especially where an act of Congress could be read to encroach upon powers constitutionally committed to a coordinate branch of government. . . .

(U) In the area of foreign affairs, and war powers in particular, the avoidance canon has special force. *See, e.g., Dept of Navy v. Egan*, 484 U.S. 518, 530 (1988) ("unless Congress specifically has provided otherwise, courts traditionally have been reluctant to intrude upon the authority of the

Executive in military and national security affairs."); *Japan Whaling Ass'n v. American Cetacean Socy,* 478 U.S. 221, 232-33 (1986) (construing federal statutes to avoid curtailment of traditional presidential prerogatives in foreign affairs). It should not be lightly assumed that Congress has acted to interfere with the President's constitutionally superior position as Chief Executive and Commander-in-Chief in the area of military operations. *See Egan,* 484 U.S. at 529 (quoting *Haig v. Agee,* 1453 U.S. 280, 293-94 (1981). *See also Agee,* 453 U.S. at 291 (deference to Executive Branch is "especially" appropriate "in the area of national security").

(U) In order to respect the President's inherent constitutional authority to manage a military campaign, 18 U.S.C. §2340A (the prohibition against torture) as well as any other potentially applicable statute must be construed as inapplicable to interrogations undertaken pursuant to his Commander-in-Chief authority. Congress lacks authority under Article I to set the terms and conditions under which the President may exercise his authority as Commander-in-Chief to control the conduct of operations during a war. The President's power to detain and interrogate enemy combatants arises out of his constitutional authority as Commander-in-Chief. A construction of Section 2340A that applied the provision to regulate the President's authority as Commander-in-Chief to determine the interrogation and treatment of enemy combatants would raise serious constitutional questions. Congress may no more regulate the President's ability to detain and interrogate enemy combatants than it may regulate his ability to direct troop movements on the battlefield. Accordingly, we would construe Section 2340A to avoid this constitutional difficulty and conclude that it does not apply to the President's detention and interrogation of enemy combatants pursuant to his Commander-in-Chief authority. . . .

(U) One of the core functions of the Commander in Chief is that of capturing, detaining, and interrogating members of the enemy. It is well settled that the President may seize and detain enemy combatants, at least for the duration of the conflict, and the laws of war make clear that prisoners may be interrogated for information concerning the enemy, its strength, and its plans. Numerous Presidents have ordered the capture, detention, and questioning of enemy combatants during virtually every major conflict in the Nation's history, including recent conflicts in Korea, Vietnam, and the Persian Gulf. Recognizing this authority, Congress has never attempted to restrict or interfere with the President's authority on this score.

(U) Any effort by Congress to regulate the interrogation of unlawful combatants would violate the Constitution's sole vesting of the Commander-in-Chief authority in the President. There can be little doubt that intelligence operations, such as the detention and interrogation of

Chapter 12. Investigating Terrorism

enemy combatants and leaders, are both necessary and proper for the effective conduct of a military campaign. Indeed, such operations may be of more importance in a war with an international terrorist organization than one with the conventional armed forces of a nation-state, due to the former's emphasis on secret operations and surprise attacks against civilians. It may be the case that only successful interrogations can provide the information necessary to prevent the success of covert terrorist attacks upon the United States and its citizens. Congress can no more interfere with the President's conduct of the interrogation of enemy combatants than it can dictate strategy or tactical decisions on the battlefield. Just as statutes that order the President to conduct warfare in a certain manner or for specific goals would be unconstitutional, so too are laws that seek to prevent the President from gaining the intelligence he believes necessary to prevent attacks upon the United States. . . .

b. Necessity

(U) The defense of necessity could be raised, under the current circumstances, to an allegation of a violation of a criminal statute. Often referred to as the "choice of evils" defense, necessity has been defined as follows:

> Conduct that the actor believes to be necessary to avoid a harm or evil to himself or to another is justifiable, provided that:
>
> (a) the harm or evil sought to be avoided by such conduct is greater than that sought to be prevented by the law defining the offense charged; and
> (b) neither the Code nor other law defining the offense provides exceptions or defenses dealing with the specific situation involved; and
> (c) a legislative purpose to exclude the justification claimed does not otherwise plainly appear.

Model Penal Code §3.02. *See also* Wayne R. LaFave & Austin W. Scott, 1 Substantive Criminal Law §5.4 at 627 (1986 & 2002 supp.) ("LaFave & Scott"). Although there is no federal statute that generally establishes necessity or other justifications as defenses to federal criminal laws, the Supreme Court has recognized the defense. *See United States v. Bailey*, 444 U.S. 394, 410 (1980) (relying on LaFave & Scott and Model Penal Code definitions of necessity defense). . . .

(U) Legal authorities identify an important exception to the necessity defense. The defense is available "only in situations wherein the legislature has not itself, in its criminal statute, made a determination of values." [LaFave & Scott] at 629. Thus, if Congress explicitly has made clear that violation of a statute cannot be outweighed by the harm avoided, courts cannot recognize the necessity defense. LaFave and Israel provide as an example an abortion statute that made clear that abortions even to save the life of the mother would still be a crime; in such cases the necessity defense would be unavailable. *Id.* at 630. Here, however, Congress has not explicitly made a determination of values vis-a-vis torture. In fact, Congress explicitly removed efforts to remove torture from the weighing of values permitted by the necessity defense.[21]

c. Self-Defense

(U) Even if a court were to find that necessity did not justify the violation of a criminal statute, a defendant could still appropriately raise a claim of self-defense. The right to self-defense, even when it involves deadly force, is deeply embedded in our law, both as to individuals and as to the nation as a whole. . . . Self-defense is a common-law defense to federal criminal law offenses, and nothing in the text, structure or history of Section 2340A precludes its application to a charge of torture. In the absence of any textual provision to the contrary, we assume self-defense can be an appropriate defense to an allegation of torture. . . .

(U) There can be little doubt that the nation's right to self-defense has been triggered under our law. The Constitution announces that one of its

---

21. In the CAT [Convention Against Torture], torture is defined as the intentional infliction of severe pain or suffering "for such purposes as obtaining from him or a third person information or a confession." CAT art 1.1. One could argue that such a definition represented an attempt to indicate that the good of obtaining information – no matter what the circumstances – could not justify an act of torture. In other words, necessity would not be a defense. In enacting Section 2340, however, Congress removed the purpose element in the definition of torture, evidencing an intention to remove any fixing of values by statute. By leaving Section 2340 silent as to the harm done by torture in comparison to other harms, Congress allowed the necessity defense to apply when appropriate.

Further, the CAT contains an additional provision that "no exceptional circumstances whatsoever, whether a state of war or a threat of war, internal political instability or any other public emergency, may be invoked as a justification of torture," CAT art. 2.2. Aware of this provision of the treaty and of the definition of the necessity defense that allows the legislature to provide *for* an exception to the defense, see Model Penal Code §3,02(b), Congress did not incorporate CAT article 2.2 into Section 2-4. Given that Congress omitted CAT's effort to bar a necessity or wartime defense, Section 2340 could be read as permitting the defense.

Chapter 12. Investigating Terrorism

purposes is "to provide for the common defense." U.S. Const., Preamble. Article I, §8 declares that Congress is to exercise its powers to "provide for the common defense." *See also* 2 Pub. Papers of Ronald Reagan 920, 921 (1988-89) (right to self-defense recognized by Article 51 of the U.N. Charter). The President has particular responsibility and power to take steps to defend the nation and its people. *In re Neagle*, 135 U.S. at 64. *See also* U.S. Const. art. IV, §4 ("The United States shall . . . protect [each of the States] against Invasion"). As Commander-in-Chief and Chief Executive, he may use the Armed Forces to protect the nation and its people. *See, e.g., United States v. Verdugo-Urquidez*, 494 U.S. 259, 273 (1990). And he may employ secret agents to aid in his work as Commander-in-Chief. *Totten v. United States*, 92 U.S. 105, 106 (1876). As the Supreme Court observed in *The Prize Cases*, 67 U.S. (2 Black) 635 (1862), in response to an armed attack on the United States "the President is not only authorized but bound to resist force by force . . . without waiting for any special legislative authority." *Id.* at 668. The September 11 events were a direct attack on the United States, and as we have explained above, the President has authorized the use of military force with the support of Congress.

(U) As DOJ has made clear in opinions involving the war on al Qaida, the nation's right to self-defense has been triggered by the events of September 11. If a government defendant were to harm an enemy combatant during an interrogation in a manner that might arguably violate criminal prohibition, he would be doing so in order to prevent further attacks on the United States by the al Qaida terrorist network. In that case, DOJ believes that he could argue that the executive branch's constitutional authority to protect the nation from attack justified his actions. This national and international version of the right to self-defense could supplement and bolster the government defendant's individual right. . . .

B. Federal Civil Statutes

1. 28 U.S.C. §1350

(U) 28 U.S.C. §1350 extends the jurisdiction of the U.S. District Courts to *"any civil action by an alien for a tort only, committed in violation of the law of nations or a treaty of the United States."*[33] Section 1350 is a vehicle by which victims of torture and other human rights violations by their native government and its agents have sought judicial remedy for the

---

33. (U) 28 U.S.C. §1350, the Alien Tort Claim Act (ATCA).

wrongs they've suffered. However, all the decided cases we have found involve foreign nationals suing in U.S. District Courts for conduct by foreign actors/governments.[34] The District Court for the District of Columbia has determined that section 1350 actions, by the GTMO detainees, against the United States or its agents acting within the scope of employment fail. This is because (1) the United States has not waived sovereign immunity to such suits like those brought by the detainees, and (2) the *Eisentrager* doctrine barring habeas access also precludes other potential avenues of jurisdiction.[35] This of course leaves interrogators vulnerable in their individual capacity for conduct a court might find to constitute torture. Assuming a court would take jurisdiction over the matter and grant standing to the detainee,[36] it is possible that this statute would provide an avenue of relief for actions of the United States or its agents found to violate customary international law. . . .

2. Torture Victims Protection Act (TVPA)

(U) In 1992, President Bush signed into law the Torture Victims Protection Act of 1991.[37] Appended to the U.S. Code as a note to section 1350, the TVPA specifically creates a cause of action for individuals (or their successors) who have been subjected to torture or extra-judicial killing by "an individual who, under actual or apparent authority, or color of law, *of any foreign nation* – (1) subjects an individual to torture shall, in a civil action, be liable for damages to that individual; or (2) subjects an individual to extra-judicial killing shall, in a civil action, be liable for damages . . . ."

---

34. (U) See, for example, *Abebe-Jira v. Negewo*, No. 93-9133, United States Court of Appeals, Eleventh Circuit, Jan. 10, 1996. In this case the 11th Circuit concluded, "the Alien Tort Claims Act establishes a federal forum where courts may fashion domestic common law remedies to give effect to violations of customary international law."

35. (U) *Al Odah v. United States* (D.D.C., 2002).

36. (U) *Filartiga v. Pena-Irala*, 630 F.2d 876 (2nd Cir. 1980) 885, note 18, "conduct of the type alleged here [torture] would be actionable under 42 U.S.C. §1983, or undoubtedly the Constitution, if performed by a government official."

37. Pub. L. No. 102-256, 106 Stat. 73, 28 U.S.C. § 1350 (note).

(emphasis added).[38] Thus, the TVPA does not apply to the conduct of U.S. agents acting under the color of law. . . .

Counter-Resistance Techniques in the War on Terrorism
April 16, 2003
http://www.defenselink.mil/news/Jun2004/d20040622doc9.pdf

Memorandum for: Commander, US Southern Command

From: Donald Rumsfeld, Secretary of Defense

(U) I have considered the report of the Working Group that I directed be established on January 15, 2003.

(U) I approve the use of specified counter-resistance techniques, subject to the following:

(U) a. The techniques I authorize are those lettered A-X, at Tab A.
(U) b. These techniques must be used with all the safeguards described at Tab B.
(U) c. Use of these techniques is limited to interrogations of unlawful combatants held at Guantanamo Bay, Cuba.
(U) d. Prior to the use of these techniques, the Chairman of the Working Group on Detainee Interrogations in the Global War on Terrorism must brief you and your staff.

(U) I reiterate that US Armed Forces shall continue to treat detainees humanely and, to the extent appropriate and consistent with military

---

38. (U) The definition of torture used in PL 102-256 is: "any act, directed against an individual in the offender's custody or physical control, by which severe pain or suffering (other than pain or suffering arising only from or inherent in, or incidental to lawful sanctions) whether physical or mental, is intentionally inflicted on that individual for such purposes as obtaining from that individual or a third person information or a confession, punishing that individual for an act that individual or a third person has committed or is suspected of having committed, intimidating or coercing that individual or a third person, or for any reason based on discrimination of any kind." This is similar, but broader, than the definition in the Torture Statute. The definition of mental pain and suffering is the same as in the Torture Statute.

necessity, in a manner consistent with the principles of the Geneva Conventions. In addition, if you intend to use techniques B, I, O, or X, you must specifically determine that military necessity requires its use and notify me in advance.

(U) If, in your view, you require additional interrogation techniques for a particular detainee, you should provide me, via the Chairman of the Joint Chiefs of Staff, a written request describing the proposed technique, recommended safeguards, and the rationale for applying it with an identified detainee.

(U) Nothing in this memorandum in any way restricts your existing authority to maintain good order and discipline among detainees.

TAB A
INTERROGATION TECHNIQUES

(U) The use of techniques A – X is subject to the general safeguards as provided below as well as specific implementation guidelines to be provided by the appropriate authority. Specific implementation guidance with respect to techniques A – Q is provided in Army Field Manual 34-52. Further implementation guidance with respect to techniques R – X will need to be developed by the appropriate authority.

(U) Of the techniques set forth below, the policy aspects of certain techniques should be considered to the extent those policy aspects reflect the views of other major U.S. partner nations. Where applicable, the description of the technique is annotated to include a summary of the policy issues that should be considered before application of the technique.

A. (U) Direct: Asking straightforward questions.

B. (U) Incentive/Removal of Incentive: Providing a reward or removing a privilege, above and beyond those that are required by the Geneva Convention, from detainees. (Caution: Other nations that believe that detainees are entitled to POW protections may consider that provision and retention of religious items (e.g., the Koran) are protected under international law (see, Geneva III, Article 34). Although the provisions of the Geneva Convention are not applicable to the interrogation of unlawful combatants, consideration should be given to these views prior to the application of the technique.)

C. (U) Emotional Love: Playing on the love a detainee has for an individual or group.

D. (U) Emotional Hate: Playing on the hatred a detainee has for an individual or group.

E. (U) Fear Up Harsh: Significantly increasing the fear level in a

Chapter 12. Investigating Terrorism 71

detainee.

F. (U) Fear Up Mild: Moderately increasing the fear level in a detainee.

G. (U) Reduced Fear: Reducing the fear level in a detainee.

H. (U) Pride and Ego Up: Boosting the ego of a detainee.

I. (U) Pride and Ego Down: Attacking or insulting the ego of a detainee, not beyond the limits that would apply to a POW. (Caution: Article 17 of the Geneva III provides, "Prisoners of war who refuse to answer may not be threatened, insulted, or exposed to any unpleasant or disadvantageous treatment of any kind." Other nations that believe that detainees are entitled to POW protections may consider this technique inconsistent with the provisions of Geneva. Although the provisions of Geneva are not applicable to the interrogation of unlawful combatants, consideration should be given to these views prior to application of the technique.)

J. (U) Futility: Invoking the feeling of futility of a detainee.

K. (U) We Know All: Convincing the detainee that the interrogator knows the answer to questions he asks the detainee.

L. (U) Establish Your Identity: Convincing the detainee that the interrogator has mistaken the detainee for someone else.

M. (U) Repetition Approach: Continuously repeating the same question to the detainee within interrogation periods of normal duration.

N. (U) File and Dossier: Convincing the detainee that the interrogator has a damning and inaccurate file, which must be fixed.

O. (U) Mutt and Jeff: A team consisting of a friendly and harsh interrogator. The harsh interrogator might employ the Pride and Ego Down technique. (Caution: Other nations that believe that POW protections apply to detainees may view this technique as inconsistent with the Geneva III, Article 13 which provides that POWs must be protected against acts of intimidation. Although the provisions of Geneva are not applicable to the interrogation of unlawful combatants, consideration should be given to these views prior to application of the technique.)

P. (U) Rapid Fire: Questioning in rapid succession without allowing detainee to answer.

Q. (U) Silence: Staring at the detainee to encourage discomfort.

R. (U) Change of Scenery Up: Removing the detainee from the standard interrogation setting (generally to a location more pleasant, but no worse).

S. (U) Change of Scenery Down: Removing the detainee from the standard interrogation setting and placing him in a setting that may be less comfortable; would not constitute a substantial change in environmental quality.

T. (U) Dietary Manipulation: Changing the diet of a detainee; no intended deprivation of food or water; no adverse medical or cultural effect and without intent to deprive subject of food or water, e.g., hot rations to MREs.

U. (U) Environmental Manipulation: Altering the environment to create moderate discomfort (e.g., adjusting temperature or introducing an unpleasant smell). Conditions would not be such that they would injure the detainee. Detainee would be accompanied by interrogator at all times. (Caution: Based on court cases in other countries, some nations may view application of this technique in certain circumstances to be inhumane. Consideration of these views should be given to use of this technique.)

V. (U) Sleep Adjustment: Adjusting the sleeping times of the detainee (e.g., reversing sleep cycles from night to day.) This technique is NOT sleep deprivation.

W. (U) False Flag: Convincing the detainee that individuals from a country other than the United States are interrogating him.

X. (U) Isolation: Isolating the detainee from other detainees while still complying with basic standards of treatment. (Caution: The use of isolation as an interrogation technique requires detailed implementation instructions, including specific guidelines regarding the length of isolation, medical and psychological review, and approval for extensions of the length of isolation by the appropriate level in the chain of command. This technique is not known to have been generally used for interrogation purposes for longer than 30 days. Those nations that believe detainees are subject to POW protections may view use of this technique as inconsistent with the requirements of Geneva III, Article 13 which provides that POWs must be protected against acts of intimidation; Article 14 which provides that POWs are entitled to respect for their person; Article 34 which prohibits coercion and Article 126 which ensures access and basic standards of treatment. Although the provisions of Geneva are not applicable to the interrogation of unlawful combatants, consideration should be given to these views prior to application of the technique.)

TAB B
GENERAL SAFEGUARDS

(U) Application of these interrogation techniques is subject to the following general safeguards: (i) limited to use only at strategic interrogation facilities; (ii) there is a good basis to believe that the detainee possesses critical intelligence; (iii) the detainee is medically and operationally evaluated as suitable (considering all techniques to be used in combination); (iv) interrogators are specifically trained for the technique(s); (v) a specific interrogation plan (including reasonable safeguards, limits on

Chapter 12. Investigating Terrorism 73

duration, intervals between applications, termination criteria and the presence or availability of qualified medical personnel) has been developed; (vi) there is appropriate supervision; and (vii) there is appropriate specified senior approval for use with any specific detainee (after considering the foregoing and receiving legal advice). . . .

NOTES AND QUESTIONS

a. Torture in General

1. *Detainee Investigations.* Several collections of documents relating to U.S. interrogation of its detainees may be found online. Among the most extensive are New York Times, *A Guide to the Memos on Torture* (n.d.), *at* http://www.nytimes.com/ref/international/24MEMO-GUIDE.html; National Security Archive, *Interrogation Documents: Debating U.S. Policy and Methods* (updated July 13, 2004), *at http://www.gwu.edu/~nsarchiv/NSA EBB/NSAEBB127*; and American Civil Liberties Union, *Government Documents on Torture* (n.d.), *at http://action.aclu.org/torturefoia/.* The Department of Defense Web site also provides links to DOD reports, independent panel and inspector general reports, briefing transcripts, and news releases and articles, at *http://www.defenselink.mil/news/detainee _investigations.html.*

2. *Definitions.* What constitutes "torture"? Not surprisingly, torture is forbidden by a number of written treaties and international conventions, by customary international law, and by U.S. statutory and constitutional law. There is, however, no universally accepted definition of "torture." Torture may be physical or psychological, and a variety of interrogation techniques may be forbidden as torture.

What are the elements of the Torture Convention's definition of "torture"? Of the United States understanding upon ratification? Do any of the techniques in Defense Secretary Rumsfeld's April 16, 2003, memo on Guantánamo exceed the limits set out in either? Which techniques? Would the same methods be lawful in Iraq? At some undisclosed off-shore location?

The Torture Statute, 18 U.S.C. §§2340-2340B, is supposed to implement the Torture Convention. Recall that in August 2002 the Justice Department's Office of Legal Counsel (OLC) offered a very narrow definition of "torture" (*see* p. 41 *supra*) and argued that the President could authorize torture. It also indicated that interrogation activities "may be cruel, in-human, or degrading, but still not produce pain and suffering of the requisite intensity" to violate §2340. Bybee Memo (*supra* p. 41 note 4, at

1). The memorandum also asserted that a specific intent to torture is required to violate the torture statute. *Id.* at 4. How would you rate this definition of the key terms against those set out in the Torture Convention and the U.S. understanding?

Two months after the public disclosure of abuses at Abu Ghraib, the August 2002 memorandum was withdrawn by OLC head Jack Goldsmith, and a new opinion superseding it was delivered to the new Deputy Attorney General for OLC on December 30, 2004. Memorandum for James B. Comey, Deputy Atty. General, from Daniel Levin, Acting Asst. Atty. General, *Legal Standards Applicable Under 18 U.S.C. 2340-2340A*, Dec. 30, 2004, *at http://www.usdoj.gov/olc/dagmemo.pdf.* The new memorandum questioned "the appropriateness and relevance of the non-statutory discussion . . . and various aspects of the statutory analysis" in the earlier memo, namely the assertion that torture required organ failure, impaired bodily function, or death. *Id.* at 1-2. The 2004 memorandum continued to maintain that it was unlikely that a person who "acted in good faith, and only after reasonable investigation establishing that his conduct would not inflict severe physical or mental pain or suffering," would possess the specific intent required to violate the torture statute. *Id.* at 17. Do you agree?

Most authorities ban conduct considered cruel, inhuman, or degrading, but they differ in their interpretation of the terms. Note that the United States conditioned its acceptance of the Torture Convention on the understanding that the United States considers itself bound by the proscription against "cruel, inhuman or degrading treatment or punishment" only to the extent such conduct is prohibited by the Fifth, Eighth, and/or Fourteenth Amendments to the Constitution. What is the practical significance of this reservation? Would a universal definition of the key terms be a good idea? Would it matter? *See* Oren Gross, *Are Torture Warrants Warranted? Pragmatic Absolutism and Official Disobedience*, 88 Minn. L. Rev. 101, 109 (2004) ("preventive interrogational torture is far too complex to be addressed by definitional juggling").

3. *"Torture Lite."* Were the interpretations of the relevant law on torture by Defense Department and Justice Department lawyers in effect endorsements of what has been referred to as "torture lite"? *See* Seth F. Kreimer, *"Torture Light," "Full Bodied" Torture, and the Insulation of Legal Conscience,* 1 J. Natl. Security L. & Poly. ___ (2005); Duncan Campbell, *U.S. Interrogators Turn to "Torture Lite,"* The Guardian, Jan. 25, 2003, at 17. Was approval by the Working Group and Secretary Rumsfeld of the techniques listed at pp. 69-73 *supra* further evidence of sanctioned "torture lite"? Did the Working Group specifically disapprove

Chapter 12. Investigating Terrorism

of any interrogation technique? Do you suppose that the resulting legal ambiguities contributed to abuses at Abu Ghraib and elsewhere?

4. *Assigning Responsibility.* There were at least three different sets of interrogation rules in place in Abu Ghraib prison at different times – from Army field manuals, from personnel who had worked earlier in Afghanistan, and from Guantánamo. Craig Gordon, *High-Pressure Tactics: Critics Say Bush Policies – Post 9/11 – Gave Interrogators Leeway to Push Beyond Normal Limits*, Newsday, May 23, 2004. General Taguba found that operating procedures and copies of the Geneva Conventions were not distributed to the guards handling the prisoners. To complicate matters, senior military commanders called for interrogators to isolate and manipulate detainees who may have "significant intelligence value." R. Jeffrey Smith, *Memo Gave Intelligence Bigger Role: Increased Pressure Sought on Prisoners*, Wash. Post, May 21, 2004.

The overall detention and interrogation picture that has emerged from official statements and documents reveals "a trail of fitful ad hoc policymaking" where interrogation techniques were authorized, then rescinded or modified, at times leading to decisions made in the field or at the Pentagon on a case-by-case basis. Dana Priest & Bradley Graham, *U.S. Struggled Over How Far to Push Tactics*, Wash. Post, June 24, 2004, at A1. The decision documents suggest that Secretary Rumsfeld was directly responsible for most of the decisions. Unlike CIA requests for expanded interrogation authority that were reviewed by the Department of Justice and the National Security Council, Defense Department interrogation policy decisions were not subjected to outside review. *Id.*

Who do you think is responsible for the abuses at Abu Ghraib? The Army announced in April 2005 that it was preparing to issue a new field manual to replace *Intelligence Interrogation* (FM 34-52), Sept. 28, 1992. The new manual reportedly will specifically prohibit the harsh techniques that came to light in the Abu Ghraib scandal and will include safeguards to prevent future misconduct. Eric Schmitt, *In New Manual, Army Limits Tactics in Interrogation*, N.Y. Times, April 28, 2005, at A1. The new manual apparently will also forbid physical and mental torture, slapping, and humiliation. Additional units trained in detention operations are planned, including 9,000 new military intelligence personnel. *Id.*

In June 2005 the Defense Department promoted or nominated for promotion the former deputy commander of U.S. forces in Iraq and the senior military lawyer for the U.S. command in Baghdad, both involved in overseeing or advising detention and interrogation operations during the Abu Ghraib scandal. The top intelligence officer in Iraq at that time was promoted earlier in the year. Eric Schmitt, *Army Moves to Advance 2*

Linked to Abu Ghraib, N.Y. Times, June 29, 2005, at A20. The *Schlesinger Report* (p. 41 n.5 *supra*) found those officers to be among those responsible for the abuses at Abu Ghraib, and the Fay Report (p. 42 n.8 *supra*) faulted the commanders for issuing and revising the interrogation rules three times in 30 days, and their legal staff for giving bad legal advice – not warning that practices permitted at Guantánamo Bay and in Afghanistan might not be lawful in Iraq. Nevertheless, the Army Inspector General cleared them of any wrongdoing. Inspector General, Dept. of the Army, *Detainee Operations Inspection,* July 21, 2004, at http://www4.army.mil/ocpa/reports/ArmyIGDetaineeAbuse/index.html.

The various Defense Department investigations of detention practices cited in this narrative found detention and interrogation abuses in Afghanistan and at Guantánamo. In each instance of documented abuse, however, only low-level interrogators or handlers have been recommended for discipline. An inquiry by Air Force Lt. Gen. Randall M. Schmidt of Guantánamo interrogation practices recommended a reprimand for Army Maj. Gen. Geoffrey C. Miller, commander of the Guantánamo facility in 2002 and 2003, for failing to oversee the interrogation of a high-value detainee who was subjected to abusive treatment. After a review of three years' practice and over 24,000 interrogations at Guantánamo, General Schmidt found three acts in violation of Army Field Manual 34-52 and the Working Group guidance. *Army Regulation 15-6: Final Report, Investigation into FBI Allegations of Detainee Abuse at Guantanamo Bay, Cuba Detention Facility,* Apr. 1, 2005, amended June 9, 2005. After referral of the recommendation, the Army Inspector General decided that Miller had not violated law or Defense Department policy. David S. Cloud, *Guantanamo Reprimand Was Sought, An Aide Says,* N.Y. Times, July 13, 2005, at A16.

At a news conference called in response to the Abu Ghraib publicity in June 2004, White House Counsel Alberto Gonzalez stated that the United States intended to "follow its treaty obligations and U.S. law, both of which prohibit the use of torture." Gonzalez denied that "the president . . . authorized ordered or directed" violations of "the standards of the torture conventions or the torture statute." *Transcript of Press Briefing by Alberto Gonzalez,* June 22, 2004, at http://www.whitehouse.gov/news/releases/2004/06020040622-14.html. What legal wiggle room does the Gonzalez statement leave for the President? Does it mean that President Bush was not responsible for the reported abuses?

5. *Who Decides What Interrogation Conduct Is Unlawful?* The policy of the United States is to condemn and prohibit torture. *See generally* U.S. Dept. of State, Introduction, Initial Report of the United States of America

Chapter 12. Investigating Terrorism

to the UN Committee Against Torture, Oct. 15, 1999, *available at* http://www.state.gov/www/global/human_rights/torture_intro.html ("Torture is prohibited by law throughout the United States. It is categorically denounced as a matter of policy and as a tool of state authority."); *Second Periodic Report of the United States of America to the Committee Against Torture,* May 6, 2005, *available at* http://www.state.gov/g/drl/rls/45738.htm ("United States is unequivocally opposed to the use and practice of torture.... No circumstance whatsoever ... may be invoked as a justification for or defense to committing torture.") Who decides how to translate the policy into enforceable rules?

6. *Ghost Detainees.* On March 19, 2004, the Justice Department's Office of Legal Counsel (OLC) drafted a confidential memo that authorized the CIA to transfer detainees out of Iraq for interrogation. The CIA then transported as many as a dozen detainees from Iraq to other countries between March and October of 2004. *See* Dana Priest, *Memo Lets CIA Take Detainees Out of Iraq,* Wash. Post, Oct. 24, 2004, A1. (The practice of "extraordinary rendition" is addressed *infra* pp. 95-102.) The memo also provided support for the CIA practice of holding "ghost detainees." Hiwa Abdul Rahman Rashul, a suspected member of the Iraqi Al-Ansar terrorist group who was nicknamed "Triple X" by CIA and military officials, was captured by Kurdish fighters in June or July 2003. He was turned over to the CIA, which rendered him to Afghanistan for interrogation. In October, then-White House Counsel Gonzalez asked OLC to advise on whether Rashul was a "protected person" under the Fourth Geneva Convention. (Article 49 of the Fourth Geneva Convention prohibits "the Deportations of protected persons from occupied territory.") OLC answered that Rashul was protected and had to be returned to Iraq. The CIA brought Rashul back and suspended renditions out of Iraq. At the same time, then-DCI George Tenet asked Defense Secretary Rumsfeld not to give Rashul a prisoner number and to hide him from the Red Cross. "Ghost detainee" Rashul was then lost in the Iraqi prison system for seven months. When asked about the legal basis for hiding Rashul, Rumsfeld replied, "We know from our knowledge that [Tenet] has authority to do this." *Id.* In June 2004, Secretary Rumsfeld acknowledged that military officials, acting on a request from the CIA, ordered military officers in Iraq to hold a detainee in Iraq but not list him on the prison rolls. Eric Schmitt & Thom Shanker, *Rumsfeld Issued an Order to Hide Detainee in Iraq,* N.Y. Times, June 17, 2004, at A1. An Army inquiry in 2004 found that the CIA held from dozens to 100 "ghost detainees." Priest, *supra.* What is wrong with hiding a detainee in this fashion? Can you imagine a legal justification for holding such "ghost detainees"? The forthcoming revised Army field manual

announced in April 2005 reportedly will forbid the CIA from keeping unregistered detainees at Army prisons. Schmitt, *supra* Note 4.

7. *The Moral Dimension.* What *should* the U.S. position on torture be? There is an undoubted and morally complex tension between the need to obtain information that could save many lives through coercive interrogation of a suspect and the condoning of torture. Is it *ever* justifiable to torture a detainee? Assume that authorities have in custody someone whom they are certain has placed an especially destructive explosive device somewhere in a large shopping mall. The explosive may go off at any time, and there may not be enough time to evacuate the mall. If the bomb detonates, thousands will die. The detainee is the only person with knowledge of the bomb, and he will not talk. Should the interrogators torture the detainee in hopes of learning the location of the bomb before it is too late? *Compare* Alan Dershowitz, *Why Terrorism Works* 142-149 (2002) (torture techniques may be morally and legally justified in some circumstances),*with* Assn. of the Bar of the City of New York, Comm. on Intl. Human Rights, Comm. on Military Affairs and Justice, *Human Rights Standards Applicable to the United States' Interrogation of Detainees*, April 30, 2004, at 8-9, *available at* http://www.abcny.org/pdf/HUMAN RIGHTS.pdf ("Condoning torture under any circumstances erodes one of the most basic principles of international law and human rights and contradicts our values as a democratic state."). The Convention Against Torture, to which the United States is a party, adopts the latter position. See p. 66 n.21 in this Supplement.

8. *Torture Warrants?* Professor Dershowitz would recognize a qualified prohibition on torture. He suggests a form of judicial "torture warrant" before permitting torture of suspected terrorists in interrogations. Dershowitz, *supra,* at 148-149, 158-163. What might be the criteria for issuing such warrants? Should a judge, for example, try to balance the credibility or gravity of a threat against the suffering or injury to be inflicted on the recalcitrant detainee? Can you articulate a process that would be helpful to the court in doing that? Can you think of other methods for keeping the "qualified" use of torture in check?

Another approach to making exceptions to a ban on torture has been recommended by Professors Philip Heymann and Juliette Kayyem. They advocate an "emergency exception" to a ban on torture, based on a written finding by the President of "an urgent and extraordinary need," reported "within a reasonable period" to appropriate congressional committees, stating the reason to believe that the information is known by the person to be interrogated, that it "concerns a specific plan that threatens U.S. lives," and that there are "no reasonable alternatives to save the lives in question." Philip B. Heymann & Juliette N. Kayyem, *Long-Term Strategy Project for Preserving Security and Democratic Freedoms in the War on Terrorism* 25-26 (2004). Is this "findings" approach preferable in the ticking bomb case to a torture warrant?

Alternatively, should we expect government officials confronted with the ticking bomb case to engage in a form of official disobedience, hoping for ratification of the disobedient conduct after the fact? *See* Gross, *supra*, 88 Minn. L. Rev. at 107; *see also* casebook pp. 86-87. Could Congress or the President make lawful through ratification torture that was undertaken in disobedience of the law?

9. *Defenses of Torture Offered by the Government.*

a. *Necessity.* The Bush administration lawyers argued that self-defense and necessity may legitimate torture. Does the presence of an arguable defense to an act of torture nullify the requirement that the torture be legally authorized? *See* William C. Banks & Peter Raven-Hansen, *Targeted Killing and Assassination: The U.S. Legal Framework,* 37 U. Richmond L. Rev. 667, 668 (2003) (basic rule of law requires positive legal authority for government actions). Would a necessity defense be available even where Congress clearly proscribed the conduct so defended? *See* Wayne R. LaFave & Austin W. Scott, I Substantive Criminal Law §5.4 at 629. Might a defense be available to someone charged with carrying out even a specious legal authorization of torture? *See* Public Committee Against Torture in Israel v. State of Israel, H.C. 5100/94, 53(4) P.D. 817 (1999).

b. *Self-Defense.* The criminal law doctrine of self-defense permits the use of force to prevent harm to another person. Does the criminal law doctrine apply in this setting to exculpate otherwise unlawful torture or inhumane treatment by an interrogator of a prisoner? Is an individual claim of self-defense portable to the executive branch in the war on terrorism? How would you rebut the argument made by the Working Group (p. 59 *supra*) that the Commander in Chief's defensive war powers legitimate what might otherwise be proscribed as torture? Unlike the Bybee Memo (p. 41 n.4 *supra*), the December 30, 2004, OLC memo (p. 74 *supra*) made no mention of the constitutional authority of the President to disregard statutory or treaty obligations regarding torture. Of what significance is the revision?

10. *Article II as a Trump Card?* The Bush administration asserted in the Working Group memorandum and elsewhere that if any of the laws

proscribing torture apply to interrogation during the war on terrorism, such laws must be subordinated to the Commander-in-Chief Clause power to conduct the military campaign. In what particular settings is the Article II argument most persuasive? Compare battlefield detentions and on-the-spot interrogations of those seized during combat with long-term detentions in remote locations away from the battle. Al Qaeda reportedly continues to plan and carry out terrorist acts that threaten national security. Based on the ongoing threat, is the capture and interrogation by torture of al Qaeda operatives merely a tactical choice in carrying out the war on terrorism by the Commander in Chief?

If information gained from interrogations may prevent future attacks, does it necessarily follow that the terms and conditions of detention and interrogation are subject solely to presidential determination? *Cf.* U.S. Const. art. I, §8 (granting Congress the power to "define and punish . . . Offenses against the Law of Nations" and to "make Rules for the government and Regulation of the land and naval forces"). How does the Use of Force resolution of September 18, 2001 (casebook p. 262) affect your answer?

If you find a constitutional limit on the authority of Congress to regulate interrogation, can you construe the laws reviewed in this section to avoid the potential constitutional problem? Did the Working Group memo persuasively apply the avoidance canon? Can Congress prohibit particular interrogatory techniques when interrogation is part of the conduct of war committed to the Commander in Chief? *See* January 2002 OLC memo, p. 45 *supra,* at 36, 39 ("Congress can no more interfere with the President's conduct of the interrogation of enemy combatants than it can dictate strategic or tactical decisions on the battlefield.").

11. Lawyers and Their Role. Many of the legal opinions in the Justice Department and Defense Department memoranda excerpted above are highly controversial. Are the opinions legally and morally defensible? Some have argued that the memoranda were designed primarily to protect potentially culpable officials from prosecution for interrogation abuses. See *Lawyers' Statement on Bush Administration's Torture Memos,* Aug. 4, 2004, *at http://www.allianceforjustice.org/spotlight/collection/spotlight_ statement0804.html* (letter signed by about 130 prominent lawyers); *Letter Sent to the United States Congress Regarding Recent Human Rights Issues in Iraq,* June 16, 2004, *at http://www.iraq-letter.com* (letter signed by more than 500 university professors). Others, including the Defense Department investigators of detention and interrogation practices, found that the confusion and ambiguity fostered by these memoranda may have contributed to the abusive practices, or to a "permissive climate in which

Chapter 12. Investigating Terrorism

abuses were more likely." Richard B. Bilder & Detlev F. Vagts, *Speaking Law to Power: Lawyers and Torture*, 98 Am. J. Intl. L. 689, 691 (2004) (citing, e.g., John Barry, Michael Hirsh & Michael Isikoff, *The Roots of Torture*, Newsweek, May 24, 2004, at 28). What are the legal and ethical responsibilities of government lawyers in the war on terror? *See* Bilder & Vagts, *supra*, at 691-695.

The *Schlesinger Report* (p. 41 n.5 *supra*) also found that in the development of Defense Department detention and interrogation policies in 2002 and 2003, "the legal resources of the Services' Judge Advocate General and General Counsels were not utilized to their full potential. Had the Secretary of Defense had a wider range of legal opinions and more robust debate regarding detainee policies and operations" the frequent policy changes between December 2002 and April 2003 might have been avoided. *Id.* at 8. Why would the Secretary not have relied on JAG lawyers and General Counsels to furnish the needed advice? What would have been gained by their perspectives? At a Senate hearing in July 2005, the judge advocates general for the Army, Air Force, and Marines stated that they complained about the Justice Department's definition of "torture" and how it would be applied in the Working Group process early in 2003. Their objections apparently were overruled by the Defense Department general counsel's office. Neil A. Lewis, *Military's Opposition to Harsh Interrogation Is Outlined*, N.Y. Times, July 28, 2005; Josh White, *Military Lawyers Fought Policy on Interrogations, JAGs Recount Objections to Definition of Torture*, Wash. Post, July 15, 2005, at A1.

Apparently, on March 17, 2005, the General Counsel of the Defense Department wrote a memo that rescinded the Working Group report and concluded that the report "does not reflect now-settled executive branch views of the relevant law.... [T]he [report] is to be considered a historical document with no standing in policy, practice, or law." *Id.* What do you suppose happened between April 2003 and March 2005 to change the executive branch views of the relevant law? In what specific ways is the new understanding different from the old one?

b. (Incorporated?) International Law on Torture

1. *The U.N. Convention Against Torture and Other Cruel, Inhuman, or Degrading Treatment or Punishment (CAT).* The instruments of ratification submitted by the United States for the CAT include a declaration making it clear that it regards CAT Articles 1 through 16 as not self-executing. *See* Office of the High Commissioner for Human Rights, *Declarations and Reservations* (as of 23 April 2004) ("United States of America" at ¶III(1)), at *http://www.unhchr.ch/html/menu2/6/cat/treaties/convention-reserv.htm*.

What is the legal significance of such a declaration? The prohibitions against torture in the CAT, qualified by the various U.S. reservations, understandings, and declarations attached to it, have been implanted in domestic law in a range of settings, and its provisions underlie the Alien Tort Claims Act and Torture Victim Protection Act, both addressed *infra*. What are the important elements of "torture" as defined in the CAT? Does it apply to military and civilian interrogators? To private persons?

One understanding of the United States in ratifying the CAT specifies that "torture" as mental pain or suffering refers to

> prolonged mental harm caused by or resulting from: (1) the intentional infliction or threatened infliction of severe physical pain or suffering; (2) the administration or application, or threatened administration or application, of mind-altering substances or other procedures calculated to disrupt profoundly the senses or the personality; (3) the threat of imminent death; or (4) the threat that another person will imminently be subjected to death, severe physical pain or suffering, or the administration or application of mind-altering substances or other procedures calculated to disrupt profoundly the senses or personality. *Id.* at ¶II(1)(a).

What is the practical significance of this understanding? What interrogation techniques are permitted by the CAT? Sleep deprivation? Starvation? Sensory deprivation or bombardment? Do any of the techniques approved by the Secretary (p. 69 *supra*) constitute "torture" or "cruel, inhuman, or degrading treatment" under the CAT?

Article 2(2) of the CAT provides that "[n]o exceptional circumstances whatsoever, whether a state of war or a threat of war, internal political instability, or any other public emergency, may be invoked as a justification of torture." What is the legal significance of this "no exceptions" provision?

Article 2(1) requires parties to take preventive measures "in any territory under its jurisdiction." How does extension of the CAT to the special maritime and territorial jurisdiction of the United States affect the rules for interrogation at Guantánamo? How do you think this Article 2 provision applies in Afghanistan or in Iraq?

2. *Cruel, Inhuman, or Degrading Treatment.* How does the prohibition against cruel, inhuman, or degrading treatment differ from the rule barring torture? As described in the Working Group memorandum, the United States reserved its implementation of the prevention of "cruel, inhuman, or degrading treatment or punishment" under CAT Article 16 to those acts that would be forbidden by the Fifth, Eighth and/or Fourteenth Amendments. Why would the United States make such a reservation? Because the case

Chapter 12. Investigating Terrorism 83

law arises in domestic criminal justice proceedings, how would you measure U.S. compliance with the "cruel, inhuman, or degrading" proviso? Do the techniques described in the *Taguba Report* or the Rumsfeld memorandum fall within the definition? See casebook p. 664, Note 8.

3. *Criminalizing Torture Under the CAT.* The criminal sanction in 18 U.S.C. §2340 was included to meet the CAT requirement that each ratifying country criminalize torture. Compare the definitions in the treaty and the Act (pp. 59-63 *supra*). Do you see any important differences? In an August 1, 2002, letter to the White House Counsel, OLC asserted that "interrogation methods that comply with Section 2340 would not violate our international obligations under the Torture Convention." *Letter to Alberto R. Gonzalez, Counsel to the President, from John C. Yoo, Deputy Asst. Atty. General*, Aug. 1, 2002, at 1, *at http://www.gwu.edu/~nschariv/ NSAEBB/NSAEBB127/020801.pdf*. If the measures of compliance with the CAT prohibition against "cruel, inhuman, or degrading treatment" are the Fifth, Eighth, and Fourteenth Amendments, do aliens held by the United States overseas have any protection from cruel, inhuman, or degrading treatment by U.S. officials under the CAT? Does the lack of domestic criminal enforcement authority extinguish U.S. obligations under the Torture Convention not to engage in "cruel, inhuman, and degrading treatment"?

In 18 U.S.C. §2340, Congress forbade conduct that is "specifically intended to inflict severe physical or mental pain or suffering." Without further statutory definitions, how would you define the key words and phrases – "severe," "severe physical pain or suffering," "severe mental pain or suffering," and "specifically intended"? See *Memorandum for James B. Comey*, p. 74 *supra*, at 5-17.

4. *Application of the Geneva Conventions.* Apply the language of the Geneva Conventions, as incorporated through the War Crimes Act (WCA), *supra* pp. 46-49, to the detentions and interrogation described in these materials. What threshold determinations must be made, and by whom?

a. *What Conflicts?* Was the conflict against the Taliban and al Qaeda in Afghanistan covered by the Geneva Conventions? Do you think Attorney General Ashcroft made a persuasive case that Geneva Convention III for the protection of POWs should not apply because Afghanistan was a "failed" state? Despite the Taliban's violent and harsh measures against Afghan citizens, its government controlled nearly all of Afghanistan when U.S. and British forces invaded that country in December 2001. *See* Hamdan v. Rumsfeld, No. 04-5393, 2005 WL 1653046 (D.C. Cir. July 15,

2005) (*infra* p. 334). In *Hamdan*, a panel of the D.C. Circuit Court of Appeals ruled that the conflict was neither an international conflict between a signatory state and an opposing power that has accepted the provisions of the convention, nor an "armed conflict not of an international character occurring in the territory of one of the High Contracting Parties" because the President had determined that the conflict was "international in scope." Does this ruling affirm the Ashcroft analysis? Does it make sense? Is there a third category of conflict that falls outside the convention altogether, which therefore escapes the convention rules altogether?

What do you think was the effect, if any, of the election of the Karzai government in Afghanistan in June 2002? Before that date, the conflict arguably was subject to the Geneva Conventions by virtue of common Article 2, which provides that the Conventions "apply to all cases of . . . armed conflict" between two or more parties to the Convention. Signatories are bound regardless of whether an additional party to the conflict is a signatory. After formation of the Karzai government, the conflict seemingly became internal, and U.S. and other foreign forces were present in Afghanistan with the consent of the government.

Do you find persuasive the argument in the Yoo/Delahunty memorandum that common Article 3, which applies to an "armed conflict not of an international character," and which requires at least "minimal" humane treatment of all detainees regardless of status, does not apply in Afghanistan, since the real enemy – al Qaeda, aided by the Taliban – is a transnational terrorist group?

Do you think it likely, as the Yoo/Delahunty memorandum argues, that the signers of the 1949 Geneva Conventions meant to exclude "small-scale" civil wars from their coverage? If so, was the conflict between U.S. and Taliban and al Qaeda forces "small-scale"?

b. *Which Combatants?* Can you say on what basis any persons detained during wartime are wholly outside the protections of the Geneva Conventions? *See* Sean D. Murphy, *Contemporary Practice of the United States Relating to International Law*, 96 Am. J. Intl. L. 461, 476-477 (2002).

The Bush administration first took the position that al Qaeda and Taliban prisoners are "unlawful combatants" and thus not protected at all by the Conventions. The White House, President George W. Bush, *Memorandum to National Security Advisors Re: Humane Treatment of al Qaeda and Taliban Detainees*, Feb. 7, 2002, *available at http://www.gwu. edu/~nsarchiv/NSAEBB/NSAEBB127/02.02.07.pdf.* It also reasoned that the Geneva Conventions have no application to non-state organizations such as al Qaeda, that the conflict was internal, and further that al Qaeda members

Chapter 12. Investigating Terrorism

failed to meet the criteria in Article 4 of Geneva Convention III. Under Article 4, combatants earn POW status if they are members of the armed forces, other than medical or chaplain personnel. The general criteria include being subject to command authority, having a "fixed distinctive sign recognizable at a distance," carrying arms openly, and conducting operations in accordance with the laws and customs of war. The Taliban also were not entitled to Geneva Convention protections, according to the Administration, because Afghanistan was not a functioning state during the conflict, and because the Taliban were not recognized as a legitimate government. *Id.* After Secretary of State Powell objected and requested that the Administration reconsider its position, President Bush announced that Geneva Convention III was applicable to the Taliban, though not to al Qaeda. But because the Taliban violated the laws of war and associated with al Qaeda, he determined that Taliban detainees do not qualify as POWs. *See White House Fact Sheet: Status of Detainees at Guantanamo*, Feb. 7, 2002, *available at http://www.whitehouse.gov/news/releases/2002/02/20020207-13.html*. Do you find support for the Administration's position in the memoranda excerpted here? If not, in what respects does the argument come up short? *Cf.* United States v. Lindh, 212 F. Supp. 2d 541 (E.D.Va. 2002) (concluding that Taliban were not covered by Geneva Convention III, since it had an insufficient internal system of military command, wore no distinctive sign, and regularly targeted civilian populations).

In cases of doubt, Article 5 of Geneva Convention III entitles detainees to a "competent tribunal" to determine their status. Does it offer a reasonable way to accommodate both sides in this debate? *See* Jennifer Elsea, *Treatment of "Battlefield Detainees" in the War on Terrorism* 35 (Cong. Res. Serv. RL31367), Jan. 13, 2005 (asserting that the United States has in the past required an individualized assessment of detainee status before denying POW status). Why do you suppose POW determination tribunals have not been established? Does the U.S. stance itself constitute a violation of the laws of war, thus providing an enemy with an argument for denying captured U.S. soldiers POW status?

The Office of Legal Counsel asserted in a March 28, 2002, letter to the State Department Legal Adviser that there can be no doubt about the POW status of any individual affiliated with the Taliban, because the organization was found not to meet the requirements of Article 4. *Letter to William H. Taft, IV, Legal Adviser, Dept. of State, from John C. Yoo, Deputy Asst. Atty. General, Office of Legal Counsel,* Mar. 28, 2002, *at http://www.cartoonbank.com/newyorker/slideshows/05YooTaft.pdf.* Does it necessarily follow that the categorical denial of POW status to a military organization makes any person allegedly a member of that organization ineligible for an Article 5 tribunal?

c. *Which Other Persons?* Defense Secretary Rumsfeld acknowledged in early 2002 in comments about the detention facility at Guantánamo Bay that "[s]ometimes when you capture a big, large group there will be someone who just happened to be in there that didn't belong in there." *Secretary Rumsfeld Media Availability En Route to Camp X-Ray*, Jan. 27, 2002, *available at http://www.defenselink.mil/transcripts/2002/t01282002_ t0127sd2.html*. What rights do these innocent bystanders have, once detained? Do Articles 4 and 5 of Geneva Convention III and Geneva Convention IV apply? Does it matter for the purposes of qualifying for Geneva Convention IV that a person may have unlawfully participated in a conflict?

d. *What Conduct Is Covered?* What constitutes a "grave breach" under the Geneva Conventions? If "torture or inhuman treatment" is such a breach, what aspects of the Conventions remain in dispute concerning detainees in the war on terrorism? For POWs, Article 17 of Geneva Convention III provides that "no physical or mental torture, nor any other form of coercion, may be inflicted on prisoners of war to secure from them information of any kind whatever." For protected civilians, Article 31 of Geneva Convention IV provides that "[n]o physical or moral coercion shall be exercised against [them], in particular to obtain information from them or from third parties." What interrogation techniques would be proscribed by these rules? How do the techniques recommended by the Working Group and approved by Secretary Rumsfeld (p. 69 *supra*) measure up under the Geneva Conventions? *See* Jennifer K. Elsea, *Lawfulness of Interrogation Techniques under the Geneva Conventions* 23-35 (Cong. Res. Serv. RL32567), Sept. 8, 2004.

e. *Liability for U.S. Personnel?* The documents excerpted above expose an underlying tension in setting the interrogation policy – providing maximum flexibility to pressure detainees to talk, while ensuring immunity from criminal sanctions if lawful boundaries are crossed. Compare the arguments on the amenability of U.S. personnel to criminal prosecution by Attorney General Ashcroft and by State Department General Counsel Taft. Which side has the better view in light of the Geneva Conventions?

f. *Are the Conventions Judicially Enforceable?* Salim Ahmed Hamdan was captured by Afghani militia forces in November 2001. He was turned over to the U.S. military and transported to Guantánamo Bay. In July 2003, President Bush determined "that there was reason to believe that [Hamdan] was a member of al Qaeda or was otherwise involved in terrorism directed

Chapter 12. Investigating Terrorism 87

against the United States," and Hamdan was designated for trial before a military commission. After Hamdan filed a petition for habeas corpus in federal district court, he was charged with a variety of terrorism-related offenses stemming from his alleged role as the personal driver for Osama bin Laden. In November 2004, the district court granted Hamdan's petition in part, holding that he could not be tried by a military commission unless a competent tribunal determined that he was not a POW under Geneva Convention III. Hamdan v. Rumsfeld, 344 F. Supp. 2d 152 (D.D.C. 2004).

On July 15, 2005, a D.C. Circuit Court of Appeals panel reversed. In Hamdan v. Rumsfeld, No. 04-5393, 2005 WL 1653046 (D.C. Cir. 2005) (*infra* p. 334), the court found that Geneva Convention III confers upon Hamdan no right to enforce its provisions in court. *Id.* at *13. The court also held that, even if the convention were judicially enforceable, Hamdan could not qualify as a POW under Article 4 because he does not claim to be a member of a group that displayed fixed insignia and complied with the laws of war. *Id.* at *14. Hamdan might, opined the court, claim POW status before the military commission under Article 4A(4) as a person who accompanied an armed force without being a member of it, but he had not made such a claim in court. The court also agreed with the government that the conflict with al Qaeda is neither a common Article 2 "international armed conflict" nor a common Article 3 conflict "not of an international character." The decision to treat the conflict with al Qaeda in Afghanistan as distinct from that against the Taliban is a "political-military decision" constitutionally committed to the President. *Id.* at *16. Finally, if common Article 3 did protect Hamdan, the court said, considerations of comity would require it to abstain until the military commission proceeding occurs. *Id.* at *16-17. Why would a treaty ratified in accordance with constitutional requirements not be judicially enforceable in U.S. courts? (For a review, see casebook pp. 214-226.) If Geneva Convention III is not a self-executing treaty, what is its legal effect as U.S. law? Other aspects of the *Hamdan* decision are considered in this Supplement at pp. 342-343.

5. *The New Paradigm?* Do the Geneva Conventions apply *at all* in the war on terrorism? White House Counsel Gonzales argued that the "nature of the new war" and the "new paradigm render[] obsolete Geneva's strict limitations" on questioning and make other Geneva provisions "quaint." How would you rebut the Gonzales interpretation? Do Gonzales' arguments apply with equal force in Afghanistan and in Iraq? To detainees captured elsewhere? *See* Derek Jinks & David Sloss, *Is the President Bound by the Geneva Conventions?*, 90 Cornell L. Rev. 97 (2004) (concluding that he is). By contrast, the Office of Legal Counsel argued that the Geneva Conventions are "quite clear," and that the President correctly determined that the Taliban and al Qaeda detainees cannot meet

the clear requirements of Geneva Convention III. *Letter to Taft from Yoo*, p. 85 *supra*. Is the OLC position more or less persuasive than that of the former White House Counsel?

In June 2004 the Senate adopted an amendment to the Defense Authorization Act that would have provided that "[n]o person in the custody or under the physical control of the United States shall be subject to torture or cruel, inhuman, or degrading treatment prohibited by the Constitution or treaties." *Humane Treatment of Detainees*, S. 2401, 108th Cong., §1057 (2004). The Bush administration opposed the provision, and a conference committee substituted a "sense of the Congress" resolution announcing a policy that no detainee in the physical control of the United States as a result of armed conflict "shall be subject to torture or cruel, inhuman, or degrading treatment that is prohibited by the Constitution, laws, or treaties of the United States." *Ronald W. Reagan National Defense Authorization Act for Fiscal Year 2005*, Pub. L. No. 108-375, §1091(a)(6), (a)(8), (b)(1), (c), 118 Stat. 2068 (2004). Why do you suppose that the Administration objected to the Senate amendment? Does the enacted "sense of the Congress" policy reflect a new paradigm?

6. *The International Covenant on Civil and Political Rights.* The ICCPR is like the CAT, in that it forbids torture and cruel, inhuman, and degrading conduct, and it is subject to the same Senate approval as the CAT. The ICCPR is non-self-executing, and the lower federal courts have found that the ICCPR creates no privately enforceable rights in U.S. courts. However, some courts cite the ICCPR as evidence that customary international law prohibits arbitrary arrest, prolonged detention, and torture. See casebook p. 239, Note 9. What is the legal basis for the Working Group position that the ICCPR does not apply to U.S. activities abroad during an armed conflict?

7. *The Role of Customary International Law and Jus Cogens.* The substantive content of customary international law in the area of torture is embodied in the CAT and ICCPR, among other instruments. The torture prohibition is also part of *jus cogens* and is so recognized by U.S. courts. *See* Restatement (Third) of Foreign Relations Law §702 (1986). It remains unclear, however, whether the prohibition against cruel, inhuman, or degrading treatment also is part of *jus cogens*. For a refresher on the role of custom and *jus cogens* as U.S. law, see casebook pp. 226-241.

Chapter 12. Investigating Terrorism

8. *Responses to Torture in Other Democracies.*

a. *Ireland.* In Republic of Ireland v. United Kingdom, 2 Eur. Ct. H.R. 25 (1978), the European Court of Human Rights applied the European Convention for the Protection of Human Rights and Fundamental Freedoms and its bar against torture and inhuman or degrading treatment or punishment. It found unlawful a range of special powers created by the Northern Ireland government that permitted interrogation techniques similar to those at issue in the war on terrorism, including wall-standing, hooding, subjection to noise, and deprivation of sleep, food, and drink. *Id.* at 59. The court acknowledged that the treatment complained of had to be severe, based on an "assessment . . . necessarily relative, depending on all the circumstances, including the duration of the treatment, its physical or mental effects and, sometimes, the sex, age or state of health of the victim." *Id.* at 26. The court also noted that the distinction between torture and inhuman or degrading treatment "derived principally from a difference in the intensity of the suffering inflicted." *Id.* The court found that the techniques employed in Northern Ireland violated the rule against inhuman or degrading treatment but did not amount to torture. *Id.* at 79-80. What outcome would follow if the criteria employed in the *Ireland* decision were applied to the treatment of detainees at Abu Ghraib? To the 24 techniques approved by Secretary Rumsfeld? What rules could you suggest for future interrogation of suspected terrorists based on these criteria?

b. *Israel.* In Judgment Concerning the Legality of the General Security Service's Interrogation Methods, 38 I.L.M. 1471 (1999), the Israeli Supreme Court declared that "terrorist organizations have established as their goal Israel's annihilation." *Id.* at 1472. In 1987, the Landau Commission of Inquiry into the Methods of Investigation of the GSS (General Security Service) Regarding Hostile Terrorist Acts concluded that psychological means and "a moderate amount of physical pressure" could not be avoided in the Israeli setting. *Reprinted in* 23 Israeli L. Rev. 146, 184 (1989). In its 1999 decision, the Court took into account the Landau Commission findings in its review of interrogation methods that included shaking, the "shabach" position (detainee has his hands tied behind his back, sits on a small and low chair with seat tilted forward and toward the ground, one hand placed inside the chair seat and back support, head covered by a hood), loud music played in the room, the "frog crouch" (detainee crouches on the tips of his toes for five-minute intervals), excessive tightening of handcuffs, and sleep deprivation. *GSS Interrogation Methods Decision,* at 1477. The Court balanced the government's duty to protect human rights and its duty to combat terrorism and concluded that these interrogation methods were unlawful and that GSS interrogators were subject to the same rules as the police. *Id.* at 1485. What are the lessons of the Israeli experience for the war on terrorism?

c. Domestic Law on Torture

1. *Applying the Constitution.* A U.S. reservation to the Convention Against Torture limits "cruel, inhuman or degrading conduct" to conduct that violates that Fifth, Eighth, and/or Fourteenth Amendments. Simply put, in the U.S. view torture and cruel, inhuman, and degrading conduct are unconstitutional. But what is the content of those constitutional protections? For contrasting views, see Seth F. Kreimer, *Too Close to the Rack and the Screw: Constitutional Constraints on Torture in the War on Terror*, 6 U. Penn. J. Constl. L. 278 (2003); and John T. Parry, *What Is Torture, Are We Doing It, and What if We Are?*, 64 U. Pitt. L. Rev. 237 (2003).

In Chavez v. Martinez, 538 U.S. 760 (2003), a badly fractured Supreme Court ruled on claims of liability asserted by a plaintiff who had been subjected to persistent police questioning while he was in the hospital incapacitated by extreme pain. Five justices voted to remand the question whether he could pursue a claim for violation of his substantive due process rights, but the Court could not agree about the scope and applicability of those rights or the related right against self-incrimination.

Three justices joined in part of an opinion by Justice Thomas asserting that the interrogation was not egregious or conscience-shocking enough to violate the plaintiff's substantive due process rights. They reasoned that "freedom from unwanted police questioning is [not] a right so fundamental that it cannot be abridged absent a 'compelling state interest.'" *Id.* at 776. For them, it was enough that the questioning was justified by *some* government interest – here the need to preserve critical evidence concerning a shooting by a police officer – and that it was not "conduct intended to injure in some way unjustifiable by any government interest." *Id.* at 774.

Justice Stevens concluded that "the interrogation of respondent was the functional equivalent of an attempt to obtain an involuntary confession from a prisoner by torturous methods," which is "a classic example of a violation of a constitutional right 'implicit in the concept of ordered liberty.'" *Id.* at 788 (Stevens, J., concurring in part, dissenting in part).

Justice Kennedy (joined on this point by Justices Stevens and Ginsburg) agreed that the use of investigatory torture violates a person's fundamental right to liberty but noted that interrogating suspects who are in pain or anguish is not necessarily torture when the police have "legitimate reasons, borne of exigency, . . . [such as] [l]ocating the victim of a kidnapping, ascertaining the whereabouts of a dangerous assailant or accomplice, or

Chapter 12. Investigating Terrorism 91

determining whether there is a rogue police officer." *Id*. at 796 (Kennedy, J., concurring in part, dissenting in part). On the other hand, he added, the police may not prolong or increase the suspect's suffering or threaten to do so to elicit a statement. The test for a constitutional violation, in Justice Kennedy's view, was whether the police "exploited" the suspect's pain to secure his statement. He found that they had done so in *Chavez*.

Under any of the tests in *Chavez* would torture in the United States of a suspected terrorist to obtain information about an imminent terrorist attack violate substantive due process? How about practices such as hooding and sleep deprivation? Do military or civilian investigators in the war on terrorism have broader authority than the police do to use coercive interrogation techniques, because of their different goals in an interrogation? *See* Marcy Strauss, *Torture*, 48 N.Y.L. Sch. L. Rev. 201, 251 (2003) (maintaining that it is unclear whether torture used to gain information violates the Fifth Amendment privilege against self-incrimination if the information is not used in a criminal prosecution; if so used, the right is violated).

Does the Eighth Amendment ban on "cruel and unusual punishment" supply an interpretive standard in the coercive interrogation context? If no judicially imposed punishment is contemplated by the interrogators, does the Eighth Amendment even apply? *See* Ingraham v. Wright, 430 U.S. 651, 671-672, n.40 (1977) ("[T]he State does not acquire the power to punish with which the Eighth Amendment is concerned until after it has secured a formal adjudication of guilt in accordance with due process of law.").

2. *Extraterritorial Application of the Constitution.* Are U.S. interrogators in Iraq, Afghanistan, or elsewhere outside the United States subject to the same constitutional constraints on their interrogation methods that limit their conduct in the United States? Are they subject to any U.S. laws? See casebook pp. 214-226. If aliens held at Guantánamo have *some* U.S. constitutional rights, *see* Rasul v. Bush, 542 U.S. 466 (2004) (p. 252 in this Supplement), do aliens held by U.S. forces in Afghanistan or Iraq have *any*?

3. *"Shocks the Conscience" Redux.* Apply the "shocks the conscience" standard described in casebook p. 663, Note 7 to unconnected aliens in this setting. Would the most abusive techniques used at Abu Ghraib ever be permitted in the United States? How about in the ticking bomb situation? *See* Oren Gross, *The Prohibition on Torture and the Limits of the Law* 2 (2004).

4. *Criminal Sanctions.* The Torture Act of 2000, 18 U.S.C. §§2340-2340B, which imposes criminal sanctions required by the Convention Against Torture, applies only to U.S. nationals or others present in the United States who commit or conspire to commit torture "outside the United States." The Working Group took pains to assert that Guantánamo is included within the special maritime jurisdiction of the United States and thus that the U.S. personnel conducting interrogations there are not subject to the Torture Act. Can you explain the basis for U.S. claims over Guantánamo for special maritime jurisdiction purposes, while rejecting claims of sovereignty over the same base for the purposes of providing a jurisdictional basis for claims by the detainees there? *See* Rasul v. Bush, 542 U.S. 466 (2004) (p. 252 in this Supplement).

The Torture Act was amended in 2004 to extend the definition of "United States" to include the several states, the District of Columbia, and the commonwealths, territories, and possessions of the United States. *Ronald W. Reagan National Defense Authorization Act for Fiscal Year 2005*, Pub. L. No. 108-375, §1089, 118 Stat. 2067, amending 18 U.S.C. §2340(3). In any case, it appears that the United States had never prosecuted a U.S. or foreign agent suspected of engaging in torture outside the United States. *See* Amnesty Intl. USA, *United States of America: A Safe Haven for Torturers*, 2002, *available at http://www.amnestyusa.org/stoptorture/safehaven.pdf*; Michael John Garcia, *U.N. Convention Against Torture (CAT): Overview and Application to Interrogation Techniques* 11-12 (Cong. Res. Serv. RL34238), Feb. 10, 2005.

The Uniform Code of Military Justice (UCMJ) provides for courts-martial to prosecute torture or inhumane acts committed within or outside the United States by members of the military and certain accompanying civilians. 10 U.S.C. §805 (UCMJ applies worldwide); 10 U.S.C. §802 (to any service member); 10 U.S.C. §802(a)(10) (to certain accompanying civilians); 10 U.S.C. §818 (for an offense against the laws of war); 10 U.S.C. §855 (torture or cruel or unusual punishment); 10 U.S.C. §934 ("disorders and neglects to the prejudice of good order and discipline in the armed forces"). To date, seven soldiers have been convicted under the UCMJ of abusing detainees at Abu Ghraib, while 29 other soldiers have been subjected to summary, special, or general courts-martial for detainee abuse in other settings. Vice Adm. Albert T. Church III, Naval Inspector General, *Unclassified Executive Summary of Review of Department of Defense Interrogation Operations*, Mar. 10, 2005, *at http://www.defenselink.mil/news/Mar2005/d20050310exe.pdf*.

Why do you suppose Congress has not enacted a statute specifically outlawing torture within the United States?

Chapter 12. Investigating Terrorism

5. *Prosecuting Civilian Contractors.* In June 2004 a federal grand jury in North Carolina indicted a contractor employed by the CIA on assault charges for allegedly beating a detainee in Afghanistan over two days in 2003. The detainee died the next day. Richard A. Oppel Jr. & Ariel Hart, *Contractor Indicted in Afghan Detainee's Beating*, N.Y. Times, June 17, 2004, at A1. The CIA refused to acknowledge whether the agency was aware that the accused had been arrested on felony assault charges before his employment by the Agency. *Id.* How might the War Crimes Act, 18 U.S.C. §2441 (pp. 46-49 in this Supplement) apply to the accused in this case?

Generally, the UCMJ has not been applied to civilians accompanying military units in peacetime. *See, e.g., Willenburg v. Neurauter*, 48 M.J. 152, 157 (C.A.A.F. 1998). The Military Extraterritorial Jurisdiction Act of 2000 (MEJA), however, now provides for federal jurisdiction over crimes committed abroad by civilians who are "accompanying or employed by" the U.S. military. 18 U.S.C. §§3261-3267. Still, after the *Taguba Report* (p. 43 n.12 *supra*) named the contracting firms Titan Corporation and CACI, Inc. as having provided translators and interrogators who were accused of engaging in detainee abuse at the Abu Ghraib prison, it appeared that the jurisdictional provisions of the MEJA would not reach the contractor who employed the accused individuals. Moreover, CACI's contract is with the Department of Interior rather than with DOD. Scott Shane, *Some U.S. Prison Contractors May Avoid Charges*, Balt. Sun, May 24, 2004, at A1. In response to this jurisdictional gap, the 2005 Defense Authorization Act broadened the range of potential defendants under the MEJA to include civilian employees, contractors or subcontractors, and their employees, of DOD or "any other Federal agency, or any provisional authority, to the extent such employment relates to supporting the mission of the Department of Defense overseas." *Ronald D. Reagan Defense Authorization Act of 2005*, Pub. L. No. 108-375, §1088, 118 Stat. 2066-2067 (2004). Do these amendments to the MEJA plug all the holes? Would it reach State Department or FBI employees? CIA personnel? *See* Frederick A. Stein, *Have We Closed the Barn Door Yet? A Look at the Current Loopholes in the Military Extraterritorial Jurisdiction Act*, 27 Hous. J. Intl. L. 579 (2005).

The MEJA creates no substantive crimes but incorporates a range of existing offenses, such as murder, assault, sexual abuse, and deprivation of rights under color of law. What ordinary crimes might be charged against civilian contractors working in facilities like Abu Ghraib? Could CIA operatives engaged in interrogational torture while operating with military units be prosecuted under the UCMJ?

6. *Civil Sanctions.* The Torture Victim Protection Act (TVPA), Pub. L. No. 102-256, 106 Stat. 73 (1992), codified at 28 U.S.C. §1350 Note, provides a civil remedy in the federal courts for U.S. persons who have been victims of torture or extrajudicial killing, while the Alien Tort Claims Act (ATCA), 28 U.S.C. §1350, confers jurisdiction in federal district courts over tort suits by aliens where a violation of the law of nations or a treaty of the United States is alleged. In Sosa v. Alvarez-Machain, 542 U.S. 692 (2004), the Supreme Court rejected the ATCA as a basis for jurisdiction in the federal courts over a tort claim related to the abduction of Alvarez-Machain by a Mexican national who acted with the approval of the DEA. (An earlier related case may be found at casebook p. 855.) The Court reasoned that the ATCA was intended to create jurisdiction to hear suits based on current international norms, but only those whose "content and acceptance among civilized nations" is no less definite than the small number of "historical paradigms" familiar when the statute was passed in 1789. *Id.* at 718. In the course of its opinion, however, the Court cited with evident approval the decision in Filartiga v. Peña-Irala, 630 F.2d 876 (2d Cir. 1980) (noted at casebook p. 240), which applied the ATCA in a torture case. (The most recent *Alvarez-Machain* decision is also considered in this Supplement at p. 6.)

What would be the measure of "torture" under these civil mechanisms? Relying on the Alien Tort Claims Act, the Center for Constitutional Rights recently sued the two prime security contractors operating for the United States in Iraq – CACI International, Inc. and Titan Corp. – on behalf of Iraqi prisoners, alleging that the contractors conspired with government officials to abuse the detainees and failed to supervise adequately their employees. *See* Renae Merle, *CACI and Titan Sued Over Iraq Operations*, Wash. Post, June 10, 2004, at E3. The suit seeks damages and an injunction to prevent the contractors from obtaining new government contracts. What problems can you foresee for the plaintiffs in this lawsuit?

In other civil suits U.S. courts have found that defendants committed actionable torture by subjecting detainees to interrogation sessions lasting 14 hours, Xuncax v. Gramajo, 886 F. Supp. 162, 170 (D. Mass. 1995); beating with hands, Tachiaona v. Mugabe, 234 F. Supp. 2d 401, 420-423 (S.D.N.Y. 2002); striking with blunt objects and boots, Mehinovic v. Vuckovic, 198 F. Supp. 2d 1322 (N.D. Ga. 2002); threatening with death, Adebe-Jira v. Negewo, 72 F.3d 844, 845 (11th Cir. 1996); and using techniques to increase pain or injury. *Id.*

6. Extraordinary Rendition

Rendition is generally understood to be the surrender of a person from one state to another state that has requested him, typically pursuant to a criminal prosecution. See casebook p. 851. In recent years, however, the United States has begun transferring detainees to foreign countries in circumstances where it is more likely than not that the individuals will be subjected to torture or to cruel, inhuman, or degrading treatment. The practice is called extraordinary rendition. Whether authorized by secret presidential directive or simply done by government officials without authorization, extraordinary rendition has apparently been utilized as an integral adjunct to coercive interrogation in the war on terrorism.

UNITED STATES DISTRICT COURT
EASTERN DISTRICT OF NEW YORK

MAHER ARAR, Plaintiff

– against –

JOHN ASHCROFT, Attorney General of the United States; LARRY D. THOMPSON, formerly Acting Deputy Attorney General [*et al.*], Defendants

04 -CV-249-DGT-VVP

COMPLAINT AND DEMAND FOR JURY TRIAL

Plaintiff MAHER ARAR, by and through his attorneys, alleges the following:

NATURE OF ACTION

1. This is a constitutional, civil, and human rights case challenging the decision by United States government ("Federal") officials to send Maher Arar, a Canadian citizen seized while he was transiting through JFK Airport to a connecting flight home, to Syria for interrogation under torture. After holding Mr. Arar in harsh and punitive conditions, coercively interrogating him for hours on end, and depriving him of contact with his family, his consulate, and his lawyer, federal officials rushed Mr. Arar off in a private jet to Jordan and then Syria. Federal officials removed Mr. Arar to Syria with the full knowledge of the existence of state-sponsored torture in that

country, and in direct contravention of the United Nations Convention Against Torture and Other Cruel, Inhuman and Degrading Treatment or Punishment (CAT), a treaty ratified by the United States in 1994. Upon information and belief, federal officials removed Mr. Arar to Syria under the Government's "extraordinary renditions" program precisely because Syria could use methods of interrogation to obtain information from Mr. Arar that would not be legally or morally acceptable in this country or in other democracies.

2. On information and belief, the decision to remove Mr. Arar to Syria for interrogation under torture was based solely on Mr. Arar's casual acquaintance with individuals thought possibly to be involved in terrorist activity. On information and belief, there was never, and is not now, any reasonable suspicion to believe that Mr. Arar was involved in such activity.

3. Plaintiff Maher Arar brings this action against Defendants John Ashcroft, Larry D. Thompson... and others, for their role in the violation of his constitutional, civil and international human rights. Defendants conspired with officials in the Syrian government and/or aided and abetted Syrian government officials in their plan to arbitrarily detain, interrogate and torture Mr. Arar.... Defendants' conduct violates the Torture Victim Protection Act, the Fifth Amendment to the United States Constitution, and treaty law....

5. Mr. Arar seeks a judgment declaring that Defendants' actions, and those of all persons acting on their behalf including their agents and/or employees are illegal and violate Mr. Arar's constitutional, civil, and human rights....

6. Mr. Arar also seeks compensatory and punitive damages for violations of his constitutionally and internationally protected rights....

STATEMENT OF FACTS

Background

23. The United States Department of State ("State Department") has long regarded Syria as a systematic practitioner of torture. The State Department lists Syria as a state sponsor of terrorism, and, for at least the past ten years, State Department Human Rights Country Reports on Syria have documented that the Syrian government practices torture.... [R]ecently, President Bush publicly condemned Syrian dictators for "a legacy of torture, oppression, misery and ruin." *Remarks by the President at the 20th Anniversary of the National Endowment for Democracy*, United States Chamber of Commerce, Washington D.C., November 6, 2003.

24. On information and belief, since September 11, 2001, the United

Chapter 12. Investigating Terrorism

States has undertaken covert "extraordinary renditions," removing non-U.S. citizens detained in this country and elsewhere and suspected – reasonably or unreasonably – of terrorist activity to countries, including Syria, where interrogations under torture are routine. The Federal officials who have adopted, ratified, and/or implemented the "extraordinary renditions" policy know full well that non-U.S. citizens removed under this policy will be interrogated under torture. . . . *See e.g.*, Rajiv Chandrasekaran and Peter Finn, *U.S. Behind Secret Transfer of Terrorist Suspects*, Wash. Post, March 11, 2002 at A01; Dana Priest and Barton Gellman, *U.S Decries Abuse but Defends Interrogations*, Wash. Post, Dec. 26, 2002, at A01; Sebastian Rotella, *Key to U.S. Case Denies Iraq-Al Qaeda Link*, L.A. Times, Feb. 1, 2003, at A01; DeNeen Brown and Dana Priest, *Deported Syrian Suspect Details Torture in Syria*, Wash. Post, Nov. 5, 2003 at A01.

Facts Specific to Plaintiff

25. While on a family vacation in Tunisia in late September 2002, Mr. Arar received an e-mail from his former employer, MathWorks, asking him to return to Ottawa to consult with a prospective client. On September 25, 2002, Mr. Arar took a flight to Zurich, leaving his wife and two children behind to continue their vacation. After stopping overnight in Zurich, he boarded a flight to Montreal, with a transfer stop at John F. Kennedy Airport, New York ("JFK").

26. At around noon, on September 26, 2002, Mr. Arar debarked at JFK in order to catch his connecting flight. He was not applying to enter the United States at this time. Mr. Arar presented his valid Canadian passport to the immigration inspector on duty. Upon entering Mr. Arar's name into a computer, the inspector instructed Mr. Arar to wait nearby.

27. At about 2 p.m., an immigration officer fingerprinted and photographed Mr. Arar. Shortly thereafter, two uniformed men searched Mr. Arar's wallet, carry-on bags, and luggage, without his consent. Concerned that he would miss his connecting flight, Mr. Arar repeatedly asked to make a telephone call home. His requests were ignored. . . .

[Arar was detained and interrogated for 13 days in the United States. When Arar was told that he was being removed to Syria, he told his interrogators that he feared that he would be tortured if removed there.]

47. Early on October 8, 2002, at about 4 a.m., Mr. Arar was taken in chains and shackles to a room where two INS officials told him that, based on Mr. Arar's casual acquaintance with certain named individuals . . . as well as classified information, [the INS regional director] had decided to remove Mr. Arar to Syria. Without elaboration, [the director] also stipulated that Mr. Arar's removal to Syria would be consistent with Article 3

of CAT. When Mr. Arar repeated his concerns about torture, the officials present simply stated that the INS is not governed by the "Geneva Convention." They further told Mr. Arar that he was barred from re-entering the United States for five years.

48. On information and belief, Defendant Thompson, Deputy Attorney General, in his capacity as Acting Attorney General, signed an order on or about October 8, 2002, removing Mr. Arar to Syria.

49. After the interrogation, Mr. Arar was taken . . . in chains and shackles to a New Jersey airfield, placed on a small private jet, and flown to Washington, D.C. From there, Mr. Arar was flown to Amman, Jordan, where he was turned over to Jordanian authorities on October 9, 2002. On information and belief, Syrian officials refused to accept Mr. Arar directly from the United States.

50. After interrogating and beating him, on or about October 9, 2002, Jordanian authorities turned Mr. Arar over to Syrian authorities. For the next 10 months, until about August 19, 2003, Mr. Arar was detained in the Palestine Branch of Syrian Military Intelligence ("the Palestine Branch").

51. For the first 12 days of his detention in Syria, Mr. Arar was interrogated for 18 hours per day. He was also subjected to physical and psychological torture. Syrian security officers regularly beat him on the palms, hips, and lower back, using a two-inch thick electric cable. They also regularly struck Mr. Arar in the stomach, face, and back of the neck with their fists. The pain was excruciating. Mr. Arar pleaded with them to stop, to no avail.

52. Syrian security officers . . . also subjected Mr. Arar to severe psychological torture. They placed him in a room where he could hear the screams of other detainees being tortured. They also repeatedly threatened to place him in the spine-breaking "chair," hang him upside down in a "tyre" and beat him, and give him electric shocks.

53. To minimize the torture, Mr. Arar falsely confessed, among other things, to having trained with terrorists in Afghanistan. In fact, Mr. Arar has never been to Afghanistan and has never been involved in terrorist activity.

54. The questions asked Mr. Arar by Syrian security officers in the Palestine Branch bore a striking similarity to those asked Mr. Arar by FBI agents at JFK in September, 2002. As with the FBI agents, Syrian security officers focused on Mr. Arar's relationship with certain individuals. . . .

55. On information and belief, Defendants provided their Syrian counterparts with a dossier on Mr. Arar, compiled in part from the interrogations at JFK. On information and belief, Defendants suggested matters to be covered by Syrian security officers during Mr. Arar's interrogation. On information and belief, Defendants handed over Mr. Arar

Chapter 12. Investigating Terrorism

to Syrian officials intending that they interrogate him under torture or knowing full well that Mr. Arar would be tortured during those interrogations.

56. On information and belief, Syrian security officers turned over to the Defendants all information coerced from Mr. Arar during his interrogations under torture in Syria. A Syrian official familiar with Mr. Arar's case stated that during Mr. Arar's detention in Syria, the Syrian government shared information gleaned from its interrogation and investigation of Mr. Arar with the United States government. *See* 1/21/04 transcript of CBS's Sixty Minutes II: "His Year In Hell".

57. On information and belief, United States officials removed Mr. Arar to Syria so that Syrian security officers could interrogate him under torture and thereby obtain information for United States counter-terrorism operations. . . .

58. When not being interrogated, Mr. Arar was placed in a tiny underground cell, measuring approximately six feet long, seven feet high, and three feet wide – hardly enough room to even move. The cell was damp and cold, especially during the winter months. The only light came through a small aperture in the ceiling above – an aperture which rats ran across and through which cats often urinated onto Mr. Arar.

59. Sanitary conditions were almost non-existent. Mr. Arar was allowed to bathe – in cold water – only once a week. He was not permitted to exercise. The food was barely edible. While detained at the Palestine Branch, Mr. Arar lost approximately 40 pounds.

60. The intensive interrogations and severe physical beatings of Mr. Arar ceased on or about October 20, 2002, the same day that the Canadian Embassy officials in Syria inquired about Mr. Arar. The next day, Syrian officials confirmed to Canadian Embassy officials that Mr. Arar was in their custody. United States officials had refused even to acknowledge to . . . Arar's immigration attorney, or to . . . the Canadian Consulate staff person who visited Mr. Arar . . . that Mr. Arar had been removed to Syria. . . .

64. On October 5, 2003, Mr. Arar was taken to the Syrian Supreme State Security Court. There, a prosecutor told him that he would be released without criminal charges. That same day, Mr. Arar was released into the custody of Canadian Embassy officials in Damascus, Syria.

65. According to Imad Moustapha, Syria's highest-ranking diplomat in Washington, Syrian officials investigated every link and relationship in order to uncover a connection between Mr. Arar and al Qaeda, but could find no such connection. . . .

66. On October 6, 2003, Mr. Arar returned home to Ottawa to his family whom he had not seen in more than a year.

67. Mr. Arar continues to suffer the effects of his ordeal. He still experiences difficulties relating to his wife and two young children. He frequently has nightmares about his treatment in the United States and Syria. People continue to call him a terrorist. The publicity surrounding his situation has made finding employment particularly difficult. His employment prospects have been further undermined by his inability to travel to the United States. . . .

NOTES AND QUESTIONS

1. *Arar v. Ashcroft.* Arar's lawsuit was filed on January 22, 2004. Based on the authorities reviewed at pp. 45-94 *supra*, can you outline his claims for relief? After a general answer denying the claims by Arar, the Justice Department asserted the state secrets privilege, arguing that the lawsuit must be dismissed because allowing it to proceed would inevitably involve the disclosure of sensitive information that would threaten national security or diplomatic relations if made public. *See* Letter from Scott Dunn, Asst. U.S. Atty., to Hon. David G. Trager, Jan. 18, 2005, *available at* http://www.ccr-ny.org/v2/legal/september_11th/docs/Arar_StateSecrets.pdf. (The state secrets privilege is discussed in the casebook at pp. 452-454, 970-979, and in this Supplement at pp. 382-390.) On March 30, 2005, media sources reported the discovery of flight records that appear to corroborate at least part of Arar's story. *See* Scott Shane, Stephen Grey & Ford Fessenden, *Detainee's Suit Gains Support from Jet's Log*, N.Y. Times, Mar. 30, 2005, at A1. Assuming the facts to be as alleged in the complaint, what is the likely outcome of Arar's lawsuit if it is heard on the merits?

2. *Scope of the Operations.* No one knows for sure how many extraordinary renditions have occurred. Reported destinations for extraordinary rendition include Egypt, Jordan, Morocco, Saudi Arabia, Yemen, and Syria, all condemned by the U.S. State Department as employing torture in interrogation. *See* Jane Mayer, *Outsourcing Torture*, New Yorker, Feb. 14, 2005, at 106. Examples of alleged extraordinary renditions, compiled from news sources, are summarized in Committee on International Human Rights of the Assn. of the Bar of the City of New York and The Center for Human Rights and Global Justice, N.Y.U. School of Law, *Torture by Proxy: International and Domestic Law Applicable to "Extraordinary Renditions"* 9-13 (2004), *available at* http://www.nyuhr.org/docs/TortureByProxy.pdf.

Chapter 12. Investigating Terrorism 101

3. *CIA Charter Flights.* Some extraordinary renditions have reportedly been carried out by the CIA, pursuant to broadly worded findings approved by the President. Douglas Jehl & David Johnston, *Rule Change Lets CIA Freely Send Suspects Abroad to Jails*, N.Y. Times, Mar. 6, 2005, at A1. An apparently private charter company, Aero Contractors, is actually a domestic centerpiece of the CIA secret air service, including flights to render suspects abroad. *See* Scott Shane, *CIA Expanding Terror Battle Under Guise of Charter Flights*, N.Y. Times, May 31, 2005, at A1. Assuming that the President's findings complied with the National Security Act (casebook pp. 524-528), are the renditions lawful? Does it matter legally if Congress is not notified about individual cases?

4. *Why Do It?* Why would the United States sponsor or participate in extraordinary renditions? One unnamed official with experience in so rendering detainees explained: "We don't kick the [expletive] out of them. We send them to other countries so they can kick the [expletive] out of them." Dana Priest & Barton Gellman, *U.S. Decries Abuse but Defends Interrogations; "Stress and Duress" Tactics Used on Terrorism Suspects Held in Secret Overseas Facilities*, Wash. Post, Dec. 26, 2002, at A1. What is wrong with CIA interrogators or their agents applying interrogation methods that are banned by U.S. law, if they do it abroad in a country that cooperates closely with the United States?

5. *Official Policy?* The Bush administration has not denied that persons have been rendered to foreign nations reputed to practice torture. However, officials have denied that renditions have occurred for the purpose of torture. R. Jeffrey Smith, *Gonzalez Defends Transfer of Detainees*, Wash. Post, Mar. 8, 2005, A3 (quoting Attorney General Gonzalez as stating that it is not U.S. policy to send persons "to countries where we believe or we know that they're going to be tortured"). How would this statement of U.S. policy affect the likelihood of Arar gaining relief in his lawsuit?

6. *The CAT and Implementing Legislation.* Review the discussion of the Convention Against Torture and its implementing legislation at pp. 81-83 *supra*. CAT art. 3 provides that no State Party "shall expel, return ('refouler') or extradite a person to another State where there are substantial grounds for believing that he would be in danger of being subjected to torture." An understanding attached to the convention by the Senate upon its advice and consent states that the requirement in art. 3 would apply when it is "more likely than not" that torture would follow such a rendition. Sen. Exec. Rpt. 101-30, *Resolution of Advice and Consent to Ratification* (1990),

at II(2). Based on what information should the lawyers asked to advise on such a question make the "more likely than not" determination? The CAT lacks a parallel provision regarding cruel, inhuman, or degrading treatment. What is the legal significance of this omission?

In 1998, Congress approved legislation implementing art. 3 of the CAT. Pub. L. No. 105-277, §2242(a)-(b), 112 Stat. 2681, 2681-822. Although Congress permitted administrative discretion in excluding from the CAT protection certain classes of aliens, at this writing, regulations prohibit the removal of all persons to states where they more likely than not would be tortured. 8 C.F.R. §§208.16-18, 1208.16-18 (2004).

The criminal sanctions implementing arts. 4 and 5 of the CAT forbid torture outside the United States. Review the specific intent required by the statute. See p. 61-63 *supra*. Would the torturer be liable if the torture occurred, say, in Syria? How about the CIA official who arranged for the extraordinary rendition?

7. *A Congressional Response.* A number of proposals have been made in Congress to provide oversight to the practice of rendition. At this writing, Congress has approved the Emergency Supplemental Appropriations Act for Defense, the Global War on Terror, and Tsunami Relief, Pub. L. No. 109-13, §1031, 119 Stat. 256 (2005), which provides:

> None of the funds appropriated or otherwise made available by this Act shall be obligated or expended to subject any person in the custody or under the physical control of the United States to torture or cruel, inhuman, or degrading treatment or punishment that is prohibited by the Constitution, laws, or treaties of the United States. [*Id.* §1031(a)(1).]

The terms "torture" and "cruel, inhuman, or degrading" are given the meanings adopted by the United States in reservations and understandings to the CAT. If this provision had been in effect when Arar was rendered to Syria, would the Act have been violated? Does it establish rights for detainees to which they otherwise are not entitled?

C. CONGRESSIONAL AUTHORITY FOR SURVEILLANCE

Page 679. Add this material at the end of Note 2.b.

Why doesn't a pen register installed by the telephone company at the FBI's request violate the Fourth Amendment? In Smith v. Maryland, 442

Chapter 12. Investigating Terrorism 103

U.S. 735 (1979), the Supreme Court explained that people do not have any actual or legitimate expectation of privacy in the numbers that they dial, because they voluntarily convey that information to the phone company and therefore assume the risk that the phone company will reveal the dialed numbers to the police. The installation of a pen register, consequently, was not a search. The Court emphasized, however, that pen registers do not record the contents of telephone communications. *Id.* at 741.

Page 679. Add this material at the end of Note 2.c.

Recall that Smith v. Maryland, upholding the constitutionality of the pen register, emphasized that pen registers do not record the contents of telephone communications. See preceding note, this Supplement. Is *Smith* authority for searching e-mail subject lines and URLs without a warrant? See subsection h. *infra.*

Page 679. Omit Note 2.d.

Page 681. Add this material to the end of Note 4.

Section 6001 of the Intelligence Reform and Terrorism Prevention Act of 2004, Pub. L. No. 108-458, 118 Stat. 3742, added a new element to the definition of "agent of a foreign power." The term now includes, *inter alia*, any person other than a United Stated who "engages in international terrorism or activities in preparation therefore [sic]." 50 U.S.C. §1801(b)(1)C). Can you see how the category of potential targets of FISA surveillance or searches has been enlarged? Why would this so-called "lone wolf" provision have been sought by the Government? Can you identify any downside risks to the expanded definition? The new provision is subject to the sunset provision in §224 of the USA PATRIOT Act, 115 Stat. 295. The expanded authority will expire on December 31, 2005, except for foreign intelligence investigations begun before that date, or where a criminal offense or potential criminal offense began before that date.

Page 683. Add this material to the end of Note 6.

In 2002 the presiding judge of the FISC complained that several applications to the court contained factual inaccuracies. In re All Matters Submitted to the Foreign Intelligence Surveillance Court, 218 F. Supp. 2d 611 (2002), noted at p. 106 in this Supplement. In response, the FBI developed FISA Verification Procedures (the so-called "Woods Procedures," named for their author, FBI lawyer Michael J. Woods) to better ensure the accuracy of the facts in each FISA application, particularly concerning what FISA calls "probable cause," and the existence and nature of any parallel criminal processes or prior or ongoing asset relationship involving the target. The procedures include FBI computer database searches and requirements to check the status of the proposed target with the Asset and Informant Unit and Criminal Division. The Woods Procedures were declassified in 2002 and are *available at http://www.fas. org/irp/agency/doj/fisa/woods/pdf.*

FBI Director Robert Mueller responded to Senate Judiciary Committee questions about the new procedures in August 2003. He stated that FBI field offices had, among other things, mistakenly reported that there were no criminal investigations ongoing concerning a target when in fact there were, and that the Bureau had failed to report that a proposed FISA target was also an FBI informant. *See* Written Questions of Senator Leahy to the Honorable Robert S. Mueller, III (Aug. 29, 2003), *at http://www.fas.org/ irp/agency/ doj/fisa/fbi082903.pdf.*

Are the Woods Procedures likely to improve the accuracy of the FISA process? How will Congress or the public know of their success or failure?

Page 687. Add this material at the end of Note 9.

The Intelligence Authorization Act for Fiscal Year 2002, Pub. L. No. 107-108, §314(a)(2)(B) & (4), 115 Stat. 1394, 1402 (2001), also extended from 24 to 72 hours the time the Attorney General has to authorize surveillance or searches before review by the FISC. 50 U.S.C. §§1805(f), 1824(e). Between 1978 and September 11, 2001, Attorneys General issued 47 emergency authorizations under FISA. Between September 11, 2001, and September 19, 2002, the Attorney General authorized 113 wiretaps and/or physical searches under FISA.

Section 225 of the Homeland Security Act expands the circumstances in which law enforcement can use pen registers and trap and trace devices without seeking a court order to include emergencies involving "an immediate threat to a national security interest." Pub. L. No. 107-296, §225(i)(3)(c), 116 Stat. 2135, 2158 (2002). Under the same section, an Internet service provider may disclose the content of electronic communications to any government agency if the ISP in "good faith" believes that the communication relates to information that involves the risk of death or serious physical injury. *Id.* §225(d)(1)(d). How, if at all, do these authorities exacerbate the judicial review and monitoring problems noted in the text?

Chapter 12. Investigating Terrorism

Page 691. Add this material after Note 11.d.

In re: Sealed Case No. 02-001, 02-002
Foreign Intelligence Surveillance Court of Review, 2002
310 F.3d 717

GUY, Senior Circuit Judge, presiding; SILBERMAN and LEAVY, Senior Circuit Judges.

PER CURIAM: This is the first appeal from the Foreign Intelligence Surveillance Court to the Court of Review since the passage of the Foreign Intelligence Surveillance Act (FISA), 50 U.S.C. §§1801-1862 (West 1991 and Supp. 2002), in 1978. The appeal is brought by the United States from a FISA court surveillance order which imposed certain restrictions on the government. . . .

I.

The court's decision from which the government appeals imposed certain requirements and limitations accompanying an order authorizing electronic surveillance of an "agent of a foreign power" as defined in FISA. There is no disagreement between the government and the FISA court as to the propriety of the electronic surveillance . . . . [T]he court ordered that

> law enforcement officials shall not make recommendations to intelligence officials concerning the initiation, operation, continuation or expansion of FISA searches or surveillances. Additionally, the FBI and the Criminal Division [of the Department of Justice] shall ensure that law enforcement officials do not direct or control the use of the FISA procedures to enhance criminal prosecution, and that advice intended to preserve the option of a criminal prosecution does not inadvertently result in the Criminal Division's directing or controlling the investigation using FISA searches and surveillances toward law enforcement objectives.

To ensure the Justice Department followed these strictures the court also fashioned what the government refers to as a "chaperone requirement"; that a unit of the Justice Department, the Office of Intelligence Policy and Review (OIPR) (composed of 31 lawyers and 25 support staff), "be invited" to all meetings between the FBI and the Criminal Division involving consultations for the purpose of coordinating efforts "to investigate or protect against foreign attack or other grave hostile acts, sabotage, international terrorism, or clandestine intelligence activities by foreign powers or their agents." If representatives of OIPR are unable to attend such meetings, "OIPR shall be appri[s]ed of the substance of the meetings forthwith in writing so that the Court may be notified at the earliest opportunity."

These restrictions are not original to the order appealed. They were actually set forth in an opinion written by the former Presiding Judge of the FISA court on May 17 of this year. [*See* In re All Matters Submitted to the Foreign Intelligence Surveillance Court, 218 F. Supp. 2d 611 (2002).] . . .

We think it fair to say, however, that the May 17 opinion of the FISA court does not clearly set forth the basis for its decision. It appears to proceed from the assumption that FISA constructed a barrier between counterintelligence/intelligence officials and law enforcement officers in the Executive Branch – indeed, it uses the word "wall" popularized by certain commentators (and journalists) to describe that supposed barrier.

The "wall" emerges from the court's implicit interpretation of FISA. The court apparently believes it can approve applications for electronic surveillance only if the government's objective is *not* primarily directed toward criminal prosecution of the foreign agents for their foreign intelligence activity. But the court neither refers to any FISA language supporting that view, nor does it reference the Patriot Act amendments, which the government contends specifically altered FISA to make clear that an application could be obtained even if criminal prosecution is the primary counter mechanism.

Instead the court relied for its imposition of the disputed restrictions on its statutory authority to approve "minimization procedures" designed to prevent the acquisition, retention, and dissemination within the government of material gathered in an electronic surveillance that is unnecessary to the government's need for foreign intelligence information. 50 U.S.C. §1801(h). . . .

II.

The government makes two main arguments. The first . . . is that the supposed pre-Patriot Act limitation in FISA that restricts the government's intention to use foreign intelligence information in criminal prosecutions is an illusion; it finds no support in either the language of FISA or its legislative history. The government does recognize that several courts of appeals, while upholding the use of FISA surveillances, have opined that FISA may be used only if the government's primary purpose in pursuing foreign intelligence information is not criminal prosecution, but the government argues that those decisions, which did not carefully analyze the statute, were incorrect in their statements, if not incorrect in their holdings.

Alternatively, the government contends that even if the primary purpose test was a legitimate construction of FISA prior to the passage of the Patriot Act, that Act's amendments to FISA eliminate that concept. And as a corollary, the government insists the FISA court's construction of the minimization procedures is far off the mark both because it is a misconstruction of those provisions *per se*, as well as an end run around the specific amendments in the Patriot Act designed to deal with the real issue underlying this case. The government, moreover, contends that the FISA court's restrictions, which the court described as minimization procedures, are so intrusive into the operation of the Department of Justice as to exceed the constitutional authority of Article III judges.

The government's brief, and its supplementary brief requested by this court, also set forth its view that the primary purpose test is not required by the Fourth Amendment. . . .

The 1978 FISA

We turn first to the statute as enacted in 1978. . . . [The court reviewed the definitions of "foreign intelligence information" and "agent of a foreign power" and noted that each is concerned with national security crimes.]

In light of these definitions, it is quite puzzling that the Justice Department, at some point during the 1980s, began to read the statute as limiting the Department's ability to obtain FISA orders if it intended to prosecute the targeted agents – even for foreign intelligence crimes. To be sure, section 1804, which sets forth the elements of an application for an order, required a national security official in the Executive Branch – typically the Director of the FBI – to certify that "the purpose" of the surveillance is to obtain foreign intelligence information (amended by the Patriot Act to read "a significant purpose"). But as the government now argues, the definition of foreign intelligence information includes evidence of crimes such as espionage, sabotage or terrorism. Indeed, it is virtually impossible to read the 1978 FISA to exclude from its purpose the prosecution of foreign intelligence crimes, most importantly because, as we have noted, the definition of an agent of a foreign power – if he or she is a U.S. person – is grounded on criminal conduct.

It does not seem that FISA, at least as originally enacted, even contemplated that the FISA court would inquire into the government's purpose in seeking foreign intelligence information. Section 1805, governing the standards a FISA court judge is to use in determining whether to grant a surveillance order, requires the judge to find that

> the application which has been filed contains all statements and certifications required by section 1804 of this title and, if the target is a

United States person, the certification or certifications are not clearly erroneous on the basis of the statement made under section 1804(a)(7)(E) of this title and any other information furnished under section 1804(d) of this title.

50 U.S.C. §1805(a)(5). And section 1804(a)(7)(E) requires that the application include "a statement of the basis of the certification that – (i) the information sought is the type of foreign intelligence information designated; and (ii) such information cannot reasonably be obtained by normal investigative techniques." That language certainly suggests that, aside from the probable cause, identification of facilities, and minimization procedures the judge is to determine and approve (also set forth in section 1805), the only other issues are whether electronic surveillance is necessary to obtain the information and whether the information sought is actually foreign intelligence information – not the government's proposed use of that information.

Nor does the legislative history cast doubt on the obvious reading of the statutory language that foreign intelligence information includes evidence of foreign intelligence crimes. . . .

The government argues persuasively that arresting and prosecuting terrorist agents of, or spies for, a foreign power may well be the best technique to prevent them from successfully continuing their terrorist or espionage activity. The government might wish to surveil the agent for some period of time to discover other participants in a conspiracy or to uncover a foreign power's plans, but typically at some point the government would wish to apprehend the agent and it might be that only a prosecution would provide sufficient incentives for the agent to cooperate with the government. . . .

Congress was concerned about the government's use of FISA surveillance to obtain information not truly intertwined with the government's efforts to protect against threats from foreign powers. Accordingly, the certification of purpose under section 1804(a)(7)(B) served to

> prevent the practice of targeting, for example, a foreign power for electronic surveillance when the true purpose of the surveillance is to gather information about an individual for other than foreign intelligence purposes. It is also designed to make explicit that the sole purpose of such surveillance is to secure "foreign intelligence information," as defined, and not to obtain some other type of information.

[H.R. Rep. No. 95-1283 (hereinafter "H. Rep.")] at 76; *see also* [S. Rep. No. 95-701 (hereinafter "S. Rep.")] at 51. But Congress did not impose any

Chapter 12. Investigating Terrorism

restrictions on the government's use of the foreign intelligence information to prosecute agents of foreign powers for foreign intelligence crimes. Admittedly, the House, at least in one statement, noted that FISA surveillances "are not primarily for the purpose of gathering evidence of a crime. They are to obtain foreign intelligence information, which when it concerns United States persons must be necessary to important national concerns." H. Rep. at 36. That, however, was an observation, not a proscription. And the House as well as the Senate made clear that prosecution is one way to combat foreign intelligence crimes. *See id.*; S. Rep. at 10-11.

The origin of what the government refers to as the false dichotomy between foreign intelligence information that is evidence of foreign intelligence crimes and that which is not appears to have been a Fourth Circuit case decided in 1980. United States v. Truong Dinh Hung, 629 F.2d 908 (4th Cir. 1980). That case, however, involved an electronic surveillance carried out prior to the passage of FISA and predicated on the President's executive power. In approving the district court's exclusion of evidence obtained through a warrantless surveillance subsequent to the point in time when the government's investigation became "primarily" driven by law enforcement objectives, the court held that the Executive Branch should be excused from securing a warrant only when "the object of the search or the surveillance is a foreign power, its agents or collaborators," and "the surveillance is conducted 'primarily' for foreign intelligence reasons." *Id.* at 915. . . .

[S]ome time in the 1980s – the exact moment is shrouded in historical mist – the Department [of Justice] applied the *Truong* analysis to an interpretation of the FISA statute. What is clear is that in 1995 the Attorney General adopted "Procedures for Contacts Between the FBI and the Criminal Division Concerning Foreign Intelligence and Foreign Counterintelligence Investigations."

Apparently to avoid running afoul of the primary purpose test used by some courts, the 1995 Procedures limited contacts between the FBI and the Criminal Division in cases where FISA surveillance or searches were being conducted by the FBI for foreign intelligence (FI) or foreign counterintelligence (FCI) purposes. The procedures state that "the FBI and Criminal Division should ensure that advice intended to preserve the option of a criminal prosecution does not inadvertently result in either the fact or the appearance of the Criminal Division's *directing or controlling* the FI or FCI investigation toward law enforcement objectives." 1995 Procedures at 2, ¶6 (emphasis added). Although these procedures provided for significant information sharing and coordination between criminal and FI or FCI investigations, based at least in part on the "directing or controlling" language, they eventually came to be narrowly interpreted within the Department of Justice, and most particularly by OIPR, as requiring OIPR to act as a "wall" to prevent the FBI intelligence officials from communicating with the Criminal Division regarding ongoing FI or FCI investigations. . . .

The Department's attitude changed somewhat after the May 2000 report by the Attorney General . . . concluded that the Department's concern over how the FISA court or other federal courts might interpret the primary purpose test has inhibited necessary coordination between intelligence and law enforcement officials. *See id.* at 721-34. . . . [T]he Attorney General, in January 2000, issued additional, interim procedures designed to address coordination problems identified in that report. In August 2001, the Deputy Attorney General issued a memorandum clarifying Department of Justice policy governing intelligence sharing and establishing additional requirements. (These actions, however, did not replace the 1995 Procedures.) . . .

The Patriot Act and the FISA Court's Decision

The passage of the Patriot Act altered and to some degree muddied the landscape. In October 2001, Congress amended FISA to change "the purpose" language in 1804(a)(7)(B) to "a significant purpose." It also added a provision allowing "Federal officers who conduct electronic surveillance to acquire foreign intelligence information" to "consult with Federal law enforcement officers to coordinate efforts to investigate or protect against" attack or other grave hostile acts, sabotage or international terrorism, or clandestine intelligence activities, by foreign powers or their agents. 50 U.S.C. §1806(k)(1). And such coordination "shall not preclude" the government's certification that a significant purpose of the surveillance is to obtain foreign intelligence information, or the issuance of an order authorizing the surveillance. *Id.* §1806(k)(2). Although the Patriot Act amendments to FISA expressly sanctioned consultation and coordination between intelligence and law enforcement officials, in response to the first applications filed by OIPR under those amendments, in November 2001, the FISA court for the first time adopted the 1995 Procedures, as augmented by the January 2000 and August 2001 Procedures, as "minimization procedures" to apply in all cases before the court.

The Attorney General interpreted the Patriot Act quite differently. On March 6, 2002, the Attorney General approved new "Intelligence Sharing Procedures" to implement the Act's amendments to FISA. The 2002 Procedures supersede prior procedures and were designed to permit the complete exchange of information and advice between intelligence and law

Chapter 12. Investigating Terrorism

enforcement officials. They eliminated the "direction and control" test and allowed the exchange of advice between the FBI, OIPR, and the Criminal Division regarding "the initiation, operation, continuation, or expansion of FISA searches or surveillance." On March 7, 2002, the government filed a motion with the FISA court, noting that the Department of Justice had adopted the 2002 Procedures and proposing to follow those procedures in all matters before the court. The government also asked the FISA court to vacate its orders adopting the prior procedures as minimization procedures in all cases and imposing special "wall" procedures in certain cases.

Unpersuaded by the Attorney General's interpretation of the Patriot Act, the court ordered that the 2002 Procedures be adopted, *with modifications*, as minimization procedures to apply in all cases. The court emphasized that the definition of minimization procedures had not been amended by the Patriot Act, and reasoned that the 2002 Procedures "cannot be used by the government to amend the Act in ways Congress has not." ...

Undeterred, the government submitted the application at issue in this appeal on July 19, 2002, and expressly proposed using the 2002 Procedures *without modification*. In an order issued the same day, the FISA judge hearing the application granted an order for surveillance of the target but modified the 2002 Procedures consistent with the court's May 17, 2002 *en banc* order. It is the July 19, 2002 order that the government appeals . . . .

Essentially, the FISA court took portions of the Attorney General's augmented 1995 Procedures – adopted to deal with the primary purpose standard – and imposed them generically as minimization procedures. In doing so, the FISA court erred. It did not provide any constitutional basis for its action – we think there is none – and misconstrued the main statutory provision on which it relied. The court mistakenly categorized the augmented 1995 Procedures as FISA minimization procedures and then compelled the government to utilize a modified version of those procedures in a way that is clearly inconsistent with the statutory purpose.

Under section 1805 of FISA, "the judge shall enter an ex parte order as requested or as modified approving the electronic surveillance if he finds that . . . the proposed minimization procedures meet the definition of minimization procedures under section 1801(h) of this title." 50 U.S.C. §1805(a)(4). [Section 1801(h)] defines minimization procedures in pertinent part as:

> (1) specific procedures, which shall be adopted by the Attorney General, that are reasonably designed in light of the purpose and technique of the particular surveillance, to minimize the acquisition and retention, and prohibit the dissemination, of nonpublicly available information concerning unconsenting United States persons consistent with the need

of the United States to obtain, produce, and disseminate foreign intelligence information; . . .

. . . [M]inimization procedures are designed to protect, as far as reasonable, against the acquisition, retention, and dissemination of nonpublic information which is not foreign intelligence information. If the data is not foreign intelligence information as defined by the statute, the procedures are to ensure that the government does not use the information to identify the target or third party, unless such identification is necessary to properly understand or assess the foreign intelligence information that is collected. *Id.* §1801(h)(2). . . .

The minimization procedures allow, however, the retention and dissemination of non-foreign intelligence information which is evidence of *ordinary crimes* for preventative or prosecutorial purposes. *See* 50 U.S.C. §1801(h)(3). Therefore, if through interceptions or searches, evidence of "a serious crime totally unrelated to intelligence matters" is incidentally acquired, the evidence is "*not* . . . required to be destroyed." H. Rep. at 62 (emphasis added). As we have explained, under the 1978 Act, "evidence of certain crimes like espionage would itself constitute 'foreign intelligence information,' as defined, because it is necessary to protect against clandestine intelligence activities by foreign powers or their agents." H. Rep. at 62; *see also id.* at 49. In light of these purposes of the minimization procedures, there is simply no basis for the FISA court's reliance on section 1801(h) to limit criminal prosecutors' ability to advise FBI intelligence officials on the initiation, operation, continuation, or expansion of FISA surveillances to obtain foreign intelligence information, even if such information includes evidence of a foreign intelligence crime.

The FISA court's decision and order not only misinterpreted and misapplied minimization procedures it was entitled to impose, but as the government argues persuasively, the FISA court may well have exceeded the constitutional bounds that restrict an Article III court. The FISA court asserted authority to govern the internal organization and investigative procedures of the Department of Justice which are the province of the Executive Branch (Article II) and the Congress (Article I). Subject to statutes dealing with the organization of the Justice Department, however, the Attorney General has the responsibility to determine how to deploy personnel resources. . . .

We also think the refusal by the FISA court to consider the legal significance of the Patriot Act's crucial amendments was error. The government, in order to avoid the requirement of meeting the "primary purpose" test, specifically sought an amendment to section 1804(a)(7)(B) which had required a certification "that the purpose of the surveillance is to

Chapter 12. Investigating Terrorism

obtain foreign intelligence information" so as to delete the article "the" before "purpose" and replace it with "a." The government made perfectly clear to Congress why it sought the legislative change. Congress, although accepting the government's explanation for the need for the amendment, adopted language which it perceived as not giving the government quite the degree of modification it wanted. Accordingly, section 1804(a)(7)(B)'s wording became "that a *significant* purpose of the surveillance is to obtain foreign intelligence information" (emphasis added). There is simply no question, however, that Congress was keenly aware that this amendment relaxed a requirement that the government show that its primary purpose was other than criminal prosecution....

... [T]here can be no doubt as to Congress' intent in amending section 1804(a)(7)(B). Indeed, it went further to emphasize its purpose in breaking down barriers between criminal law enforcement and intelligence (or counterintelligence) gathering by adding section 1806(k):

> (k) Consultation with Federal law enforcement officer
> (1) Federal officers who conduct electronic surveillance to acquire foreign intelligence information under this title may consult with Federal law enforcement officers to coordinate efforts to investigate or protect against
> > (A) actual or potential attack or other grave hostile acts of a foreign power or an agent of a foreign power; or
> > (B) sabotage or international terrorism by a foreign power or an agent of a foreign power; or
> > (C) clandestine intelligence activities by an intelligence service or network of a foreign power or by an agent of a foreign power.
> (2) Coordination authorized under paragraph (1) shall not preclude the certification required by section [1804](a)(7)(B) of this title or the entry of an order under section [1805] of this title....

... [W]hen Congress explicitly authorizes consultation and coordination between different offices in the government, without even suggesting a limitation on who is to direct and control, it necessarily implies that either could be taking the lead....

Accordingly, the Patriot Act amendments clearly disapprove the primary purpose test. And as a matter of straightforward logic, if a FISA application can be granted even if "foreign intelligence" is only a significant – not a primary – purpose, another purpose can be primary. One other legitimate purpose that could exist is to prosecute a target for a foreign intelligence crime....

... [I]t is our task to do our best to read the statute to honor congressional intent. The better reading, it seems to us, excludes from the purpose of gaining foreign intelligence information a sole objective of criminal prosecution. We therefore reject the government's argument to the contrary. Yet this may not make much practical difference. Because, as the government points out, when it commences an electronic surveillance of a foreign agent, typically it will not have decided whether to prosecute the agent (whatever may be the subjective intent of the investigators or lawyers who initiate an investigation). So long as the government entertains a realistic option of dealing with the agent other than through criminal prosecution, it satisfies the significant purpose test.

The important point is – and here we agree with the government – the Patriot Act amendment, by using the word "significant," eliminated any justification for the FISA court to balance the relative weight the government places on criminal prosecution as compared to other counterintelligence responses. If the certification of the application's purpose articulates a broader objective than criminal prosecution – such as stopping an ongoing conspiracy – and includes other potential non-prosecutorial responses, the government meets the statutory test. Of course, if the court concluded that the government's sole objective was merely to gain evidence of past criminal conduct – even foreign intelligence crimes – to punish the agent rather than halt ongoing espionage or terrorist activity, the application should be denied.

... It can be argued, however, that by providing that an application is to be granted if the government has only a "significant purpose" of gaining foreign intelligence information, the Patriot Act allows the government to have a primary objective of prosecuting an agent for a non-foreign intelligence crime. Yet we think that would be an anomalous reading of the amendment. For we see not the slightest indication that Congress meant to give that power to the Executive Branch. Accordingly, the manifestation of such a purpose, it seems to us, would continue to disqualify an application. That is not to deny that ordinary crimes might be inextricably intertwined with foreign intelligence crimes. For example, if a group of international terrorists were to engage in bank robberies in order to finance the manufacture of a bomb, evidence of the bank robbery should be treated just as evidence of the terrorist act itself. But the FISA process cannot be used as a device to investigate wholly unrelated ordinary crimes.

One final point; we think the government's purpose as set forth in a section 1804(a)(7)(B) certification is to be judged by the national security official's articulation and not by a FISA court inquiry into the origins of an investigation nor an examination of the personnel involved. It is up to the Director of the FBI, who typically certifies, to determine the government's national security purpose, as approved by the Attorney General or Deputy

Chapter 12. Investigating Terrorism

Attorney General. This is not a standard whose application the FISA court legitimately reviews by seeking to inquire into which Justice Department officials were instigators of an investigation. . . .

III.

Having determined that FISA, as amended, does not oblige the government to demonstrate to the FISA court that its primary purpose in conducting electronic surveillance is not criminal prosecution, we are obliged to consider whether the statute as amended is consistent with the Fourth Amendment. . . . The FISA court indicated that its disapproval of the Attorney General's 2002 Procedures was based on the need to safeguard the "privacy of Americans in these highly intrusive surveillances and searches," which implies the invocation of the Fourth Amendment. The government, recognizing the Fourth Amendment's shadow effect on the FISA court's opinion, has affirmatively argued that FISA is constitutional. . . .

The FISA court expressed concern that unless FISA were "construed" in the fashion that it did, the government could use a FISA order as an improper substitute for an ordinary criminal warrant under Title III. That concern seems to suggest that the FISA court thought Title III procedures are constitutionally mandated if the government has a prosecutorial objective regarding an agent of a foreign power. But in United States v. United States District Court (*Keith*), 407 U.S. 297, 322 (1972) – in which the Supreme Court explicitly declined to consider foreign intelligence surveillance – the Court indicated that, even with respect to domestic national security intelligence gathering for prosecutorial purposes where a warrant was mandated, Title III procedures were not constitutionally required: "[W]e do not hold that the same type of standards and procedures prescribed by Title III are necessarily applicable to this case. We recognize that domestic security surveillance may involve different policy and practical considerations from the surveillance of 'ordinary crime.'" Nevertheless, in asking whether FISA procedures can be regarded as reasonable under the Fourth Amendment, we think it is instructive to compare those procedures and requirements with their Title III counterparts. Obviously, the closer those FISA procedures are to Title III procedures, the lesser are our constitutional concerns.

Comparison of FISA Procedures with Title III

. . . [W]hile Title III contains some protections that are not in FISA, in many significant respects the two statutes are equivalent, and in some, FISA contains additional protections. Still, to the extent the two statutes diverge in constitutionally relevant areas – in particular, in their probable cause and particularity showings – a FISA order may not be a "warrant" contemplated by the Fourth Amendment. . . . We do not decide the issue but note that to the extent a FISA order comes close to meeting Title III, that certainly bears on its reasonableness under the Fourth Amendment.

Did Truong *Articulate the Appropriate Constitutional Standard?*

Ultimately, the question becomes whether FISA, as amended by the Patriot Act, is a reasonable response based on a balance of the legitimate need of the government for foreign intelligence information to protect against national security threats with the protected rights of citizens. . . .

It will be recalled that the case that set forth the primary purpose test *as constitutionally required* was *Truong*. The Fourth Circuit thought that *Keith*'s balancing standard implied the adoption of the primary purpose test. We reiterate that *Truong* dealt with a pre-FISA surveillance based on the President's constitutional responsibility to conduct the foreign affairs of the United States. 629 F.2d at 914. Although *Truong* suggested the line it drew was a constitutional minimum that would apply to a FISA surveillance, *see id.* at 914 n.4, it had no occasion to consider the application of the statute carefully. The *Truong* court, as did all the other courts to have decided the issue, held that the President did have inherent authority to conduct warrantless searches to obtain foreign intelligence information. It was incumbent upon the court, therefore, to determine the boundaries of that constitutional authority in the case before it. We take for granted that the President does have that authority and, assuming that is so, FISA could not encroach on the President's constitutional power. The question before us is the reverse, does FISA amplify the President's power by providing a mechanism that at least approaches a classic warrant and which therefore supports the government's contention that FISA searches are constitutionally reasonable.

The district court in the *Truong* case had excluded evidence obtained from electronic surveillance after the government's investigation – the court found – had converted from one conducted for foreign intelligence reasons to one conducted primarily as a criminal investigation. . . . The court of appeals endorsed that approach, stating:

> We think that the district court adopted the proper test, because once surveillance becomes primarily a criminal investigation, the courts are entirely competent to make the usual probable cause determination, and because, importantly, individual privacy interests come to the fore *and government foreign policy concerns recede* when the government is

Chapter 12. Investigating Terrorism

primarily attempting to form the basis of a criminal prosecution.

Id. at 915 (emphasis added).

That analysis, in our view, rested on a false premise and the line the court sought to draw was inherently unstable, unrealistic, and confusing. The false premise was the assertion that once the government moves to criminal prosecution, its "foreign policy concerns" recede. As we have discussed in the first part of the opinion, that is simply not true as it relates to counterintelligence. In that field the government's primary purpose is to halt the espionage or terrorism efforts, and criminal prosecutions can be, and usually are, interrelated with other techniques used to frustrate a foreign power's efforts. . . .

Recent testimony before the Joint Intelligence Committee amply demonstrates that the *Truong* line is a very difficult one to administer. Indeed, it was suggested that the FISA court requirements based on *Truong* may well have contributed, whether correctly understood or not, to the FBI missing opportunities to anticipate the September 11, 2001 attacks. That is not to say that we should be prepared to jettison Fourth Amendment requirements in the interest of national security. Rather, assuming *arguendo* that FISA orders are not Fourth Amendment warrants, the question becomes, are the searches constitutionally reasonable. And in judging reasonableness, the instability of the *Truong* line is a relevant consideration. . . .

Supreme Court's Special Needs Cases

The distinction between ordinary criminal prosecutions and extraordinary situations underlies the Supreme Court's approval of entirely warrantless and even suspicionless searches that are designed to serve the government's "special needs, beyond the normal need for law enforcement." Vernonia School Dist. 47J v. Acton, 515 U.S. 646, 653 (1995) (quoting Griffin v. Wisconsin, 483 U.S. 868, 873 (1987) (internal quotation marks omitted)) (random drug-testing of student athletes). Apprehending drunk drivers and securing the border constitute such unique interests beyond ordinary, general law enforcement. *Id.* at 654 (citing Michigan Dep't of State Police v. Sitz, 496 U.S. 444 (1990), and United States v. Martinez-Fuerte, 428 U.S. 543 (1976)). . . .

. . . The nature of the "emergency," which is simply another word for threat, takes the matter out of the realm of ordinary crime control.

Conclusion

FISA's general programmatic purpose, to protect the nation against terrorists and espionage threats directed by foreign powers, has from its outset been distinguishable from "ordinary crime control." After the events of September 11, 2001, though, it is hard to imagine greater emergencies facing Americans than those experienced on that date.

We acknowledge, however, that the constitutional question presented by this case – whether Congress's disapproval of the primary purpose test is consistent with the Fourth Amendment – has no definitive jurisprudential answer. The Supreme Court's special needs cases involve random stops (seizures) not electronic searches. In one sense, they can be thought of as a greater encroachment into personal privacy because they are not based on any particular suspicion. On the other hand, wiretapping is a good deal more intrusive than an automobile stop accompanied by questioning.

... Our case may well involve the most serious threat our country faces. Even without taking into account the President's inherent constitutional authority to conduct warrantless foreign intelligence surveillance, we think the procedures and government showings required under FISA, if they do not meet the minimum Fourth Amendment warrant standards, certainly come close. We, therefore, believe firmly, applying the balancing test drawn from *Keith*, that FISA as amended is constitutional because the surveillances it authorizes are reasonable.

Accordingly, we reverse the FISA court's orders in this case to the extent they imposed conditions on the grant of the government's applications, vacate the FISA court's Rule 11, and remand with instructions to grant the applications as submitted and proceed henceforth in accordance with this opinion.

NOTES AND QUESTIONS

1. *Defending the FISC (and the Public?) on Appeal.* No target of a FISC surveillance order ever learns about the issuance of the order, unless the information collected is later used in a criminal prosecution, as in *Duggan,* or turns up in a FOIA or Privacy Act request (see casebook Chapter 15). As a practical matter, therefore, there was no one who had a legally protected interest to process an appeal of the *FISCR* decision to the Supreme Court – or at least no one who knew she had such an interest. Nonetheless, public interest groups led by the ACLU filed a petition for leave to intervene and a petition for certiorari in the Supreme Court. Can you outline their likely positions, both on their right to intervene and on the merits? On March 24, 2003, the Supreme Court dismissed the petition.

Chapter 12. Investigating Terrorism

American Civil Liberties Union v. United States, 123 S. Ct. 1615 (2003) (Mem.). *See* Linda Greenhouse, *Opponents Lose Challenge to Government's Broader Use of Wiretaps to Fight Terrorism*, N.Y. Times, Mar. 25, 2003, at A12.

2. *The Holding.* What is the holding of the *FISCR* decision? Is the holding based on FISA, on the Constitution, or both? Can you reconcile the holding in the *FISCR* decision with *Keith*? With *Truong*?

3. *Purpose vs. Use.* If it has been the case since 1978 that foreign intelligence information includes evidence of foreign intelligence crimes, does this frequent overlap in the nature of the information bear upon the objective of the planned surveillance? Are the FISA limits concerned with the objective of the surveillance or the nature and subsequent uses of the information to be obtained?

The *FISC* decision emphasized the importance of preserving the foreign intelligence objectives of FISA. In view of those objectives, on what basis did the FISCR object to forbidding the Criminal Division from directing or controlling the use of FISA procedures? Is the alleged flaw in the FISC order based on the PATRIOT Act amendments to FISA, or would the infirmity have been present even if FISA had not been amended?

Can you now describe the significance of the PATRIOT Act amendment to the "purpose" requirement? Did the information-sharing additions to FISA in the PATRIOT Act contribute to the result? If so, how? Should Congress revisit the "purpose" standard in FISA? If so, should Congress codify the "primary purpose" requirement, or should it more clearly abandon any required foreign intelligence objectives in shaping requests to the FISC?

A sampling of scholarly reaction to the *FISCR* decision and the PATRIOT Act changes to FISA includes William C. Banks, *And the Wall Came Tumbling Down: Secret Surveillance After the Terror*, 57 U. Miami L. Rev. 1147 (2003); David Hardin, *The Fuss Over Two Small Words: The Unconstitutionality of the USA Patriot Act Amendments to FISA Under the Fourth Amendment*, 71 Geo. Wash. L. Rev. 291 (2003); George P. Varghese, *A Sense of Purpose: The Role of Law Enforcement in Foreign Intelligence Surveillance*, 152 U. Pa. L. Rev. 385 (2003).

4. *The Minimization Requirements.* Why was the FISC in error for relying on the minimization requirements in FISA to justify its order? Do the minimization procedures imply a "wall" between the law enforcement and intelligence investigators?

5. *The "Special Needs" Precedents.* Are you persuaded that the Supreme Court's "special needs" cases are based on considerations that are analogous to the Justice Department procedures at issue in this appeal?

6. *The Aftermath.* Approximately six months after the *FISCR* decision, Justice Department officials reported to the House Judiciary Committee that the procedures approved by the FISCR have "allowed the Department of Justice to investigate cases in a more orderly, efficient, and knowledgeable way, and ha[ve] permitted all involved personnel, both law enforcement and intelligence, to discuss openly legal, factual, and tactical issues arising during the course of investigations. . . . The Department has developed counterterrorism tools and methods that plainly would not have been possible under the previous standards." Letter from Jamie E. Brown, Acting Asst. Attorney General, Off. of Legislative Affairs, U.S. Dept. of Justice, to F. James Sensenbrenner, Jr., Chair, House Comm. on the Judiciary, May 13, 2003, at 15-16. The Department also reported that approximately 4,500 open intelligence files were shared with criminal prosecutors since October 2002 to allow the law enforcement personnel to determine whether criminal investigations should be initiated concerning any of those intelligence targets. *Id.*

In 2003 the FBI issued a classified field directive to further dismantle the wall between law enforcement and intelligence investigations. The directive spells out the Model Counterterrorism Investigations Strategy (MCIS) and new requirements that criminal and intelligence investigators physically work as part of the same teams investigating terrorism. All terrorism investigations are now treated as intelligence investigations, are formally run by the counterterrorism division at FBI headquarters, and will be able to use FISA procedures and methods. Dan Eggen, *FBI Applies New Rules to Surveillance*, Wash. Post, Dec. 13, 2003, A1. FBI officials stated that the new system will deemphasize criminal prosecution in favor of longer-term intelligence surveillance. When a criminal case is brought, however, prosecutors will be able to use the FISA-derived evidence at trial. *Id.* Does the MCIS satisfy the requirements outlined in the FISCR decision? Is the new strategy constitutional?

Page 696. Add this material to Note 1.

The FISC approved a record 1724 applications for searches or electronic surveillance in 2003, compared to 1228 in 2002. Although four applications were denied by the court, two of those were subsequently approved in revised applications. The FISC also made substantive modifications to the government's proposed orders in 79 applications

Chapter 12. Investigating Terrorism 121

presented to the court. The 2003 annual report to Congress on FISA is *available at http://www.fas.org/irp/agency/doj/fisa/2003rept.pdf*. During calendar year 2004, 1758 applications were made, and 1754 were approved by the FISC. Three applications were withdrawn by the Government prior to a FISC ruling, and one was approved in 2003 and received a docket number in 2004. The FISC did not deny any application submitted by the Government in 2004. The 2004 annual report is *available at http://www.fas.org/irp/agency/doj/fisa/2004rept.pdf*. Although the numbers reveal a nearly doubled volume of applications to the FISC since 2000, it remains unclear how many investigations are covered by the aggregate number, which ones are for physical search and which for electronic surveillance, and how many target U.S. persons. Section 6002 of the Intelligence Reform and Terrorism Prevention Act of 2004, Pub. L. No. 108-458, 118 Stat. 3742, expanded the reporting under FISA to require semiannual reports to the intelligence and judiciary committees of the House and Senate that include aggregate number of persons targeted, and breakdowns for electronic surveillance, physical searches, pen registers, access to records, and "lone wolf" orders (see p. 103 in this Supplement). The new reports also must indicate the number of times the Attorney General has authorized information derived from FISA surveillance to be used in a criminal proceeding, provide summaries of significant legal interpretations of FISA by DOJ before the FISC or FISCR, and provide copies of all decisions or opinions of the FISC or FISCR that include "significant construction or interpretation" of FISA. *Id*. In what ways do you think that the new reports will be useful?

Page 697. Add this material after Note 5.

6. *Intelligence Reform Act and FISA*. Enactment of the Intelligence Reform and Terrorism Prevention Act of 2004, Pub. L. No. 108-458, 118 Stat. 3638, affected FISA in a number of ways. In addition to the "lone wolf" and reporting provisions noted above, the new Director of National Intelligence (DNI) was given responsibility "to establish requirements and priorities for foreign intelligence information to be collected" under FISA and assist the Attorney General to ensure that FISA intelligence "may be used efficiently and effectively for foreign intelligence purposes, except that the Director shall have no authority to direct, manage, or undertake" surveillance or search operations under FISA "unless otherwise authorized by statute or Executive order." *Id*. §102(A)(f)(6), 118 Stat. 3650. The authorities and duties of the DNI are considered in this Supplement, Chapter 10 *supra*. What do you think will be the practical importance of this new player in the FISA processes? What legal issues would be raised

by an Executive Order provision that authorized the DNI to direct or undertake FISA surveillance? Another section of the Intelligence Reform Act provided that, "Nothing in this act shall be construed as affecting the role of the Department of Justice or the Attorney General with respect to applications under" FISA. *Id.* §102(A)(f)(8), 118 Stat. 3650.

h. Electronic Communications and Transactional Records

Doe v. Ashcroft
United States District Court, Southern District of New York, 2004
334 F. Supp. 2d 471

MARRERO, J. . . .

I. INTRODUCTION

Plaintiffs in this case challenge the constitutionality of 18 U.S.C. §2709 ("§2709"). That statute authorizes the Federal Bureau of Investigation ("FBI") to compel communications firms, such as internet service providers ("ISPs") or telephone companies, to produce certain customer records whenever the FBI certifies that those records are "relevant to an authorized investigation to protect against international terrorism or clandestine intelligence activities."[24] The FBI's demands under §2709 are issued in the form of national security letters ("NSLs"), which constitute a unique form of administrative subpoena cloaked in secrecy and pertaining to national security issues. The statute bars all NSL recipients from ever disclosing that the FBI has issued an NSL.[25]

The lead plaintiff, called "John Doe" ("Doe") for purposes of this litigation, is described in the complaint as an internet access firm that received an NSL. . . .

II. BACKGROUND . . .

A. Doe's Receipt of an NSL

After receiving a call from an FBI agent informing him that he would

---

24. 18 U.S.C. §2709.

25. *Id.* §2709(c).

Chapter 12. Investigating Terrorism

be served with an NSL, Doe received a document, printed on FBI letterhead, which stated that, "pursuant to Title 18, United States Code (U.S.C.), Section 2709" Doe was "directed" to provide certain information to the Government. As required by the terms of §2709, in the NSL the FBI "certif[ied] that the information sought [was] relevant to an authorized investigation to protect against international terrorism or clandestine intelligence activities." Doe was "further advised" that §2709(c) prohibited him, or his officers, agents, or employees, "from disclosing to *any person* that the FBI has sought or obtained access to information or records under these provisions." Doe was "requested to provide records responsive to [the] request *personally"* to a designated individual, and to not transmit the records by mail or even mention the NSL in *any* telephone conversation. . . .

. . . Doe has not complied with the NSL request, and has instead engaged counsel to bring the present lawsuit.

B. §2709 in General

As stated above, §2709 authorizes the FBI to issue NSLs to compel communications firms to produce certain customer records whenever the FBI certifies that those records are relevant to an authorized international terrorism or counterintelligence investigation, and the statute also categorically bars NSL recipients from disclosing the inquiry. In relevant part, it states:

> (a) Duty to provide. – A wire or electronic communication service provider shall comply with a request for subscriber information and toll billing records information, or electronic communication transactional records in its custody or possession made by the Director of the Federal Bureau of Investigation under subsection (b) of this section.
> (b) Required certification. – The Director of the Federal Bureau of Investigation, or his designee in a position not lower than Deputy Assistant Director at Bureau headquarters or a Special Agent in Charge in a Bureau field office designated by the Director, may –
>> (1) request the name, address, length of service, and local and long distance toll billing records of a person or entity if the Director (or his designee) certifies in writing to the wire or electronic communication service provider to which the request is made that the name, address, length of service, and toll billing records sought are relevant to an authorized investigation to protect against international terrorism or clandestine intelligence activities, provided that such an investigation of a United States person is not conducted solely on the basis of activities protected by the first amendment to the Constitution of the United States. . . .

(c) Prohibition of certain disclosure. – No wire or electronic communication service provider, or officer, employee, or agent thereof, shall disclose to any person that the Federal Bureau of Investigation has sought or obtained access to information or records under this section.[15] . . .

Section 2709 is one of only a handful of statutes authorizing the Government to issue NSLs. The other NSL statutes authorize the Government to compel disclosure of certain financial and credit records which it certifies are relevant to international terrorism or counterintelligence investigations, and to compel disclosure of certain records of current or former government employees who have (or have had) access to classified information.[17] . . .

C. Legislative History

Section 2709 was enacted as part of Title II of the Electronic Communications Privacy Act of 1986 ("ECPA"),[19] which sought to "protect privacy interests" in "stored wire and electronic communications" while also "protecting the Government's legitimate law enforcement needs."[20] . . .

. . . As first enacted, §2709 required electronic communication service providers to produce subscriber information," "toll billing records information," or "electronic communication transactional records," upon the FBI's internal certification that (1) the information was "relevant to an authorized foreign counterintelligence investigation" and that (2) there were "specific and articulable facts giving reason to believe that the person or entity to whom the information sought pertains [was] a foreign power or an agent of a foreign power."[28] . . .

The . . . most recent major revision to §2709 occurred in October 2001,

---

15. *Id.*

17. *See* 12 U.S.C. §3414 (financial records); 15 U.S.C. §§1681u, 1681v (credit records); 50 U.S.C. §436 (government employee records).

19. *See* Pub. L. No. 99-508, §201, 100 Stat. 1848, 1867 (1986).

20. S. Rep. No. 99-541, at 3 (1986), *reprinted in* 1986 U.S.C.C.A.N. 3555, 3557.

28. 18 U.S.C. §2709 (1988).

Chapter 12. Investigating Terrorism

as part of the USA PATRIOT Act of 2001 ("Patriot Act").[39] In short, the Patriot Act removed the previous requirement that §2709 inquiries have a nexus to a foreign power, replacing that prerequisite with a broad standard of relevance to investigations of terrorism or clandestine intelligence activities. In hearings before the House Judiciary Committee on September 24, 2001, the Administration submitted the following explanation for the proposed change:

> NSL authority requires both a showing of relevance and a showing of links to an "agent of a foreign power." In this respect, [it is] substantially more demanding than the analogous criminal authorities, which require only a certification of relevance. Because the NSLs require documentation of the facts supporting the "agent of a foreign power" predicate and because they require the signature of a high-ranking official at FBI headquarters, they often take months to be issued. This is in stark contrast to criminal subpoenas, which can be used to obtain the same information, and are issued rapidly at the local level. In many cases, counterintelligence and counterterrorism investigations suffer substantial delays while waiting for NSLs to be prepared, returned from headquarters, and served. The section would streamline the process of obtaining NSL authority....[41]

The House Judiciary Committee agreed that "[s]uch delays are unacceptable" and stated in its October 11, 2001, report that the Patriot Act would "harmonize[ ]" §2709 "with existing criminal law where an Assistant United States Attorney may issue a grand jury subpoena for all such records in a criminal case."

D. NSLs and Other Information-gathering Authority

It is instructive to place the Government's NSL authority in the context of other means by which the Government gathers information of the type covered by §2709 because Congress (in passing and amending the NSL statutes) and the parties here (in contesting §2709's constitutionality) have drawn analogies to those other authorities as grounds for or against its validity. The relationship of §2709 to other related statutes supplies a

---

39. *See* Pub. L. 107-56, §505, 115 Stat. 272, 365 (2001).

41. *Administration's Draft Anti-Terrorism Act of 2001: Hearing Before the House Comm. on the Judiciary,* 107th Cong. 57-58 (2001), *available at* http://www.house.gov/judiciary/75288.pdf (section-by-section analysis of the Anti-Terrorism Act of 2001).

backdrop for assessing congressional intent and judging the validity of the law on its face and as applied. In addition, an analysis of these analogous information-gathering methods indicates that NSLs such as the ones authorized by §2709 provide fewer procedural protections to the recipient than any other information-gathering technique the Government employs to procure information similar to that which it obtains pursuant to §2709.

1. Administrative Subpoenas

The most important set of statutes relevant to this case are those authorizing federal agencies to issue administrative subpoenas for the purpose of executing the particular agency's function. Ordinary administrative subpoenas, which are far more common than NSLs, may be issued by most federal agencies, as authorized by the hundreds of applicable statutes in federal law. For example, the Internal Revenue Service (IRS) may issue subpoenas to investigate possible violations of the tax code, and the Securities Exchange Commission (SEC) may issue subpoenas to investigate possible violations of the securities laws. . . .

There is a wide body of law which pertains to administrative subpoenas generally. According to the Government's central theory in this case, those standing rules would presumably also apply to NSLs, even if not so explicitly stated in the text of the statute. Where an agency seeks a court order to enforce a subpoena against a resisting subpoena recipient, courts will enforce the subpoena as long as: (1) the agency's investigation is being conducted pursuant to a legitimate purpose, (2) the inquiry is relevant to that purpose, (3) the information is not already within the agency's possession, and (4) the proper procedures have been followed.[47] The Second Circuit has described these standards as "minimal."[48] Even if an administrative subpoena meets these initial criteria to be enforceable, its recipient may nevertheless affirmatively challenge the subpoena on other grounds, such as an allegation that it was issued with an improper purpose or that the information sought is privileged.

Unlike the NSL statutes, most administrative subpoena laws either contain no provision requiring secrecy, or allow for only limited secrecy in special cases. For example, some administrative subpoena statutes permit the investigating agency to apply for a court order to temporarily bar disclosure of the inquiry, generally during specific renewable increments or

---

47. *See United States v. Powell,* 379 U.S. 48 , 57-58 (1964).

48. *See United States v. White,* 853 F.2d 107, 111 (2d Cir. 1988). . . .

for an appropriate period of time fixed by the court, where such disclosure could jeopardize the investigation. . . .

2. Subpoena Authority in the Criminal Context

In its role as a party to a federal criminal proceeding (including a grand jury proceeding), the Government has broad authority to issue a subpoena to obtain witness testimony or *"any* books, papers, documents, data, or other objects the subpoena designates."[52] Although such subpoenas "are issued in the name of the district court over the signature of the clerk, they are issued pro forma and in blank to anyone requesting them," and the "court exercises no prior control whatsoever upon their use."[53]

The court becomes involved in the subpoena process only if the subpoenaed party moves to quash the request as "unreasonable or oppressive,"[54] or if the Government seeks to compel compliance with the subpoena. The reasonableness of a subpoena depends on the context. For example, to survive a motion to quash, a subpoena issued in connection with a criminal trial must make a reasonably specific request for information that would be both relevant and admissible at trial."[55] By contrast, a grand jury subpoena is generally enforced as long as there is a "reasonable possibility that the category of materials the Government seeks will produce information relevant to the general subject of the grand jury's investigation."[56] Considering the grand jury's broad investigatory power and minimal court supervision, it is accurate to observe, as the Second Circuit did long ago, that "[b]asically the grand jury is a law enforcement agency."[57]

While materials presented in a criminal trial setting are generally public,

---

52. Fed. R. Crim. P. 17(a), (c)(1) (emphasis added).

53. *In re Grand Jury Proceedings,* 486 F.2d 85, 90 (3d Cir. 1973); *see also* Fed R. Crim. P. 17(a) ("The clerk must issue a blank subpoena – signed and sealed – to the party requesting it. . . .").

54. Fed. R. Crim. P. 17(c)(2).

55. *United States v. R. Enters., Inc.,* 498 U.S. 292, 299 (1991) (citing *United States v. Nixon,* 418 U.S. 683, 700 (1974)).

56. *Id.* at 301.

57. *United States v. Cleary,* 265 F.2d 459, 461 (2d Cir. 1959).

the federal rules impose stringent secrecy requirements on certain grand jury participants, including the attorneys, court reporters, and grand jurors.[59] . . .

In certain contexts, the Government may issue subpoenas related to criminal investigations even without initiating a formal criminal proceeding. For example, the United States Attorney General is authorized to issue administrative subpoenas, without convening a grand jury, to investigate federal narcotics crimes, racketeering crimes, health care related crimes, and crimes involving the exploitation of children. In each of these instances, the administrative process is governed by the general rules described above, providing safeguards of judicial review.

3. Background Rules Governing Disclosure of Stored Electronic Communications

Title II of the ECPA [also called the Stored Communications Act], in which §2709 was enacted, sets forth an intricate framework by which electronic communications providers, such as ISPs and phone companies, may be compelled to disclose stored electronic information to the Government. The framework described below operates independently of the rules governing NSLs issued pursuant to §2709, but may aid with interpretation of §2709.

The Government may obtain basic subscriber information[69] merely by issuing an authorized administrative subpoena, trial subpoena, or grand jury subpoena, and the Government need not notify the subscriber of the request.

If the Government gives prior notice to the subscriber, or otherwise complies with certain delayed notice procedures, the Government may also subpoena the *contents* of electronic communications which are either (1) retained on a system for storage purposes (*e.g.,* opened email which remains on an ISP's server), or (2) retained, for more than 180 days, in intermediate or temporary storage (*e.g.,* unopened email on an ISP's server). For the Government to obtain the contents of electronic communications kept for

---

59. *See* Fed. R. Crim. P. 6(e).

69. Basic subscriber information includes: (1) a subscriber's name and (2) address; (3) the subscriber's local and long distance telephone connection records, or records of session times and durations; (4) the subscriber's length of service and types of service he has utilized; (5) any telephone or instrument number or other subscriber number or identity, including any temporarily assigned network address; and (6) the subscriber's means and source of payment for the service. *See* 18 U.S.C. §2703(c)(2).

Chapter 12. Investigating Terrorism

180 days or less in intermediate or temporary storage (*e.g.,* unopened email on an ISP's server), it must obtain a search warrant under Federal Rule of Criminal Procedure 41, or the state equivalent. In other words, the Government would have to appear before a neutral magistrate and make a showing of probable cause. The Government may also obtain a court order requiring an electronic communications service provider to turn over transactional and content information by setting forth "specific and articulable facts showing that there are reasonable grounds to believe that" the information sought is "relevant and material to an ongoing criminal investigation."[75]

The ECPA permits the Government to seek a court order prohibiting the communications provider from revealing the Government's inquiry "for such period as the court deems appropriate" if the court determines that such disclosure, among other things, would result in "destruction of or tampering with evidence" or "seriously jeopardizing an investigation or unduly delaying a trial."[76]

4. Mail

Government law enforcement agencies are authorized to request the Postal Inspector to initiate a so-called "mail cover" to obtain any information appearing on the outside of a particular piece of mail.[77] Among other grounds, the law enforcement agency can obtain a mail cover by "specify[ing] the reasonable grounds to demonstrate the mail cover is necessary" to "[p]rotect the national security" or to "[o]btain information regarding the commission or attempted commission of a crime."[78] There is no requirement that the mail sender or recipient be notified of the mail cover.

The Government must obtain a warrant based upon probable cause to open and inspect sealed mail because the contents of mail are protected by the Fourth Amendment. As the Supreme Court established long ago: "Whilst in the mail, [a person's papers] can only be opened and examined under like warrant, issued upon similar oath or affirmation, particularly

---

75. 18 U.S.C. §2703(d).

76. *Id.* §2705(b).

77. *See* 39 C.F.R. §233.3.

78. *See id.* §233.3(e)(2).

describing the thing to be seized, as is required when papers are subjected to search in one's own household."[80]

5. Pen Registers and Trap and Trace Devices

Pen registers and trap and trace devices record certain electronic communications data indicating the origins and destinations of various "dialing, routing, addressing, or signaling information," *e.g.,* the phone numbers dialed to and from a telephone.[81] In criminal investigations, the Government must apply for a court order, renewable in 60-day increments, to install or collect data from such devices, though the standard for issuing such an order is relatively low. The Government need only show that "the information likely to be obtained by such installation and use is relevant to an ongoing criminal investigation."[83]

The person owning the communications device is prohibited, unless otherwise directed by court order, from disclosing the fact that a pen register or trap and trace device is in effect.

6. Wiretaps and Electronic Eavesdropping

The Fourth Amendment protects against warrantless Government wiretapping. Federal legislation specifies the procedures by which law enforcement officials may obtain a court order to conduct wiretaps and other forms of electronic eavesdropping. The requirements are rigorous. Among other things, the Government must show that: (1) "there is probable cause for belief that an individual is committing, has committed, or is about to commit" one of a list of enumerated crimes; (2) "there is probable cause for belief that particular communications concerning that offense will be obtained through such interception"; and (3) "normal investigative procedures have been tried and have failed or reasonably appear to be unlikely to succeed if tried or to be too dangerous."[87] Such orders are not available "for any period longer than is necessary to achieve the objective

---

80. *Id.*

81. *See* 18 U.S.C. §3127(3)-(4).

83. *Id.* §3123(a).

87. [18 U.S.C.] §2518(3).

Chapter 12. Investigating Terrorism 131

of the authorization," subject to a renewable maximum of 30 days.[88] The communications provider is prohibited from disclosing that a wiretap or electronic surveillance is in place, "except as may otherwise be required by legal process and then only after prior notification" to the appropriate law enforcement authorities.[89]

7. Foreign Intelligence Surveillance Act . . .

[The court summarized the procedures for obtaining an order of the Foreign Intelligence Surveillance Court for electronic surveillance under FISA.]

The FISA also authorizes the Government to apply to the FISA court "for an order requiring the production of any tangible things (including books, records, papers, documents, and other items) for an investigation to obtain foreign intelligence information not concerning a United States person or to protect against international terrorism or clandestine intelligence activities. . . ."[99] Such an application need only specify that the inquiry is part of an authorized investigation and in accordance with the appropriate guidelines.[100] Recipients of such an order are prohibited from disclosing to anyone (except those whose assistance is necessary to comply with the subpoena) that the inquiry was made.[101]

Finally, FISA authorizes the Government to apply to the FISA court for an order, renewable in 90-day increments, to install a pen register or trap and trace device as part of "any investigation to obtain foreign intelligence information not concerning a United States person or to protect against international terrorism or clandestine intelligence activities."[102] The Government need only certify to the court that it will likely obtain

---

88. *Id.* §2518(5).

89. *Id.* §2511(2)(a)(ii).

99. 50 U.S.C. §1861(a). [This authority was added by Section 215 of the USA PATRIOT Act, Pub. L. No. 107-108, §215, 115 Stat. 272, 287-288 (2001), and is therefore sometimes called a "Section 215 Order." Section 215 authority is set to expire on December 31, 2005. Eds.]

100. *See id.* §§1861(b), (c).

101. *See id.* §1861(d).

102. 50 U.S.C. §1842(a)(1).

information relevant to a proper inquiry.[103] Just as in the criminal context, the person owning the communications device is prohibited, unless otherwise directed by court order, from disclosing the fact that a pen register or trap and trace device is in effect.[104]. . .

IV. DISCUSSION . . .

B. As Applied Here, Section 2709 Lacks Procedural Protections Necessary to Vindicate Constitutional Rights

1. Section 2709 and The Fourth Amendment[118] . . .

. . . The Fourth Amendment's protection against unreasonable searches applies to administrative subpoenas, even though issuing a subpoena does not involve a literal physical intrusion or search.[121] In so doing, the Supreme Court explained that the Fourth Amendment is not "confined literally to searches and seizures as such, but extends as well to the orderly taking under compulsion of process."[122]

---

103. *See id.* §1842(c).

104. 50 U.S.C. §1842(d)(2)(B)(ii)(I).

118. To be clear, the Fourth Amendment rights at issue here belong to the person or entity receiving the NSL, not to the person or entity to whom the subpoenaed records pertain. Individuals possess a limited Fourth Amendment interest in records which they voluntarily convey to a third party. *See Smith* [v. Maryland], 442 U.S. [735 (1979),] at 742-746; [United States v.] *Miller*, 425 U.S. [435 (1976),] at 440-443. Nevertheless, as discussed below, many potential NSL recipients may have particular interests in resisting an NSL, *e.g.,* because they have contractually obligated themselves to protect the anonymity of their subscribers or because their own rights are uniquely implicated by what they regard as an intrusive and secretive NSL regime. For example, since the definition of "wire or electronic communication service provider," 18 U.S.C. §2709(a), is so vague, the statute could (and may currently) be used to seek subscriber lists or other information from an association that also provides electronic communication services (e.g., email addresses) to its members, or to seek records from libraries that many, including the *amici* appearing in this proceeding, fear will chill speech and use of these invaluable public institutions. . . .

121. *See United States v. Morton Salt Co.,* 338 U.S. 632, 651-52 (1950).

122. *Id.*

Chapter 12. Investigating Terrorism

However, because administrative subpoenas are "at best, constructive searches," there is no requirement that they be issued pursuant to a warrant or that they be supported by probable cause.[123] Instead, an administrative subpoena needs only to be "reasonable," which the Supreme Court has interpreted to mean that (1) the administrative subpoena is "within the authority of the agency;" (2) that the demand is "not too indefinite;" and (3) that the information sought is "reasonably relevant" to a proper inquiry.[124]

While the Fourth Amendment reasonableness standard is permissive in the context of administrative subpoenas, the constitutionality of the administrative subpoena is predicated on the availability of a neutral tribunal to determine, after a subpoena is issued, whether the subpoena actually complies with the Fourth Amendment's demands. In contrast to an actual physical search, which must be justified by the warrant and probable cause requirements occurring *before* the search, an administrative subpoena "is regulated by, and its justification derives from, [judicial] process" available *after* the subpoena is issued.[125]

Accordingly, the Supreme Court has held that an administrative subpoena "may not be made and enforced" by the administrative agency; rather, the subpoenaed party must be able to "obtain judicial review of the reasonableness of the demand prior to suffering penalties for refusing to comply."[126] In sum, longstanding Supreme Court doctrine makes clear that an administrative subpoena statute is consistent with the Fourth Amendment when it is subject to "judicial supervision" and "surrounded by every safeguard of judicial restraint."[127]

Plaintiffs contend that §2709 violates this Fourth Amendment process-based guarantee because it gives the FBI alone the power to issue as well as enforce its own NSLs, instead of contemplating some form of judicial

---

123. *Gimbel v. Federal Deposit Ins. Corp. (In re Gimbel)*, 77 F.3d 593, 596 (2d Cir. 1996) (internal quotation marks and citation omitted).

124. *Morton Salt Co.*, 338 U.S. at 652; *see also Oklahoma Press Pub. Co. v. Walling*, 327 U.S. 186, 208 (1946) ("The gist of the protection is . . . that the disclosure sought shall not be unreasonable.").

125. United States v. Bailey (*In re Subpoena Duces Tecum*), 228 F.3d 341, 348 (4th Cir. 2000).

126. *See v. City of Seattle*, 387 U.S. 541, 544-45 (1967); *see also Oklahoma Press*, 327 U.S. at 217.

127. *Oklahoma Press*, 327 U.S. at 217.

review. Although Plaintiffs appear to concede that the statute does not authorize the FBI to literally enforce the terms of an NSL by, for example, unilaterally seizing documents or imposing fines, Plaintiffs contend that §2709 has the *practical* effect of coercing compliance. . . .

The crux of the problem is that the form NSL, like the one issued in this case, which is preceded by a personal call from an FBI agent, is framed in imposing language on FBI letterhead and which, citing the authorizing statute, orders a combination of disclosure *in person* and in complete secrecy, essentially coerces the reasonable recipient into immediate compliance. Objectively viewed, it is improbable that an FBI summons invoking the authority of a certified "investigation to protect against international terrorism or clandestine intelligence activities," and phrased in tones sounding virtually as biblical commandment, would not be perceived with some apprehension by an ordinary person and therefore elicit passive obedience from a reasonable NSL recipient. The full weight of this ominous writ is especially felt when the NSL's plain language, in a measure that enhances its aura as an expression of public will, prohibits disclosing the issuance of the NSL to "any person." Reading such strictures, it is also highly unlikely that an NSL recipient reasonably would know that he may have a right to contest the NSL, and that a process to do so may exist through a judicial proceeding.

Because neither the statute, nor an NSL, nor the FBI agents dealing with the recipient say as much, all but the most mettlesome and undaunted NSL recipients would consider themselves effectively barred from consulting an attorney or anyone else who might advise them otherwise, as well as bound to absolute silence about the very existence of the NSL. . . .

The evidence in this case bears out the hypothesis that NSLs work coercively in this way. The ACLU obtained, via the Freedom of Information Act ("FOIA"), and presented to the Court in this proceeding, a document listing all the NSLs the Government issued from October 2001 through January 2003. Although the entire substance of the document is redacted, it is apparent that hundreds of NSL requests were made during that period. Because §2709 has been available to the FBI since 1986 (and its financial records counterpart in RFPA since 1978), the Court concludes that there must have been hundreds more NSLs issued in that long time span. The evidence suggests that, until now, none of those NSLs was ever challenged in any court. . . .

. . . The Court thus concludes that in practice NSLs are essentially unreviewable because, as explained, given the language and tone of the statute as carried into the NSL by the FBI, the recipient would consider himself, in virtually every case, obliged to comply, with no other option but to immediately obey and stay quiet. . . .

Chapter 12. Investigating Terrorism

Accordingly, the Court concludes that §2709, as applied here, must be invalidated because in all but the exceptional case it has the effect of authorizing coercive searches effectively immune from any judicial process, in violation of the Fourth Amendment. . . .

2. NSLs May Violate ISP Subscribers' Rights

Plaintiffs have focused on the possibility that §2709 could be used to infringe subscribers' First Amendment rights of anonymous speech and association. Though it is not necessary to precisely define the scope of ISP subscribers' First Amendment rights, the Court concludes that §2709 may, in a given case, violate a subscriber's First Amendment privacy rights, as well as other legal rights, if judicial review is not readily available to an ISP that receives an NSL. . . .

The Supreme Court has recognized the First Amendment right to anonymous speech at least since *Talley v. California*,[161] which invalidated a California law requiring that handbills distributed to the public contain certain identifying information about the source of the handbills. The Court stated that the "identification requirement would tend to restrict freedom to distribute information and thereby freedom of expression."[162] The Supreme Court has also invalidated identification requirements pertaining to persons distributing campaign literature, persons circulating petitions for state ballot initiatives, and persons engaging in door-to-door religious advocacy.

In a related doctrine, the Supreme Court has held that "compelled disclosure of affiliation with groups engaged in advocacy" amounts to a "restraint on freedom of association" where disclosure could expose the members to "public hostility."[166] Laws mandating such disclosures will be upheld only where the Government interest is compelling.

The Court concludes that such First Amendment rights may be infringed by application of §2709 in a given case. For example, the FBI theoretically could issue to a political campaign's computer systems operator a §2709 NSL compelling production of the names of all persons who have email addresses through the campaign's computer systems. The FBI theoretically could also issue an NSL under §2709 to discern the

---

161. 362 U.S. 60 (1960).

162. *Id.* at 64.

166. *NAACP v. Alabama ex rel. Patterson*, 357 U.S. 449, 462 (1958). . . .

identity of someone whose anonymous online web log, or "blog," is critical of the Government. Such inquiries might be beyond the permissible scope of the FBI's power under §2709 because the targeted information might not be relevant to an authorized investigation to protect against international terrorism or clandestine intelligence activities, or because the inquiry might be conducted solely on the basis of activities protected by the First Amendment. These prospects only highlight the potential danger of the FBI's self-certification process and the absence of judicial oversight.

Other rights may also be violated by the disclosure contemplated by the statute; the statute's reference to "transactional records" creates ambiguity regarding the scope of the information required to be produced by the NSL recipient. If the recipient – who in the NSL is called upon to exercise judgment in determining the extent to which complying materials constitute transactional records rather than content – interprets the NSL broadly as requiring production of all e-mail header information, including subject lines, for example, some disclosures conceivably may reveal information protected by the subscriber's attorney-client privilege, *e.g.,* a communication with an attorney where the subject line conveys privileged or possibly incriminating information. Indeed, the practical absence of judicial review may lead ISPs to disclose information that is protected from disclosure by the NSL statute itself, such as in a case where the NSL was initiated solely in retaliation for the subscriber's exercise of his First Amendment rights, as prohibited by §2709(b)(1)-(b)(2). Only a court would be able to definitively construe the statutory and First Amendment rights at issue in the "First Amendment retaliation" provision of the statute, and to strike a proper balance among those interests.

The Government asserts that disclosure of the information sought under §2709 could not violate a subscriber's rights (and thus demands no judicial process) because the information which a §2709 NSL seeks has been voluntarily conveyed to the ISP who receives the NSL. According to the Government, an internet speaker relinquishes any interest in any anonymity, and any protected claim to that information, as soon as he releases his identity and other information to his ISP. In support of its position, the Government cites the Supreme Court's holding [in *Smith* and *Miller*] that, at least in the Fourth Amendment context involving the Government installing a pen register or obtaining bank records, when a person voluntarily conveys information to third parties, he assumes the risk that the

Chapter 12. Investigating Terrorism

information will be turned over to the Government.[169] . . .

The evidence on the record now before this Court demonstrates that the information available through a §2709 NSL served upon an ISP could easily be used to disclose vast amounts of anonymous speech and associational activity. For instance, §2709 imposes a duty to provide "electronic communication transactional records,"[173] a phrase which, though undefined in the statute, certainly encompasses a log of email addresses with whom a subscriber has corresponded and the web pages that a subscriber visits. Those transactional records can reveal, among other things, the anonymous message boards to which a person logs on or posts, the electronic newsletters to which he subscribes, and the advocacy websites he visits. Moreover, §2709 imposes a duty on ISPs to provide the names and addresses of subscribers,[174] thus enabling the Government to specifically identify someone who has written anonymously on the internet.[175] As discussed above, given that an NSL recipient is directed by the FBI to turn over all information *"which you consider to be* an electronic communication transactional record," the §2709 NSL could also reasonably be interpreted by an ISP to require, at minimum, disclosure of all e-mail header information, including subject lines.

In stark contrast to this potential to compile elaborate dossiers on internet users, the information obtainable by a pen register is far more limited. As the Supreme Court in *Smith* was careful to note:

---

169. *See Smith v. Maryland*, 442 U.S. 735 (1979) (holding that installing a pen register does not violate the Fourth Amendment rights of phone customers); *United States v. Miller*, 425 U.S. 435 (1976) (holding that a bank customer does not have any Fourth Amendment protection against the Government obtaining financial records maintained by a bank).

173. 18 U.S.C. §2709(a).

174. *See id.* §2709(b).

175. NSLs can potentially reveal far more than constitutionally-protected associational activity or anonymous speech. By revealing the websites one visits, the Government can learn, among many other potential examples, what books the subscriber enjoys reading or where a subscriber shops. As one commentator has observed, the records compiled by ISPs can "enable the government to assemble a profile of an individual's finances, health, psychology, beliefs, politics, interests, and lifestyle." Daniel J. Solove, *Digital Dossiers and the Dissipation of Fourth Amendment Privacy*, 75 S. Cal. L. Rev. 1083, 1084 (2002).

[Pen registers] disclose only the telephone numbers that have been dialed – a means of establishing communication. Neither the purport of any communication between the caller and the recipient of the call, their identities, nor whether the call was even completed is disclosed by pen registers.[177]

The Court doubts that the result in *Smith* would have been the same if a pen register operated as a key to the most intimate details and passions of a person's private life.

The more apt Supreme Court case for evaluating the assumption of risk argument at issue here is *Katz v. United States*,[178] the seminal decision underlying both *Smith* and *Miller*. *Katz* held that the Fourth Amendment's privacy protections applied where the Government wiretapped a telephone call placed from a public phone booth.[179] Especially noteworthy and pertinent to this case is the Supreme Court's remark that: "The Government's activities in electronically listening to and recording the petitioner's words violated the privacy upon which he justifiably relied while using the telephone booth and thus constituted a 'search and seizure' within the meaning of the Fourth Amendment."[180] The Supreme Court also stated that a person entering a phone booth who "shuts the door behind him" is "surely entitled to assume that the words he utters into the mouthpiece will not be broadcast to the world," and held that, "[t]o read the Constitution more narrowly is to ignore the vital role that the public telephone has come to play in private communication."[181]

Applying that reasoning to anonymous internet speech and associational activity is relatively straightforward. A person who signs onto an anonymous forum under a pseudonym, for example, is essentially "shut[ting] the door behind him," and is surely entitled to a reasonable expectation that his speech, whatever form the expression assumes, will not be accessible to the Government to be broadcast to the world absent appropriate legal process. To hold otherwise would ignore the role of the

---

177. *Smith,* 442 U.S. at 741 (quoting *United States v. New York Tel. Co.,* 434 U.S. 159, 167 (1977)).

178. 389 U.S. 347 (1967).

179. *See id.* at 353.

180. *Id.*

181. *Id.* at 352.

Chapter 12. Investigating Terrorism

internet as a remarkably powerful forum for private communication and association. Even the Government concedes here that the internet is an "important vehicle for the free exchange of ideas and facilitates associations."

To be sure, the Court is keenly mindful of the Government's reminder that the internet may also serve as a vehicle for crime. The Court equally recognizes that circumstances exist in which the First Amendment rights of association and anonymity must yield to a more compelling Government interest in obtaining records from internet firms. To this end, the Court re-emphasizes that it does not here purport to set forth the scope of these First Amendment rights in general, or define them in this or any other case. The Court holds only that such fundamental rights are certainly implicated in some cases in which the Government may employ §2709 broadly to gather information, thus requiring that the process incorporate the safeguards of some judicial review to ensure that if an infringement of those rights is asserted, they are adequately protected through fair process in an independent neutral tribunal. Because the necessary procedural protections are wholly absent here, the Court finds on this ground additional cause for invalidating §2709 as applied.

C. Constitutionality of the Non-Disclosure Provision

Finally, the Court turns to the issue of whether the Government may properly enforce §2709(c), the non-disclosure provision, against Doe or any other person who has previously received an NSL. Section 2709(c) states: "No wire or electronic communication service provider, or officer, employee, or agent thereof, shall disclose to any person that the Federal Bureau of Investigation has sought or obtained access to information or records under this section."[184]

A threshold question concerning this issue is whether, as Plaintiffs contend, §2709(c) is subject to strict scrutiny as either a prior restraint on speech or a content-based speech restriction, or whether, as the Government responds, §2709(c) is subject to the more relaxed judicial review of intermediate scrutiny. The difference is crucial. A speech restriction which is either content-based or which imposes a prior restraint on speech is presumed invalid and may be upheld only if it is "narrowly tailored to

---

184. 18 U.S.C. §2709(c).

promote a compelling Government interest."[185] If "less restrictive alternatives would be at least as effective in achieving the legitimate purpose that the statute was enacted to serve," then the speech restriction is not narrowly tailored and may be invalidated.[186] Under intermediate scrutiny, a speech restriction may be upheld as long as "it advances important governmental interests unrelated to the suppression of free speech and does not burden substantially more speech than necessary to further those interests."[187]

The Court agrees with Plaintiffs that §2709(c) works as both a prior restraint on speech and as a content-based restriction, and hence, is subject to strict scrutiny. First, axiomatically the categorical non-disclosure mandate embodied in §2709(c) functions as prior restraint because of the straightforward observation that it prohibits speech before the speech occurs. As the Supreme Court articulated the threshold inquiry: "The relevant question is whether the challenged regulation authorizes suppression of speech in advance of its expression. . . ."[189] . . .

Second, the Court considers §2709(c) to be a content-based speech restriction. . . .

The Government . . . argues that §2709(c) is content-neutral because it prohibits certain disclosures irrespective of any particular speaker's views on NSLs, terrorism, or anything else. . . .

The Government's argument is unpersuasive. It fails to recognize that even a *viewpoint*-neutral restriction can be *content*-based, if the restriction pertains to an entire category of speech. The Supreme Court has clearly expressed this principle: "The First Amendment's hostility to content-based regulation extends not only to restrictions on particular viewpoints, but also to prohibition of public discussion of an entire topic."[197] Section 2709(c) prohibits any discussion of the first-hand experiences of NSL recipients, and of their officers, employees, and agents, and thus closes off that "entire

---

185. *United States v. Playboy Entm't Group, Inc.*, 529 U.S. 803, 813 (2000) (applying strict scrutiny to a content-based restriction). . . .

186. *See Reno v. ACLU*, 521 U.S. 844, 874 (1997).

187. *Turner Broad. Sys., Inc. v. FCC*, 520 U.S. 180, 189 (1997).

189. *Ward v. Rock Against Racism*, 491 U.S. 781, 795 n.5 (1989) (emphasis omitted).

197. *Id.*

Chapter 12. Investigating Terrorism

topic" from public discourse.[198] Those persons are forever barred from speaking to anyone about their knowledge and role in the underlying events pertaining to the issuance of an NSL, however substantively limited or temporally remote that role may be, even at a time when disclosure of the occurrence of the investigation may have ceased to generate legitimate national security concerns and instead may hold historical or scholarly value then bearing relatively greater interest to the general public. The restriction would also categorically bar the recipient and its agents from ever discussing their roles even if other persons may be free to do so – because, for example, the matter may have become public or the FBI itself may have revealed the information or publicly brought the investigation to closure. The absolute and permanent ban on disclosure §2709(c) commands forecloses an objective weighing of these competing public policy interests by a neutral arbiter even as the relative merits of the respective claims may alter over time. . . .

. . . As stated, §2709(c) may survive strict scrutiny if it is "narrowly tailored to promote a compelling Government interest,"[199] and there are no "less restrictive alternatives [which] would be at least as effective in achieving the legitimate purpose that the statute was enacted to serve."[200] The Supreme Court has instructed that, in the courts' assessment of these considerations, "[p]recision of regulation must be the touchstone" of the inquiry.[201] . . .

The Government's claim to perpetual secrecy surrounding the FBI's issuance of NSLs, by its theory as advanced here an authority neither restrained by the FBI's own internal discretion nor reviewable by any form of judicial process, presupposes a category of information, and thus a class of speech, that, for reasons not satisfactorily explained, must forever be kept from public view, cloaked by an official seal that will always overshadow the public's right to know. In general, as our sunshine laws and judicial doctrine attest, democracy abhors undue secrecy, in recognition that public knowledge secures freedom. Hence, an unlimited government warrant to conceal, effectively a form of secrecy *per se*, has no place in our open society. Such a claim is especially inimical to democratic values for

---

198. *Id.*

199. *Playboy Entm't Group*, 529 U.S. at 813.

200. *Reno v. ACLU*, 521 U.S. at 874.

201. *See NAACP v. Button*, 371 U.S. 415, 438 (1963).

reasons borne out by painful experience. Under the mantle of secrecy, the self-preservation that ordinarily impels our government to censorship and secrecy may potentially be turned on ourselves as a weapon of self-destruction. When withholding information from disclosure is no longer justified, when it ceases to foster the proper aims that initially may have supported confidentiality, a categorical and uncritical extension of non-disclosure may become the cover for spurious ends that government may then deem too inconvenient, inexpedient, merely embarrassing, or even illicit to ever expose to the light of day. At that point, secrecy's protective shield may serve not as much to secure a safe country as simply to save face. . . .

. . . Section 2709(c) does not countenance the possibility that the FBI could permit modification of the NSL's no-disclosure order even in those or any other similar situations no longer implicating legitimate national security interests and presenting factual or legal issues that any court could reasonably adjudicate. Bluntly stated, the statute simply does not allow for that balancing of competing public interests to be made by an independent tribunal at any point. In this regard, it is conceivable that "less restrictive alternatives would be at least as effective in achieving the legitimate purpose that the statute was enacted to serve."[243] For instance, Congress could require the FBI to make at least *some* determination concerning need before requiring secrecy, and ultimately it could provide a forum and define at least *some* circumstances in which an NSL recipient could ask the FBI or a court for a subsequent determination whether continuing secrecy was still warranted. . . .

In this Court's judgment, . . . authorities persuasively confirm that the Government should be accorded a due measure of deference when it asserts that secrecy is necessary for national security purposes in a *particular situation* involving *particular persons* at a *particular time*. Here, however, the Government cites no authority supporting the open-ended proposition that it may universally apply these general principles to impose perpetual secrecy upon an entire category of future cases whose details are unknown and whose particular twists and turns may not justify, for all time and all places, demanding unremitting concealment and imposing a disproportionate burden on free speech. . . .

VI. CONCLUSION

To summarize, the Court concludes that the compulsory, secret, and

---

243. *Reno v. ACLU,* 521 U.S. at 874.

Chapter 12. Investigating Terrorism 143

unreviewable production of information required by the FBI's application of 18 U.S.C. §2709 violates the Fourth Amendment, and that the non-disclosure provision of 18 U.S.C. §2709(c) violates the First Amendment. The Government is therefore enjoined from issuing NSLs under §2709 or from enforcing the non-disclosure provision in this or any other case, but enforcement of the Court's judgment will be stayed pending appeal, or if no appeal is filed, for 90 days. . . .

NOTES AND QUESTIONS

1. *Transactional Information.* "Transactional information broadly describes information that documents financial or communications transactions without necessarily revealing the substance of those transactions." Michael J. Woods, *Counterintelligence and Access to Transactional Records: A Practical History of USA PATRIOT Act Section 215*, 1 J. Natl. Security L. & Poly. 37, 41 (2005). Those documents include telephone billing records that list numbers dialed, an internet service provider's records showing a customer's internet use, records of banking transactions and money transfers, credit card records, and travel records. They have proven invaluable in counter-terrorist investigations. Terrorists can try to encrypt or otherwise disguise the substance of their communications, "but it is far more difficult for them to cover their transactional footsteps." *Id.* at 41-42. Counter-terrorist analysts can use transactional information to perform "link analysis" to tie suspects together and thus help identify cells (*see* McCormick Tribune Foundation (Cantigny Conf. Rpt.), *Counterterrorism Technology and Privacy* 53 (Patrick J. McMahon rapp., 2005)). An example is the retrospective link analysis of the 9/11 hijackers. Woods, *supra*, at 42. It can also be used for pattern analysis and profiling to identify suspects.

2. *The Expectation of Privacy in Transactional Records.* In United States v. Miller, 425 U.S. 435 (1976), the Court held that police seizure of bank records under a defective subpoena duces tecum was lawful because the depositor had no protected Fourth Amendment privacy interest in checks, deposit slips, and other financial information that she voluntarily conveyed to banks. "The depositor takes the risk, in revealing his affairs to another, that the information will be conveyed by that person to the Government." *Id.* at 443. Recall that the Court used the same logic in Smith v. Maryland, 442 U.S. 735 (1979), to uphold the constitutionality of a pen register, which records dialed numbers of outgoing calls.

Is this logic sound? Do you, subjectively, have any expectation of privacy when you convey transactional data to a bank or commercial vendor? Or telephone numbers to the phone company? Of course, you do not expect to keep the information private from the bank, vendor, or phone company; you know that they need the data to complete the transaction that you initiated. But does that need not also define the scope of your intended disclosure? Do you expect the phone company, bank, or vendor to show the information to anyone who is not essential to completing the transaction? In fact, don't some vendors promise you just the opposite, sometimes even providing a checkbox or button for you to indicate whether you want them to share the data with others?

Under Katz v. United States, 389 U.S. 347 (1967), a subjective expectation of privacy for Fourth Amendment purposes is legitimate — protectible — only if it is also "one that society is prepared to recognize as 'reasonable.'" *Id.* at 361. If your expectation is that such transactional information will be disclosed by the bank, vendor, or phone company only as needed to complete the transaction, would society recognize it as reasonable? In the late 1970s, the Court thought not. In the late 1990s, was the answer the same? If it had changed by the late 1990s, did it change again after September 11, 2001?

3. *Matching Legal Thresholds and Processes with Government Surveillance and Collection Techniques.* Professor Orin Kerr identifies the following legal thresholds (standards for obtaining the information) and attendant processes (administrative or judicial or both) for government surveillance in ascending order of strictness:

1. No standard or legal process. The government just gets the information.
2. Internal administrative process. There is no bifurcation between the issuing and enforcing authority.
3. Grand jury or administrative subpoena. The issuing and enforcing authority are bifurcated.
4. Certification court order. The government needs a court order, but gets it simply by certifying relevancy. The court does not decide whether the certification is justified.
5. Articulable facts court order. The government needs a court order and must offer specific and articulable facts to establish relevancy.
6. Probable cause search warrant. The traditional criminal law standard and the predicate preferred by the Fourth Amendment.
7. "Super" search warrant. Same, but government must first exhaust all other investigatory techniques or meet some other "plus" requirement beyond showing probable cause.
8. Prohibition. The government is forbidden from getting the information.

Adapted from Orin Kerr, *Internet Surveillance Law After the USA Patriot*

Act: The Big Brother That Isn't, 97 Nw. U. L. Rev. 607, 620-621 (2003). Match one of these thresholds to each of the surveillance and collection techniques cataloged in Doe v. Ashcroft. Recall that FISA electronic surveillance has its own unique threshold. Where would you place it in the hierarchy? What about the threshold for national security surveillance ordered by the President on his own authority, if he still has it? You may need to prepare a table of techniques and standards to do this exercise. Is there any logic or pattern to the matches reflected in your table?

Should you have to make a table to figure all this out? Looking just at electronic surveillance techniques, Professor Daniel Solove remarks, "The intricacy of electronic surveillance law is remarkable because it is supposed to apply not just to the FBI, but to state and local police – and even to private citizens. Given its complexity, however, it is unfair to expect these varying groups to comprehend what they can and cannot do." Daniel J. Solove, *Reconstructing Electronic Surveillance Law*, 72 Geo. Wash. L. Rev. 1264, 1293 (2004). If you agree, and if you believe that inclusion of non-electronic surveillance techniques as well only compounds the complexity, should the law be simplified? How?

4. *The Relevancy Standard.* Prior to the USA PATRIOT Act, FISA orders for selected business records required a showing of a counterintelligence purpose and of "specific and articulable facts giving reason to believe that the person to whom the records pertain is a foreign power or agent of a foreign power." Pub. L. No. 105-272, §602, 112 Stat. 2396, 2410-2412. The USA PATRIOT Act broadened eligible information to "tangible things" and substituted a showing that the production was for an authorized investigation to protect against international terrorism, as long as such an investigation of a U.S. person is not conducted solely upon the basis of activities protected by the First Amendment. USA PATRIOT Act, Pub. L. No. 107-56, §215, 115 Stat. 287. This is effectively a relevancy standard. It is the same standard adopted in FISA for pen registers and trap and trace devices. *Id.* §214, 112 Stat. 286.

How does the substitution of the relevancy standard for the FISA probable cause standard in obtaining §215 orders affect the scope of resulting government surveillance authority? Consider the following assessment.

> Previously, the FBI could get the credit card records of anyone suspected of being a foreign agent. Under the PATRIOT Act, broadly read, the FBI can get the entire database of the credit card company. Under prior law, the FBI could get library borrowing records only with a subpoena in a criminal investigation, and generally had to ask for the records of a

specific patron. Under the PATRIOT Act, broadly read, the FBI can go into a public library and ask for the records on everybody who ever used the library, or who used it on a certain day, or who checked out certain kinds of books. It can do the same at any bank, telephone company, hotel or motel, hospital, or university – merely upon the claim that the information is . . . sought for . . . an investigation to protect against international terrorism or clandestine intelligence activities.

Terrorism Investigations and the Constitution: Hearing Before the Subcomm. on the Constitution of the House Comm. on the Judiciary, 108th Cong. (2003) (statement of James X. Dempsey, Exec. Director, Center for Democracy & Technology), *available at 2003 WL 21153545*. This critique overstates the scope of resulting investigatory authority, however, because FBI investigations are still subject to any limits established by the Attorney General's Guidelines. Woods (p. 143 *supra*) at 65. *See infra* pp. 152-165 (excerpts of Guidelines).

5. *National Security Letters and the Constitution.* National security letters have been described as "the intelligence corollary to . . . administrative subpoena[s]." Lee S. Strickland, *New Information-Related Laws and the Impact on Civil Liberties*, Bull. Am. Soc. for Info. Sci. & Tech, Feb./Mar. 2002, *at http://www.asis.org/Bulletin/Mar-02/strickland2. html*. Neither administrative subpoenas nor national security letters require a court order. Why are the former lawful under the Fourth Amendment, but not the latter, according to the court? How, if at all, can the infirmity be cured without compromising national security? *See infra* Note 7.

In Doe v. Ashcroft, the court also finds that national security letters for electronic communications records may impermissibly infringe on First Amendment rights. Whose rights? (Hint: more than one category of person.) How are they infringed? How is this infringement different from that resulting from pen registers? How, if at all, could this infirmity be cured without compromising national security?

The former chief of the FBI's National Security Law Unit writes that the pre-9/11 "regulatory scheme governing counterintelligence, the higher legal standards for counter-intelligence authorities, and even the 'wall' separating intelligence and criminal law enforcement have all functioned to counter-balance and contain a tendency toward excessive secrecy in this area." Woods (p. 143 *supra*) at 67. Does the post-9/11 lowering of the legal standards and dismantling of the wall (*see supra* pp. 105-120) upset that balance, supporting the conclusion that the non-disclosure provisions of the NSL statutes fail strict scrutiny?

Chapter 12. Investigating Terrorism
147

6. *Section 215 Orders.* Although FISA §215 requires an order of the FISC for FBI access to "tangible things," its relevancy standard is so low that the order is arguably boilerplate. The government has itself suggested that the FISC's role is simply to ascertain that the government has made the required certification of relevancy, not whether the certification is justified. *See* Letter from Jamie E. Brown, *supra* p. 120, at 3.

This low standard has been defended on the basis of the Supreme Court's reasoning in *Smith* and *Miller* that a person who voluntarily conveys information to a third party to consummate a transaction has no legitimate privacy interest in the information. Section 215, however, is not on its face limited to transactional information; it applies to "any tangible things (including books, records, papers, documents, and other items) . . . ." 50 U.S.C. §1861(a)(1). Does the Court's reasoning, even if correct, support the full breadth of §215? Suppose you entrust your personal diary to your brother. Would a §215 order to your brother be supported by the Court's reasoning?

You have to tell the library what book you are borrowing. Do you intend that it, in turn, will tell the government? No potential application of §215 authority has drawn more criticism that its application to library records, although as of April 2005, the government denied having yet used it for that purpose. *See Attorney General Defends Patriot Act,* CNN.com, Apr. 5, 2005, *at http://www.cnn.com/2005/POLITICS/04/05/patriot.act/.* Can you speculate why, using both the Fourth Amendment and the First Amendment? If library records enjoy a distinct First Amendment protection, should they be excluded from Section 215 authority? On June 15, 2005, the House passed a bill that would do so. H.R. 2862, 109th Cong. (2005).

7. *An FBI Administrative Subpoena?* At this writing, the Senate Intelligence Committee has reported out a bill that would authorize the FBI to issue administrative subpoenas requiring "production of records or other material that are relevant to an authorized" counter-terrorist investigation. S. 1266, 109th Cong., §213 (2005). The Attorney General would be authorized to seek enforcement of such a subpoena in federal district court or the FISC, which could hold closed hearings and act on secret information, if necessary. The court could modify or set aside the subpoena "if compliance would be unreasonable or oppressive." *Id.* §213(a).

Given the scope of existing national security letter and §215 authorities, does the FBI need this additional authority? The bill would direct the FBI to stop using national security letters six months after getting the subpoena authority and direct the Attorney General and Director of National Intelligence to report after one year on the "continuing need" for these tools in light of the proposed subpoena authority. The Committee minority, however, asserts for the same reason that there is no need for the subpoena authority, except in emergency situations. S. Rep. No. 109-85, 109th Cong., 1st Sess. 39-40 (minority views) (June 16, 2005).

Is the proposed subpoena authority broader or narrower than existing authorities? Do the provisions described here meet the legal objections and questions raised in Doe v. Ashcroft and these notes to the authorities it might replace?

The Committee minority objected to the subpoena authority partly because, "absent an emergency, maintaining pre-issuance judicial review of requests for orders to produce business records is an important check against potential abuse in the investigative process." *Id.* In light of the prior notes, is this correct, as a practical matter? Would the judicial review provided by the proposed bill afford a stronger check?

8. *The Question* Smith *and* Miller *Did Not Ask.* The Supreme Court focused in *Smith* and *Miller* on the surveillance and collection techniques (pen registers recording dialed numbers and subpoenas for bank records), not on what became of the information they yield. The Court's focus was understandable from the perspective of traditionally reactive criminal law enforcement, which builds one case at a time. But in the fight against terrorism, reactive law enforcement has given way to proactive and preventive law enforcement. *See* Peter Raven-Hansen, *Security's Conquest of Law Enforcement*, in *In Democracy's Shadow* ch. 12 (Raskin & LeVan eds., 2005). Data are collected and stored in databases maintained for the continuing preventive effort. Law enforcement agents tracking potential terrorists may use data mining across consumer, financial and credit, travel, telephone, internet, and other databases to search for patterns and to build profiles, as well as to perform link analysis.

Does this prospect affect the expectation of privacy? Do you have a different and greater expectation of privacy in your aggregate data than in its parts? For example, are you willing to risk that airlines might disclose your travel data to the government, yet not want those data linked to your consumer and credit data? Should courts gauge the legitimacy of privacy expectations in the original data by the possibility that it will be aggregated for data mining to establish patterns and profiles about the person to whom the data pertain?

Chapter 12. Investigating Terrorism

D. EXECUTIVE AUTHORITY FOR NATIONAL SECURITY INVESTIGATIONS

1. Initiating Investigation

Page 698. Replace all material on pp. 698-712 with the following:

The Attorney General is expressly vested with "primary investigative authority for all Federal crimes of terrorism." 18 U.S.C. §2332b(f) (2000). The FBI, in contrast, has scant statutory authority to carry out its mission. Lacking a legislative charter, the FBI operates on the basis of the Attorney General's authority in 28 U.S.C. §533 (2000) to appoint officials:

(1) to detect and prosecute crimes against the United States;
(2) to assist in the protection of the person of the President; and
(3) to conduct such other investigations regarding official matters under the control of the Department of Justice and the Department of State as may be directed by the Attorney General.

In addition to the powers granted to it by FISA, the FBI, lacking a statutory charter, conducts all of its investigations under the authority of guidelines promulgated by the Attorney General and a 1981 executive order that directs the activities of all the agencies that make up the intelligence community. The *Attorney General's Guidelines on General Crimes, Racketeering Enterprise and Domestic Security/Terrorism Investigations*, Mar. 7, 1983, 32 Crim. L. Rep. 3087 (hereinafter *Domestic Security Guidelines*), "provide guidance for all investigations by the FBI of crimes and crime-related activities." *Id.*, Preamble. On May 30, 2002, the FBI issued three new sets of guidelines for investigations that significantly revise the 1983 *Domestic Security Guidelines*. They are the *Attorney General's Guidelines on General Crimes, Racketeering Enterprise and Terrorism Enterprise Investigations*; the *Attorney General's Guidelines on the Use of Confidential Informants*; and the *Attorney General's Guidelines on Federal Bureau of Investigation Undercover Operations*, available at http://www.usdoj.gov/olp/index.html#agguide. The 1983 *Attorney General Foreign Counterintelligence (FCI) Guidelines* were replaced on November 5, 2003, by the *Attorney General's Guidelines for FBI National Security Investigations and Foreign Intelligence Collection (NSI Guidelines)*. These guidelines support FBI collection of foreign intelligence and national security information. Excerpts of the current guidelines, as revised, along with a portion of Executive Order No. 12,333, are set out below.

Executive Order No. 12,333[27]
46 Fed. Reg. 59,941 (1981)

1.8 The Central Intelligence Agency. All duties and responsibilities of the CIA shall be related to the intelligence functions set out below. As authorized by this Order; the National Security Act of 1947, as amended; the CIA Act of 1949, as amended; appropriate directives or other applicable law, the CIA shall:

(a) Collect, produce and disseminate foreign intelligence and counterintelligence, including information not otherwise obtainable. The collection of foreign intelligence or counterintelligence within the United States shall be coordinated with the FBI as required by procedures agreed upon by the [DCI] and the Attorney General; . . .

(c) Conduct counterintelligence activities outside the United States and, without assuming or performing any internal security functions, conduct counterintelligence activities within the United States in coordination with the FBI as required by procedures agreed upon by the [DCI] and the Attorney General; . . .

2.3 Collection of Information. Agencies within the Intelligence Community are authorized to collect, retain or disseminate information concerning United States persons only in accordance with procedures established by the head of the agency concerned and approved by the Attorney General . . . . Those procedures shall permit collection, retention and dissemination of the following types of information: . . .

(b) Information constituting foreign intelligence or counter-intelligence, including such information concerning corporations or other commercial organizations. Collection within the United States of foreign intelligence not otherwise obtainable shall be undertaken by the FBI or, when significant foreign intelligence is sought, by other authorized agencies of the Intelligence Community, provided that no foreign intelligence collection by such agencies may be undertaken for the purpose of acquiring information concerning the domestic activities of United States persons; . . .

2.5 Attorney General Approval. The Attorney General hereby is delegated the power to approve the use for intelligence purposes, within the United States or against a United States person abroad, of any technique for

---

[27. Portions of Exec. Order No. 12,333 are reproduced at casebook p. 464.]

Chapter 12. Investigating Terrorism

which a warrant would be required if undertaken for law enforcement purposes, provided that such techniques shall not be undertaken unless the Attorney General has determined in each case that there is probable cause to believe that the technique is directed against a foreign power or an agent of a foreign power. Electronic surveillance, as defined in the Foreign Intelligence Surveillance Act of 1978, shall be conducted in accordance with that Act, as well as this Order.

2.6 Assistance to Law Enforcement Authorities. Agencies within the Intelligence Community are authorized to: . . .

(b) Unless otherwise precluded by law or this Order, participate in law enforcement activities to investigate or prevent clandestine intelligence activities by foreign powers, or international terrorist or narcotics activities; . . .

2.8 Consistency With Other Laws. Nothing in this Order shall be construed to authorize any activity in violation of the Constitution or statutes of the United States.

2.9 Undisclosed Participation in Organizations Within the United States. No one acting on behalf of agencies within the Intelligence Community may join or otherwise participate in any organization in the United States on behalf of any agency within the Intelligence Community without disclosing his intelligence affiliation to appropriate officials of the organization, except in accordance with procedures established by the head of the agency concerned and approved by the Attorney General. Such participation shall be authorized only if it is essential to achieving lawful purposes as determined by the agency head or designee. No such participation may be undertaken for the purpose of influencing the activity of the organization or its members except in cases where:

(a) The participation is undertaken on behalf of the FBI in the course of a lawful investigation; or

(b) The organization concerned is composed primarily of individuals who are not United States persons and is reasonably believed to be acting on behalf of a foreign power. . . .

Attorney General's Guidelines on General Crimes, Racketeering Enterprise and Terrorism Enterprise Investigations [*Domestic Security Guidelines*]

Department of Justice (May, 2002)
http://www.usdoj.gov/olp/index.html#agguide

I. General Principles

Preliminary inquiries and investigations governed by these Guidelines are conducted for the purpose of preventing, detecting, or prosecuting violations of federal law. The FBI shall fully utilize the methods authorized by these Guidelines to maximize the realization of these objectives. . . .

All preliminary inquiries shall be conducted pursuant to the General Crime Guidelines. There is no separate provision for a preliminary inquiries under the Criminal Intelligence guidelines. . . . A preliminary inquiry shall be promptly terminated when it becomes apparent that a full investigation is not warranted. If, on the basis of information discovered in the course of a preliminary inquiry an investigation is warranted, it may be conducted as a general crimes investigation, or a criminal intelligence investigation, or both. All such investigations, however, shall be based on a reasonable factual predicate and shall have a valid law enforcement purpose.

In its efforts to anticipate or prevent crime, the FBI must at times initiate investigations in advance of criminal conduct. It is important that such investigations not be based solely on activities protected by the First Amendment or on the lawful exercise of any other rights secured by the Constitution or laws of the United States. When, however, statements advocate criminal activity or indicate an apparent intent to engage in crime, particularly crimes of violence, an investigation under these Guidelines may be warranted unless it is apparent, from the circumstances or the context in which the statements are made, that there is no prospect of harm. . . .

II. General Crimes Investigations . . .

B. Preliminary Inquiries

(1) On some occasions the FBI may receive information or an allegation not warranting a full investigation – because there is not yet a "reasonable indication" of criminal activities – but whose responsible handling requires some further scrutiny beyond the prompt and extremely limited checking out of initial leads. In such circumstances, though the

Chapter 12. Investigating Terrorism

factual predicate for an investigation has not been met, the FBI may initiate an "inquiry" involving some measured review, contact, or observation activities in response to the allegation or information indicated the possibility of criminal activity.

This authority to conduct inquiries short of a full investigation allows the government to respond in a measured way to ambiguous or incomplete information and to do so with as little intrusion as the needs of the situation permit. This is especially important . . . when an allegation or information is received from a source of unknown reliability. . . .

(2) The FBI supervisor authorizing an inquiry shall assure that the allegation or other information which warranted the inquiry has been recorded in writing . . . .

(4) The choice of investigative techniques in an inquiry is a matter of judgment, which should take account of: (i) the objectives of the inquiry and available investigative resources, (ii) the intrusiveness of a technique, considering such factors as the effect on the privacy of individuals and potential damage to reputation, (iii) the seriousness of the possible crime, and (iv) the strength of the information indicating its existence or future commission. Where the conduct of an inquiry presents a choice between the use of more or less intrusive methods, the FBI should consider whether the information could be obtained in a timely and effective way by the less intrusive means. The FBI should not hesitate to use any lawful techniques consistent with these Guidelines in an inquiry, even if intrusive, where the intrusiveness is warranted in light of the seriousness of the possible crime or the strength of the information indicating its existence or future commission. This point is to be particularly observed in inquiries relating to possible terrorist activities.

(5) All lawful investigative techniques may be used in an inquiry except:

    (a) Mail openings; and

    (b) Nonconsensual electronic surveillance or any other investigative technique covered by chapter 119 of title 18, United States Code (18 U.S.C. 2510-2522).

(6) The following investigative techniques may be used in an inquiry without any prior authorization from a supervisory agent:

    (a) Examination of FBI indices and files;

    (b) Examination of records available to the public and other public sources of information;

    (c) Examination of available federal, state and local government records;

    (d) Interview of the complainant, previously established informants and confidential sources;

(e) Interview of the potential subject;

(f) Interview of persons who would readily be able to corroborate or deny the truth of the allegation, except this does not include pretest interviews or interviews of a potential subject's employer or co-workers unless the interviewee was the complainant;

(g) Physical or photographic surveillance of any person.

The use of any other lawful investigative technique in an inquiry shall require prior approval by a supervisory agent, except in exigent circumstances. . . .

(7) Where a preliminary inquiry fails to disclose sufficient information to justify an investigation, the FBI shall terminate the inquiry and make a record of the closing. . . .

III. Terrorism Enterprise Investigations

This section authorizes the FBI to conduct criminal intelligence investigations of certain enterprises who seek either to obtain monetary or commercial gains or profits through racketeering activities or to further political or social goals through activities that involve criminal violence. These investigations differ from general crimes investigations, authorized by Section II, in several important respects. As a general rule, an investigation of a completed criminal act is normally confined to determining who committed that act and with securing evidence to establish the elements of the particular offense. It is in this respect, self-defining. An intelligence investigation of an ongoing criminal enterprise must determine the size and composition of the group involved, its geographic dimensions, its past acts and intended criminal goals, and its capacity for harm. While a standard criminal investigation terminates with the decision to prosecute or not to prosecute, the investigation of a criminal enterprise does not necessarily end, even though one or more of the participants may have been prosecuted. . . .

B. Domestic Security/Terrorism Investigations . . .

1. General Authority

a. A terrorism enterprise investigation may be initiated when facts or circumstances reasonably indicate that two or more persons are engaged in an enterprise for the purpose of: (i) furthering political or social goals wholly or in part through activities that involve force or violence and a violation of federal criminal law, (ii) engaging in terrorism as defined in 18 U.S.C. 2331(1) or (5) that involves a violation of federal criminal law, or

Chapter 12. Investigating Terrorism

(iii) committing any offense described in 18 U.S.C. 2332b(g)(5)(B). A terrorism enterprise investigation may also be initiated when facts or circumstances reasonably indicate that two or more persons are engaged in a pattern of racketeering activity as defined in the RICO statute, 18 U.S.C. 1961(5), that involves an offense or offenses described in 18 U.S.C. 2332b(g)(5)(B). The standard of "reasonable indication" is identical to that governing the initiation of a general crimes investigation under Part II. In determining whether an investigation should be conducted, the FBI shall consider all of the circumstances including: (i) the magnitude of the threatened harm; (ii) the likelihood it will occur; (iii) the immediacy of the threat; and (iv) any danger to privacy or free expression posed by an investigation. . . .

c. Mere speculation that force or violence might occur during the course of an otherwise peaceable demonstration is not sufficient grounds for initiation of an investigation under this Subpart, but where facts or circumstances reasonably indicate that a group or enterprise has engaged or aims to engage in activities involving force or violence or other criminal conduct described in paragraph (1)(a) in a demonstration, an investigation may be initiated in conformity with the standards of that paragraph. . . . This does not limit the collection of information about public demonstrations by enterprises that are under active investigation pursuant to paragraph (1)(a) above. . . .

4. Authorization and Renewal

a. A terrorism enterprise investigation may be authorized by the Special Agent in Charge, with notification to FBIHQ, upon a written recommendation setting forth the facts or circumstances reasonably indictating the existence of an enterprise as described in paragraph (1)(a). . . .

IV. Investigative Techniques

A. When conducting investigations under these guidelines the FBI may use any lawful investigative technique. . . . When the conduct of an investigation presents a choice between the use of more or less intrusive methods, the FBI should consider whether the information could be obtained in a timely and effective way by less intrusive means. . . .

B. All requirements for use of a technique set by statute, Department regulations and policies, and Attorney General Guidelines must be complied with. The investigative techniques listed below are subject to the noted restrictions:

1. Informants and confidential sources must be used in compliance with the Attorney General's Guidelines on the Use of Informants and Confidential Sources;
2. Undercover operations must be conducted in compliance with the Attorney General's Guidelines of FBI Undercover Operations; . . .
4. Nonconsensual electronic surveillance must be conducted pursuant to the warrant procedures and requirements of Title III. . . .
7. Consensual electronic monitoring must be authorized pursuant to Department policy. . . .
8. Searches and seizures must be conducted under the authority of a valid warrant unless the search or seizure comes within a judicially recognized exception to the warrant requirements. . . .

V. Dissemination of Information

A. The FBI may disseminate information during investigations conducted pursuant to these guidelines to another Federal agency or to a State or local criminal justice agency when such information:

1. falls within the investigative or protective jurisdiction or litigative responsibility of the agency;
2. may assist in preventing a crime or the use of violence or any other conduct dangerous to human life; . . .
4. is required to be disseminated by statute, interagency agreement approved by the Attorney General, or Presidential Directive;

and to other persons and agencies as permitted by Sections 552 and 552a of Title V, U.S.C. . . .

VI. Counterterrorism Activities and Other Authorizations

A. Counterterrorism Activities

1. Information Systems

The FBI is authorized to operate and participate in identification, tracking, and information systems for the purpose of identifying and locating terrorists. . . . Systems within the scope of this paragraph may draw on and retain pertinent information from any source permitted by law, including information derived from past or ongoing investigative activities;

other information collected or provided by governmental entities, such as foreign intelligence information and lookout list information; publicly available information, whether obtained directly or through services or resources (whether nonprofit or commercial) that compile or analyze such information; and information voluntarily provided by private entities. Any such system operated by the FBI shall be reviewed periodically for compliance with all applicable statutory provisions, Department regulations and policies, and Attorney General Guidelines.

2. Visiting Public Places and Events

For the purpose of detecting or preventing terrorist activities, the FBI is authorized to visit any place and attend any event that is open to the public, on the same terms and conditions as members of the public generally. No information obtained from such visits shall be retained unless it relates to potential or terrorist activity.

VII. Reservation . . .

C. These guidelines are set forth solely for the purpose of internal Department of Justice guidance. They are not intended to, do not, and may not be relied upon to create any rights, substantive or procedural, enforceable at law by any party in any manner, civil or criminal, nor do they place any limitation on otherwise lawful investigative and litigative prerogatives of the Department of Justice.

The Attorney General's Guidelines for FBI National Security Investigations and Foreign Intelligence Collection (U)[28] [*NSI Guidelines*]
Department of Justice (October 2003)
available at *http://www.usdoj.gov/olp/nsiguidelines.pdf*

INTRODUCTION (U)

. . . These Guidelines generally authorize investigation by the FBI of threats to the national security of the United States; investigative assistance

---

[28. The guidelines are partly classified. "(U)" means that a particular provision is unclassified.]

by the FBI to state, local, and foreign governments in relation to matters affecting the national security; the collection of foreign intelligence by the FBI; the production of strategic analysis by the FBI; and the retention and dissemination of information resulting from the foregoing activities. This includes guidance for the activities of the FBI pursuant to Executive Order 12333, "United States Intelligence Activities" (Dec. 4, 1981). (U)

The general objective of these Guidelines is the full utilization of all authorities and investigative techniques, consistent with the Constitution and laws of the United States, so as to protect the United States and its people from terrorism and other threats to the national security. (U) . . .

The activities of the FBI under these Guidelines are part of the overall response of the United States to threats to the national security, which includes cooperative efforts and sharing of information with other agencies, including other entities in the Intelligence Community and the Department of Homeland Security. The overriding priority in these efforts is preventing, preempting, and disrupting terrorist threats to the United States. In some cases, this priority will dictate the provision of information to other agencies even where doing so may affect criminal prosecutions or ongoing law enforcement or intelligence operations. To the greatest extent possible that is consistent with this overriding priority, the FBI shall also act in a manner to protect other significant interests, including the protection of intelligence and sensitive law enforcement sources and methods, other classified information, and sensitive operational and prosecutorial information. (U)

A. National Security Investigations (U)

. . . The investigations authorized by these Guidelines serve to protect the national security by providing the basis for, and informing decisions concerning, a variety of measures to deal with threats to the national security. These measures may include, for example, recruitment of double agents and other assets; excluding or removing persons involved in terrorism or espionage from the United States; freezing assets of organizations that engage in or support terrorism; securing targets of terrorism or espionage; providing threat information and warnings to other federal agencies and officials, state and local governments, and private entities; diplomatic or military actions; and actions by other intelligence agencies to counter international terrorism or other national security threats. In addition, the matters identified by these Guidelines as threats to the national security, including international terrorism and espionage, almost invariably involve possible violations of criminal statutes. Detecting, solving, and preventing these crimes – and in many cases, arresting and

Chapter 12. Investigating Terrorism

prosecuting the perpetrators – are crucial objectives of national security investigations under these Guidelines. Thus, these investigations are usually both "counterintelligence" investigations and "criminal" investigations. (U)

The authority to conduct national security investigations under these Guidelines does not supplant or limit the authority to carry out activities under other Attorney General guidelines or pursuant to other lawful authorities of the FBI. (U) . . .

Part II of these Guidelines authorizes three levels of investigative activity in national security investigations: (1) threat assessments, (2) preliminary investigations, and (3) full investigations: (U)

> (1) *Threat assessments.* To carry out its central mission of preventing the commission of terrorist acts against the United States and its people, the FBI must proactively draw on available sources of information to identify terrorist threats and activities. It cannot be content to wait for leads to come in through the actions of others, but rather must be vigilant in detecting terrorist activities to the full extent permitted by law, with an eye towards early intervention and prevention of acts of terrorism before they occur. (U)
>
> Part II.A of these Guidelines accordingly authorizes the proactive collection of information concerning threats to the national security, including information on individuals, groups, and organizations of possible investigative interest, and information on possible targets of international terrorist activities or other national security threats (such as infrastructure and computer systems vulnerabilities). (U) . . .
>
> In addition to allowing proactive information collection for national security purposes, the authority to conduct threat assessments may be used in cases in which information or an allegation concerning possible terrorist (or other national security-threatening) activity by an individual, group, or organization is received, and the matter can be checked out promptly through the relatively non-intrusive techniques authorized in threat assessments. This can avoid the need to open a formal preliminary or full investigation, if the threat assessment indicates that further investigation is not warranted. In this function, threat assessments under these Guidelines are comparable to the checking of initial leads in ordinary criminal investigations. (U)
>
> (2) *Preliminary investigations.* . . . Preliminary investigations may relate to individuals, groups, organizations, and possible criminal violations, as specified in Part II.B. . . .

(3) *Full investigations.* Like preliminary investigations, full investigations may relate to individuals, groups, or organizations and possible criminal violations, as specified in Part II.B. . . .

Part II.E. of these Guidelines sets out conditions and approval requirements for extraterritorial activities. As provided in Part II.E, these activities require a request from or approval of the Director of Central Intelligence or a designee. This requirement ensures that extraterritorial activities under these Guidelines are properly coordinated with other agencies in the Intelligence Community, so that their authorities and capabilities are also brought to bear as appropriate to protect the national security, consistent with Executive Order 12333 or a successor order.

The FBI may also provide assistance to state and local governments, and to foreign law enforcement, intelligence, and security agencies, in investigations relating to threats to the national security. Part III of these Guidelines specifies standards and procedures for the provisions of such assistance. (U) . . .

B. Foreign Intelligence Collection (U)

The FBI's functions pursuant to Executive Order 12333 §§ 1.6, 1.14, 2.3, and 2.4 include engaging in foreign intelligence collection and providing operational support for other components of the U.S. Intelligence Community. This role is frequently critical in collecting foreign intelligence within the United States because the authorized domestic activities of other intelligence agencies are more constrained than those of the FBI under applicable statutory law and Executive Order 12333. (U) . . .

I. GENERAL AUTHORITIES AND PRINCIPLES (U)

A. General Authorities (U)

1. The FBI is authorized to conduct investigations to obtain information concerning or to protect against threats to the national security, including investigations of crimes involved in or related to threats to the national security, as provided in Parts II and V of these Guidelines. Threats to the national security are:

Chapter 12. Investigating Terrorism

    a. International terrorism.

    b. Espionage and other intelligence activities, sabotage, or assassination, conducted by, for, or on behalf of foreign powers, organizations, or persons.

    c. Foreign computer intrusions.

    d. Other matters as determined by the Attorney General, consistent with Executive Order 12333 or a successor order. (U) . . .

B. Use of Authorities and Method (U) . . .

2. Choice of Methods (U)

The conduct of investigations and other activities authorized by these Guidelines may present choices between the use of information collection methods that are more or less intrusive, considering such factors as the effect on the privacy of individuals, and potential damage or reputation. As Executive Order 12333 §2.4 provides, "the latest intrusive collection techniques feasible" are to be used in such situations. It is recognized, however, that the choice of techniques is a matter of judgment. The FBI shall not hesitate to use any lawful techniques consistent with these Guidelines, even if intrusive, where the degree of intrusiveness is warranted in light of the seriousness of a threat to the national security or the strength of the information indicating its existence. This point is to be particularly observed in investigations relating to terrorism. (U)

3. Respect for Legal Rights (U)

These Guidelines do not authorize investigating or maintaining information on United States persons solely for the purpose of monitoring activities protected by the First Amendment or the lawful exercise of other rights secured by the Constitution or laws of the United States. Rather, all activities under these Guidelines must have a valid purpose consistent with these Guidelines, and must be carried out in conformity with the Constitution and all applicable statutes, executive orders, Department of Justice regulations and policies, and Attorney General Guidelines. . . .

C. Determination of United States Person Status (U) . . .

3. Determination Whether Certain Groups are Substantially Composed of United States Persons (U)

In determining whether a group or organization in the United States that is affiliated with a foreign-based international organization is substantially composed of United States persons, the relationship between the two shall be considered. If the U.S.-based group or organization operates directly under the control of the international organization and has no independent program or activities in the United States, the membership of the entire international organization shall be considered in determining if it is substantially composed of United States persons. If, however, the U.S.-based group or organization has programs or activities separate from, or in addition to, those directed by the international organization, only its membership in the United States shall be considered in determining whether it is substantially composed of United States persons. (U)

D. Nature and Application of the Guidelines (U)

1. Status as Internal Guidance (U)

These Guidelines are set forth solely for the purpose of internal Department of Justice guidance. They are not intended to, do not, and may not be relied upon to create any rights, substantive or procedural, enforceable by law by any party in any matter, civil or criminal, nor do they place any limitation on otherwise lawful investigative and litigative prerogatives of the Department of Justice. (U)

2. Departures from the Guidelines (U)

Departures from these Guidelines must be approved by the Attorney General, the Deputy Attorney General, or an official designated by the Attorney General. If a departure from these Guidelines is necessary without such prior approval because of the immediacy or gravity of a threat to the national security or to the safety of persons or property and the need to take immediate action to protect against such a threat, the Attorney General, the Deputy Attorney General, or an official designated by the Attorney General shall be notified as soon thereafter as practicable. The FBI shall provide timely written notice of departures from these Guidelines to the Office of Intelligence Policy and Review. Notwithstanding this paragraph, all activities in all circumstances must be carried out in a manner consistent

Chapter 12. Investigating Terrorism

with the Constitution and laws of the United States. (U) . . .

II. NATIONAL SECURITY INVESTIGATIONS (U) . . .

B. Common Provisions for Preliminary and Full Investigations (U) . .

3. Investigations of Groups and Organizations (U)

a. Preliminary and full investigations of groups and organizations should focus on activities related to threats to the national security, not on unrelated First Amendment activities. . . .

E. Extraterritorial Operations (U)

1. The FBI may conduct investigations abroad, participate with foreign officials in investigations abroad, or otherwise conduct activities outside the United States with the written request or approval of the Director of Central Intelligence and the Attorney General or their designees. . . . The involvement of the Director of Central Intelligence or designee in the authorization of these extraterritorial activities reflects the coordinating and liaison roles of the Director of Central Intelligence and the Central Intelligence Agency in this area in accordance with the National Security Act of 1947 and Executive Order 12333, including §§1.5(e), 1.8(c)-(d), 1.14(b) of that Order, and helps to ensure that the collective resources and capabilities of the broader Intelligence Community will be used in the most effective manner to protect the national security. . . .

IV. FOREIGN INTELLIGENCE COLLECTION AND ASSISTANCE TO INTELLIGENCE AGENCIES (U)

A. Foreign Intelligence Collection (U)

1. The FBI may collect foreign intelligence in response to requirements of topical interest published by an entity authorized by the Director of Central Intelligence to establish such requirements, including, but not limited to, the National HUMINT Requirements Tasking Center. When approved by the Attorney General, the Deputy Attorney General, or an official designated by the Attorney General, the FBI may collect other foreign intelligence in response to tasking specifically levied on the FBI by an official of the Intelligence Community designated by the President. Upon a request by an official of the Intelligence Community designated by the President, the FBI may also collect foreign intelligence to clarify or

complete foreign intelligence previously disseminated by the FBI. Copies of such requests shall be provided to the Office of Intelligence Policy and Review. (U)

2. The FBI may also collect foreign intelligence, if consistent with Executive Order 12333 or a successor order, as directed by the Attorney General, the Deputy Attorney General, or an official designated by the Attorney General. (U) . . .

B. Operational Support (U)

1. When approved by the Attorney General, the Deputy Attorney General, or an official designated by the Attorney General, the FBI may provide operational support to authorized intelligence activities of other entities of the Intelligence Community upon a request made or confirmed in writing by an official of the Intelligence Community designated by the President. The request shall describe the type and duration of support required, the reasons why the FBI is being requested to furnish the assistance, and the techniques that are expected to be utilized, and shall certify that such assistance is necessary to an authorized activity of the requesting entity. (U)

2. The support may include techniques set forth in the approved request and, with the approval of FBI headquarters, any other technique that does not substantially alter the character of the support. The FBI shall promptly notify the Office of Intelligence Policy and Review of the utilization of any such additional techniques. (U)

3. The FBI may recruit new assets to obtain information or services needed to furnish the requested support, subject to the same standards and procedures applicable to other FBI assets. (U) . . .

VII. RETENTION AND DISSEMINATION OF INFORMATION . . .

B. Information Sharing (U)

Legal rules and Department of Justice policies regarding information sharing and interagency coordination have been significantly modified since the September 11, 2001, terrorist attack by statutory reforms and new Attorney General guidelines. The general principle reflected in current laws and policies is that information should be shared as consistently and fully as possible among agencies with relevant responsibilities to protect the United States and its people from terrorism and other threats to the national security, except as limited by specific constraints on such sharing. Under this general principle, the FBI shall provide information expeditiously to

Chapter 12. Investigating Terrorism

other agencies in the Intelligence Community, so that these agencies can take action in a timely manner to protect the national security in accordance with their lawful functions. (U) . . .

NOTES AND QUESTIONS

a. Executive Order 12,333

1. *Investigatory Authorizations Under Executive Order No. 12,333.* What constitutes a "lawful" FBI investigation within the meaning of Executive Order No. 12,333? What are the likely elements of a probable cause determination under §2.5?

According to the executive order, the most important factor in assessing executive power to conduct national security investigations is the presence or absence of a connection between the target of surveillance and a foreign power. To this extent, the executive order tracks FISA. The 1994 amendments to FISA extended the FISA procedures to applications for a physical search for foreign intelligence information where the target is a foreign power or agent of a foreign power. See casebook p. 679. In Executive Order No. 12,949, 60 Fed. Reg. 8169 (Feb. 9, 1995), President Clinton updated Executive Order No. 12,333 to authorize the Attorney General to approve applications to the FISC for physical searches for foreign intelligence purposes, following the certifications required by FISA. *Id.* §2. Bearing in mind the provisions of FISA, what "technique[s] for which a warrant would be required if undertaken for law enforcement purposes" (§2.5) continue to be governed by Executive Order 12,333 and FBI guidelines?

2. *Infiltration.* Is CIA or FBI infiltration of domestic organizations permitted by the executive order? On the basis of what information will the "agency head or designee" determine that infiltration is "essential to achieving lawful purposes"? If infiltration is authorized outside the limits of the order, what redress would be available to aggrieved persons? *See* Sherri J. Conrad, Note, *Executive Order 12,333: Unleashing the CIA Violates the Leash Law,* 70 Cornell L. Rev. 968 (1985).

3. *12,333 and the National Security Act of 1947.* Compare §§1.8 and 2.3(b) of the executive order to the National Security Act of 1947 (casebook pp. 428-429). Does the order adequately respect the statutory mandate that the CIA not engage in "internal security functions"? How may the CIA "conduct counterintelligence activities within the United States in coordination with

the FBI" without performing any "internal security functions"? In what ways will the reorganization of the intelligence community and the creation of the Director of National Intelligence (DNI), as prescribed in the Intelligence Reform and Terrorism Prevention Act of 2004 (described in this Supplement, pp. 21-29 *supra*) affect the CIA/FBI relationship in national security investigations?

4. *Making of Guidelines for Investigation.* Several sections of Executive Order No. 12,333 provide that procedures for intelligence collection are to be independently established by each agency, subject to approval by the Attorney General. Should a citizen be able to participate in setting such procedures? Where would they be published?

b. Domestic Security Guidelines

1. *Authority for Guidelines.* Does the FBI have statutory authority to promulgate the guidelines set out above? In addition to the authority granted by 28 U.S.C. §533, the Attorney General "may from time to time make such provisions as he considers appropriate authorizing the performance by any other officer, employee, or agency of the Department of Justice of any function of the Attorney General." *Id.* §510. Do you think Congress should provide more explicit statutory authority for the FBI to conduct national security investigations?

2. *The Guidelines and FISA.* What purposes are served by these guidelines that are not met by FISA? Can you see where the prescriptions in FISA end and those of the two sets of guidelines begin?

3. *Application.* Compare the coverage of the two sets of guidelines. How can you tell which set applies to a potential investigation?

4. *Preliminary Investigation.* Are the standards for beginning a preliminary inquiry in the domestic security setting clear? What purpose is served by the preliminary inquiry? Can you predict when agents might opt for a preliminary inquiry instead of a full investigation? Are the rights of the targets of an inquiry safeguarded adequately by the *Domestic Security Guidelines*?

The Introduction to the *2002 Domestic Security Guidelines* describes and explains the checking of leads and preliminary inquiries:

> The lowest level of investigative activity is the "prompt and extremely limited checking out of initial leads," which should be

undertaken whenever information is received of such a nature that some follow-up as to the possibility of criminal activity is warranted. This limited activity should be conducted with an eye toward promptly determining whether further investigation (either a preliminary inquiry or a full investigation) should be conducted.

The next level of investigative activity, a preliminary inquiry, should be undertaken when there is information or an allegation which indicates the possibility of criminal activity and whose responsible handling requires some further scrutiny beyond checking initial leads. This authority allows FBI agents to respond to information that is ambiguous or incomplete. Even where the available information meets only this threshold, the range of available investigative techniques is broad. . . .

Whether it is appropriate to open a preliminary inquiry immediately, or instead to engage first in a limited checking out of leads, depends on the circumstances presented. If, for example, an agent receives an allegation that an individual or group has advocated the commission of criminal violence, and no other facts are available, an appropriate first step would be checking out of leads to determine whether the individual, group, or members of the audience have the apparent ability or intent to carry out the advocated crime. A similar response would be appropriate on the basis of non-verbal conduct of an ambiguous character – for example, where a report is received that an individual has accumulated explosives that could be used either in a legitimate business or to commit a terrorist act. Where the limited checking out of leads discloses a possibility or reasonable indication of criminal activity, a preliminary inquiry or full investigation may then be initiated. However, if the available information shows at the outset that the threshold standard for a preliminary inquiry or full investigation is satisfied, then the appropriate investigative activity may be initiated immediately, without progressing through more limited investigative stages.

The application of these Guidelines' standards for inquiries merits special attention in cases that involve efforts by individuals or groups to obtain, for no apparent reason, biological, chemical, radiological, or nuclear materials whose use or possession is constrained by such statutes as 18 U.S.C. 175, 229, or 831. For example, FBI agents are not required to possess information relating to an individual's intended criminal use of dangerous biological agents or toxins prior to initiating investigative activity. On the contrary, if an individual or group has attempted to obtain such materials, or has indicated a desire to acquire them, and the reason is not apparent, investigative action, such as conducting a checking out of leads or initiating a preliminary inquiry, may be appropriate to determine whether there is a legitimate purpose for the possession of the materials by the individual or group. Likewise, where individuals or groups engage in efforts to acquire or show an interest in acquiring, without apparent reason, toxic chemicals or their precursors or radiological or nuclear materials, investigative action to determine whether there is a legitimate purpose may be justified.

Upon what authority do FBI agents check leads or conduct preliminary inquiries? Do you see a risk that these authorities could be exercised in a way that burdens constitutional liberties?

5. *Full Investigation.* How would you describe the threshold test for initiating a full investigation under the *Domestic Security Guidelines*? The guidelines define "reasonable indication" as: "substantially lower than probable cause . . . . [T]he standard does require specific facts or circumstances indicating a post, current, or impending violation. There must be an objective, factual basis for initiating the investigation; a mere hunch is insufficient." *2002 Domestic Security Guidelines*, §II.C.1. Does the definition clarify or muddy "reasonable indication"? The 2002 guidelines add that a full investigation "may be conducted to prevent, solve, or prosecute" criminal activity. *Id.* Does the "reasonable indication" standard continue to provide an adequate benchmark for preserving privacy or First Amendment interests?

6. *Informants.* Compare the provisions for the use of informants in the executive order with those in the *Domestic Security Guidelines*. While interviews and photographic surveillance in a domestic security investigation do not require prior authorization, the use of an informant to infiltrate a group "in a manner that may influence the exercise of rights protected by the First Amendment" must be approved by FBI headquarters with notice to the Department of Justice. *Domestic Security Guidelines* §IV.B.3. By contrast, during a preliminary "inquiry," informants and infiltrators may be used based on uncorroborated allegations; no reasonable suspicion of an illegal act is required. *Id.* §§I, IIB. What accounts for the differing treatment of the use of informants in these rules? Do the guidelines provide sufficient protection for individual liberties in this respect?

The 2002 guidelines change the "undisclosed participation" strictures, providing instead that any such investigation that could raise "potential constitutional concerns relating to activities of the organization protected by the First Amendment" must comply with the *Attorney General's*

Chapter 12. Investigating Terrorism

Guidelines on FBI Undercover Operations and the *Attorney General's Guidelines Regarding the Use of Informants*. 2002 *Domestic Security Guidelines* §IV.B.3.

An undercover operation uses a government employee whose relationship with the FBI is concealed from third parties in the course of an investigation, *Undercover Operations Guidelines, supra*, §§II.B, C, while a confidential informant is any person who provides useful and credible information. *Confidential Informants Guidelines* §I.B.6. The *Confidential Informants Guidelines* do not mention the First Amendment interests of groups that may be infiltrated by an informant or undercover agent, and the *Undercover Operations Guidelines* simply say that any official empowered to authorize an undercover operation should give "careful consideration" to the "risk of invasion of privacy or interference with privileged or confidential relationships and any potential constitutional concerns or other legal concerns" in deciding whether to approve an application. *Undercover Operations Guidelines* §IV.A.(3). Do you think that these provisions are constitutional?

7. *Mail Covers and New Techniques.* The 2002 *Domestic Security Guidelines* removed mail covers from the list of forbidden techniques during preliminary inquiries. §II.B.5. Mail covers consist of viewing and recording information on the outside covers of mail. The Postal Inspector is authorized by regulation to initiate a mail cover at the request of a law enforcement agency. 39 C.F.R. §233.3 (2005). Is this change lawful? They also added potentially important and constitutionally controversial new authority for FBI investigations in counterterrorism, in reaction to September 11 and the continuing threat of terrorism. Three broad investigative activities are authorized: (1) surfing the Internet to identify Web sites, bulletin boards, chat rooms, and the like where terrorist or other criminal activities might be detected; (2) attending public events and visiting public places for the purpose of detecting terrorist activity; and (3) using data-mining services to search for terrorists and terrorist activities. *See Domestic Security Guidelines* §§VI.A.1, 2; VI.B. According to DOJ officials, the decision to spell out the authorities in these three areas was based on the fact that the prior guidelines were widely regarded as exclusive; if something was not explicitly permitted, it was viewed as barred. *See New Rules Allow FBI Greater Use of Web, Visits to Public Places in Terrorism Probes*, 70 U.S.L.W. 2779 (June 11, 2002). What are the implications of the DOJ explanation for the scope and meaning of the new guidelines?

Some groups reacted by claiming that the new authorities would permit "fishing expeditions" and would chill protected expression in places like mosques, libraries, and Internet chat rooms, and at public gatherings in support of Palestinian or Islamic causes. *See* Center for Democracy & Technology, *CDT's Analysis of New FBI Guidelines*, May 30, 2002, available at *http://www.cdt.org/wiretap/020530guidelines.shtml*; Adam Liptak, *Changing the Standard: Despite Civil Liberties Fears, FBI Faces No Legal Obstacles on Domestic Spying*, N.Y. Times, May 31, 2002, A1.

According to the Justice Department, under the previous guidelines "agents were reluctant to follow suspected terrorists into mosques." Brown, *supra*, at 39. Was the agents' reluctance justified as a matter of law? Do the new guidelines solve whatever problem might have existed?

Section VI.B of the 2002 *Domestic Security Guidelines* authorizes the FBI to carry out "general topical research" online, defined as "concerning subject areas that are relevant for the purpose of facilitation or supporting the discharge of investigative responsibilities . . . [but] does not include online searches for information by individuals' names or other individual identifiers, except where such searches are incidental to topical research, such as searching to locate writings on a topic by searching under the names of authors who write on the topic, or searching by the name of a party to a case in conducting legal research." The introduction to Section VI states that the activities described may be carried out without regard to the predicates for the levels of investigative activity described in the guidelines.

8. *Enforceability of Guidelines*. The *Domestic Security Guidelines* explain that they are "solely for the purpose of internal Department of Justice guidelines" and are thus not judicially enforceable. §VII.C. If the guidelines are not judicially enforceable, do they serve any useful purpose? Would they have any importance in a judicial proceeding?

c. NSI Guidelines

1. *Comparing the Guidelines*. What are the principal differences between the *Domestic Security* and *NSI Guidelines*? What best explains the need for a separate set of *NSI Guidelines*? What guidance to investigators is supplied by the *NSI Guidelines* that is not already available under Executive Order 12,333, FISA, other statutes, and the Constitution?

2. *Threat Assessments*. The authorization for conducting threat assessments is new in the 2003 *NSI Guidelines*. Roughly equivalent to the checking of leads in the *Domestic Security Guidelines*, the threat assessment activity is designed to permit early intervention and prevention of terrorist attacks. The authorization for "proactive collection" of publicly available

Chapter 12. Investigating Terrorism 171

information was not part of the previous *FCI Guidelines*. Why do you think the *Guidelines* were changed in this way? The predicate criteria for conducting threat assessments are redacted from the *Guidelines*, as is the threshold for initiating such an assessment. Can you imagine what the redactions say?

3. *Initiating and Conducting NSI Investigations.* Like the prior *FCI Guidelines*, significant portions of the *NSI Guidelines* are classified. Review the threshold for opening and the techniques for conducting an investigation under the *Domestic Security Guidelines*. Based on those guidelines and what you know from FISA and Executive Order 12,333, can you predict the triggering requirements for opening a NSI investigation? Can you say what techniques are permitted or foreclosed?

4. *Choice of Methods.* Note that the *NSI Guidelines* contain language roughly similar to the *Domestic Security Guidelines* stating that the FBI should "not hesitate to use any lawful techniques" if warranted by the circumstances. Of what value is such an instruction?

5. *United States Persons.* What is the idea behind the presumption that the entire membership of an international organization with no independent activities in the United States be counted in determining whether the organization is substantially composed of United States persons? Why is making the "U.S. persons" determination important under the *NSI Guidelines*?

6. *Extraterritorial Investigations.* Why is the written request or approval of the DCI and the Attorney General required before the FBI conducts investigations abroad? Does Executive Order 12,333 further prescribe the standards for extraterritorial investigations by the FBI? If not, what limits are there on such investigations?

7. *CIA and DOD Activities in the United States?* One entirely redacted section in the *NSI Guidelines* is entitled "Central Intelligence Agency and Department of Defense Activities Within the United States." In light of the National Security Act and Executive Order 12,333, can you imagine what the redacted language says? What CIA or DOD activities would be legally permissible in the United States?

8. *Sharing Information.* How will FBI officials decide when it is appropriate to share "certain information gathered in national security investigations" with state and local officials? What kinds of information do

you think would be shared in this way? How will the agencies share information without threatening personal privacy? How will state and local officials benefit if much of the information they may find valuable is classified?

9. *Enforceability.* Like the *Domestic Security Guidelines*, the *NSI Guidelines* state that they are not judicially enforceable. Do the *NSI Guidelines* serve any useful purpose? Would they ever be relevant in a judicial proceeding?

10. *Departures.* What is the purpose of providing a process for exceeding the authority given by the Guidelines? What is the legal effect, if any, of a departure that is approved by or noticed to the Attorney General?

Page 716. Add this material before the first full paragraph.

The Homeland Security Act further amended FISA by permitting intelligence officers to consult with state and local law enforcement officers regarding foreign intelligence information. Pub. L. No. 107-296, §898, 116 Stat. 2258 (2002), amending 50 U.S.C. §1806(k)(1).

Page 717. Add the following material after Note 4.

4. Balancing Privacy and Security

Scientia Est Potentia (knowledge is power) was the motto of the ill-fated Total Information Awareness (TIA) program, announced in 2002 by the Pentagon's Defense Advanced Research Projects Agency (DARPA). TIA was a research project to develop new counterterrorism technology. It included software for machine language translation and devices that could recognize individuals by their facial features or walking gait. Other software would permit "data mining" – the collection of government and private electronic data – from "an indefinitely expandable universe of databases," automatically integrate and search those data on a real-time basis for patterns suggestive of terrorist activity, then transmit appropriate warnings to law enforcement and intelligence officials. *See* Gina Marie Stevens, *Privacy: Total Information Awareness Programs and Related Information Access, Collection, and Protection Laws* (Cong. Res. Serv. RL31730) (2003). Personal information in the database might include records of medical treatment, credit card transactions, ATM withdrawals, airline reservations, and more. An individual's purchase of a book about

Chapter 12. Investigating Terrorism

bomb making, for example, followed by her procurement of explosive materials, would be noted by federal authorities. In any case, personal data about the good and the bad, the guilty as well as the innocent, would necessarily be swept up in the process. *See* Office of the Inspector General, Dept. of Defense, *Information Technology Management: Terrorism Information Awareness Program,* Dec. 12, 2003.

For some, TIA conjured up memories of Cold War domestic spy programs in the 1960s and '70s, like the CIA's Operation CHAOS and the FBI's COINTELPRO (casebook pp. 448-455), as well as Army domestic intelligence activities (this Supplement p. 200), when government agents conducted surveillance and compiled dossiers on politically active Americans and groups who were campaigning for civil rights and against the Vietnam War. TIA attracted even more attention than it might otherwise have because it was led by John Poindexter, the National Security Adviser in the Reagan administration who appeared to be at the center of the Iran-Contra Affair (casebook pp. 473-517). Negative reactions from across the ideological spectrum led Congress to defund most of the TIA program in 2003. Department of Defense Appropriations Act, 2004, Pub. L. No. 108-87, §8131, 117 Stat. 1054, 1102. At the time of its demise, TIA included no protocols for the protection of personal privacy. It also had not complied with §208(b) of the E-Government Act of 2002, Pub. L. No. 107-347, 116 Stat. 2899, 2921-2922, which requires agencies to prepare a "privacy impact assessment" before developing or procuring a new information technology system.

Nevertheless, similar data mining programs currently exist or are under development in at least six other agencies, some of them administered by the Department of Homeland Security. One such program, Novel Intelligence from Massive Data (NIMD), resides in an obscure agency called Intelligence Community Advanced Research and Development Activity (ARDA) at NSA headquarters. NIMD is supposed to be capable of processing a "petabyte" or more of data, an amount equal to 40 pages of text for every member of the human race. *See* Advanced Research and Development Activity, *Novel Intelligence from Massive Data, at* http://ic-arda.org/Novel_Intelligence/index.html. *See generally* Jeffrey W. Seifert, *Data Mining: An Overview* (Cong. Res. Serv. RL31798), May 3, 2004.

The Fourth Amendment may afford only limited protection against inappropriate government mining of personal information from private databases, since individuals are thought to have no "reasonable expectation of privacy" concerning data voluntarily provided to third parties. United States v. Miller, 425 U.S. 435 (1976). Moreover, neither the Privacy Act, 5 U.S.C. §552a (2000), nor the Foreign Intelligence Surveillance Act, 50 U.S.C. §§1801-1829 (2000 & Supp. I 2001), can necessarily ensure that an agency will collect, store, or share only personal data that are timely, accurate, and relevant to the agency's mission. See p. 200-201 in this Supplement.

For example, in 2004, the Transportation Security Administration (TSA), began development of a program, called Secure Flight, for prescreening domestic airline passengers. In tests, TSA collected personal data not only from airline reservation records but also from commercial data brokers – altogether more than 100 million records on some 240,000 names. According to the GAO, TSA violated the Privacy Act by failing to fully inform the public of: (1) the persons targeted, (2) the types of data collected, (3) the purpose of the collection, (4) how the data would be stored and maintained, and (5) how individuals could access and amend their personal data. Government Accountability Office, *Aviation Security: Transportation Security Administration Did Not Fully Disclose Uses of Personal Information* (GAO-05-864R), July 22, 2005.

TIA and programs like it have spurred proposals for government-wide limits on data mining. *See, e.g.,* Technology and Privacy Advisory Committee, *Safeguarding Privacy in the Fight Against Terrorism* (Mar. 2004), *available at http://www.sainc.com/TAPAC*; Paul Rosenzweig, *Proposals for Implementing the Total Information Awareness System,* Legal Memorandum (Heritage Fdn.), Aug. 7, 2003; K.A. Taipale, *Data-Mining and Domestic Security: Connecting the Dots to Make Sense of Data,* 5 Colum. Sci. & Tech. L. Rev. 2 (2003). These include recommendations that personal data be "anonymized" when collected, then linked to a particular individual only if a terrorist threat is detected, and then only following the issuance of a judicial order. It is generally agreed that special measures should be adopted to protect the security of stored personal information, and that any manipulation of a government database should automatically create a tamper-proof audit trail. Some would permit an agency to collect, keep, or share only data relevant to its mission. Others would require congressional approval before deployment of any data-mining technology, or would impose civil and criminal penalties for abuses. *See, e.g.,* Rosenzweig, *supra.*

NOTES AND QUESTIONS

1. *Privacy: A Purely Personal Matter?* How important is it to you to keep records of your credit card purchases out of government databases? What about your medical history, social activities, reading habits, and religious practices? Can you say why? Do you think your concern for personal privacy has changed since the September 11 terrorist attacks?

Chapter 12. Investigating Terrorism 175

2. *Balancing Privacy and Security.* If trade-offs are required to keep us safe, what kinds of personal information would you feel comfortable having stored in government databases? For how long? Would you care which agencies – federal, state, or local – collected the data? Which ones had access to the information? Would you be more likely to approve if a high government official or a judge authorized the collection or sharing of data?

3. *Availability of Technological Safeguards.* There is considerable doubt that software can be invented that would ensure observance of the proposed limits on data mining described above. Should the deployment of data-mining programs await the creation of such protective software?

Do you think that non-technological measures could furnish privacy protections that would be reasonable under the circumstances? Can you briefly outline such measures? Do you think these measures could be made enforceable?

E. PROFILING SUSPECTS FOR INVESTIGATION

Page 726. Add this material after the carryover paragraph.

On June 17, 2003, the Bush Administration issued guidelines barring federal agents from using race or ethnicity in investigations. However, the policy explicitly exempts national security and terrorism investigations and permits agents to use race and ethnicity in "narrow" circumstances. Eric Lichtblau, *Bush Issues Racial Profiling Ban But Exempts Security Inquiries*, N.Y. Times, June 18, 2003, at A1. The Justice Department offered examples of how the policy applies, including one which asserts that when officials learn that "terrorists from a particular ethnic group are planning to use commercial jetliners as weapons by hijacking them at an airport in California during the next week, . . . men of that ethnic group" boarding planes in California may be subjected to "heightened scrutiny." *Justice Department Guidance Regarding the Use of Race by Federal Law Enforcement Agencies*, www.usdoj.gov/crt/split/documents/guidance_on_race.htm. What is the legal effect of the new policy? Do you see any potential legal problems with implementing the policy in the California hijacking situation?

In a Justice Department report released earlier in June 2003, the DOJ Inspector General found that in the months after the September 11 attacks, many illegal immigrants with no connection to terrorism were detained under harsh conditions for lengthy periods. *See* Michael Moss, *False Terrorism Tips to FBI Uproot the Lives of Suspects*, N.Y. Times, June 19, 2003, at A1. The detention report is considered below. A New York Times investigation of court records and interviews also showed "that even seemingly plausible information from tipsters who eagerly came forward to identify themselves has led to misguided investigations." *Id.* Does the Bush administration's profiling policy respond effectively to the problem of relying on questionable sources to launch terrorism investigations? Can you outline a better policy?

F. PREVENTIVE DETENTION

Page 732. Add this material before Notes and Questions.

Office of the Inspector General, Department of Justice, Press Release, The September 11 Detainees: A Review of the Treatment of Aliens Held on Immigration Charges in Connection with the Investigation of the September 11 Attacks
June 2, 2003
http://www.usdoj.gov/oig/special/03-06/press.htm

After the September 11 terrorist attacks, the Department of Justice (Department) used federal immigration laws to detain aliens in the United States who were suspected of having ties to the attacks or connections to terrorism, or who were encountered during the course of the Federal Bureau of Investigation's (FBI) investigation into the attacks. In the 11 months after the attacks, 762 aliens were detained in connection with the FBI terrorism investigation for various immigration offenses, including overstaying their visas and entering the country illegally.

The Office of the Inspector General (OIG) examined the treatment of these detainees, including their processing, bond decisions related to them, the timing of their removal from the United States or their release from custody, their access to counsel, and their conditions of confinement. . . .

Among the specific findings in the OIG's report:

Arrest, Charging & Assignment to a Detention Facility

• The FBI in New York City made little attempt to distinguish between aliens who were subjects of the FBI terrorism investigation (called "PENTTBOM") and those encountered coincidentally to a

PENTTBOM lead. The OIG report concluded that, even in the chaotic aftermath of the September 11 attacks, the FBI should have expended more effort attempting to distinguish between aliens who it actually suspected of having a connection to terrorism from [sic] those aliens who, while possibly guilty of violating federal immigration law, had no connection to terrorism but simply were encountered in connection with a PENTTBOM lead.

• The INS did not consistently serve the September 11 detainees with notice of the charges under which they were being held within the INS's stated goal of 72 hours. The review found that some detainees did not receive these charging documents (called a "Notice to Appear" or NTA) for more than a month after being arrested. This delay affected the detainees' ability to understand why they were being held, obtain legal counsel, and request a bond hearing. . . .

• The Department instituted a policy that all aliens in whom the FBI had an interest in connection with the PENTTBOM investigation required clearance by the FBI of any connection to terrorism before they could be removed or released. Although not communicated in writing, this "hold until cleared" policy was clearly understood and applied throughout the Department. The policy was based on the belief – which turned out to be erroneous – that the FBI's clearance process would proceed quickly. FBI agents responsible for clearance investigations often were assigned other duties and were not able to focus on the detainee cases. The result was that detainees remained in custody – many in extremely restrictive conditions of confinement – for weeks and months with no clearance investigations being conducted. The OIG review found that, instead of taking a few days as anticipated, the FBI clearance process took an average of 80 days, primarily because it was understaffed and not given sufficient priority by the FBI.

Bond and Removal Issues

• The Department instituted a "no bond" policy for all September 11 detainees as part of its effort to keep the detainees confined until the FBI could complete its clearance investigations. The OIG review found that the INS raised concerns about this blanket "no bond" policy, particularly when it became clear that the FBI's clearance process was much slower than anticipated and the INS had little information in many individual cases on which to base its continued opposition to bond in immigration hearings. INS officials also were concerned about continuing to hold detainees while the FBI conducted clearance investigations where detainees had received a final removal or voluntary departure order. The OIG review found that the INS and the Department did not timely address conflicting interpretations of federal immigration law about detaining aliens with final orders of removal who wanted and were able to leave the country, but who had not been cleared by the FBI.

• In January 2002, when the FBI brought the issue of the extent of the INS's detention authority to the Department's attention, the Department abruptly changed its position as to whether the INS should continue to hold aliens after they had received a final departure or removal order until the FBI had completed the clearance process. After this time, the Department allowed the INS to remove aliens with final orders without FBI clearance. In addition, in many cases the INS failed to review the detainees' custody determination as required by federal regulations.

The FBI's initial assessment of the September 11 detainees' possible connections to terrorism and the slow pace of the clearance process had significant ramifications on the detainees' conditions of confinement. Our review found that 84 September 11 detainees were housed at the MDC [Metropolitan Detention Center] in Brooklyn under highly restrictive conditions. These conditions included "lock down" for at least 23 hours per day; escort procedures that included a "4-man hold" with handcuffs, leg irons, and heavy chains any time the detainees were moved outside their cells; and a limit of one legal telephone call per week and one social call per month.

Among the OIG review's findings regarding the treatment of detainees held at the MDC and Passaic are:

Conditions of Confinement

• BOP officials imposed a communications blackout for September 11 detainees immediately after the terrorist attacks that lasted several weeks. After the blackout period ended, the MDC's designation of the September 11 detainees as "Witness Security" inmates frustrated efforts by detainees' attorneys, families, and even law enforcement officials, to determine where the detainees were being held. We found that MDC staff frequently – and mistakenly – told people who inquired about a specific September 11 detainee that the detainee was not held at the facility when, in fact, the opposite was true.

• The MDC's restrictive and inconsistent policies on telephone access for detainees prevented some detainees from obtaining legal counsel in a timely manner. Most of the September 11 detainees did not have legal representation prior to their detention at the MDC. Consequently, the policy developed by the MDC that permitted detainees one legal call per week – while complying with broad BOP national standards – severely limited the detainees' ability to obtain and consult with legal counsel. In addition, we found that in many instances MDC staff did not ask detainees if they wanted their one legal call each week. We also found that the list of pro bono attorneys provided to the detainees contained inaccurate and outdated information.

• With regard to allegations of abuse at the MDC, the evidence

Chapter 12. Investigating Terrorism 179

indicates a pattern of physical and verbal abuse by some correctional officers at the MDC against some September 11 detainees, particularly during the first months after the attacks and during intake and movement of prisoners. Although the allegations of abuse have been declined for criminal prosecution, the OIG is continuing to investigate these matters administratively.

• The OIG review found that certain conditions of confinement at the MDC were unduly harsh, such as subjecting the September 11 detainees to having two lights illuminated in their cells 24 hours a day for several months longer than necessary, even after electricians rewired the cellblock to allow the lights to be turned off individually. We also found that MDC staff failed to inform MDC detainees in a timely manner about the process for filing formal complaints about their treatment.

• By contrast, the OIG review found that the detainees confined at Passaic had much different, and significantly less harsh, experiences than the MDC detainees. According to INS data, Passaic housed 400 September 11 detainees from the date of the terrorist attacks through May 30, 2002, the largest number of September 11 detainees held at any single U.S. detention facility. Passaic detainees housed in the general population were treated like "regular" INS detainees who also were held at the facility. Although we received some allegations of physical and verbal abuse, we did not find the evidence indicated a pattern of abuse at Passaic. However, the INS did not conduct sufficient and regular visits to Passaic to ensure the September 11 detainees' conditions of confinement were appropriate.

"The Justice Department faced enormous challenges as a result of the September 11 terrorist attacks, and its employees worked with dedication to meet these challenges," [Inspector General] Fine said. "The findings of our review should in no way diminish their work. However, while the chaotic situation and the uncertainties surrounding the detainees' connections to terrorism explain some of the problems we found in our review, they do not explain them all," Fine said. . . .

Page 732. Add this material at the end of Note 1.

In Denmore v. Hyung Joon Kim, 538 U.S. 510 (2003), Justice Souter summarized the due process requirements for preventive detention as follows:

> [D]ue process requires a "special justification" for physical detention that "outweighs the individual's constitutionally protected interest in avoiding physical restraint" as well as "adequate procedural protections." "There must be a 'sufficiently compelling' governmental interest to justify such an action, usually a punitive interest in imprisoning the convicted criminal

or a regulatory interest in forestalling danger to the community." The class of persons subject to confinement must be commensurately narrow and the duration of confinement limited accordingly. . . . Finally, procedural due process requires, at a minimum, that a detainee have the benefit of an impartial decisionmaker able to consider particular circumstances on the issue of necessity.

Id. at 557 (Souter, J., concurring in part and dissenting in part).

Applying such standards, in United States v. Salerno, 481 U.S. 739 (1987), a divided Supreme Court upheld the provisions of the Bail Reform Act of 1984, 18 U.S.C. §3142(e), which authorized preventive detention (denial of bail) of arrestees on the grounds of flight risk or future dangerousness. The majority found that the Act authorized a "regulatory," rather than punitive, detention that was reasonably related to compelling government interests. The Court noted that regulatory interests in community safety can outweigh an individual's liberty interest, "[f]or example, in times of war and insurrection." 481 U.S. at 748. But it emphasized that the Bail Reform Act authorized detention of an arrestee only when: (a) he has been arrested and indicted on probable cause of having committed one or more specified extremely dangerous offenses, (b) a court conducts a full-blown adversary hearing on denial of bail at which the arrestee is entitled to be represented by his own counsel, (c) the government persuades the court by clear and convincing evidence that no conditions of release can assure the presence of the arrestee or the safety of the community, and (d) the arrestee is given a right of appeal from the court's decision.

Do the post-September 11 detentions described above satisfy the due process standards? Even if they do, does the Bail Reform Act occupy the field of preventive detention (leaving aside immigration detentions)?

Page 733. Add this material at the end of Note 2.

More recently, the Administration has asserted that terrorism investigations resulted in charges against more than 400 suspects, half of whom were convicted. A Washington Post study of the Department of Justice's own list of prosecutions, however, indicated that only 39 of these convictions were for crimes related to terrorism or national security. Dan Eggen & Julie Tate, *U.S. Campaign Produces Few Convictions of Terrorism Charges*, Wash. Post, June 12, 2005, at A1. The majority were for minor crimes such as fraud, making false statements, and passport violations, for which the median sentence was just 11 months.

The Justice Department defend the numbers by arguing that many

Chapter 12. Investigating Terrorism

defendants were prosecuted for "spitting on the sidewalk" in exchange for non-public information that was valuable in other terrorism probes. *Id.* The former Associate Attorney General who headed the Office of Legal Policy had an additional explanation. "You're talking about a violation of law that may or may not rise to the level of what might usually be called a federal case. But the calculation does not happen in isolation; you are not just talking about the [minor] crime itself, but the suspicion of terrorism. . . . That skews the calculation in favor of prosecution." *Id.* (quoting Viet D. Dinh). In other words, the Post paraphrased, "the primary strategy is to use 'prosecutorial discretion' to detain suspicious individuals by charging them with minor crimes." *Id.* Replied a defense attorney, "That's fine if you take it as a given that you have the devil there," citing Al Capone (who was eventually prosecuted for income tax evasion) as an example, but "the problem is . . . [that] you're going to make mistakes and you're going to hurt innocent people." *Id.*

Page 734. Add this material at the end of Note 3.

Although the government has not disclosed how many persons it has held as material witnesses in counter-terrorist investigations, Human Rights Watch reported that their research had identified 70 such persons as of June 2005. Human Rights Watch, *Witness to Abuse: Human Rights Abuses Under the Material Witness Law Since September 11*, 17 Hum. Rts. Watch 1, June 2005, at 2, 15, *available at http://hrw.org/reports/2005/us0605/us0605.pdf.*

The Second Circuit Court of Appeals rejected a challenge to one of these detentions, finding that it was lawful to detain material witnesses in connection with a grand jury investigation, and not just for trial, as the challenger had argued. United States v. Awadallah, 349 F.3d 42, 52 (2d Cir. 2003). At the same time, however, the court cautioned that "it would be improper for the government to use [material witness detention] for other ends, such as the detention of persons suspected of criminal activity for which probable cause has not yet been established." *Id.* at 59.

Human Rights Watch found, nevertheless, that fewer than half of the 9/11 material witnesses were ever brought before a grand jury or court to testify; many were apparently held as suspects rather than witnesses. *Witness to Abuse, supra*, at 2. The government has not been shy about explaining this use of the statute. For example, after acknowledging that the United States has no general preventive detention law, one architect of the post-9/11 detention policy said that "the material witness statute *gives the government effectively the same power* . . . . To the extent that it is a suspect involved in terror, you hold them on a material witness warrant, and you get the information until you find out what's going on." *Id.* at 19 (quoting former U.S. Attorney for the Southern District of New York, Mary Jo White) (emphasis added). Is this view of the statutory power consistent with the Second Circuit dictum?

The Second Circuit also found that the material witness statute made a deposition available as an alternative to detention for obtaining grand jury testimony, effectively giving the detainee a key to his jail cell. *Awadallah,* 349 F.3d at 52. Human Rights Watch reports, however, that the government has consistently opposed depositions or stalled taking them, citing national security reasons. *Witness to Abuse, supra,* at 79. Moreover, the government reportedly failed to advise many detainees of the reasons for their arrests, their right to an attorney and to have an attorney present at their interrogations, and their right to remain silent. *Id.* at 4.

Page 734. Add this material at the end of Note 4.

As the OIG report suggests, immigration laws, like the Bail Reform Act (see *supra*), authorize immigration judges to deny bond for a detained immigrant if the government provides evidence of flight risk or dangerousness. The FBI, however, provided no information to sustain such determinations in many cases. Nevertheless, INS lawyers were apparently ordered to argue the "no bond" position in court without any evidence, using "boilerplate" affidavits like the Rolince affidavit set out in the casebook at p. 729. *See* Office of the Inspector General, U.S. Dept. of Justice, *The September 11 Detainees: A Review of the Treatment of Aliens Held on Immigration Charges in Connection With the Investigation of the September 11 Attacks* 78-80 (June 2003). Was this ethical? *Id.* at 79, 81. In some cases, the alien succeeded in obtaining a bond order and posting bond, but the INS, without appealing the order, continued to hold him anyway. Was this lawful? *Id.* at 87 (reporting that one INS official admitted not knowing what to tell the immigrant's lawyer, "because I cannot bring myself to say that the INS no longer feels compelled to obey the law"). How far may a government lawyer go in defending preventive detention if he is instructed that it is essential to a terrorism investigation?

In Denmore v. Hyung Joon Kim, 538 U.S. 510 (2003), the Supreme Court revisited the issue of immigration detention, this time considering a statutory provision for mandatory detention of criminal aliens pending their removal hearings. Admitting that individualized bond hearings might be feasible, the majority nevertheless concluded that "when the Government deals with deportable aliens, the Due Process Clause does not require it to employ the least burdensome means to accomplish its goal." *Id.* at 528. The Court therefore upheld the mandatory detention law, but emphasized

Chapter 12. Investigating Terrorism 183

that such detentions pending removal were for less than 90 days in the majority of cases. Joining in the opinion, Justice Kennedy noted that if the removal proceedings were unreasonably delayed, "it could become necessary then to inquire whether the detention is not to facilitate deportation, or to protect against risk of flight or dangerousness, but to incarcerate for other reasons." *Id.* at 532-533 (Kennedy, J., concurring). How would the post-September 11 immigration detentions described in the OIG report fare by these standards?

Recent data show that since March 2003, the government filed immigration charges against more than 500 people who were under scrutiny in terrorism investigations. Mary Beth Sheridan, *Immigration Law as an Anti-Terrorism Tool*, Wash. Post, June 13, 2005, at A1. The Washington Post reports that 768 suspects were "secretly processed on immigration charges" in the 9/11 investigations, most being deported after being cleared of terrorism connections. *Id.*

Authorities explained that immigration charges are a good way to detain persons suspected of terrorism connections when the government lacks sufficient evidence to prove the connections. *Id.* Civil liberties activists disagree. They allege that immigration laws are being selectively enforced against Muslims and Arabs and largely ignored with respect to the rest of the immigrant population. "The approach is basically to target the Muslim and Arab community with a kind of zero-tolerance immigration policy. No other community is treated to zero-tolerance enforcement," said Professor David Cole. *Id.*

Page 735. Add this material at the end of Note 6.

At the same time that it repealed the Emergency Detention Act, Congress adopted a measure stating, "No citizen shall be imprisoned or otherwise detained by the United States except pursuant to an Act of Congress." 18 U.S.C. §4001(a). Does this provision apply to the detention of suspected terrorists? Application of §4001(a) was considered in two recent cases, set out at pp. 208 and 235 in this Supplement.

Page 736. Add this material at the end of Note 7.

Which, if any, of the foregoing rights were violated during the post-September 11 detention of immigrants described in the OIG report? Shortly after publication of the report, a divided panel of the D.C. Circuit Court of Appeals found that various public interest groups had no right under the Freedom of Information Act or First Amendment to assorted details of the post-September 11 detentions, which they sought in part to ascertain the legality of the detentions and conditions of confinement. Center for National Security Studies v. United States Dept. of Justice, 331 F.3d 918 (D.C. Cir. 2003), *cert. denied*, 540 U.S. 1104 (2004). Based presumably on the government's representations, a majority of the panel assumed that the immigrant detainees "have had access to counsel, and the INS has provided detainees with lists of attorneys willing to represent them. . . . They have also been free to disclose their names to the public." *Id.* In light of the OIG report, were these assumptions warranted?

13

Consequence Management: When the Worst Happens

B. WHO'S IN CHARGE? TAKING COMMAND OF THE SITUATION

1. Assigning Lead Agency Responsibility

Page 750. Add this material after Note 8.

d. *The Department of Homeland Security*

In July 2002, the Office of Homeland Security published the *National Strategy for Homeland Security*, available at http://www.whitehouse.gov/homeland/book/. In line with earlier recommendations, this document recognized a need to "clarify lines of responsibility for homeland security in the executive branch, . . . mobilize our entire society, . . . and manage risk and allocate resources judiciously." *Id.* at 3. It called for planning to defend against terrorist attacks using conventional weapons as well as weapons of mass destruction, cyber attacks, and new or unexpected tactics. To accomplish these goals, it proposed the establishment of a new Department of Homeland Security (DHS), which would assume primary responsibility for intelligence and warning of a domestic attack, border and transportation security, domestic counterterrorism, protection of critical infrastructure, and response and recovery from any future terrorist attack. DHS would also respond to natural disasters. By consolidating emergency activities into one "genuinely all-discipline, all-hazard plan," the Department would also eliminate the distinction between "crisis" and "consequence" management that so plagued earlier planners. *Id.* at 42.

The new department was created later the same year with passage of the Homeland Security Act of 2002, Pub. L. No. 107-296, 116 Stat. 2135

(2002), to be codified at 6 U.S.C. §§101-557 and scattered sections of other titles. The act merges all or portions of 22 federal agencies and 170,000 employees into the DHS. Included are the Coast Guard, Customs Service, Transportation Security Administration, Federal Emergency Management Agency (FEMA), Secret Service, parts of the Immigration and Naturalization Service, and a long list of less well-known federal entities. The startup of this huge new enterprise is traced in Harold C. Relyea, *Homeland Security: Department Organization and Management – Implementation Phase* (Cong. Res. Serv. RL31751), Jan. 3, 2005.

The Homeland Security Act breaks the new department functionally into four directorates: Science and Technology, Border and Transportation Security, Information Analysis and Infrastructure Protection, and Emergency Preparedness and Response. Our main concern here is with the last two of these.

(1) Information Analysis and Infrastructure Protection

Section 201 of the Homeland Security Act of 2002 created an ambitious new program, the Directorate for Information Analysis and Infrastructure Protection (IAIP). Its overall mission is described in §201(d) this way:

(1) To access, receive, and analyze law enforcement information, intelligence information, and other information from agencies of the Federal Government, State and local government agencies (including law enforcement agencies), and private sector entities, and to integrate such information in order to –
(A) identify and assess the nature and scope of terrorist threats to the homeland; . . .
(2) To carry out comprehensive assessments of the vulnerabilities of the key resources and critical infrastructure of the United States, including the performance of risk assessments to determine the risks posed by particular types of terrorist attacks within the United States . . . .
(3) To integrate relevant information, analyses, and vulnerability assessments . . . in order to identify priorities for protective and support measures by the Department, other agencies of the Federal Government, State and local government agencies and authorities, the private sector, and other entities. . . .
(5) To develop a comprehensive national plan for securing the key resources and critical infrastructure of the United States, including power production, generation, and distribution systems, information technology and telecommunications systems (including satellites), electronic financial and property record storage and transmission systems, emergency preparedness communications systems, and the physical and technological assets that support such systems. . . .

(7) To administer the Homeland Security Advisory System, including:

(A) exercising primary responsibility for public advisories related to threats to homeland security; and

(B) in coordination with other agencies of the Federal Government, providing specific warning information, and advice about appropriate protective measures and countermeasures, to State and local government agencies and authorities, the private sector, other entities, and the public. . . .

(9) To disseminate, as appropriate, information analyzed by the Department within the Department, to other agencies of the Federal Government with responsibilities relating to homeland security, and to agencies of State and local governments and private sector entities with such responsibilities in order to assist in the deterrence, prevention, preemption of, or response to, terrorist attacks against the United States. . . .

(12) To ensure that –

(A) any material received pursuant to this Act is protected from unauthorized disclosure and handled and used only for the performance of official duties; and

(B) any intelligence information under this Act is shared, retained, and disseminated consistent with the authority of the Director of Central Intelligence to protect intelligence sources and methods under the National Security Act of 1947 . . . and related procedures and, as appropriate, similar authorities of the Attorney General concerning sensitive law enforcement information. . . .

(14) To establish and utilize, in conjunction with the chief information officer of the Department, a secure communications and information technology infrastructure, including data-mining and other advanced analytical tools, in order to access, receive, and analyze data and information in furtherance of the responsibilities under this section, and to disseminate information acquired and analyzed by the Department, as appropriate. . . .

(17) To coordinate with elements of the intelligence community and with Federal, State, and local law enforcement agencies, and the private sector, as appropriate.

(18) To provide intelligence and information analysis and support to other elements of the Department.

(19) To perform such other duties relating to such responsibilities as the Secretary may provide.

In a separate provision, all agencies of the federal government are directed to send DHS all reports, assessments, and analytical information relating to threats of terrorism, as well as information about U.S. vulnerability to terrorism. §202(b)(2). Part of IAIP's job, in other words, is to collect and analyze data from every possible source, government and private, that might bear on DHS's domestic counterterrorism mission, then to use those data directly and make them available to others in aid of that mission. Personnel from a variety of other defense and intelligence agencies are detailed to IAIP to help in this work. §201(f).

Independently of the Homeland Security Act, in his 2003 State of the Union address, President Bush announced the creation of a Terrorist Threat Integration Center (TTIC), to be managed by the Director of Central Intelligence. *See* White House News Release, *Fact Sheet: Strengthening Intelligence to Better Protect America,* Jan. 28, 2003. Like IAIP, TTIC's job was to collect intelligence from agencies throughout the government, analyze it, and disseminate it again for use in counterterrorism. And like IAIP, its purpose was to "connect the dots" in order to avoid the kind of intelligence failures that preceded 9/11. TTIC also was to maintain a database of known and suspected terrorists that would be available to federal and non-federal officials. Unlike IAIP, TTIC was directed to collect data on threats to American interests abroad, but not on purely homegrown threats. Also unlike IAIP, TTIC lacked any legislative limits or, for that matter, any charter.

Nine months later, President Bush directed the creation of another counterterrorism intelligence entity, this one within the Justice Department. Homeland Security Presidential Directive/HSPD-6, *Integration and Use of Screening Information,* Sept. 16, 2003. The mission of the Terrorist Screening Center (TSC), administered by the FBI, is to "consolidate watchlists and provide 24/7 operational support for thousands of federal screeners across the country and around the world." Office of the Press Secretary, Dept. of Homeland Security, *New Terrorist Screening Center Established,* Sept. 16, 2003. *See* William J. Krouse, *Terrorist Identification, Screening, and Tracking Under Homeland Security Directive 6* (Cong. Res. Serv. RL32366) (Apr. 21, 2004).

There was a very considerable overlap in the functions of these three entities – IAIP, TSC, and TTIC – as well as some confusion within the federal government and among state and local governments about their respective roles. The report of the 9/11 Commission lamented what it called "structural barriers to performing joint intelligence work" and "divided management of intelligence capabilities," and it recommended the unification of such functions under a new National Intelligence Director. National Commission on Terrorist Attacks Upon the United States, *The 9/11 Commission Report* 408-415 (2004).

In August 2004, President Bush ordered the creation of a new National Counterterrorism Center (NCTC), Exec. Order No. 13,354, *National Counterterrorism Center,* 69 Fed. Reg. 53,589 (Aug. 27, 2004), to take over the duties of TTIC. NCTC's mandate is much more expansive, however.

Chapter 13. Consequence Management: When the Worst Happens

The new center is described as "the primary organization in the United States Government for analyzing and integrating all intelligence possessed or acquired by the [government] pertaining to terrorism and counterterrorism, except purely domestic counterterrorism information." *Id.* §3(a). (The exception is understood to refer to eco-terrorists, violent animal rights activists, and the like.) NCTC is directed to "conduct strategic operational planning for counterterrorism activities, integrating all instruments of national power, including diplomatic, financial, military, intelligence, homeland security, and law enforcement activities within and among agencies." *Id.* §3(b). And it is authorized to "assign operational responsibilities to lead agencies for counterterrorism activities," but not to direct the execution of operations. *Id.* §3(c).

At the end of 2004, Congress used almost identical language in describing the mission of an NCTC within the office of the new Director of National Intelligence. Intelligence Reform and Terrorism Prevention Act of 2004, Pub. L. No. 108-458, §1021, 118 Stat. 3638, 3672 (2004). This legislative NCTC may, however, receive, retain, and disseminate "intelligence pertaining exclusively to domestic counterterrorism." *Id.*, adding §119(e) to the National Security Act of 1947. In addition, under the Intelligence Reform Act, the Director of the NCTC reports directly to the President, rather than to the DCI (or even DNI), with respect to "planning and progress of joint counterterrorism operations (other than intelligence operations)." *Id.*, adding §119(c)(3). Other differences are spelled out in Todd M. Masse, *The National Counterterrorism Center: Implementation Challenges and Issues for Congress* (Cong. Res. Serv. RL32816), Mar. 24, 2005 (asserting that the legislative language is controlling).

In July 2005, DHS announced an extensive internal reorganization, including the creation of a new Office of Intelligence and Analysis that will perform the IA function described in the Homeland Security Act. Office of the Press Secretary, Dept. of Homeland Security, *Homeland Security Secretary Michael Chertoff Announces Six-Point Agenda for Department of Homeland Security*, July 13, 2005, at http://www.dhs.gov/dhspublic/display?content=4598. A new Homeland Security Operations Center will serve as "the nation's nerve center for information sharing and domestic incident management on a 24/7/365 basis." And a new Directorate for Preparedness will consolidate and manage preparedness activities across the Department. FEMA's responsibilities will be limited to response and recovery.

Another part of DHS's mission is to "develop a comprehensive national plan for securing the key resources and critical infrastructure of the United States." Homeland Security Act §201(d)(5). "Critical infrastructure" includes telecommunications, pipelines, rail and road systems, shipping and aviation, mass transit, chemical plants, the postal service, and cyber communications. The goal here is to protect against terrorist acts that could:

(a) cause catastrophic health effects or mass casualties . . . ;
(b) impair Federal departments and agencies' abilities to perform essential missions, or to ensure the public's health and safety;
(c) undermine State and local government capabilities to maintain order . . . ;
(d) damage the private sector's capability to ensure the orderly functioning of the economy and delivery of essential services;
(e) have a negative effect on the economy . . . ; or
(f) undermine the public's morale and confidence in our national economic and political institutions.

Homeland Security Presidential Directive/HSPD-7, *Critical Infrastructure Identification, Prioritization, and Protection,* Dec. 17, 2003, at ¶7. To do this, DHS is to work closely with other agencies at all levels of government, as well as with the private sector. In practical terms, for example, the Department has ordered the Coast Guard to step up its protection of shipping, pipelines, and coastwise industries, it has developed a system to provide warnings of cyber attacks, and it is working with the Departments of Agriculture and Health and Human Services to secure American food supplies.

One part of the critical infrastructure program has proven to be very controversial. Section 214(a) of the Act invites private sector concerns to "voluntarily" submit to DHS "critical infrastructure information," which would then become exempt from disclosure under the Freedom of Information Act (casebook pp. 923-949), and which could not without the consent of the submitter be used in any civil action by another agency or a third party. Some worry that regulated industries may try to use this provision to immunize themselves against tort liability or enforcement of workplace safety, public health, racial discrimination, or environmental protection laws. *See, e.g.,* Rena I. Steinzor, *"Democracies Die Behind Closed Doors": The Homeland Security Act and Corporate Accountability,* 12 Kan. J.L. & Pub. Poly. 641 (2003). Regulations implementing the section appear at 6 C.F.R. pt. 29 (2004).

One program that has attracted a lot of attention is the Homeland Security Advisory System, which uses color-coded alert levels to keep Americans advised about the current risk of another terrorist attack. The levels range from Green (low risk) to Red (severe risk). *See* Homeland Security Presidential Directive-3, Mar. 11, 2002. Announcement of an increase in threat levels is supposed to be accompanied by "as much

Chapter 13. Consequence Management: When the Worst Happens 191

information regarding the threat as possible, consistent with the safety of the Nation." *Id.* But thus far the occasional increases from Yellow (elevated), the usual condition since the system was adopted, to Orange (high) have produced only the vaguest descriptions of the risks. While the increases have triggered additional protective measures like enhanced police presence at public events, a recent study found "continuing confusion" among officials at all levels of government about how they should respond. General Accounting Office, *Homeland Security: Communication Protocols and Risk Communication Principles* (GAO-04-682) (July 2004), at 39. A different study found that "inconsistent messages regarding threats to the homeland have led to an erosion of confidence in the information conveyed to the nation" by DHS. *See* John Mintz, *Skepticism of Terrorism Alerts Cited,* Wash. Post, May 4, 2005, at A17.

Members of the public have been given only general advice about how to react either to changes in threat levels or to an actual attack. Some information is available on a DHS Web site called Ready.gov. There one may find guidance on assembly of an emergency kit containing food, clothing, and personal items, as well as plastic sheeting and duct tape. One is advised to make a family communications plan and to monitor TV and radio news reports for instructions. The site also contains very rudimentary instructions for responding specifically to a biological, chemical, nuclear, or radiological attack. More detailed guidance is provided by a Rand Corporation monograph, Lynn E. Davis et al., *Individual Preparedness and Response to Chemical, Radiological, Nuclear, and Biological Terrorist Attacks: A Quick Guide* (2003), *available at http://www.rand.org/pubs/ monograph_reports/2005/RAND_MR1731.1.pdf.*

None of the advice available to the public from DHS so far addresses the possibility of a quarantine, the need to undergo physical examination or inoculation, or the availability of medical care. And no mention is made of the possible involvement of military forces in the response to an attack. Presumably, DHS intends to supply the answers to these kinds of questions as they are needed, in the midst of a crisis.

DHS is unique among federal agencies in having statutorily mandated oversight offices for privacy and for civil rights and civil liberties. Homeland Security Act §§222 and 705. These offices might help to provide a measure of accountability, at least internally, for the department's intelligence activities, and they could even open a public window into those activities. Nevertheless, the Secretary of Homeland Security may block any audit or investigation by the DHS Inspector General if the Secretary deems it necessary to protect "sensitive information, . . . to preserve the national security, or to prevent a significant impairment to the interests of the United States." Consolidated Appropriations Resolution, 2003, Pub. L. No. 108-7,

Div. L, §104(b)(3), 117 Stat. 11, 527 (2003).

(2) Emergency Response and Recovery

One of the principal goals of DHS is to provide a unified federal response to a terrorist incident. To do this the department has absorbed FEMA, which responds to both man-made and natural disasters under the Stafford Act (see casebook p. 742), along with parts of other agencies like the Department of Energy that have more specialized duties in a crisis. DHS is now the focal point for communications between and among federal, state, and local agencies, and it is supposed to provide an authoritative voice of the government in keeping the public informed about emergency responses.

In February 2003, the White House published Homeland Security Presidential Directive/HSPD-5, entitled *Management of Domestic Incidents.* It is meant to "ensure that all levels of the government across the Nation have the capability to work efficiently and effectively together, using a national approach to domestic incident management," *id.* ¶(3), and it declares that the Secretary of Homeland Security is the "principal Federal official for domestic incident management." *Id.* at ¶(4). On the other hand, the Attorney General is given lead responsibility for criminal investigations of terrorist threats or acts within the United States, and she is directed to "coordinate the activities of other members of the law enforcement to detect, prevent, preempt, and disrupt terrorist attacks against the United States." *Id.* at ¶(8). In addition, the Defense Department may provide military support to civil authorities in a domestic incident, but always under the command of the Secretary of Defense. *Id.* at ¶(9).

HSPD-5 also ordered the creation of a National Incident Managment System (NIMS), to provide a flexible national framework within which governments at all levels and private entities could work together to manage domestic "incidents." The NIMS was rolled out a year later. Dept. of Homeland Security, National Incident Managment System, March 1, 2004, *available at http://www.dhs.gov/interweb/assetlibrary/NIMS-90-web.pdf.*

Finally, HSPD-5 called for development of a *National Response Plan* (NRP) to replace the existing *Federal Response Plan* and CONPLAN (casebook pp. 743-746). The new NRP was published in January 2005. Dept. of Homeland Security, *National Response Plan*, Dec. 2004, *available at http://www.dhs.gov/interweb/assetlibrary/NRP_FullText.pdf.* Like the earlier plans, it provides for a coordinated, all-hazards approach to "incident management," spelling out in broad terms the roles of all relevant elements of the national government, and calling for communications and operational coordination by offices within DHS. It also sets out a framework for federal interaction with state, local, and tribal governments and with the private sector in an emergency. It also includes an annex describing a federal law enforcement and investigation response to threats or acts of terrorism.

NOTES AND QUESTIONS

1. *Connecting the Dots.* One of the lessons learned from the tragedy of 9/11 is that we must do a better job of sharing information among agencies at all levels of government. In response to that lesson, we now have offices for the collection, analysis, and dissemination of counterterrorism data not only at IAIP, NCTC, and the FBI's TSC, but also at the Defense Department's NORTHCOM (*infra* p. 201 in this Supplement). Why do you suppose this redundancy exists? Do you think it is justified by the threat? Do you see a downside to the duplication of functions?

2. *Domestic Intelligence and DHS.* Review the portions of §201 excerpted above. What would you say Congress sought to accomplish in providing domestic intelligence authorities to DHS? In what circumstances would IAIP provide intelligence to other elements of the Department?

3. *Bringing DHS into the Information Sharing Community.* In 2003, an interagency memorandum of understanding established guidelines for the sharing of terrorism information among law enforcement and intelligence agencies. *Memorandum of Understanding Between the Intelligence Community, Federal Law Enforcement Agencies, and the Department of Homeland Security Concerning Information Sharing,* Mar. 4, 2003, *available at http://www.fas.org/sgp/othergov/mou.infoshar.pdf.* The memorandum was signed by the Attorney General, the DCI, and the Secretary of Homeland Security. It states that "preventing, preempting, and disrupting terrorist threats to our homeland" is an "overriding priority" that takes precedence over "the protection of intelligence . . . sources and methods." *Id.* §3a. What is the legal effect of this provision, in light of the National Security Act "sources and methods" provision?

4. *Trading Liberty for Security?* Since 9/11, the establishment of government agencies to collect and integrate personal information from government files and private sources, together with the development of powerful computer data-mining technology, may pose serious threats to personal privacy and associated liberties. See *supra* pp. 172-174 in this Supplement. Would you say the trade-off of liberty for safety is justified?

Can you imagine ways to limit such information-sharing to that which is clearly necessary?

5. *Transparency in Emergency Planning.* Obviously, every detail of planning for a terrorist emergency cannot be made public, lest terrorists exploit those plans in mounting an attack. But where should the line be drawn between what to publicize and what to keep secret? And who should draw the line? Can you describe a planning process that would provide needed security and yet some measure of public accountability? What are the implications of these questions for democratic government?

Based on what you now know, do you believe that DHS has a coherent plan for responding to a major terrorist attack that uses weapons of mass destruction? If you do not know the answer, can you say how that fact could make the nation more vulnerable to a terrorist attack than it might otherwise be?

6. *Public Reaction to a Terrorist Incident.* Why do you think DHS has not furnished more detailed information to the public in raising the terrorism threat level from time to time? Should it do so?

As a member of the public with an above-average interest in emergency planning, do you know now what you would do if word reached you that terrorists had released pneumonic plague in your community or set off a "dirty" bomb? Can you predict the reactions of your neighbors upon learning of such an event?

Why do you suppose DHS has not mounted an extensive campaign to educate members of the public about preparations for a terrorist emergency and responses to an actual attack? If it is preferable, in your view, to rely on a more flexible response to an inherently unpredictable future event, what difficulties can you foresee in implementing authoritative directions to the public in a crisis? Can you think of ways to make the public's reaction more predictable?

7. *Prospects for a Truly Unified Response.* Despite abandonment of the distinction between crisis management and consequence management, HSPD-5 divides the responsibility for the federal response to a domestic terrorist incident between the Department of Homeland Security and the Justice Department. In practice, these responsibilities seem bound to overlap to some degree. Can you think of ways to minimize the potential for confusion and conflict between the two departments in an actual incident?

Chapter 13. Consequence Management: When the Worst Happens

2. Addressing Medical Emergencies

a. Case Study: A Plague on Your City

Page 754. Add this material before Notes and Questions.

A subsequent exercise, in May 2003, is described in Department of Homeland Security, *Top Officials (TOPOFF) Exercise Series: TOPOFF 2 – After Action Summary Report* (Dec. 19, 2003). It featured a simulated radiological attack in Seattle, a dispersal of plague bacilli in Chicago, a cyber attack, and terrorism threats in other locations. One conclusion was that "additional clarity . . . would be helpful" regarding authorities and resources available under the Stafford Act (casebook pp. 742-743) and the Public Health Act (casebook pp. 755-761). *Id.* at 4. Unlike the earlier TOPOFF exercise, however, in TOPOFF 2 participants were notified well in advance. The resulting lack of unpredictability and spontaneity may have reduced its value as either a test of preparedness or an aid in planning. A similar TOPOFF 3 exercise was conducted in early 2005. *See* Eric Lipton, *Fictional Doomsday Team Plays Out Scene After Scene*, N.Y. Times, Mar. 26, 2005, at A11.

b. Statutory and Regulatory Authority

Page 760. Add this material to Note 1.

Section 70.6 of the quarantine regulations has been changed to allow prompter responses to emerging threats. It now allows new pathogens of concern to be listed in an executive order, instead of going through the rule-making process for new regulations. An April 2003 order lists several diseases not contained previously in §70.6, including hemorrhagic fevers and SARS. Exec. Order No. 13295, *Revised List of Quarantinable Communicable Diseases,* 68 Fed. Reg. 17244 (Apr. 4, 2003). A more recent one aimed at halting the spread of bird flu adds "influenza caused by novel or reemergent influenza viruses that are causing, or have the potential to cause, a pandemic." *Executive Order: Amendment to E.O. 13295 Relating to Certain Influenza Viruses and Quarantinable Communicable Diseases,* Apr. 1, 2005. *available at http://www.whitehouse.gov/news/releases/2005/04/20050401-6.html.*

Page 760. Add this material to Note 2.

A Defense Department-sponsored report concluded that the anthrax letter attacks "revealed weaknesses in almost every aspect of U.S. biopreparedness and response." David Heyman, *Lessons from the Anthrax Attacks: Implications for U.S. Bioterrorism Preparedness*, Apr. 2002 (partly redacted), *available at http://www.fas.org/irp/threat/cbw/dtra02.pdf.* See also Keith Rhodes, *Diffuse Security Threats: Information on U.S. Domestic Anthrax Attacks* (GAO-03-0323T), Dec. 10, 2002, available at pp. 808-822 of another report *at http://www.fas.org/irp/congress/2002_rpt/911rept.pdf*; *Bioterrorism: Public Health Responses to Anthrax Incidents of 2001* (GAO-04-152), Oct. 2003.

Page 760. Add this material to Note 3.

An excellent summary of CDC planning for a smallpox outbreak may be found in Centers for Disease Control and Prevention (CDC), *CDC Guidance for Post-Event Smallpox Planning,* Oct. 29, 2002, *at http://www.bt.cdc.gov/agent/smallpox/prep/post-event-guidance.asp.* It includes this advice: "To address public questions, minimize false rumors and misinformation, and reassure the public that the public health system is responding effectively, it is imperative that public health officials acknowledge the seriousness of a smallpox outbreak and provide accurate, timely information to the public through the media." *Id.* at 2. In a separate document, CDC declares, "No one will be forced to be vaccinated, even if they have been exposed to smallpox. . . . [However, to] prevent smallpox from spreading, anyone who has been in contact with a person with smallpox but who decides not to get the vaccine may need to be isolated for at least 18 days. . . . People placed in isolation will not be able to go to work." *Fact Sheet: What You Should Know About a Smallpox Outbreak,* Mar. 29, 2004, *at http://www.bt.cdc.gov/agent/smallpox/basics/outbreak.asp.* Much more detail is available in *CDC Smallpox Response Plan and Guidelines (Version 3.0),* Nov. 26, 2002 (with updates), *at http://www.bt.cdc.gov/agent/smallpox/response-plan/index.asp.*

Page 761. Add this material after Note 6.

7. *Recent Developments in Biodefense.* The Public Health Security and Bioterrorism Preparedness and Response Act, Pub. L. No. 107-188, 116 Stat. 594 (2002), is a wide-ranging measure designed to bolster the nation's ability to respond to a bioterrorism emergency. It creates a new Assistant Secretary of Health and Human Services for Public Health Emergency Preparedness. *Id.* §102. It also provides, *inter alia,* enhanced support for state and local bioterrorism preparedness, improvements in communications among public health services, and fast-track authority for the development

Chapter 13. Consequence Management: When the Worst Happens 197

of new drugs for emergency use. Details of the new act are set out in C. Stephen Redhead & Mary E. Tiemann, *Public Health Security and Bioterrorism Preparedness and Response Act (P.L. 107-188): Provisions and Changes to Preexisting Law* (Cong. Res. Serv. RL31263) (2002).

In April 2004, President Bush issued a directive billed as providing "a comprehensive framework for our nation's biodefense." *HSPD-10: Biodefense for the 21st Century*, available at http://www.dhs.gov/dhpublic/display?theme=43&content=3522&print=true. It declared that while "the public health philosophy of the 20th Century – emphasizing prevention – is ideal for addressing natural disease outbreaks, it is not sufficient to confront 21st Century threats where adversaries may use biological weapons agents as part of a long-term campaign of aggression and terror." It offered federal support to state, local, and private resources to provide "layered defenses" against attacks. It also called for improvements in intelligence capabilities, new international nonpro-liferation efforts, and added protection for infrastructure related to medical care, food, water, and energy. And it directed the creation of new capabilities for early warning, forensics, and recovery from an attack. Details, however, may be found only in a classified version of the directive. Some of the same goals are described, but in considerably more detail, in Centers for Disease Control and Prevention, *A National Public Health Strategy for Terrorism Preparedness and Response 2003-2008* (Mar. 2004).

Another initiative concerns pharmaceuticals that could be used in responding to a terrorist threat or attack. Project BioShield was announced by President Bush in his 2003 State of the Union address and approved by Congress in July 2004. The Project Bioshield Act of 2004, Pub. L. No. 108-276, 118 Stat. 835 (2004), amends the Public Health Service Act to direct new research and development of drugs for use in a terrorist emergency, permits the waiver of normal guidelines for procurement of products and services, and reorders management of the Strategic National Stockpile of drugs for emergency use (see casebook p. 764, Note 3). It also allows the administration in an emergency of pharmaceuticals not yet approved for routine general use.

c. *Civil Liberties Implications*

Page 763. Add this material to Note 1.

The CDC guidance for smallpox includes this summary, from a recent conference, of public health powers needed for an adequate response to a bioterrorism event:

Chapter 13. Consequence Management: When the Worst Happens

1. Collection of Records and Data
   a. Reporting of diseases, unusual clusters, and suspicious events
   b. Access to hospital and provider records
   c. Data sharing with law enforcement agencies
   d. Veterinary reporting
   e. Reporting of workplace absenteeism
   f. Reporting from pharmacies
2. Control of Property
   a. Right of access to suspicious premises
   b. Emergency closure of facilities
   c. Temporary use of hospitals and ability to transfer patients
   d. Temporary use of hotel rooms and drive-through facilities
   e. Procurement or confiscation of medicines and vaccines
   f. Seizure of cell phones and other "walkie-talkie" type equipment . . .
3. Management of Persons
   a. Identification of exposed persons
   b. Mandatory medical examinations
   c. Collect lab specimens and perform tests
   d. Rationing of medicines
   e. Tracking and follow-up of persons
   f. Isolation and quarantine . . .
   h. Enforcement authority through police or National Guard . . .

Cantigny Conference, *State Emergency Health Powers and the Bioterrorism Threat*, Apr. 26-27, 2001, *available at http://www.nationalstrategy.com/april%20conference.htm*, excerpted at *http://www.bt.cdc.gov/agent/smallpox/response-plan/files/guide-c-part-2.doc*. These measures implicate a wide range of individual liberty and property issues. Can you describe current legal authority for each one of them? Can you say how you would respond to their implementation, and why?

Can you argue that government personnel responsible for enforcement of a *cordon sanitaire* around a city following an outbreak of, say, plague would be authorized to shoot anyone trying to escape the quarantine? Do you think they have that authority currently? Do you believe that lesser measures would protect the public safety?

Page 764. Add the following materials after Note 3.

4. *SARS and the Locus of Authority.* The Sudden Acute Respiratory Syndrome (SARS) epidemic that mysteriously appeared in the spring of 2003 caused public health officials to revisit the prospect of quarantine as a public health measure. On April 1, when seven passengers on an American Airlines flight from Tokyo to San Jose, California, experienced

Chapter 13. Consequence Management: When the Worst Happens

flu-like symptoms, Santa Clara County health officials surrounded the aircraft with emergency vehicles after it landed. The passengers were given a choice – go with county officials for examination and potential quarantine, or go home and about their business, at the risk of spreading SARS. Five went with the county teams, two went home, and none developed SARS. Santa Clara County officials then complained that they lacked authority to order detention or confinement of possible SARS victims. Melissa Healy, *Are Quarantines Back?*, L.A. Times, Apr. 14, 2003. Was the officials' concern well-founded? On April 4, President Bush added SARS to the list of diseases for which federal officials may quarantine citizens. Exec. Order No. 13,295, 68 Fed. Reg. 17,255 (2003). Does the new order provide adequate authority for public health officials to respond to the threat of SARS? Should Santa Clara County take additional measures? If so, which ones?

5. *Smallpox Vaccination Plan Update.* The federal campaign to vaccinate 500,000 health care workers against smallpox stalled in the first months of 2003 when only about 35,000 workers agreed to be inoculated. Because adequate numbers of volunteers did not come forward, public health officials revised smallpox preparedness plans to acknowledge the likely need to vaccinate doctors and nurses after, rather than before, an outbreak begins. Christian Davenport, *Smallpox Strategies Shifting: Inoculations Fall Far Short of Goals of Nation, Region*, Wash. Post, May 12, 2003, at A1. More than 450,000 military personnel were also vaccinated by June 2003. Both the civilian and military programs were "paused" in June 2003; the military program was halted because it had already inoculated everyone who was eligible. Donald G. McNeil, Jr., *2 Programs to Vaccinate for Smallpox Are "Paused,"* N.Y. Times, June 19, 2003, at A13.

3. The Role of the Armed Forces

a. The Military in American Society

Page 776. Replace Note 9 with the following material.

9. *A Domestic Role for Military Intelligence?* Since the earliest days of the Republic, military intelligence units have supported domestic uses of military force. They have also been used occasionally to collect personal information about Americans who posed no real threat to national security. This activity reached a peak in the late 1960s, when the Pentagon compiled data on more than 100,000 politically active Americans, in an effort to quell

civil rights and anti-Vietnam War demonstrations and to discredit protestors. The Army deployed 1,500 plainclothes agents to watch demonstrators, infiltrate organizations, and circulate blacklists. Military officials claimed that they were preparing for the use of troops to put down insurrections. *See* Christopher H. Pyle, *Military Surveillance of Civilian Politics, 1961-1971* (1986). In 1976, the Church Committee, looking into a variety of intelligence community abuses, called the Army program "the worst intrusion that military intelligence has ever made into the civilian community." *Improper Surveillance of Private Citizens by the Military, Final Report of the Senate Select Comm. to Study Governmental Operations with Respect to Intelligence Activities*, S. Rep. No. 755, 94th Cong. 356 (1976), Book III at 792 [*Church Committee Report*]. Today the Pentagon describes what happened then as a classic example of "mission creep."

When these actions were revealed, political activists sued to stop them, claiming that their First Amendment rights of free expression and association were "chilled" by Army surveillance and record collection. They also worried that the improper use of information about their political activities might jeopardize their jobs and reputations. The Supreme Court dismissed the case on standing grounds. Laird v. Tatum, 408 U.S. 1 (1972).

Congress reacted to these and other domestic intelligence abuses by passing the Privacy Act in 1974, 5 U.S.C. §552a (2000), and the Foreign Intelligence Surveillance Act (FISA) in 1978 (casebook pp. 666-697). Both measures limit the collection, retention, and sharing of information about how individuals exercise rights guaranteed by the First Amendment, as well as information not relevant to the mission of an agency. But serious doubts exist about the efficacy of these laws in safeguarding personal privacy. *See, e.g.,* William C. Banks, *And the Wall Came Tumbling Down: Secret Surveillance After the Terror*, 57 U. Miami L. Rev. 1147 (2002); Steven W. Becker, *Maintaining Secret Government Dossiers on the First Amendment Activities of American Citizens: The Law Enforcement Activity Exception to the Privacy Act,* 50 DePaul L. Rev. 675 (2000).

Several developments in the wake of 9/11 point to a possible expanded domestic role for military intelligence. The Department of Homeland Security's Directorate for Information Analysis and Infrastructure Protection (IAIP) (pp. 186 in this Supplement) collects, analyzes, and disseminates data about possible domestic terrorist threats from government and private sources, including the military's intelligence components. The National Counterterrorism Center (NCTC) (pp. 188-189 in this Supplement) performs many of the same functions. Military intelligence personnel work in both of these agencies, where they become both suppliers and recipients of personal information about U.S. persons, some of which may have no clear relevance to the Pentagon's homeland defense mission. Congress has

Chapter 13. Consequence Management: When the Worst Happens 201

also approved the creation of a new Under Secretary of Defense for Intelligence, Pub. L. No. 107-314, §901, 116 Stat. 2458, 2465 (2002), who is supposed to provide "more coordinated, better focused intelligence support for pressing national concerns like homeland security." Dept. of Defense, *Report to Congress on the Role of the Department of Defense in Supporting Homeland Security* 3, Sept. 2003.

In 2002, DOD created the Northern Command (NORTHCOM), based in Colorado, to assist in homeland defense. *See generally* http://www. northcom.mil. Like IAIP and NCTC, NORTHCOM collects and "fuses" intelligence and law enforcement information from various sources, then redistributes it widely to federal, state, and local agencies. Unlike the two civilian agencies, however, NORTHCOM also collects domestic data directly, utilizing a Pentagon organization called Counterintelligence Field Activity (CIFA). *See* DOD Dir. 5105.67, *DoD Counterintelligence Field Activity* (Feb. 19, 2002). CIFA is charged to maintain "a domestic law enforcement database" and to develop a data-mining capability. But NORTHCOM has not spelled out any limits on these activities, aside from the Pentagon's own domestic intelligence rules, *see* DOD Dir. 5240.1-R, *Procedures Governing the Activities of DoD Intelligence Components That Affect United States Persons* (Dec. 1982), and these rules make no provision for outside oversight or accountability.

In 1976, the Church Committee proposed a "precisely drawn legislative charter" that would, *inter alia,* "limit military investigations to activities in the civilian community which are necessary and pertinent to the military mission, and which cannot feasibly be accomplished by civilian agencies." *Church Committee Report, supra,* Book II at 310-311. The committee apparently believed that military intelligence units could make no unique contribution to the domestic security efforts of the FBI, local law enforcement, and other civilian agencies. If that was true three decades ago, when the threat of terrorism was not such an abiding concern, do you think it is true today? Or do you believe an expanded military intelligence role at home would make us more secure? If so, would it be worth the possible trade-offs in privacy and related liberties? Are your answers affected by the availability of new data mining technology (pp. 172-174 in this Supplement)? Can you outline a charter for domestic military intelligence activities that reflects whatever concerns you have? *See generally* Stephen Dycus, *The Role of Military Intelligence in Homeland Security,* 64 La. L. Rev. 779 (2004).

b. Military Responsibility for "Homeland Security"

Page 781. At the bottom of the page, delete the excerpt from §1023 of the FY 2000 Defense Authorization Act (which expired by its terms on September 30, 2004).

Page 782. Add the following material after the first full paragraph.

In 2002, the Defense Department's new Northern Command (NORTHCOM) assumed responsibility for DOD's homeland defense efforts and for provision of military support to civil authorities. *See* Scott Shepherd & Steve Bowman, *Homeland Security: Establishment and Implementation of the United States Northern Command* (Cong. Res. Serv. RS21322) (2005). It manages military responses to all kinds of threats, from terrorism to hurricanes, working closely with the Department of Homeland Security and directing the activities of the Joint Task Force-Civil Support. Details of NORTHCOM's organization and responsibilities, as well as those of various DOD components, are spelled out in considerable detail in *Report to Congress on the Role of the Department of Defense in Supporting Homeland Security* (p. 201 *supra*); Dept. of Defense, *The DoD Role in Homeland Security: Defense Study and Report to Congress*, July 2003.

In mid-2005, a new DOD policy document appeared that may signal a significantly more expansive Pentagon homeland security role. Dept. of Defense, *Strategy for Homeland Defense and Civil Support*, June 2005, available at http://www.defenselink.mil/news/June2005/d20050630home land.pdf. "Our adversaries consider US territory an inte-gral part of a global theater of combat," it declared. "We must therefore have a strategy that applies to the domestic context the key principles that are driving the transformation of US power projection and joint expeditionary warfare." *Id.* at 1. The new policy envisions an "active, layered" defense that could deal with "simultaneous, mass casualty attacks." *Id.* at 7, 10. It expects to "reorient its intelligence capabilities" to enable it to, *inter alia*, "[c]ollect homeland defense threat information from relevant private and public sector sources, consistent with US constitutional authorities and privacy law," and to "[d]evelop automated tools to improve data fusion, analysis, and management, to track systematically large amounts of data, and to detect, fuse, and analyze aberrant patterns of activity, consistent with US privacy protections." *Id.* at 21. This last is an apparent reference to a data-mining system like DARPA's much-maligned Total Information Awareness program. *See supra* p. 172. DOD will work to "diminish existing cultural, technological, and bureaucratic obstacles to information sharing" among

Chapter 13. Consequence Management: When the Worst Happens

federal agencies, with state, local, and tribal governments, with private entities, and with "key foreign partners." *Id.* at 23. Finally, while recognizing that "[d]omestic security is primarily a civilian law enforcement function," the strategy declares that when "directed by the President, the Department will execute land-based military operations to detect, deter, and defeat foreign terrorist attacks within the United States." *Id.* at 26.

Page 785. Add the following material after Note 6.

7. *Additional Resources.* A recent flurry of articles and other writings about the military's role in homeland security includes Steve Bowman, *Homeland Security: The Department of Defense's Role* (Cong. Res. Serv. RL31615) (2003); Defense Science Board, *DoD Roles and Missions in Homeland Security* (2003), *available at http://www.fas.org/irp/agency/dod/dsb/homelandss.pdf*; Charles Doyle, *Terrorism: Some Legal Restrictions on Military Assistance to Domestic Authorities Following a Terrorist Attack* (Cong. Res. Serv. RS21012) (2005); Jennifer Elsea, *The Posse Comitatus Act and Related Matters: A Sketch* (Cong. Res. Serv. RS20590) (2005); Charles Bloeser, *A Statute in Need of Teeth: Revisiting the Posse Comitatus Act After 9/11*, 50-MAY Fed. Law. 24 (2003); Nathan Canestaro, *Homeland Defense: Another Nail in the Coffin for Posse Comitatus,* 12 Wash. U. J.L. & Poly. 99 (2003); Tom A. Gizzo & Tama S. Monoson, *A Call to Arms: The Posse Comitatus Act and the Use of the Military in the Struggle Against International Terrorism,* 15 Pace Intl. L. Rev. 149 (2003); Sean J. Kealy, *Reexamining the Posse Comitatus Act: Toward a Right to Civil Law Enforcement,* 21 Yale J.L. & Poly. Rev. 383 (2003); and Richard H. Kohn, *Using the Military at Home: Yesterday, Today, and Tomorrow,* 4 Chi. J. Intl. L. 165 (2003).

Page 795. Substitute these materials for Chapter 13C, parts 1 and 2, pp. 795-816.

C. WARTIME DETENTION AND SUSPENSION OF THE WRIT

During war, national security may require the detention of both non-combatants and combatants for the duration of hostilities, and the military may participate in the detention. Here we consider the law governing such detentions, postponing the closely related topic of military trial until Chapter 14. Part 1 treats the wartime detention of non-combatants before

9/11. The privilege of petitioning a court for the "Great Writ" has historically been available to detainees in England and the United States to challenge the legality of their detention, but even this privilege may be suspended in this country "when in Cases of Rebellion or Invasion the public Safety may require it." U.S. Const. art. I, §9, cl. 2. Part 2 considers suspension of the writ of habeas corpus in cases of war or national emergency. Part 3 sets out two seminal pre-9/11 cases regarding military authority over putative enemy combatants. Although they deal primarily with military trials rather than detention, their reasoning has influenced the law of military detention and military trials alike because detention is a predicate for trial. We return to them in Chapter 14 when we deal with trial by military commission. Part 4 considers the evolving topic of the military detention of U.S. citizens as enemy combatants after 9/11. Finally, in Part 5, we turn to the also evolving subject of the military detention of alien combatants after 9/11.

1. Detention of Non-Combatants Before 9/11

Alien Enemy Act
50 U.S.C. §21 (2000)

Whenever there is a declared war between the United States and any foreign nation or government, or any invasion or predatory incursion is perpetrated, attempted, or threatened against the territory of the United States by any foreign nation or government, and the President makes public proclamation of the event, all natives, citizens, denizens, or subjects of the hostile nation or government, being of the age of fourteen years and upward, who shall be within the United States and not actually naturalized, shall be liable to be apprehended, restrained, secured, and removed as alien enemies. The President is authorized in any such event, by his proclamation thereof, or other public act, to direct the conduct to be observed, on the part of the United States, toward the aliens who become so liable; the manner and degree of the restraint to which they shall be subject and in what cases, and upon what security their residence shall be permitted, and to provide for the removal of those who, not being permitted to reside within the United States, refuse or neglect to depart therefrom; and to establish any other regulations which are found necessary in the premises and for the public safety.

Korematsu v. United States
United States Supreme Court, 1944
323 U.S. 214

[The opinion is set forth at casebook p. 796.]

NOTES AND QUESTIONS

Aliens. Why did the government not invoke the Alien Enemy Act to intern Korematsu and his fellow internees? Could the government have invoked it to justify the detention of immigrants described in the OIG report at p. 176 in this Supplement? If so, by this act has Congress occupied the field of alien detention during war or invasion?

[The remaining Notes and Questions are set forth at casebook pp. 802-810.]

2. Suspension of the Writ of Habeas Corpus

Article I, §9, clause 2 of the Constitution provides, "The privilege of the Writ of Habeas Corpus shall not be suspended unless when in Cases of Rebellion or Invasion the public Safety may require it." Although the quoted language appears in the part of the Constitution devoted to an enumeration of legislative powers, there is no other textual clue about who possesses the power to suspend the writ. The question arose in an early Civil War era case, Ex parte Merryman, 17 F. Cas. 144 (C.C.D. Md. 1861) (No. 9487), when Chief Justice Taney, sitting as a circuit court judge, ordered the release of a Southern sympathizer imprisoned at Fort McHenry. Merryman had been seized after President Lincoln signed an order authorizing suspension of the writ of habeas corpus. Said the Chief Justice, "I had supposed it to be one of those points in constitutional law upon which there was no difference of Opinion . . . that the privilege of the writ could not be suspended, except by act of congress." *Id.* at 148. However, Taney's decree was ignored by the President, and Merryman remained in prison for a time. A month later, in a message to a special session of Congress, Lincoln remarked that Taney's interpretation of the constitutional requirement would allow

> all the laws, but one, to go unexecuted, and the government itself go to pieces, lest that one be violated. . . . [T]he Constitution itself, is silent as to which, or who, is to exercise the power; and as the provision was plainly made for a dangerous emergency, it cannot be believed the framers

of the instrument intended, that in every case, the danger should run its course, until Congress could be called together; the very assembling of which might be prevented, as was intended in this case, by the rebellion. [4 *Collected Works of Abraham Lincoln* 430-431 (Roy P. Basler ed., 1953).]

Congress responded in 1863 by authorizing the President to suspend the writ. Three years later, the full Supreme Court considered the effects of that authorization.

Ex parte Milligan
United States Supreme Court, 1866
71 U.S. (4 Wall.) 2

[Lambdin P. Milligan, a resident of Indiana, was arrested on October 5, 1864, at his home by order of General Alvin P. Hovey, commander of the military district of Indiana, for planning to raid a federal arsenal in Indiana and use the munitions seized there to free Confederate prisoners, for inciting insurrection, and for plotting to assassinate the governor. Congress had authorized the President "during the present rebellion" to suspend the writ of habeas corpus in any case throughout the United States "whenever, in his judgment, the public safety may require it." It provided that when he suspended the writ,

> no military or other officer shall be compelled, in answer to any writ of habeas corpus, to return the body of any person or persons detained by him by authority of the President . . . [and] further proceedings under the writ of habeas corpus shall be suspended by the judge or court having issued the said writ, so long as said suspension by the President shall remain in force, and said rebellion continue. [Act of March 8, 1863, 115 Stat. 755 (1863).]

The act required the government within twenty days of the statute's enactment or of any subsequent arrest to furnish the names of citizens "held as prisoners of the United States, by order or authority of the President . . . as state or political prisoners, or otherwise than as prisoners of war," to the courts in jurisdictions "in which the administration of the laws has continued unimpaired." *Id.* "In all cases where a grand jury, having attended any of said courts having jurisdiction in the premises, . . . after the furnishing of said list, . . . has terminated its session without finding an indictment or presentment," the act required the court to order discharge of the prisoner. *Id.*

On January 2, 1865, the United States Circuit Court for Indiana met at

Chapter 13. Consequence Management: When the Worst Happens

Indianapolis and empaneled a grand jury to inquire whether any laws of the United States had been broken by anyone, and to make presentments. The grand jury did not find any bill of indictment or make any presentment against Milligan, and on January 27 the court adjourned after discharging the grand jury from further service. Milligan, in the meantime, was tried by a military commission for violating the laws of war, found guilty, and sentenced to death. He petitioned the Circuit Court for his release, arguing that the military tribunal had no jurisdiction to try him.]

[The Court's opinion and additional relevant text are set forth at casebook pp. 811-813.]

NOTES AND QUESTIONS

[Read notes 1-5 at casebook pp. 813-815, omitting note 6.]

3. Detention of Combatants Before 9/11

Ex parte Milligan
United States Supreme Court, 1866
71 U.S. (4 Wall.) 2

[Read the part of the opinion set forth at casebook p. 889.]

Ex parte Quirin
United States Supreme Court, 1942
317 U.S. 1

[This opinion is set forth at casebook p. 893.]

NOTES AND QUESTIONS

[Read Notes 1-5 at casebook pp. 901-904, omitting note 6.]

4. Detention of U.S. Citizens as Enemy Combatants After 9/11

After 9/11, the government placed two U.S. citizens in military detention, citing Ex parte Quirin as authority. We consider first the case of Yaser Hamdi, who reportedly was captured on the battlefield in Afghanistan. We then turn to the military detention of José Padilla, originally arrested in Chicago as a material witness. The President subsequently designated him an enemy combatant as a basis for his transfer to military custody. Although the Second Circuit Court of Appeals decided *Padilla* before the Supreme Court decided *Hamdi*, we leave *Padilla* for last because we believe that his detention represents a further extension of detention authority, from a citizen captured on the battlefield abroad to one arrested on U.S. soil.

Hamdi v. Rumsfeld
United States Supreme Court, 2004
542 U.S. 507

Justice O'CONNOR announced the judgment of the Court and delivered an opinion, in which THE CHIEF JUSTICE, Justice KENNEDY, and Justice BREYER join. . . .

[During the U.S. military operations in Afghanistan that followed the 9/11 terrorist attacks, petitioner Hamdi was captured by Afghan Northern Alliance forces. He was subsequently transferred to U.S. military custody in Afghanistan and sent to Guantánamo. When it was discovered that he had been born in Louisiana, making him a U.S. citizen, he was transferred to the United States as an enemy combatant and detained at a Navy brig in Charleston, South Carolina. Hamdi's father filed this habeas petition on behalf of his son under 28 U.S.C. §2241, alleging that the government held him in violation of the Fifth and Fourteenth Amendments. In the ensuing proceeding, the government filed an affidavit by Department of Defense official Michael Mobbs, setting forth the foregoing facts as hearsay.]

II

The threshold question before us is whether the Executive has the authority to detain citizens who qualify as "enemy combatants." There is some debate as to the proper scope of this term, and the Government has never provided any court with the full criteria that it uses in classifying individuals as such. It has made clear, however, that, for purposes of this case, the "enemy combatant" that it is seeking to detain is an individual who, it alleges, was "part of or supporting forces hostile to the United States or coalition partners" in Afghanistan and who "engaged in an armed conflict against the United States" there. We therefore answer only the narrow question before us: whether the detention of citizens falling within that definition is authorized.

Chapter 13. Consequence Management: When the Worst Happens 209

The Government maintains that no explicit congressional authorization is required, because the Executive possesses plenary authority to detain pursuant to Article II of the Constitution. We do not reach the question whether Article II provides such authority, however, because we agree with the Government's alternative position, that Congress has in fact authorized Hamdi's detention, through the AUMF [Authorization for Use of Military Force, Pub. L. No. 107-40, 115 Stat. 224 (2001), casebook p. 262].

Our analysis on that point, set forth below, substantially overlaps with our analysis of Hamdi's principal argument for the illegality of his detention. He posits that his detention is forbidden by 18 U.S.C. §4001(a). Section 4001(a) states that "[n]o citizen shall be imprisoned or otherwise detained by the United States except pursuant to an Act of Congress." Congress passed §4001(a) in 1971 as part of a bill to repeal the Emergency Detention Act of 1950, 50 U.S.C. §811 *et seq.*, which provided procedures for executive detention, during times of emergency, of individuals deemed likely to engage in espionage or sabotage. Congress was particularly concerned about the possibility that the Act could be used to reprise the Japanese internment camps of World War II. The Government again presses two alternative positions. First, it argues that §4001(a), in light of its legislative history and its location in Title 18, applies only to "the control of civilian prisons and related detentions," not to military detentions. Second, it maintains that §4001(a) is satisfied, because Hamdi is being detained "pursuant to an Act of Congress" – the AUMF. Again, because we conclude that the Government's second assertion is correct, we do not address the first. In other words, for the reasons that follow, we conclude that the AUMF is explicit congressional authorization for the detention of individuals in the narrow category we describe (assuming, without deciding, that such authorization is required), and that the AUMF satisfied §4001(a)'s requirement that a detention be "pursuant to an Act of Congress" (assuming, without deciding, that §4001(a) applies to military detentions).

The AUMF authorizes the President to use "all necessary and appropriate force" against "nations, organizations, or persons" associated with the September 11, 2001, terrorist attacks. 115 Stat. 224. There can be no doubt that individuals who fought against the United States in Afghanistan as part of the Taliban, an organization known to have supported the al Qaeda terrorist network responsible for those attacks, are individuals Congress sought to target in passing the AUMF. We conclude that detention of individuals falling into the limited category we are considering, for the duration of the particular conflict in which they were captured, is so fundamental and accepted an incident to war as to be an exercise of the "necessary and appropriate force" Congress has authorized the President to use.

The capture and detention of lawful combatants and the capture, detention, and trial of unlawful combatants, by "universal agreement and practice," are "important incident[s] of war." *Ex parte Quirin,* 317 U.S. [1 (1942)], at 28. The purpose of detention is to prevent captured individuals from returning to the field of battle and taking up arms once again.

There is no bar to this Nation's holding one of its own citizens as an enemy combatant. In *Quirin,* one of the detainees, Haupt, alleged that he was a naturalized United States citizen. 317 U.S., at 20. We held that "[c]itizens who associate themselves with the military arm of the enemy government, and with its aid, guidance and direction enter this country bent on hostile acts, are enemy belligerents within the meaning of . . . the law of war." *Id.,* at 37-38. While Haupt was tried for violations of the law of war, nothing in *Quirin* suggests that his citizenship would have precluded his mere detention for the duration of the relevant hostilities. See *id.,* at 30-31. Nor can we see any reason for drawing such a line here. A citizen, no less than an alien, can be "part of or supporting forces hostile to the United States or coalition partners" and "engaged in an armed conflict against the United States"; such a citizen, if released, would pose the same threat of returning to the front during the ongoing conflict.

In light of these principles, it is of no moment that the AUMF does not use specific language of detention. Because detention to prevent a combatant's return to the battlefield is a fundamental incident of waging war, in permitting the use of "necessary and appropriate force," Congress has clearly and unmistakably authorized detention in the narrow circumstances considered here. . . .

Hamdi contends that the AUMF does not authorize indefinite or perpetual detention. Certainly, we agree that indefinite detention for the purpose of interrogation is not authorized. Further, we understand Congress' grant of authority for the use of "necessary and appropriate force" to include the authority to detain for the duration of the relevant conflict, and our understanding is based on longstanding law-of-war principles. If the practical circumstances of a given conflict are entirely unlike those of the conflicts that informed the development of the law of war, that understanding may unravel. But that is not the situation we face as of this date. Active combat operations against Taliban fighters apparently are ongoing in Afghanistan. The United States may detain, for the duration of these hostilities, individuals legitimately determined to be Taliban combatants who "engaged in an armed conflict against the United States." If the record establishes that United States troops are still involved in active combat in Afghanistan, those detentions are part of the exercise of "necessary and appropriate force," and therefore are authorized by the AUMF.

Ex parte Milligan, [71 U.S. (4 Wall.) 2 (1866)], does not undermine our holding about the Government's authority to seize enemy combatants, as we define that term today. In that case, the Court made repeated reference to the fact that its inquiry into whether the military tribunal had jurisdiction to try and punish Milligan turned in large part on the fact that Milligan was not a prisoner of war, but a resident of Indiana arrested while at home there. *Id.,* at 118, 131. That fact was central to its conclusion. Had Milligan been captured while he was assisting Confederate soldiers by carrying a rifle against Union troops on a Confederate battlefield, the holding of the Court might well have been different. The Court's repeated explanations that Milligan was not a prisoner of war suggest that had these different circumstances been present he could have been detained under military authority for the duration of the conflict, whether or not he was a citizen. . . .

III

Even in cases in which the detention of enemy combatants is legally authorized, there remains the question of what process is constitutionally due to a citizen who disputes his enemy-combatant status. . . .

A

Though they reach radically different conclusions on the process that ought to attend the present proceeding, the parties begin on common ground. All agree that, absent suspension, the writ of habeas corpus remains available to every individual detained within the United States. U.S. Const., Art. I, §9, cl. 2 ("The Privilege of the Writ of Habeas Corpus shall not be suspended, unless when in Cases of Rebellion or Invasion the public Safety may require it"). Only in the rarest of circumstances has Congress seen fit to suspend the writ. . . . All agree suspension of the writ has not occurred here. Thus, it is undisputed that Hamdi was properly before an Article III court to challenge his detention under 28 U.S.C. §2241. Further, all agree that §2241 and its companion provisions provide at least a skeletal outline of the procedures to be afforded a petitioner in federal habeas review. Most notably, §2243 provides that "the person detained may, under oath, deny any of the facts set forth in the return or allege any other material facts," and §2246 allows the taking of evidence in habeas proceedings by deposition, affidavit, or interrogatories.

The simple outline of §2241 makes clear both that Congress envisioned that habeas petitioners would have some opportunity to present and rebut facts and that courts in cases like this retain some ability to vary the ways in which they do so as mandated by due process. The Government recognizes the basic procedural protections required by the habeas statute, but asks us to hold that, given both the flexibility of the habeas mechanism and the circumstances presented in this case, the presentation of the Mobbs Declaration to the habeas court completed the required factual development. It suggests two separate reasons for its position that no further process is due.

B

First, the Government urges the adoption of the Fourth Circuit's holding below – that because it is "undisputed" that Hamdi's seizure took place in a combat zone, the habeas determination can be made purely as a matter of law, with no further hearing or factfinding necessary. This argument is easily rejected. As the dissenters from the denial of rehearing en banc noted, the circumstances surrounding Hamdi's seizure cannot in any way be characterized as "undisputed," as "those circumstances are neither conceded in fact, nor susceptible to concession in law, because Hamdi has not been permitted to speak for himself or even through counsel as to those circumstances." 337 F.3d 335, 357 (Luttig, J., dissenting from denial of rehearing en banc). Further, the "facts" that constitute the alleged concession are insufficient to support Hamdi's detention. Under the definition of enemy combatant that we accept today as falling within the scope of Congress' authorization, Hamdi would need to be "part of or supporting forces hostile to the United States or coalition partners" and "engaged in an armed conflict against the United States" to justify his detention in the United States for the duration of the relevant conflict. The habeas petition states only that "[w]hen seized by the United States Government, Mr. Hamdi resided in Afghanistan." An assertion that one *resided* in a country in which combat operations are taking place is not a concession that one was "*captured* in a zone of active combat operations in a foreign theater of war," 316 F.3d, at 459 (emphasis added), and certainly is not a concession that one was "part of or supporting forces hostile to the United States or coalition partners" and "engaged in an armed conflict against the United States." Accordingly, we reject any argument that Hamdi has made concessions that eliminate any right to further process.

C

The Government's second argument requires closer consideration. This is the argument that further factual exploration is unwarranted and inappropriate in light of the extraordinary constitutional interests at stake. Under the Government's most extreme rendition of this argument, "[r]espect for separation of powers and the limited institutional capabilities of courts in matters of military decision-making in connection with an ongoing conflict" ought to eliminate entirely any individual process, restricting the courts to investigating only whether legal authorization exists for the broader detention scheme. At most, the Government argues, courts should review its determination that a citizen is an enemy combatant under a very deferential "some evidence" standard. [Brief for Respondents] 34 ("Under the some evidence standard, the focus is exclusively on the factual basis supplied by the Executive to support its own determination" (citing *Superintendent, Mass. Correctional Institution at Walpole v. Hill,* 472 U.S. 445, 455-457 (1985) (explaining that the some evidence standard "does not require" a "weighing of the evidence," but rather calls for assessing "whether there is any evidence in the record that could support the conclusion")). Under this review, a court would assume the accuracy of the Government's articulated basis for Hamdi's detention, as set forth in the Mobbs Declaration, and assess only whether that articulated basis was a legitimate one.

In response, Hamdi emphasizes that this Court consistently has recognized that an individual challenging his detention may not be held at the will of the Executive without recourse to some proceeding before a neutral tribunal to determine whether the Executive's asserted justifications for that detention have basis in fact and warrant in law. See, *e.g., Zadvydas v. Davis,* 533 U.S. 678, 690 (2001). . . .

. . . The ordinary mechanism that we use for balancing such serious competing interests, and for determining the procedures that are necessary to ensure that a citizen is not "deprived of life, liberty, or property, without due process of law," U.S. Const., Amdt. 5, is the test that we articulated in *Mathews v. Eldridge,* 424 U.S. 319 (1976). *Mathews* dictates that the process due in any given instance is determined by weighing "the private interest that will be affected by the official action" against the Government's asserted interest, "including the function involved" and the burdens the Government would face in providing greater process. 424 U.S., at 335. The *Mathews* calculus then contemplates a judicious balancing of these concerns, through an analysis of "the risk of an erroneous deprivation" of the private interest if the process were reduced and the "probable value, if any, of additional or substitute safeguards." *Ibid.* We take each of these steps in turn.

1

It is beyond question that substantial interests lie on both sides of the scale in this case. Hamdi's "private interest . . . affected by the official action," *ibid.,* is the most elemental of liberty interests – the interest in being free from physical detention by one's own government. "In our society liberty is the norm," and detention without trial "is the carefully limited exception." [United States v. Salerno, 481 U.S. 739 (1987)], at 755. . . .

Nor is the weight on this side of the *Mathews* scale offset by the circumstances of war or the accusation of treasonous behavior, for "[i]t is clear that commitment for *any* purpose constitutes a significant deprivation of liberty that requires due process protection," *Jones v. United States,* 463 U.S. 354, 361 (1983) (emphasis added; internal quotation marks omitted), and at this stage in the *Mathews* calculus, we consider the interest of the *erroneously* detained individual. Indeed, as *amicus* briefs from media and relief organizations emphasize, the risk of erroneous deprivation of a citizen's liberty in the absence of sufficient process here is very real. See Brief for AmeriCares et al. as *Amici Curiae* 13-22 (noting ways in which "[t]he nature of humanitarian relief work and journalism present a significant risk of mistaken military detentions"). Moreover, as critical as the Government's interest may be in detaining those who actually pose an immediate threat to the national security of the United States during ongoing international conflict, history and common sense teach us that an unchecked system of detention carries the potential to become a means for oppression and abuse of others who do not present that sort of threat. . . .

2

On the other side of the scale are the weighty and sensitive governmental interests in ensuring that those who have in fact fought with the enemy during a war do not return to battle against the United States. As discussed above, the law of war and the realities of combat may render such detentions both necessary and appropriate, and our due process analysis need not blink at those realities. Without doubt, our Constitution recognizes that core strategic matters of warmaking belong in the hands of those who are best positioned and most politically accountable for making them. *Department of Navy v. Egan,* 484 U.S. 518, 530 (1988) (noting the reluctance of the courts "to intrude upon the authority of the Executive in military and national security affairs"); *Youngstown Sheet & Tube Co. v. Sawyer,* 343 U.S. 579, 587 (1952) (acknowledging "broad powers in military commanders engaged in day-to-day fighting in a theater of war").

The Government also argues at some length that its interests in reducing the process available to alleged enemy combatants are heightened by the practical difficulties that would accompany a system of trial-like process. In its view, military officers who are engaged in the serious work of waging battle would be unnecessarily and dangerously distracted by litigation half a world away, and discovery into military operations would both intrude on the sensitive secrets of national defense and result in a futile search for evidence buried under the rubble of war. To the extent that these burdens are triggered by heightened procedures, they are properly taken into account in our due process analysis.

3

Striking the proper constitutional balance here is of great importance to the Nation during this period of ongoing combat. But it is equally vital that our calculus not give short shrift to the values that this country holds dear or to the privilege that is American citizenship. It is during our most challenging and uncertain moments that our Nation's commitment to due process is most severely tested; and it is in those times that we must preserve our commitment at home to the principles for which we fight abroad.

With due recognition of these competing concerns, we believe that neither the process proposed by the Government nor the process apparently envisioned by the District Court below strikes the proper constitutional balance when a United States citizen is detained in the United States as an enemy combatant. That is, "the risk of erroneous deprivation" of a detainee's liberty interest is unacceptably high under the Government's proposed rule, while some of the "additional or substitute procedural safeguards" suggested by the District Court are unwarranted in light of their limited "probable value" and the burdens they may impose on the military in such cases. *Mathews,* 424 U.S., at 335.

We therefore hold that a citizen-detainee seeking to challenge his classification as an enemy combatant must receive notice of the factual basis for his classification, and a fair opportunity to rebut the Government's factual assertions before a neutral decisionmaker. "For more than a century the central meaning of procedural due process has been clear: 'Parties whose rights are to be affected are entitled to be heard; and in order that they may enjoy that right they must first be notified.' It is equally fundamental that the right to notice and an opportunity to be heard 'must be granted at a meaningful time and in a meaningful manner.'" *Fuentes v. Shevin,* 407 U.S. 67, 80 (1972). These essential constitutional promises may not be eroded.

At the same time, the exigencies of the circumstances may demand that, aside from these core elements, enemy combatant proceedings may be tailored to alleviate their uncommon potential to burden the Executive at a time of ongoing military conflict. Hearsay, for example, may need to be accepted as the most reliable available evidence from the Government in such a proceeding. Likewise, the Constitution would not be offended by a presumption in favor of the Government's evidence, so long as that presumption remained a rebuttable one and fair opportunity for rebuttal were provided. Thus, once the Government puts forth credible evidence that the habeas petitioner meets the enemy-combatant criteria, the onus could shift to the petitioner to rebut that evidence with more persuasive evidence that he falls outside the criteria. A burden-shifting scheme of this sort would meet the goal of ensuring that the errant tourist, embedded journalist, or local aid worker has a chance to prove military error while giving due regard to the Executive once it has put forth meaningful support for its conclusion that the detainee is in fact an enemy combatant. In the words of *Mathews,* process of this sort would sufficiently address the "risk of erroneous deprivation" of a detainee's liberty interest while eliminating certain procedures that have questionable additional value in light of the burden on the Government. 424 U.S., at 335.

We think it unlikely that this basic process will have the dire impact on the central functions of warmaking that the Government forecasts. The parties agree that initial captures on the battlefield need not receive the process we have discussed here; that process is due only when the determination is made to *continue* to hold those who have been seized. The Government has made clear in its briefing that documentation regarding battlefield detainees already is kept in the ordinary course of military affairs. Any factfinding imposition created by requiring a knowledgeable affiant to summarize these records to an independent tribunal is a minimal one. Likewise, arguments that military officers ought not have to wage war under the threat of litigation lose much of their steam when factual disputes at enemy-combatant hearings are limited to the alleged combatant's acts. This focus meddles little, if at all, in the strategy or conduct of war, inquiring only into the appropriateness of continuing to detain an individual claimed to have taken up arms against the United States. While we accord the greatest respect and consideration to the judgments of military authorities in matters relating to the actual prosecution of a war, and recognize that the scope of that discretion necessarily is wide, it does not infringe on the core role of the military for the courts to exercise their own time-honored and constitutionally mandated roles of reviewing and resolving claims like those presented here. Cf. *Korematsu v. United States,* 323 U.S. 214, 233-234 (1944) (Murphy, J., dissenting) ("[L]ike other claims conflicting with the asserted constitutional rights of the individual, the military claim must subject itself to the judicial process of having its reasonableness determined and its conflicts with other interests reconciled"); *Sterling v. Constantin,* 287 U.S. 378, 401 (1932) ("What are the allowable limits of military discretion, and whether or not they have been overstepped in a particular case, are judicial questions").

In sum, while the full protections that accompany challenges to detentions in other settings may prove unworkable and inappropriate in the enemy-combatant setting, the threats to military operations posed by a basic system of independent review are not so weighty as to trump a citizen's core rights to challenge meaningfully the Government's case and to be heard by an impartial adjudicator.

D

In so holding, we necessarily reject the Government's assertion that separation of powers principles mandate a heavily circumscribed role for the courts in such circumstances. Indeed, the position that the courts must forgo any examination of the individual case and focus exclusively on the legality of the broader detention scheme cannot be mandated by any reasonable view of separation of powers, as this approach serves only to *condense* power into a single branch of government. We have long since made clear that a state of war is not a blank check for the President when it comes to the rights of the Nation's citizens. *Youngstown Sheet & Tube,* 343 U.S., at 587. Whatever power the United States Constitution envisions for the Executive in its exchanges with other nations or with enemy organizations in times of conflict, it most assuredly envisions a role for all three branches when individual liberties are at stake. *Mistretta v. United States,* 488 U.S. 361, 380 (1989) (it was "the central judgment of the Framers of the Constitution that, within our political scheme, the separation of governmental powers into three coordinate Branches is essential to the preservation of liberty"); *Home Building & Loan Assn. v. Blaisdell,* 290 U.S. 398, 426 (1934) (The war power "is a power to wage war successfully, and thus it permits the harnessing of the entire energies of the people in a supreme cooperative effort to preserve the nation. But even the war power does not remove constitutional limitations safeguarding essential liberties"). Likewise, we have made clear that, unless Congress acts to suspend it, the Great Writ of habeas corpus allows the Judicial Branch to play a necessary role in maintaining this delicate balance of governance, serving as an important judicial check on the Executive's discretion in the realm of detentions. See *INS v. St. Cyr,* 533 U.S. 289, 301 (2001) ("At its historical core, the writ of habeas corpus has served as a means of reviewing the legality of Executive detention, and it is in that context that its protections have been strongest"). Thus, while we do not question that our due process assessment must pay keen attention to the particular burdens faced by the Executive in the context of military action, it would turn our system of checks and balances on its head to suggest that a citizen could not make his way to court with a challenge to the factual basis for his detention by his government, simply because the Executive opposes making available such a challenge. Absent suspension of the writ by Congress, a citizen detained as an enemy combatant is entitled to this process.

Because we conclude that due process demands some system for a citizen detainee to refute his classification, the proposed "some evidence" standard is inadequate. Any process in which the Executive's factual assertions go wholly unchallenged or are simply presumed correct without any opportunity for the alleged combatant to demonstrate otherwise falls constitutionally short. As the Government itself has recognized, we have utilized the "some evidence" standard in the past as a standard of review, not as a standard of proof. That is, it primarily has been employed by courts in examining an administrative record developed after an adversarial proceeding – one with process at least of the sort that we today hold is constitutionally mandated in the citizen enemy-combatant setting. This standard therefore is ill suited to the situation in which a habeas petitioner has received no prior proceedings before any tribunal and had no prior opportunity to rebut the Executive's factual assertions before a neutral decisionmaker.

Today we are faced only with such a case. Aside from unspecified "screening" processes, and military interrogations in which the Government suggests Hamdi could have contested his classification, Hamdi has received no process. An interrogation by one's captor, however effective an intelligence-gathering tool, hardly constitutes a constitutionally adequate factfinding before a neutral decisionmaker. Compare Brief for Respondents 42-43 (discussing the "secure interrogation environment," and noting that military interrogations require a controlled "interrogation dynamic" and "a relationship of trust and dependency" and are "a critical source" of "timely and effective intelligence") with *Concrete Pipe* [and Products of California, Inc. v. Construction Laborers Pension Trust], 508 U.S. 602, 617-618 (1993) ("one is entitled as a matter of due process of law to an adjudicator who is not in a situation which would offer a possible temptation to the average man as a judge . . . which might lead him not to hold the balance nice, clear and true" (internal quotation marks omitted)). That even purportedly fair adjudicators "are disqualified by their interest in the controversy to be decided is, of course, the general rule." *Tumey v. Ohio,* 273 U.S. 510, 522 (1927). Plainly, the "process" Hamdi has received is not that to which he is entitled under the Due Process Clause.

There remains the possibility that the standards we have articulated could be met by an appropriately authorized and properly constituted military tribunal. Indeed, it is notable that military regulations already provide for such process in related instances, dictating that tribunals be made available to determine the status of enemy detainees who assert prisoner-of-war status under the Geneva Convention. See Enemy Prisoners of War, Retained Personnel, Civilian Internees and Other Detainees, Army Regulation 190-8, §1-6 (1997). In the absence of such process, however, a court that receives a petition for a writ of habeas corpus from an alleged enemy combatant must itself ensure that the minimum requirements of due process are achieved. . . . As we have discussed, a habeas court in a case such as this may accept affidavit evidence like that contained in the Mobbs Declaration, so long as it also permits the alleged combatant to present his own factual case to rebut the Government's return. We anticipate that a District Court would proceed with the caution that we have indicated is necessary in this setting, engaging in a factfinding process that is both prudent and incremental. We have no reason to doubt that courts faced with these sensitive matters will pay proper heed both to the matters of national security that might arise in an individual case and to the constitutional limitations safeguarding essential liberties that remain vibrant even in times of security concerns.

IV

Hamdi asks us to hold that the Fourth Circuit also erred by denying him immediate access to counsel upon his detention and by disposing of the case without permitting him to meet with an attorney. Since our grant of certiorari in this case, Hamdi has been appointed counsel, with whom he has met for consultation purposes on several occasions, and with whom he is now being granted unmonitored meetings. He unquestionably has the right to access to counsel in connection with the proceedings on remand. No further consideration of this issue is necessary at this stage of the case. . . .

The judgment of the United States Court of Appeals for the Fourth Circuit is vacated, and the case is remanded for further proceedings.

It is so ordered.

Justice SOUTER. with whom Justice GINSBURG joins, concurring in part, dissenting in part, and concurring in the judgment. . . . The plurality rejects [the government's "some evidence"] limit on the exercise of habeas jurisdiction and so far I agree with its opinion. The plurality does, however, accept the Government's position that if Hamdi's designation as an enemy combatant is correct, his detention (at least as to some period) is authorized by an Act of Congress as required by §4001(a), that is, by the Authorization for Use of Military Force, 115 Stat. 224 (hereinafter Force Resolution). Here, I disagree and respectfully dissent. . . .

II

The threshold issue is how broadly or narrowly to read the Non-Detention Act, the tone of which is severe: "No citizen shall be imprisoned or otherwise detained by the United States except pursuant to an Act of Congress." . . . For a number of reasons, the prohibition within §4001(a) has to be read broadly to accord the statute a long reach and to impose a burden of justification on the Government.

First, the circumstances in which the Act was adopted point the way to this interpretation. The provision superseded a cold-war statute, the Emergency Detention Act of 1950, which had authorized the Attorney General, in time of emergency, to detain anyone reasonably thought likely to engage in espionage or sabotage. That statute was repealed in 1971 out of fear that it could authorize a repetition of the World War II internment of citizens of Japanese ancestry; Congress meant to preclude another episode like the one described in *Korematsu v. United States,* 323 U.S. 214 (1944). . . .

. . . To appreciate what is most significant, one must only recall that the internments of the 1940's were accomplished by Executive action. Although an Act of Congress ratified and confirmed an Executive order authorizing the military to exclude individuals from defined areas and to accommodate those it might remove, see *Ex parte Endo,* 323 U.S. 283, 285-288 (1944), the statute said nothing whatever about the detention of those who might be removed; internment camps were creatures of the Executive, and confinement in them rested on assertion of Executive authority. When, therefore, Congress repealed the 1950 Act and adopted §4001(a) for the purpose of avoiding another *Korematsu,* it intended to preclude reliance on vague congressional authority (for example, providing "accommodations" for those subject to removal) as authority for detention or imprisonment at the discretion of the Executive (maintaining detention camps of American citizens, for example). In requiring that any Executive detention be "pursuant to an Act of Congress," then, Congress necessarily meant to require a congressional enactment that clearly authorized detention or imprisonment.

Second, when Congress passed §4001(a) it was acting in light of an interpretive regime that subjected enactments limiting liberty in wartime to the requirement of a clear statement and it presumably intended §4001(a) to be read accordingly. This need for clarity was unmistakably expressed in *Ex parte Endo, supra,* decided the same day as *Korematsu.* . . . The petitioner was held entitled to habeas relief in an opinion that set out this principle for scrutinizing wartime statutes in derogation of customary

Chapter 13. Consequence Management: When the Worst Happens

liberty:

> "In interpreting a wartime measure we must assume that [its] purpose was to allow for the greatest possible accommodation between . . . liberties and the exigencies of war. We must assume, when asked to find implied powers in a grant of legislative or executive authority, that the law makers intended to place no greater restraint on the citizen than was clearly and unmistakably indicated by the language they used." *Id.*, at 300.

Congress's understanding of the need for clear authority before citizens are kept detained is itself therefore clear, and §4001(a) must be read to have teeth in its demand for congressional authorization.

Finally, even if history had spared us the cautionary example of the internments in World War II, even if there had been no *Korematsu*, and *Endo* had set out no principle of statutory interpretation, there would be a compelling reason to read §4001(a) to demand manifest authority to detain before detention is authorized. The defining character of American constitutional government is its constant tension between security and liberty, serving both by partial helpings of each. In a government of separated powers, deciding finally on what is a reasonable degree of guaranteed liberty whether in peace or war (or some condition in between) is not well entrusted to the Executive Branch of Government, whose particular responsibility is to maintain security. For reasons of inescapable human nature, the branch of the Government asked to counter a serious threat is not the branch on which to rest the Nation's entire reliance in striking the balance between the will to win and the cost in liberty on the way to victory; the responsibility for security will naturally amplify the claim that security legitimately raises. A reasonable balance is more likely to be reached on the judgment of a different branch, just as Madison said in remarking that "the constant aim is to divide and arrange the several offices in such a manner as that each may be a check on the other – that the private interest of every individual may be a sentinel over the public rights." The Federalist No. 51, p. 349 (J. Cooke ed.1961). Hence the need for an assessment by Congress before citizens are subject to lockup, and likewise the need for a clearly expressed congressional resolution of the competing claims.

III

Under this principle of reading §4001(a) robustly to require a clear statement of authorization to detain, none of the Government's arguments suffices to justify Hamdi's detention.

A

First, there is the argument that §4001(a) does not even apply to wartime military detentions, a position resting on the placement of §4001(a) in Title 18 of the United States Code, the gathering of federal criminal law. . . . [The] legislative history indicates that Congress was aware that §4001(a) would limit the Executive's power to detain citizens in wartime to protect national security, and it is fair to say that the prohibition was thus intended to extend not only to the exercise of power to vindicate the interests underlying domestic criminal law, but to statutorily unauthorized detention by the Executive for reasons of security in wartime, just as Hamdi claims.[2]

B

Next, there is the Government's claim, accepted by the Court, that the terms of the Force Resolution are adequate to authorize detention of an enemy combatant under the circumstances described,[3] a claim the Government fails to support sufficiently to satisfy §4001(a) as read to require a clear statement of authority to detain. Since the Force Resolution was adopted one week after the attacks of September 11, 2001, it naturally speaks with some generality, but its focus is clear, and that is on the use of military power. It is fairly read to authorize the use of armies and weapons, whether against other armies or individual terrorists. But, like the statute discussed in *Endo,* it never so much as uses the word detention, and there is no reason to think Congress might have perceived any need to augment

---

2. Nor is it possible to distinguish between civilian and military authority to detain based on the congressional object of avoiding another *Korematsu v. United States,* 323 U.S. 214 (1944). Although a civilian agency authorized by Executive order ran the detention camps, the relocation and detention of American citizens was ordered by the military under authority of the President as Commander in Chief. See *Ex parte Endo,* 323 U.S. 283, 285-288 (1944). The World War II internment was thus ordered under the same Presidential power invoked here and the intent to bar a repetition goes to the action taken and authority claimed here.

3. . . . [T]he Government argues that a required Act of Congress is to be found in a statutory authorization to spend money appropriated for the care of prisoners of war and of other, similar prisoners, 10 U.S.C. §956(5). It is enough to say that this statute is an authorization to spend money if there are prisoners, not an authorization to imprison anyone to provide the occasion for spending money.

Chapter 13. Consequence Management: When the Worst Happens

Executive power to deal with dangerous citizens within the United States, given the well-stocked statutory arsenal of defined criminal offenses covering the gamut of actions that a citizen sympathetic to terrorists might commit. See, *e.g.*, 18 U.S.C. §2339A (material support for various terrorist acts); §2339B (material support to a foreign terrorist organization); §2332a (use of a weapon of mass destruction, including conspiracy and attempt); §2332b(a)(1) (acts of terrorism "transcending national boundaries," including threats, conspiracy, and attempt); 18 U.S.C.A. §2339C (financing of certain terrorist acts); see also 18 U.S.C. §3142(e) (pretrial detention).

C

Even so, there is one argument for treating the Force Resolution as sufficiently clear to authorize detention of a citizen consistently with §4001(a). Assuming the argument to be sound, however, the Government is in no position to claim its advantage.

Because the Force Resolution authorizes the use of military force in acts of war by the United States, the argument goes, it is reasonably clear that the military and its Commander in Chief are authorized to deal with enemy belligerents according to the treaties and customs known collectively as the laws of war. Accordingly, the United States may detain captured enemies, and *Ex parte Quirin,* 317 U.S. 1 (1942), may perhaps be claimed for the proposition that the American citizenship of such a captive does not as such limit the Government's power to deal with him under the usages of war. Thus, the Government here repeatedly argues that Hamdi's detention amounts to nothing more than customary detention of a captive taken on the field of battle: if the usages of war are fairly authorized by the Force Resolution, Hamdi's detention is authorized for purposes of §4001(a). . . .

By holding him incommunicado, however, the Government obviously has not been treating him as a prisoner of war, and in fact the Government claims that no Taliban detainee is entitled to prisoner of war status. This treatment appears to be a violation of the Geneva Convention provision that even in cases of doubt, captives are entitled to be treated as prisoners of war "until such time as their status has been determined by a competent tribunal." Art. 5, 6 U.S.T., at 3324. . . .

Whether, or to what degree, the Government is in fact violating the Geneva Convention and is thus acting outside the customary usages of war are not matters I can resolve at this point. What I can say, though, is that the Government has not made out its claim that in detaining Hamdi in the manner described, it is acting in accord with the laws of war authorized to be applied against citizens by the Force Resolution. I conclude accordingly that the Government has failed to support the position that the Force

Resolution authorizes the described detention of Hamdi for purposes of §4001(a).

It is worth adding a further reason for requiring the Government to bear the burden of clearly justifying its claim to be exercising recognized war powers before declaring §4001(a) satisfied. Thirty-eight days after adopting the Force Resolution, Congress passed the statute entitled Uniting and Strengthening America by Providing Appropriate Tools Required to Intercept and Obstruct Terrorism Act of 2001 (USA PATRIOT ACT), 115 Stat. 272; that Act authorized the detention of alien terrorists for no more than seven days in the absence of criminal charges or deportation proceedings, 8 U.S.C. §1226a(a)(5) (2000 ed., Supp. I). It is very difficult to believe that the same Congress that carefully circumscribed Executive power over alien terrorists on home soil would not have meant to require the Government to justify clearly its detention of an American citizen held on home soil incommunicado.

D

Since the Government has given no reason either to deflect the application of §4001(a) or to hold it to be satisfied, I need to go no further; the Government hints of a constitutional challenge to the statute, but it presents none here. I will, however, stray across the line between statutory and constitutional territory just far enough to note the weakness of the Government's mixed claim of inherent, extrastatutory authority under a combination of Article II of the Constitution and the usages of war. It is in fact in this connection that the Government developed its argument that the exercise of war powers justifies the detention, and what I have just said about its inadequacy applies here as well. Beyond that, it is instructive to recall Justice Jackson's observation that the President is not Commander in Chief of the country, only of the military. *Youngstown Sheet & Tube Co. v. Sawyer*, 343 U.S. 579, 643-644 (1952) (concurring opinion); see also *id.*, at 637-638 (Presidential authority is "at its lowest ebb" where the President acts contrary to congressional will).

There may be room for one qualification to Justice Jackson's statement, however: in a moment of genuine emergency, when the Government must act with no time for deliberation, the Executive may be able to detain a citizen if there is reason to fear he is an imminent threat to the safety of the Nation and its people (though I doubt there is any want of statutory authority). This case, however, does not present that question, because an emergency power of necessity must at least be limited by the emergency; Hamdi has been locked up for over two years. Cf. *Ex parte Milligan*, 4 Wall. 2, 127 (1866) (martial law justified only by "actual and present" necessity as in a genuine invasion that closes civilian courts). . . .

IV . . .

It should go without saying that in joining with the plurality to produce a judgment, I do not adopt the plurality's resolution of constitutional issues that I would not reach. It is not that I could disagree with the plurality's determinations (given the plurality's view of the Force Resolution) that someone in Hamdi's position is entitled at a minimum to notice of the Government's claimed factual basis for holding him, and to a fair chance to rebut it before a neutral decision maker; nor, of course, could I disagree with the plurality's affirmation of Hamdi's right to counsel. On the other hand, I do not mean to imply agreement that the Government could claim an evidentiary presumption casting the burden of rebuttal on Hamdi, or that an opportunity to litigate before a military tribunal might obviate or truncate enquiry by a court on habeas.

Subject to these qualifications, I join with the plurality in a judgment of the Court vacating the Fourth Circuit's judgment and remanding the case.

Justice SCALIA with whom Justice STEVENS joins, dissenting. . . . Where the Government accuses a citizen of waging war against it, our constitutional tradition has been to prosecute him in federal court for treason or some other crime. Where the exigencies of war prevent that, the Constitution's Suspension Clause, Art. I, §9, cl. 2, allows Congress to relax the usual protections temporarily. Absent suspension, however, the Executive's assertion of military exigency has not been thought sufficient to permit detention without charge. No one contends that the congressional Authorization for Use of Military Force, on which the Government relies to justify its actions here, is an implementation of the Suspension Clause. Accordingly, I would reverse the decision below.

I

The very core of liberty secured by our Anglo-Saxon system of separated powers has been freedom from indefinite imprisonment at the will of the Executive. Blackstone stated this principle clearly:

> "Of great importance to the public is the preservation of this personal liberty: for if once it were left in the power of any, the highest, magistrate to imprison arbitrarily whomever he or his officers thought proper . . . there would soon be an end of all other rights and immunities. . . . To bereave a man of life, or by violence to confiscate his estate, without accusa-

tion or trial, would be so gross and notorious an act of despotism, as must at once convey the alarm of tyranny throughout the whole kingdom. But confinement of the person, by secretly hurrying him to gaol, where his sufferings are unknown or forgotten; is a less public, a less striking, and therefore a more dangerous engine of arbitrary government. . . .

"To make imprisonment lawful, it must either be, by process from the courts of judicature, or by warrant from some legal officer, having authority to commit to prison; which warrant must be in writing, under the hand and seal of the magistrate, and express the causes of the commitment, in order to be examined into (if necessary) upon a *habeas corpus*. If there be no cause expressed, the gaoler is not bound to detain the prisoner. For the law judges in this respect, . . . that it is unreasonable to send a prisoner, and not to signify withal the crimes alleged against him." 1 W. Blackstone, Commentaries on the Laws of England 132-133 (1765) (hereinafter Blackstone).

These words were well known to the Founders. Hamilton quoted from this very passage in The Federalist No. 84, p. 444 (G. Carey & J. McClellan eds. 2001). The two ideas central to Blackstone's understanding — due process as the right secured, and habeas corpus as the instrument by which due process could be insisted upon by a citizen illegally imprisoned — found expression in the Constitution's Due Process and Suspension Clauses. See Amdt. 5; Art. I, §9, cl. 2.

The gist of the Due Process Clause, as understood at the founding and since, was to force the Government to follow those common-law procedures traditionally deemed necessary before depriving a person of life, liberty, or property. When a citizen was deprived of liberty because of alleged criminal conduct, those procedures typically required committal by a magistrate followed by indictment and trial. . . .

II

The allegations here, of course, are no ordinary accusations of criminal activity. Yaser Esam Hamdi has been imprisoned because the Government believes he participated in the waging of war against the United States. The relevant question, then, is whether there is a different, special procedure for imprisonment of a citizen accused of wrongdoing *by aiding the enemy in wartime.*

A

Justice O'CONNOR writing for a plurality of this Court, asserts that captured enemy combatants (other than those suspected of war crimes) have traditionally been detained until the cessation of hostilities and then released. That is probably an accurate description of wartime practice with respect to enemy *aliens.* The tradition with respect to American citizens, however, has been quite different. Citizens aiding the enemy have been treated as traitors subject to the criminal process. . . .

The modern treason statute is 18 U.S.C. §2381; it basically tracks the language of the constitutional provision. Other provisions of Title 18 criminalize various acts of warmaking and adherence to the enemy. The only citizen other than Hamdi known to be imprisoned in connection with military hostilities in Afghanistan against the United States *was* subjected to criminal process and convicted upon a guilty plea. See *United States v. Lindh,* 212 F. Supp. 2d 541 (E.D. Va. 2002) (denying motions for dismissal).

B

There are times when military exigency renders resort to the traditional criminal process impracticable. English law accommodated such exigencies by allowing legislative suspension of the writ of habeas corpus for brief periods. Blackstone explained:

> "And yet sometimes, when the state is in real danger, even this [*i.e.,* executive detention] may be a necessary measure. But the happiness of our constitution is, that it is not left to the executive power to determine when the danger of the state is so great, as to render this measure expedient. For the parliament only, or legislative power, whenever it sees proper, can authorize the crown, by suspending the *habeas corpus* act for a short and limited time, to imprison suspected persons without giving any reason for so doing . . . . In like manner this experiment ought only to be tried in case of extreme emergency; and in these the nation parts with it[s] liberty for a while, in order to preserve it for ever." 1 Blackstone 132. . . .

Our Federal Constitution contains a provision explicitly permitting suspension, but limiting the situations in which it may be invoked: "The privilege of the Writ of Habeas Corpus shall not be suspended, unless when in Cases of Rebellion or Invasion the public Safety may require it." Art. I, §9, cl. 2. Although this provision does not state that suspension must be effected by, or authorized by, a legislative act, it has been so understood, consistent with English practice and the Clause's placement in Article I.

The Suspension Clause was by design a safety valve, the Constitution's only "express provision for exercise of extraordinary authority because of a crisis," *Youngstown Sheet & Tube Co. v. Sawyer,* 343 U.S. 579, 650 (1952) (Jackson, J., concurring). . . .

III . . .

Writings from the founding generation also suggest that, without exception, the only constitutional alternatives are to charge the crime or suspend the writ. In 1788, Thomas Jefferson wrote to James Madison questioning the need for a Suspension Clause in cases of rebellion in the proposed Constitution. His letter illustrates the constraints under which the Founders understood themselves to operate:

> "Why suspend the Hab. corp. in insurrections and rebellions? The parties who may be arrested may be charged instantly with a well defined crime. Of course the judge will remand them. If the publick safety requires that the government should have a man imprisoned on less probable testimony in those than in other emergencies; let him be taken and tried, retaken and retried, while the necessity continues, only giving him redress against the government for damages." 13 Papers of Thomas Jefferson 442 (July 31, 1788) (J. Boyd ed.1956). . . .

Further evidence comes from this Court's decision in *Ex parte Milligan,* [71 U.S. (4 Wall.) 2] (1866). There, the Court issued the writ to an American citizen who had been tried by military commission for offenses that included conspiring to overthrow the Government, seize munitions, and liberate prisoners of war. The Court rejected in no uncertain terms the Government's assertion that military jurisdiction was proper "under the 'laws and usages of war,'" *id.,* at 121:

> "It can serve no useful purpose to inquire what those laws and usages are, whence they originated, where found, and on whom they operate; they can never be applied to citizens in states which have upheld the authority of the government, and where the courts are open and their process unobstructed." *Ibid.*[1]

---

1. As I shall discuss presently, the Court purported to limit this language in *Ex parte Quirin,* 317 U.S. 1, 45 (1942). Whatever *Quirin's* effect on *Milligan's* precedential value, however, it cannot undermine its value as an indicator of original meaning. Cf. *Reid v. Covert,* 354 U.S. 1, 30 (1957) (plurality opinion) (*Milligan* remains "one of the great landmarks in this Court's history").

Milligan is not exactly this case, of course, since the petitioner was threatened with death, not merely imprisonment. But the reasoning and conclusion of *Milligan* logically cover the present case. The Government justifies imprisonment of Hamdi on principles of the law of war and admits that, absent the war, it would have no such authority. But if the law of war cannot be applied to citizens where courts are open, then Hamdi's imprisonment without criminal trial is no less unlawful than Milligan's trial by military tribunal.

Milligan responded to the argument, repeated by the Government in this case, that it is dangerous to leave suspected traitors at large in time of war:

> "If it was dangerous, in the distracted condition of affairs, to leave Milligan unrestrained of his liberty, because he 'conspired against the government, afforded aid and comfort to rebels, and incited the people to insurrection,' the *law* said arrest him, confine him closely, render him powerless to do further mischief; and then present his case to the grand jury of the district, with proofs of his guilt, and, if indicted, try him according to the course of the common law. If this had been done, the Constitution would have been vindicated, the law of 1863 enforced, and the securities for personal liberty preserved and defended." *Id.,* at 122.

Thus, criminal process was viewed as the primary means – and the only means absent congressional action suspending the writ – not only to punish traitors, but to incapacitate them.

The proposition that the Executive lacks indefinite wartime detention authority over citizens is consistent with the Founders' general mistrust of military power permanently at the Executive's disposal. In the Founders' view, the "blessings of liberty" were threatened by "those military establishments which must gradually poison its very fountain." The Federalist No. 45, p. 238 (J. Madison). No fewer than 10 issues of the Federalist were devoted in whole or part to allaying fears of oppression from the proposed Constitution's authorization of standing armies in peacetime. Many safeguards in the Constitution reflect these concerns. Congress's authority "[t]o raise and support Armies" was hedged with the proviso that "no Appropriation of Money to that Use shall be for a longer Term than two Years." U.S. Const., Art. 1, §8, cl. 12. Except for the actual command of military forces, all authorization for their maintenance and all explicit authorization for their use is placed in the control of Congress under Article I, rather than the President under Article II. . . . A view of the Constitution that gives the Executive authority to use military force rather than the force of law against citizens on American soil flies in the face of the mistrust that engendered these provisions.

IV

The Government argues that our more recent jurisprudence ratifies its indefinite imprisonment of a citizen within the territorial jurisdiction of federal courts. It places primary reliance upon *Ex parte Quirin,* 317 U.S. 1 (1942), a World War II case upholding the trial by military commission of eight German saboteurs, one of whom, Hans Haupt, was a U.S. citizen. The case was not this Court's finest hour. The Court upheld the commission and denied relief in a brief *per curiam* issued the day after oral argument concluded; a week later the Government carried out the commission's death sentence upon six saboteurs, including Haupt. The Court eventually explained its reasoning in a written opinion issued several months later.

Only three paragraphs of the Court's lengthy opinion dealt with the particular circumstances of Haupt's case. The Government argued that Haupt, like the other petitioners, could be tried by military commission under the laws of war. In agreeing with that contention, *Quirin* purported to interpret the language of *Milligan* quoted above (the law of war "can never be applied to citizens in states which have upheld the authority of the government, and where the courts are open and their process unobstructed") in the following manner:

> "Elsewhere in its opinion . . . the Court was at pains to point out that Milligan, a citizen twenty years resident in Indiana, who had never been a resident of any of the states in rebellion, was not an enemy belligerent either entitled to the status of a prisoner of war or subject to the penalties imposed upon unlawful belligerents. We construe the Court's statement as to the inapplicability of the law of war to Milligan's case as having particular reference to the facts before it. From them the Court concluded that Milligan, not being a part of or associated with the armed forces of the enemy, was a non-belligerent, not subject to the law of war . . . ." 317 U.S., at 45.

In my view this seeks to revise *Milligan* rather than describe it. *Milligan* had involved (among other issues) two separate questions: (1) whether the military trial of Milligan was justified by the laws of war, and if not (2) whether the President's suspension of the writ, pursuant to congressional authorization, prevented the issuance of habeas corpus. The Court's categorical language about the law of war's inapplicability to citizens where the courts are open (with no exception mentioned for citizens who were prisoners of war) was contained in its discussion of the first point. See 4 Wall., at 121. The factors pertaining to whether Milligan could reasonably be considered a belligerent and prisoner of war, while mentioned earlier in the opinion, were made relevant and brought to bear in the Court's later discussion of whether Milligan came within the statutory provision that effectively made an exception to Congress's authorized suspension of the writ for (as the Court described it) "all parties, not prisoners of war, resident in their respective jurisdictions, . . . who were citizens of states in which the administration of the laws in the Federal tribunals was unimpaired," *id.* at 116. *Milligan* thus understood was in accord with the traditional law of habeas corpus I have described: Though treason often occurred in wartime, there was, absent provision for special treatment in a congressional suspension of the writ, no exception to the right to trial by jury for citizens who could be called "belligerents" or "prisoners of war."

But even if *Quirin* gave a correct description of *Milligan,* or made an irrevocable revision of it, *Quirin* would still not justify denial of the writ here. In *Quirin* it was uncontested that the petitioners were members of enemy forces. They were "*admitted* enemy invaders," 317 U.S., at 47 (emphasis added), and it was "undisputed" that they had landed in the United States in service of German forces, *id.,* at 20. The specific holding of the Court was only that, "upon the *conceded* facts," the petitioners were "plainly within [the] boundaries" of military jurisdiction, *id.,* at 46 (emphasis added). But where those jurisdictional facts are *not* conceded – where the petitioner insists that he is *not* a belligerent – *Quirin* left the pre-existing law in place: Absent suspension of the writ, a citizen held where the courts are open is entitled either to criminal trial or to a judicial decree requiring his release.

V

It follows from what I have said that Hamdi is entitled to a habeas decree requiring his release unless (1) criminal proceedings are promptly brought, or (2) Congress has suspended the writ of habeas corpus. A suspension of the writ could, of course, lay down conditions for continued detention, similar to those that today's opinion prescribes under the Due Process Clause. But there is a world of difference between the people's representatives' determining the need for that suspension (and prescribing the conditions for it), and this Court's doing so.

The plurality finds justification for Hamdi's imprisonment in the Authorization for Use of Military Force, 115 Stat. 224. . . . This is not remotely a congressional suspension of the writ, and no one claims that it is. Contrary to the plurality's view, I do not think this statute even authorizes detention of a citizen with the clarity necessary to satisfy the interpretive canon that statutes should be construed so as to avoid grave constitutional concerns; with the clarity necessary to comport with cases such as *Ex parte Endo,* 323 U.S. 283, 300 (1944), and *Duncan v. Kahanamoku,* 327 U.S. 304, 314-316, 324 (1946); or with the clarity necessary to overcome the statutory prescription that "[n]o citizen shall be imprisoned or otherwise detained by the United States except pursuant to an Act of Congress." 18 U.S.C. §4001(a).[5] But even if it did, I would not permit it to overcome Hamdi's entitlement to habeas corpus relief. The Suspension Clause of the Constitution, which carefully circumscribes the conditions under which the writ can be withheld, would be a sham if it could be evaded by congressional prescription of requirements *other than the common-law requirement of committal for criminal prosecution* that render the writ, though available, unavailing. If the Suspension Clause does not guarantee the citizen that he will either be tried or released, unless the conditions for suspending the writ exist and the grave action of suspending the writ has been taken; if it merely guarantees the citizen that he will not be detained unless Congress by ordinary legislation says he can be detained; it guarantees him very little indeed.

It should not be thought, however, that the plurality's evisceration of the Suspension Clause augments, principally, the power of Congress. As usual, the major effect of its constitutional improvisation is to increase the power of the Court. Having found a congressional authorization for detention of citizens where none clearly exists; and having discarded the categorical procedural protection of the Suspension Clause; the plurality then proceeds, under the guise of the Due Process Clause, to prescribe what procedural protections *it* thinks appropriate. . . .

. . . This judicial remediation of executive default is unheard of. The role of habeas corpus is to determine the legality of executive detention, not to supply the omitted process necessary to make it legal. . . .

There is a certain harmony of approach in the plurality's making up for Congress's failure to invoke the Suspension Clause and its making up for the Executive's failure to apply what it says are needed procedures – an

---

5. The plurality rejects any need for "specific language of detention" on the ground that detention of alleged combatants is a "fundamental incident of waging war." Its authorities do not support that holding in the context of the present case. Some are irrelevant because they do not address the detention of *American citizens.* The plurality's assertion that detentions of citizen and alien combatants are equally authorized has no basis in law or common sense. Citizens and noncitizens, even if equally dangerous, are not similarly situated. See, *e.g., Milligan, supra; Johnson v. Eisentrager,* 339 U.S. 763 (1950); Rev. Stat. 4067, 50 U.S.C. §21 (Alien Enemy Act). That captivity may be consistent with the principles of international law does not prove that it also complies with the restrictions that the Constitution places on the American Government's treatment of its own citizens. . . .

approach that reflects what might be called a Mr. Fix-it Mentality. The plurality seems to view it as its mission to Make Everything Come Out Right, rather than merely to decree the consequences, as far as individual rights are concerned, of the other two branches' actions and omissions. Has the Legislature failed to suspend the writ in the current dire emergency? Well, we will remedy that failure by prescribing the reasonable conditions that a suspension should have included. And has the Executive failed to live up to those reasonable conditions? Well, we will ourselves make that failure good, so that this dangerous fellow (if he is dangerous) need not be set free. The problem with this approach is not only that it steps out of the courts' modest and limited role in a democratic society; but that by repeatedly doing what it thinks the political branches ought to do it encourages their lassitude and saps the vitality of government by the people.

VI

Several limitations give my views in this matter a relatively narrow compass. They apply only to citizens, accused of being enemy combatants, who are detained within the territorial jurisdiction of a federal court. This is not likely to be a numerous group; currently we know of only two, Hamdi and Jose Padilla. Where the citizen is captured outside and held outside the United States, the constitutional requirements may be different. Cf. *Johnson v. Eisentrager,* 339 U.S. 763, 769-771 (1950); *Reid v. Covert,* 354 U.S. 1, 74-75 (1957) (Harlan, J., concurring in result); *Rasul v. Bush,* [2004 WL 1432134 (U.S. June 28, 2004)] (Scalia, J., dissenting). Moreover, even within the United States, the accused citizen-enemy combatant may lawfully be detained once prosecution is in progress or in contemplation. . . .

. . . If the situation demands it, the Executive can ask Congress to authorize suspension of the writ — which can be made subject to whatever conditions Congress deems appropriate, including even the procedural novelties invented by the plurality today. To be sure, suspension is limited by the Constitution to cases of rebellion or invasion. But whether the attacks of September 11, 2001, constitute an "invasion," and whether those attacks still justify suspension several years later, are questions for Congress rather than this Court. . . .

Justice THOMAS, dissenting. The Executive Branch, acting pursuant to the powers vested in the President by the Constitution and with explicit congressional approval, has determined that Yaser Hamdi is an enemy combatant and should be detained. This detention falls squarely within the Federal Government's war powers, and we lack the expertise and capacity to second-guess that decision. As such, petitioners' habeas challenge should fail, and there is no reason to remand the case. . . . I do not think that the Federal Government's war powers can be balanced away by this Court. Arguably, Congress could provide for additional procedural protections, but until it does, we have no right to insist upon them. But even if I were to agree with the general approach the plurality takes, I could not accept the particulars. The plurality utterly fails to account for the Government's compelling interests and for our own institutional inability to weigh competing concerns correctly. I respectfully dissent. . . .

Order by President George W. Bush to the Secretary of Defense

June 9, 2002
Appendix A, Padilla v. Rumsfeld, 352 F.2d 695 (2d Cir. 2003)

TO THE SECRETARY OF DEFENSE:

Based on the information available to me from all sources,

REDACTED

In accordance with the Constitution and consistent with the laws of the United States, including the Authorization for Use of Military Force Joint Resolution (Public Law 107-40);

I, GEORGE W. BUSH, as President of the United States and Commander in Chief of the U.S. armed forces, hereby DETERMINE for the United States of America that:

(1) Jose Padilla, who is under the control of the Department of Justice and who is a U.S. citizen, is, and at the time he entered the United States in May 2002 was, an enemy combatant;
(2) Mr. Padilla is closely associated with al Qaeda, an international terrorist organization with which the United States is at war;
(3) Mr. Padilla engaged in conduct that constituted hostile and war-like acts, including conduct in preparation for acts of international terrorism that had the aim to cause injury to or adverse effects on the United States;
(4) Mr. Padilla possesses intelligence, including intelligence about personnel and activities of al Qaeda, that, if communicated to the U.S.,

would aid U.S. efforts to prevent attacks by al Qaeda on the United States or its armed forces, other governmental personnel, or citizens;

(5) Mr. Padilla represents a continuing, present and grave danger to the national security of the United States, and detention of Mr. Padilla is necessary to prevent him from aiding al Qaeda in its efforts to attack the United States or its armed forces, other governmental personnel, or citizens;

(6) it is in the interest of the United States that the Secretary of Defense detain Mr. Padilla as an enemy combatant; and

(7) it is REDACTED consistent with U.S. law and the laws of war for the Secretary of Defense to detain Mr. Padilla as an enemy combatant.

Accordingly, you are directed to receive Mr. Padilla from the Department of Justice and to detain him as an enemy combatant.

Padilla v. Rumsfeld
United States Court of Appeals, Second Circuit, 2003
352 F.3d 695, *rev'd and remanded for lack of jurisdiction,* 542 U.S. 426

POOLER and B.D. PARKER, JR., Circuit Judges. . . .

[José Padilla was arrested on May 8, 2002, in Chicago on a material witness warrant. On June 9, 2002, President Bush ordered Padilla's military detention as an enemy combatant based on facts subsequently submitted to the court in an affidavit by a Department of Defense official, Michael Mobbs. The Mobbs declaration alleged as hearsay that Padilla was "closely associated with al Qaeda," that in 2001 he had approached Osama Bin Laden with a proposal to steal radioactive material in the United States for building and detonating a "radiological dispersal device," also known as "a dirty bomb," and that he had traveled to the United States to that end. It also alleged that confidential sources did not believe that Padilla was actually a member of al Quaeda, but that he had received training from the organization and had been sent by it to the United States to conduct reconnaissance and/or conduct attacks on its behalf.

Padilla petitioned for a writ of habeas corpus. The district court held that the government was authorized to detain him if it could adduce "some evidence" that he was an enemy combatant, but that Padilla was entitled to an evidentiary hearing on that question and to have access to counsel in order to participate meaningfully in such hearing. This appeal by Padilla followed.]

I. Preliminary Issues

[The court held that Secretary Rumsfeld was a proper respondent for the habeas petition and that he had sufficient contact with the Southern District of New York to give it personal jurisdiction over him.] . . . .

II. Power to Detain

A. Introduction

The District Court concluded, and the government maintains here, that the indefinite detention of Padilla was a proper exercise of the President's power as Commander-in-Chief. The power to detain Padilla is said to derive from the President's authority, settled by Ex parte Quirin, 317 U.S. 1 (1942) [casebook at p. 893], to detain enemy combatants in wartime – authority that is argued to encompass the detention of United States citizens seized on United States soil. This power, the court below reasoned, may be exercised without a formal declaration of war by Congress and "even if Congressional authorization were deemed necessary, the Joint Resolution, passed by both houses of Congress [Pub. L. No. 107-40, 115 Stat. 224 (2001), set out at casebook p. 262] . . . engages the President's full powers as Commander in Chief." Specifically, the District Court found that the Joint Resolution acted as express congressional authorization under 18 U.S.C. §4001(a), which prohibits the detention of American citizens absent such authorization. In addition, the government claims that 10 U.S.C. §956(5), a statute that allows the military to use authorized funds for certain detentions, grants authority to detain American citizens.

These alternative arguments require us to examine the scope of the President's inherent power and, if this is found insufficient to support Padilla's detention, whether Congress has authorized such detentions of American citizens. We reemphasize, however, that our review is limited to the case of an American citizen arrested in the United States, not on a foreign battlefield or while actively engaged in armed conflict against the United States. As the Fourth Circuit recently – and accurately – noted in Hamdi v. Rumsfeld, "[t]o compare this battlefield capture [of Hamdi] to the domestic arrest in Padilla v. Rumsfeld is to compare apples and oranges." 337 F.3d 335, 344 (4th Cir. 2003) (*"Hamdi IV"*) (Wilkinson, J., concurring).

B. The Youngstown Analysis

Our review of the exercise by the President of war powers in the domestic sphere starts with the template the Supreme Court constructed in *Youngstown* [Sheet & Tube Co. v. Sawyer], 343 U.S. [579 (1952),] at 635-38 (Jackson, J., concurring) [casebook at pp. 38-39]. . . .

Here, we find that the President lacks inherent constitutional authority as Commander-in-Chief to detain American citizens on American soil outside a zone of combat. We also conclude that the Non-Detention Act serves as an explicit congressional "denial of authority" within the meaning of *Youngstown*, thus placing us in *Youngstown*'s third category. Finally, we conclude that because the Joint Resolution does not authorize the President to detain American citizens seized on American soil, we remain within *Youngstown*'s third category.

i. Inherent Power

The government contends that the President has the inherent authority to detain those who take up arms against this country pursuant to Article II, Section 2, of the Constitution, which makes him the Commander-in-Chief, and that the exercise of these powers domestically does not require congressional authorization. Moreover, the argument goes, it was settled by *Quirin* that the military's authority to detain enemy combatants in wartime applies to American citizens as well as to foreign combatants. There the Supreme Court explained that "universal agreement and practice" under "the law of war" holds that "[l]awful combatants are subject to capture and detention as prisoners of war by opposing military forces" and "[u]nlawful combatants are likewise subject to capture and detention, but in addition they are subject to trial and punishment by military tribunals for acts which render their belligerency unlawful." 317 U.S. at 30-31. Finally, since the designation of an enemy combatant bears the closest imaginable connection to the President's constitutional responsibilities, principles of judicial deference are said by the government to assume heightened significance.

We agree that great deference is afforded the President's exercise of his authority as Commander-in-Chief. We also agree that whether a state of armed conflict exists against an enemy to which the laws of war apply is a political question for the President, not the courts. *See Johnson v. Eisentrager*, 339 U.S. 763, 789 (1950) ("Certainly it is not the function of the Judiciary to entertain private litigation – even by a citizen – which challenges the legality, the wisdom, or the propriety of the Commander-in-Chief in sending our armed forces abroad or to any particular region."); *The Prize Cases*, 67 U.S. (2 Black) 635, 670 (1862). Because we have no authority to do so, we do not address the government's underlying assumption that an undeclared war exists between al Qaeda and the United States. . . .

However, it is a different proposition entirely to argue that the President even in times of grave national security threats or war, whether declared or undeclared, can lay claim to any of the powers, express or implied, allocated to Congress. The deference due to the Executive in its exercise of its war powers therefore only starts the inquiry; it does not end it. Where the exercise of Commander-in-Chief powers, no matter how well intentioned, is challenged on the ground that it collides with the powers assigned by the Constitution to Congress, a fundamental role exists for the courts. *See Marbury v. Madison*, 5 U.S. (1 Cranch) 137 (1803). To be sure, when Congress and the President act together in the conduct of war, "it is not for any court to sit in review of the wisdom of their action or substitute its judgment for theirs." *Hirabayashi v. United States*, 320 U.S. 81, 93 (1943). But when the Executive acts, even in the conduct of war, in the face of apparent congressional disapproval, challenges to his authority must be examined and resolved by the Article III courts. *See Youngstown*, 343 U.S. at 638 (Jackson, J., concurring).

These separation of powers concerns are heightened when the Commander-in-Chief's powers are exercised in the domestic sphere. The Supreme Court has long counseled that while the Executive should be "indulge[d] the widest latitude of interpretation to sustain his exclusive function to command the instruments of national force, at least when turned against the outside world for the security of our society," he enjoys "no such indulgence" when "it is turned inward." *Youngstown*, 343 U.S. at 645 (Jackson, J., concurring). This is because "the federal power over external affairs [is] in origin and essential character different from that over internal affairs," and "congressional legislation which is to be made effective through negotiation and inquiry within the international field must often accord to the President a degree of discretion and freedom from statutory restriction which would not be admissible were domestic affairs alone involved." [United States v.] *Curtiss-Wright* [Export Corp.], 299 U.S. 304 (1936),] at 319, 320. But, "Congress, not the Executive, should control utilization of the war power as an instrument of domestic policy." *Youngstown*, 343 U.S. at 644 (Jackson, J., concurring). Thus, we do not concern ourselves with the Executive's inherent wartime power . . . to detain enemy combatants on the battlefield. Rather, we are called on to decide whether the Constitution gives the President the power to detain an American citizen seized in this country until the war with al Qaeda ends. . . .

The Constitution entrusts the ability to define and punish offenses against the law of nations to the Congress, not the Executive. U.S. Const. art. I, §8, cl. 10. Padilla contends that the June 9 Order mandating his detention as an "enemy combatant" was not the result of congressional action defining the category of "enemy combatant." He also argues that there has been no other legislative articulation of what constitutes an "enemy combatant," what circumstances trigger the designation, or when it ends. As in *Youngstown*, Padilla maintains that "[t]he President's order does not direct that a congressional policy be executed in a manner prescribed by Congress – it directs that a presidential policy be executed in a manner prescribed by the President." *Youngstown*, 343 U.S. at 588.

The Constitution envisions grave national emergencies and contemplates significant domestic abridgements of individual liberties during such times. Here, the Executive lays claim to the inherent emergency powers necessary to effect such abridgements, but we agree with Padilla that the Constitution lodges these powers with Congress, not the President. *See Youngstown*, 343 U.S. at 649-50 (Jackson, J., concurring).

First, the Constitution explicitly provides for the suspension of the writ of habeas corpus "when in Cases of Rebellion or Invasion the public Safety may require it." U.S. Const. art. I, §9, cl. 2. This power, however, lies only with Congress. *Ex parte Bollman*, 8 U.S. (4 Cranch) 75, 101 (1807). Further, determinations about the scope of the writ are for Congress. *Lonchar v. Thomas*, 517 U.S. 314, 323 (1996).

Moreover, the Third Amendment's prohibition on the quartering of troops during times of peace reflected the Framers' deep-seated beliefs about the sanctity of the home and the need to prevent military intrusion into civilian life. At the same time they understood that in times of war – of serious national crisis – military concerns prevailed and such intrusions could occur. But significantly, decisions as to the nature and scope of these intrusions were to be made "in a manner to be prescribed by law." U.S. Const. amend. III. The only valid process for making "law" under the Constitution is, of course, via bicameral passage and presentment to the President, whose possible veto is subject to congressional override, provided in Article I, Section 7. *See* [Immigration & Naturalization Service v.] *Chadha*, 462 U.S. [919 (1983),] at 946-51.

The Constitution's explicit grant of the powers authorized in the Offenses Clause, the Suspension Clause, and the Third Amendment, to Congress is a powerful indication that, absent express congressional authorization, the President's Commander-in-Chief powers do not support Padilla's confinement. The level of specificity with which the Framers allocated these domestic powers to Congress and the lack of any even near-equivalent grant of authority in Article II's catalogue of executive powers compels us to decline to read any such power into the

Commander-in-Chief Clause. In sum, while Congress – otherwise acting consistently with the Constitution – may have the power to authorize the detention of United States citizens under the circumstances of Padilla's case, the President, acting alone, does not.

. . . The government contends that *Quirin* conclusively establishes the President's authority to exercise military jurisdiction over American citizens.

We do not agree that *Quirin* controls. First, and most importantly, the *Quirin* Court's decision to uphold military jurisdiction rested on express congressional authorization of the use of military tribunals to try combatants who violated the laws of war. Specifically, the Court found it "unnecessary for present purposes to determine to what extent the President as Commander in Chief has constitutional power to create military commissions without the support of Congressional legislation." [317 U.S.] at 29. Accordingly, *Quirin* does not speak to whether, or to what degree, the President may impose military authority upon United States citizens domestically without clear congressional authorization. We are reluctant to read into *Quirin* a principle that the *Quirin* Court itself specifically declined to promulgate.

Moreover, there are other important distinctions between *Quirin* and this case. First, when *Quirin* was decided in 1942, section 4001(a) had not yet been enacted. The *Quirin* Court consequently had no occasion to consider the effects of legislation prohibiting the detention of American citizens absent statutory authorization. As a result, *Quirin* was premised on the conclusion – indisputable at the time – that the Executive's domestic projection of military authority had been authorized by Congress. Because the *Quirin* Court did not have to contend with section 4001(a), its usefulness is now sharply attenuated.

Second, the petitioners in *Quirin* admitted that they were soldiers in the armed forces of a nation against whom the United States had formally declared war. The *Quirin* Court deemed it unnecessary to consider the dispositive issue here – the boundaries of the Executive's military jurisdiction – because the *Quirin* petitioners "upon the conceded facts, were plainly within those boundaries." Padilla makes no such concession. To the contrary, he, from all indications, intends to dispute his designation as an enemy combatant, and points to the fact that the civilian accomplices of the *Quirin* saboteurs – citizens who advanced the sabotage plots but who were not members of the German armed forces – were charged and tried as civilians in civilian courts, not as enemy combatants subject to military authority. *Haupt v. United States*, 330 U.S. 631; *Cramer v. United States*, 325 U.S. 1 (1945).

In *Ex parte Milligan*, 71 U.S. (4 Wall.) (1866) [casebook at p. 889], the

Chapter 13. Consequence Management: When the Worst Happens

government unsuccessfully attempted to prosecute before a military tribunal a citizen who, never having belonged to or received training from the Confederate Army, "conspired with bad men" to engage in acts of war and sabotage against the United States. 71 U.S. at 131. Although *Quirin* distinguished *Milligan* on the ground that "Milligan, not being a part of or associated with the armed forces of the enemy, was a non-belligerent, [and] not subject to the law of war," 317 U.S. at 45, a more germane distinction rests on the different statutes involved in *Milligan* and *Quirin*. During the Civil War, Congress authorized the President to suspend the writ of habeas corpus. *Milligan*, 71 U.S. at 4. However, it also limited his power to detain indefinitely "citizens of States in which the administration of the laws had continued unimpaired in the Federal courts, who were then held, or might thereafter be held, as prisoners of the United States, under the authority of the President, otherwise than as prisoners of war." *Id.* at 5.

This limitation was embodied in a requirement that the Executive furnish a list of such prisoners to the district and circuit courts and, upon request by a prisoner, release him if the grand jury failed to return an indictment. *Id.* The grand jury sitting when Milligan was detained failed to indict him. The Court concluded that because "Congress could grant no . . . power" to authorize the military trial of a civilian in a state where the courts remained open and functioning, and because Congress had not attempted to do so, Milligan could not be tried by a military tribunal. Thus, both *Quirin* and *Milligan* are consistent with the principle that primary authority for imposing military jurisdiction upon American citizens lies with Congress. Even though *Quirin* limits to a certain extent the broader holding in *Milligan* that citizens cannot be subjected to military jurisdiction while the courts continue to function, *Quirin* and *Milligan* both teach that – at a minimum – an Act of Congress is required to expand military jurisdiction. . . .

The dissent also relies on *The Prize Cases*, which, like *Milligan*, arose out of the Civil War, to conclude that the President has the inherent constitutional authority to protect the nation when met with belligerency and to determine what degree of responsive force is necessary. Neither the facts nor the holding of *The Prize Cases* supports such a broad construction.

First, *The Prize Cases* dealt with the capture of enemy property – not the detention of persons. The Court had no occasion to address the strong constitutional arguments against deprivations of personal liberty, or the question of whether the President could infringe upon individual liberty rights through the exercise of his wartime powers outside a zone of combat.

Second, the dissent would have us read *The Prize Cases* as resolving any question as to whether the President may detain Padilla as an enemy combatant without congressional authorization. The Court did not, however, rest its decision upholding the exercise of the President's military authority solely on his constitutional powers without regard to congressional authorization. Rather, it noted that the President's authority to "call[ ] out the militia and use the military and naval forces of the United States in case of invasion by foreign nations, and to suppress insurrection against the government" stemmed from "the Acts of Congress of February 28th, 1795, and 3d of March, 1807." In any event, Congress's subsequent ratification of the President's wartime orders mooted any questions of presidential authority. *Id.* at 670. Finally, the Court in *The Prize Cases* was not faced with the Non-Detention Act specifically limiting the President's authority to detain American citizens absent express congressional authorization.

Based on the text of the Constitution and the cases interpreting it, we reject the government's contention that the President has inherent constitutional power to detain Padilla under the circumstances presented here. Therefore, under *Youngstown*, we must now consider whether Congress has authorized such detentions.

ii. Congressional Acts

a. The Non-Detention Act

As we have seen, the Non-Detention Act provides: "No citizen shall be imprisoned or otherwise detained by the United States except pursuant to an Act of Congress." 18 U.S.C. §4001(a). The District Court held that this language "encompasses all detentions of United States citizens." . . .

We read the plain language of section 4001(a) to prohibit all detentions of citizens – a conclusion first reached by the Supreme Court. *Howe v. Smith*, 452 U.S. 473, 479 n. 3 (1981) (characterizing the Non-Detention Act as "proscribing detention *of any kind* by the United States" (emphasis in original)). Not only has the government not made an extraordinary showing of contrary intentions, but the legislative history of the Non-Detention Act is fully consistent with our reading of it. . . .

. . . Moreover, this interpretation poses no risk of unconstitutionally abridging the President's war powers because, as we have also discussed above, the President, acting alone, possesses no inherent constitutional authority to detain American citizens seized within the United States, away from a zone of combat, as enemy combatants. . . .

b. Specific Statutory Authorization

Since we conclude that the Non-Detention Act applies to military detentions such as Padilla's, we would need to find specific statutory authorization in order to uphold the detention. The government claims that both the Joint Resolution, which authorized the use of force against the perpetrators of the September 11 terrorist attacks, and 10 U.S.C. §956(5), passed in 1984, which provides funding for military detentions, authorize the detention of enemy combatants. . . .

First, we note that the Joint Resolution contains no language authorizing detention. . . .

The plain language of the Joint Resolution contains nothing authorizing the detention of American citizens captured on United States soil, much less the express authorization required by section 4001(a) and the "clear," "unmistakable" language required by *Endo* [323 U.S. 283 (1944)]. While it may be possible to infer a power of detention from the Joint Resolution in the battlefield context where detentions are necessary to carry out the war, there is no reason to suspect from the language of the Joint Resolution that Congress believed it would be authorizing the detention of an American citizen already held in a federal correctional institution and not "arrayed against our troops" in the field of battle.

Further, the Joint Resolution expressly provides that it is "intended to constitute specific statutory authorization within the meaning of . . . the War Powers Resolution." Joint Resolution §2(b); 50 U.S.C. §1541 et seq. The War Powers Resolution requires the President to cease military operations within 60 days unless Congress has declared war or specifically authorized the use of the armed forces. 50 U.S.C. §1544(b). It is unlikely – indeed, inconceivable – that Congress would expressly provide in the Joint Resolution an authorization required by the War Powers Resolution but, at the same time, leave unstated and to inference something so significant and unprecedented as authorization to detain American citizens under the Non-Detention Act.

Next, the Secretary argues that Padilla's detention is authorized by 10 U.S.C. §956(5), which allows the use of appropriated funds for "expenses incident to the maintenance, pay, and allowances of prisoners of war, other persons in the custody of the Army, Navy or Air Force whose status is determined by the Secretary concerned to be similar to prisoners of war, and persons detained in the custody of [the Armed Services] pursuant to Presidential proclamation." 10 U.S.C. §956(5). . . .

. . . Section 965(5) authorizes nothing beyond the expenditure of money. *Endo* unquestionably teaches that an authorization of funds devoid of language "clearly" and "unmistakably" authorizing the detention of American citizens seized here is insufficient. See 323 U.S. at 303 n. 24 (acknowledging that Congress may ratify past actions of the Executive through appropriations acts but refusing to find in the appropriations acts at issue an intent to allow the Executive to detain a citizen indefinitely because the appropriation did not allocate funds "earmarked" for that type of detention). In light of *Endo*, the Non-Detention Act's requirement that Congress specifically authorize detentions of American citizens, and the guarantees of the Fourth and Fifth Amendments to the Constitution, we decline to impose on section 956(5) loads it cannot bear.

CONCLUSION

In sum, we hold that (1) Donna Newman, Esq., may pursue habeas relief on behalf of Jose Padilla; (2) Secretary of Defense Rumsfeld is a proper respondent to the habeas petition and the District Court had personal jurisdiction over him; (3) in the domestic context, the President's inherent constitutional powers do not extend to the detention as an enemy combatant of an American citizen seized within the country away from a zone of combat; (4) the Non-Detention Act prohibits the detention of American citizens without express congressional authorization; and (5) neither the Joint Resolution nor 10 U.S.C. §956(5) constitutes such authorization under section 4001(a). . . . And if the President believes this authority to be insufficient, he can ask Congress – which has shown its responsiveness – to authorize additional powers. To reiterate, we remand to the District Court with instructions to issue a writ of habeas corpus directing the Secretary of Defense to release Padilla from military custody within 30 days. The government can transfer Padilla to appropriate civilian authorities who can bring criminal charges against him. Also, if appropriate, Padilla can be held as a material witness in connection with grand jury proceedings. In any case, Padilla will be entitled to the constitutional protections extended to other citizens.

WESLEY, Circuit Judge, concurring in part, dissenting in part. . . . *The Prize Cases* demonstrates that congressional authorization is not necessary for the Executive to exercise his constitutional authority to prosecute armed conflicts when, as on September 11, 2001, the United States is attacked.

My colleagues appear to agree with this premise but conclude that somehow the President has no power to deal with acts of a belligerent on U.S. soil "away from a zone of combat" absent express authorization from Congress. That would seem to imply that the President does have some war power authority to detain a citizen on U.S. soil if the "zone of combat" was the United States. The majority does not tell us who has the authority to define a "zone of combat" or to designate a geopolitical area as such. Given the majority's view that "the Constitution lodges . . . [inherent national

Chapter 13. Consequence Management: When the Worst Happens

emergency powers][1] with Congress, not the President," it would seem that the majority views this responsibility as also the singular province of Congress. That produces a startling conclusion. The President would be without any authority to detain a terrorist citizen dangerously close to a violent or destructive act on U.S. soil unless Congress declared the area in question a zone of combat or authorized the detention. Curiously, even Mr. Padilla's attorney conceded that the President could detain a terrorist without Congressional authorization if the attack were imminent.

But the scope of the President's inherent war powers under Article II does not end the matter, for in my view Congress clearly and specifically authorized the President's actions here. . .

. . . The Joint Resolution is quite clear in its mandate. Congress noted that the 9-11 attacks made it "both necessary and appropriate that the United States exercise its rights to self-defense and to protect United States citizens both at home and abroad." *Id.* It seems clear to me that Congress understood that in light of the 9-11 attacks the United States had become a zone of combat.

Organizations such as al Qaeda are comprised of people. Congress could not have intended to limit the President's authority to only those al Qaeda operatives who actually planned or took part in 9-11. That would do little to prevent future attacks. The fate of the participants is well known. And surely Congress did not intend to limit the President to pursue only those individuals who were al Qaeda operatives as of September 11, 2001. But even if it did, Mr. Padilla fits within the class for by September of 2001, he had already been under the tutelage and direction of senior al Qaeda officers for three years. Clearly, Congress recognized that al Qaeda and those who now do its bidding are a continuing threat to the United States. Thus, the Joint Resolution does have teeth and whether Padilla is a loaded weapon of al Qaeda would appear to be a fact question. A hearing, as ordered by the district court, would have settled the matter.

The majority suggests, however, that the President's actions are ultra vires because "the Joint Resolution does not specifically authorize detentions." To read the resolution as the majority suggests would create a false distinction between the use of force and the ability to detain. It would be curious if the resolution authorized the interdiction and shooting of an al Qaeda operative but not the detention of that person. . . .

. . . And if, as the majority asserts, §4001(a) is an impenetrable barrier to the President detaining a U.S. citizen who is alleged to have ties to the belligerent and who is part of a plan for belligerency on U.S. soil, then

---

[1. Inserted material in the original.]

§4001(a), in my view, is unconstitutional. . . .

NOTES AND QUESTIONS

1. *Hamdi After Remand.* After the Supreme Court remanded, Hamdi and the government negotiated an agreement for his release to his family in Saudi Arabia. The government asserted that he no longer had any intelligence value and posed no threat. Under the agreement, Hamdi gave up his U.S. citizenship, renounced terrorism, waived any civil claim he had for his detention, and accepted certain travel restrictions, including a ten-year ban on returning to the United States. *See* Motion to Stay Proceedings, Hamdi v. Rumsfeld, No. 2:02CV439 (E.D. Va. Sept. 24, 2004), *available at http://notablecases.vaed.uscourts.gov/2:02-cv-00439/docs/70223/0.pdf*; *"Enemy Combatant" Hamdi Returned to Saudi Arabia After Three Years Detention*, NewsMax.com Wires, Oct. 11, 2004, *available at http://www.newsmax.com/archives/articles/2004/10/11/121754.shtml.*

2. *Padilla Continued.* The Supreme Court reversed and remanded *Padilla* because it found that Padilla's habeas petition had to be filed in the district in which his immediate custodian (a naval commander, not Secretary Rumsfeld) could be found — South Carolina — and that the district court for the Southern District of New York therefore lacked jurisdiction. Rumsfeld v. Padilla, 542 U.S. 426 (2004). The remand order directed entry of an order of dismissal "without prejudice."

Padilla promptly refiled his petition in the District Court for South Carolina. That court granted summary judgment for Padilla, following much the same reasoning as the Second Circuit. It concluded:

> Simply stated, this is a law enforcement matter, not a military matter. . . . At the time that [Padilla] was arrested pursuant to the material arrest warrant, any alleged terrorist plans that he harbored were thwarted. From then on, he was available to be questioned — and was indeed questioned — just like any citizen accused of criminal conduct. . . .
>
> . . . There can be no debate that this country's laws amply provide for the investigation, detention and prosecution of citizen and non-citizen terrorists alike. . . .
>
> The difference between invocation of the criminal process and the power claimed by the President here, however, is one of accountability. The criminal justice system requires that defendants and witnesses be afforded access to counsel, imposes judicial supervision over government action, and places congressionally imposed limits on incarceration.

Padilla v. Hanft, No. 2:04-2221-26AJ, 2005 WL 465691, at *12, 13 (D.S.C.

Feb. 28, 2005). The government has appealed the decision and at this writing is still holding Padilla in a military brig in South Carolina.

3. *Necessity for Military Detention.* Detention under the law of war is based on military necessity, a premise echoed in the AUMF authorization for use of *"necessary* and appropriate force." *See* §2(a), at casebook p. 262 (emphasis supplied). What is that necessity?

"The purpose of detention is to prevent captured individuals from returning to the field of battle and taking up arms once again," Justice O'Connor noted in *Hamdi.* They are detained, in other words, both to enable U.S. forces to carry out their mission and to provide force protection. In addition, such individuals are detained to obtain operational intelligence by interrogation. Indeed, their detention may itself be instrumental to a successful interrogation, because the isolation of the detainees and their consequent dependence on their captors may induce them to talk. Bringing such persons before a judge, or even holding some kind of hearing, may be impracticable in the midst of hostilities, while the bullets are flying. Moving detainees back from the front lines may not be a cure, because it is often still impractical to withdraw troops from the front to give testimony or to preserve evidence during the fighting. *Cf. Odah* v. United States, 321 F.3d 1134, 1150 (D.C. Cir. 2003) (Randolph, J., concurring) (asserting with respect to military detainees at Camp X-Ray in Guantánamo Naval Base, Cuba, that "[t]he historical meaning of 'in the field' was not restricted to the field of battle. It applied as well to 'organized camps stationed in remote places where civil courts did not exist.'"), *rev'd and remanded by* Rasul v. Bush, 542 U.S. 466 (2004) (p. 252 in this Supplement).

How, if at all, did the Court in *Hamdi* respond to such arguments of military necessity? How should it have responded? If these arguments apply to Hamdi, do they also apply to Padilla? What if the government believes Padilla to be an imminent threat to set off a dirty bomb but lacks probable cause to arrest him? What response does Justice Souter suggest for such an emergency?

How would you reframe the authority for military detention to confine it strictly to situations of military necessity? Does the length of the detention affect the necessity, and, if so, how would you reflect this consideration in your specification of detention authority?

4. *The Greater Includes the Lesser?* In both *Hamdi* and *Padilla* the courts assume that Supreme Court precedents concerning trial by military commission, especially *Quirin,* are apposite to the legality of military detention. *Quirin* did say that both lawful and unlawful combatants "are subject to capture and *detention,*" and that unlawful combatants are

additionally subject to military trial and punishment (casebook p. 895 (emphasis supplied)). This the lower court in *Padilla* understood to reflect the Supreme Court's belief that "detention alone . . . [is] certainly the lesser of the consequences an unlawful combatant could face." Padilla v. Bush, 233 F. Supp. 2d 564, 595 (S.D.N.Y. 2002), *rev'd*, 352 F.3d 685 (2d Cir. 2003), *rev'd and remanded*, 542 U.S. 426 (2004).

But is that always true? The unlawful combatant who is tried at least will see a resolution of his status. *See Rasul*, p. 258 in this Supplement (Kennedy, J., concurring in judgment) (distinguishing *Eisentrager*, involving aliens being detained after having been convicted by military commission, from *Rasul*, involving aliens "being held indefinitely, and without benefit of any legal proceeding to determine their status"). What about the combatant who is detained by the military without trial or even charges indefinitely, or until the political branches determine that the war is over? If detention is not the "lesser" consequence for such a combatant, is case law establishing the legality of a military *trial* really apposite to the legality of *detention*?

5. *Section 4001(a)*. A plurality in *Hamdi* assumes, but does not decide, that §4001(a) applies to military detentions and then finds it satisfied by the AUMF. In light of its history (*see* casebook p. 735, Note 6 and p. 183 in this Supplement) and the Court of Appeals decision in *Padilla*, do you think §4001(a) applies to military detentions? If it does, and the AUMF is invoked as a statutory exception within the contemplation of §4001(a), should we apply the clear statement requirement to the AUMF as Justices Souter and Ginsburg insist in *Hamdi*, and the court in *Padilla* held? What rebuttal to a clear statement claim could you pose based on analogy to the Posse Comitatus Act and War Powers Resolution? *Compare* 18 U.S.C. §4001(a) *with* 18 U.S.C. §1385 (Posse Comitatus Act) (reproduced at casebook p. 766) and the War Powers Resolution §8(a) (casebook p. 306).

On the other hand, even without insisting on a clear statement, does a natural reading of AUMF embrace uses of force (and, by implication, military detention) *within* the United States, or just in Afghanistan? *See* Stephen I. Vladeck, Comment, *A Small Problem of Precedent: 18 U.S.C. §4001(a) and the Detention of U.S. Citizen "Enemy Combatants,"* 112 Yale L.J. 961, 967 (2003) (arguing that AUMF fails to satisfy §4001(a)).

6. *"Plenary" Military Authority*. In *Hamdi*, the government argued that the executive has plenary authority under Article II to detain enemy combatants, presumably a "war power" of the Commander in Chief. Though the plurality did not reach this claim, it agrees that the capture and military detention of combatants are "'important incident[s] of war,"

Chapter 13. Consequence Management: When the Worst Happens   249

quoting *Quirin,* and Justice Thomas dissents on the ground that Hamdi's "detention falls squarely within the Federal Government's war powers" vested in the executive branch. The assertion of war power presents several thorny questions.

First, if the war power presupposes a war, is a state of war as the Supreme Court defined that term in *The Prize Cases* (casebook p. 73) sufficient, or must the war be expressly authorized by Congress? Was a war authorized by the AUMF (casebook p. 262)? If so, what is its scope, both geographical and temporal? Does the AUMF trigger all the war powers of the President, or just some? Note, for example, that a use-of-force authorization would apparently not trigger the Alien Enemy Act (p. 204 in this Supplement). Does the AUMF override the Alien Enemy Act? If not, does this mean that the President has war power under the AUMF to detain U.S. citizen combatants but not aliens in the United States?

Second, how should we define "enemy combatants" subject to military detention under the law of war? How does the *Hamdi* Court define them? Recall the differences in the status of Milligan and of Quirin. Is Hamdi more like Milligan or like Quirin? What about Padilla? What definition of "enemy combatant" would you construct from *Milligan, Quirin,* and *Hamdi*? Or are we looking in the wrong place? If war is authorized by declaration or use-of-force statute, should we not look to the authorization for a definition of the enemy?

Suppose Congress had not authorized the use of force against terrorist organizations like al Qaeda, but the President had gone ahead anyway on the theory of repelling attack. Would military detention of combatants in that war be authorized? How are they defined? What about persons detained as terrorists generally in an undeclared "war on terrorism"?

7. *Determining Combatant Status of U.S. Citizens.* The plurality in *Hamdi* decided what procedures were required for determining his status by conducting a due process balancing. To test your understanding of where they came out, consider the alternatives.

First, why was combatant status not an issue in *Quirin*? All are agreed that the answer is that the German saboteurs admitted their status. If there is no factual dispute, then even a due process balancing presumably does not require any procedure to decide that status. Why did the Court reject the government's argument that Hamdi's status was undisputed?

If the detainee's combatant status *is* disputed and he is entitled to petition for a writ of habeas corpus, then the habeas statute, 28 U.S.C. §2241, itself suggests some evidentiary proceeding. Can you see why from the Court's account of the statute?

But what evidence and what kind of proceeding? The government suggested that "some evidence" would suffice, a conclusion reached by the district court in *Padilla* as well. The government therefore argued that the court's role on habeas was only to decide whether the evidence stated in the Mobbs declaration was sufficient standing alone. Is that consistent with the habeas statute? Or with due process?

The Court rejected the "some evidence" standard partly on the grounds "it primarily has been employed by courts in examining an administrative record developed after an adversarial proceeding . . . ." But the government has asserted that it has developed an administrative record after an elaborate internal process for determining combatant status of U.S. citizens that incorporated information developed by the Department of Defense, the Central Intelligence Agency, and the Department of Justice, written assessments by the same agencies, a formal legal opinion by the Office of Legal Counsel, recommendations by the Attorney General and the Secretary of Defense, and a final recommendation to and briefing for the President by the White House Counsel.[2] If such procedures were actually used to designate Hamdi and Padilla enemy combatants and to generate the factual predicate for their military detention, why is not the "some evidence" standard sufficient?

Finally, consider the procedures that the plurality found were required by a due process balancing. Are these sufficient to reduce the risk of inaccuracy in light of the interests at stake? What more would Justices Souter and Ginsburg require, if they found that Congress had authorized military detention? What would you find necessary if you performed the balancing?

In light of the foregoing, are Justices Scalia and Stevens right – is this a job for Congress? If so, what procedures would you recommend that Congress require?

8. *The Right to Assistance of Counsel.* Is any proceeding for determining Hamdi's or Padilla's status fair without his input? Can he give that input without a lawyer? Many have argued that the right to assistance of counsel is the most important right of a person detained or prosecuted by the government because it is essential to effectively asserting every other right.

---

2. Alberto R. Gonzales, Counsel to the President, Remarks at the American Bar Assn. Standing Comm. on Law and Natl. Sec. at 11 (Feb. 24, 2004) (transcript *available at http://www.fas.org/irp/news/2004/02/Gonzales.pdf*) (asserting also, however, that neither these procedures nor any other specific procedures were required by law, but that they were adopted instead simply by administrative grace).

The government responded to such concerns that "[t]he rights the Constitution affords persons in the criminal justice system simply do not apply in the context of detention of enemy combatants." Letter from Daniel J. Bryant (Assistant Attorney General, U.S. Dept. of Justice) to Carl Levin (Chairman of the Senate Committee on Armed Services) (Nov. 26, 2002), at 4. But doesn't this beg the question whether a detainee *is* an "enemy combatant"? Even if military detention and trial operate in some legal universe parallel to the Constitution, does it follow that the President alone is gatekeeper to that universe? If the court has some gatekeeping function as well, how can it fulfill that function without help from the detainee and his counsel?

Consider the following recommendations from the American Bar Association Task Force on Treatment of Enemy Combatants:

> RESOLVED, That the American Bar Association urges that U.S. citizens and residents who are detained within the United States based on their designation as "enemy combatants" be afforded the opportunity for meaningful judicial review of their status, under a standard according such deference to the designation as the review court determines to be appropriate to accommodate the needs of the detainee and the requirements of national security; and
>
> FURTHER RESOLVED, That the American Bar Association urges that U.S. citizens and residents who are detained within the United States based on their designations as "enemy combatants" not be denied access to counsel in connection with the opportunity for such review, subject to appropriate conditions as may be set by the court to accommodate the needs of the detainee and the requirements of national security . . . .

American Bar Association, Task Force on Treatment of Enemy Combatants, *Report to the House of Delegates* (2003).

Even before *Hamdi*, the government tried to moot this issue on the eve of oral argument by giving both Hamdi and Padilla limited access to counsel. If you were counsel to Hamdi, would you have wanted to meet with him before oral argument in his case? Why might you prefer that such an opportunity come after argument?

As the plurality in *Hamdi* observed, by the time of the argument

> Hamdi has been appointed counsel, with whom he has met for consultation purposes on several occasions, and with whom he is now being granted unmonitored meetings. He unquestionably has the right to access to counsel in connection with proceedings on remand. No further consideration of this issue is necessary at this stage of the case. [This Supplement at p. 219 *supra*.]

Did the plurality decide that access to counsel is part of the procedure owed Hamdi by due process? How would you decide that question?

5. Detention of Alien Enemy Combatants After 9/11

Military Order of November 13, 2001 Detention, Treatment, and Trial of Certain Non-Citizens in the War Against Terrorism

[This order is set forth at casebook p. 897.]

Rasul v. Bush
United States Supreme Court, 2004
542 U.S. 466

Justice STEVENS delivered the opinion of the Court. These two cases present the narrow but important question whether United States courts lack jurisdiction to consider challenges to the legality of the detention of foreign nationals captured abroad in connection with hostilities and incarcerated at the Guantanamo Bay Naval Base, Cuba.

I . . .

. . . Acting pursuant to [statutory] authorization [casebook p. 262], the President sent U.S. Armed Forces into Afghanistan [in late 2001] to wage a military campaign against al Qaeda and the Taliban regime that had supported it.

Petitioners in these cases are 2 Australian citizens and 12 Kuwaiti citizens who were captured abroad during hostilities between the United States and the Taliban. Since early 2002, the U.S. military has held them – along with, according to the Government's estimate, approximately 640 other non-Americans captured abroad – at the Naval Base at Guantanamo Bay. The United States occupies the Base, which comprises 45 square miles of land and water along the southeast coast of Cuba, pursuant to a 1903 Lease Agreement executed with the newly independent Republic of Cuba in the aftermath of the Spanish-American War. Under the Agreement, "the United States recognizes the continuance of the ultimate sovereignty of the Republic of Cuba over the [leased areas]," while "the Republic of

Chapter 13. Consequence Management: When the Worst Happens 253

Cuba consents that during the period of the occupation by the United States . . . the United States shall exercise complete jurisdiction and control over and within said areas."[2] In 1934, the parties entered into a treaty providing that, absent an agreement to modify or abrogate the lease, the lease would remain in effect "[s]o long as the United States of America shall not abandon the . . . naval station of Guantanamo."[3]

In 2002, petitioners, through relatives acting as their next friends, filed various actions in the U.S. District Court for the District of Columbia challenging the legality of their detention at the Base. All alleged that none of the petitioners has ever been a combatant against the United States or has ever engaged in any terrorist acts. They also alleged that none has been charged with any wrongdoing, permitted to consult with counsel, or provided access to the courts or any other tribunal.

The two Australians, Mamdouh Habib and David Hicks, each filed a petition for writ of habeas corpus, seeking release from custody, access to counsel, freedom from interrogations, and other relief. Fawzi Khalid Abdullah Fahad Al Odah and the 11 other Kuwaiti detainees filed a complaint seeking to be informed of the charges against them, to be allowed to meet with their families and with counsel, and to have access to the courts or some other impartial tribunal. They claimed that denial of these rights violates the Constitution, international law, and treaties of the United States. . . .

Construing all three actions as petitions for writs of habeas corpus, the District Court dismissed them for want of jurisdiction. The court held, in reliance on our opinion in *Johnson v. Eisentrager*, 339 U.S. 763 (1950), that "aliens detained outside the sovereign territory of the United States [may not] invok[e] a petition for a writ of habeas corpus." 215 F. Supp. 2d 55, 68 (D.D.C. 2002). The Court of Appeals affirmed. . . .

II

Congress has granted federal district courts, "within their respective jurisdictions," the authority to hear applications for habeas corpus by any person who claims to be held "in custody in violation of the Constitution or laws or treaties of the United States." 28 U.S.C. §§2241(a), (c)(3). . . .

---

2. Lease of Lands for Coaling and Naval Stations, Feb. 23, 1903, U.S.-Cuba, Art. III, T.S. No. 418 (hereinafter 1903 Lease Agreement). . . .

3. Treaty Defining Relations with Cuba, May 29, 1934, U. S.-Cuba, Art. III, 48 Stat. 1683, T. S. No. 866 (hereinafter 1934 Treaty).

Habeas corpus is, however, "a writ antecedent to statute, . . . throwing its root deep into the genius of our common law." *Williams v. Kaiser,* 323 U.S. 471, 484, n. 2 (1945) (internal quotation marks omitted). The writ appeared in English law several centuries ago, became "an integral part of our common-law heritage" by the time the Colonies achieved independence, *Preiser v. Rodriguez,* 411 U.S. 475, 485 (1973), and received explicit recognition in the Constitution, which forbids suspension of "[t]he Privilege of the Writ of Habeas Corpus . . . unless when in Cases of Rebellion or Invasion the public Safety may require it," Art. I, §9, cl. 2.

As it has evolved over the past two centuries, the habeas statute clearly has expanded habeas corpus "beyond the limits that obtained during the 17th and 18th centuries." *Swain v. Pressley,* 430 U.S. 372, 380, n. 13 (1977). But "[a]t its historical core, the writ of habeas corpus has served as a means of reviewing the legality of Executive detention, and it is in that context that its protections have been strongest." *INS v. St. Cyr,* 533 U.S. 289, 301 (2001). As Justice Jackson wrote in an opinion respecting the availability of habeas corpus to aliens held in U.S. custody:

> "Executive imprisonment has been considered oppressive and lawless since John, at Runnymede, pledged that no free man should be imprisoned, dispossessed, outlawed, or exiled save by the judgment of his peers or by the law of the land. The judges of England developed the writ of habeas corpus largely to preserve these immunities from executive restraint." *Shaughnessy v. United States ex rel. Mezei,* 345 U.S. 206, 218-219 (1953) (dissenting opinion).

Consistent with the historic purpose of the writ, this Court has recognized the federal courts' power to review applications for habeas relief in a wide variety of cases involving Executive detention, in wartime as well as in times of peace. The Court has, for example, entertained the habeas petitions of an American citizen who plotted an attack on military installations during the Civil War, *Ex parte Milligan,* 4 Wall. 2 (1866), and of admitted enemy aliens convicted of war crimes during a declared war and held in the United States, *Ex parte Quirin,* 317 U.S. 1 (1942), and its insular possessions, *In re Yamashita,* 327 U.S. 1 (1946).

The question now before us is whether the habeas statute confers a right to judicial review of the legality of Executive detention of aliens in a territory over which the United States exercises plenary and exclusive jurisdiction, but not "ultimate sovereignty."

III

Respondents' primary submission is that the answer to the jurisdictional question is controlled by our decision in *Eisentrager*. In that case, we held that a Federal District Court lacked authority to issue a writ of habeas corpus to 21 German citizens who had been captured by U.S. forces in China, tried and convicted of war crimes by an American military commission headquartered in Nanking, and incarcerated in the Landsberg Prison in occupied Germany. . . . [T]his Court summarized the six critical facts in the case:

> "We are here confronted with a decision whose basic premise is that these prisoners are entitled, as a constitutional right, to sue in some court of the United States for a writ of *habeas corpus*. To support that assumption we must hold that a prisoner of our military authorities is constitutionally entitled to the writ, even though he (a) is an enemy alien; (b) has never been or resided in the United States; (c) was captured outside of our territory and there held in military custody as a prisoner of war; (d) was tried and convicted by a Military Commission sitting outside the United States; (e) for offenses against laws of war committed outside the United States; (f) and is at all times imprisoned outside the United States." 39 U.S., at 777.

On this set of facts, the Court concluded, "no right to the writ of *habeas corpus* appears." *Id.,* at 781.

Petitioners in these cases differ from the *Eisentrager* detainees in important respects: They are not nationals of countries at war with the United States, and they deny that they have engaged in or plotted acts of aggression against the United States; they have never been afforded access to any tribunal, much less charged with and convicted of wrongdoing; and for more than two years they have been imprisoned in territory over which the United States exercises exclusive jurisdiction and control.

Not only are petitioners differently situated from the *Eisentrager* detainees, but the Court in *Eisentrager* made quite clear that all six of the facts critical to its disposition were relevant only to the question of the prisoners' *constitutional* entitlement to habeas corpus. *Id.,* at 777. The Court had far less to say on the question of the petitioners' *statutory* entitlement to habeas review. Its only statement on the subject was a passing reference to the absence of statutory authorization: "Nothing in the text of the Constitution extends such a right, nor does anything in our statutes." *Id.,* at 768. . . .

[Here the Court notes that the *Eisentrager* Court relied on an earlier decision, Ahrens v. Clark, 335 U.S. 188 (1948), holding that the habeas statute did not permit a district court to issue the writ for a detainee outside the court's territorial jurisdiction.]

. . . [However,] persons detained outside the territorial jurisdiction of any federal district court no longer need rely on the Constitution as the source of their right to federal habeas review. In *Braden v. 30th Judicial Circuit Court of Ky.*, 410 U.S. 484, 495 (1973), this Court held, contrary to *Ahrens,* that the prisoner's presence within the territorial jurisdiction of the district court is not "an invariable prerequisite" to the exercise of district court jurisdiction under the federal habeas statute. Rather, because "the writ of habeas corpus does not act upon the prisoner who seeks relief, but upon the person who holds him in what is alleged to be unlawful custody," a district court acts "within [its] respective jurisdiction" within the meaning of §2241 as long as "the custodian can be reached by service of process." 410 U.S., at 494-495. . . . *Braden* thus established that *Ahrens* can no longer be viewed as establishing "an inflexible jurisdictional rule," and is strictly relevant only to the question of the appropriate forum, not to whether the claim can be heard at all. 410 U.S., at 499-500.

Because *Braden* overruled the statutory predicate to *Eisentrager*'s holding, *Eisentrager* plainly does not preclude the exercise of §2241 jurisdiction over petitioners' claims.

IV

Putting *Eisentrager* and *Ahrens* to one side, respondents contend that we can discern a limit on §2241 through application of the "longstanding principle of American law" that congressional legislation is presumed not to have extraterritorial application unless such intent is clearly manifested. *EEOC v. Arabian American Oil Co.*, 499 U.S. 244, 248 (1991). Whatever traction the presumption against extraterritoriality might have in other contexts, it certainly has no application to the operation of the habeas statute with respect to persons detained within "the territorial jurisdiction" of the United States. *Foley Bros., Inc. v. Filardo,* 336 U.S. 281, 285 (1949). By the express terms of its agreements with Cuba, the United States exercises "complete jurisdiction and control" over the Guantanamo Bay Naval Base, and may continue to exercise such control permanently if it so chooses. 1903 Lease Agreement, Art. III; 1934 Treaty, Art. III. Respondents themselves concede that the habeas statute would create federal-court jurisdiction over the claims of an American citizen held at the base. Considering that the statute draws no distinction between Americans and aliens held in federal custody, there is little reason to think that Congress intended the geographical coverage of the statute to vary depending on the detainee's citizenship. Aliens held at the base, no less than American

Chapter 13. Consequence Management: When the Worst Happens

citizens, are entitled to invoke the federal courts' authority under §2241.

Application of the habeas statute to persons detained at the base is consistent with the historical reach of the writ of habeas corpus. At common law, courts exercised habeas jurisdiction over the claims of aliens detained within sovereign territory of the realm, as well as the claims of persons detained in the so-called "exempt jurisdictions," where ordinary writs did not run, and all other dominions under the sovereign's control....

In the end, the answer to the question presented is clear. Petitioners contend that they are being held in federal custody in violation of the laws of the United States.[15] No party questions the District Court's jurisdiction over petitioners' custodians. Cf. *Braden,* 410 U.S., at 495. Section 2241, by its terms, requires nothing more. We therefore hold that §2241 confers on the District Court jurisdiction to hear petitioners' habeas corpus challenges to the legality of their detention at the Guantanamo Bay Naval Base.

V

In addition to invoking the District Court's jurisdiction under §2241, the *Al Odah* petitioners' complaint invoked the court's jurisdiction under 28 U.S.C. §1331, the federal question statute, as well as §1350, the Alien Tort Statute. The Court of Appeals, again relying on *Eisentrager,* held that the District Court correctly dismissed the claims founded on §1331 and §1350 for lack of jurisdiction, even to the extent that these claims "deal only with conditions of confinement and do not sound in habeas," because petitioners lack the "privilege of litigation" in U.S. courts. 321 F.3d, at 1144 (internal quotation marks omitted)....

... But ... nothing in *Eisentrager* or in any of our other cases categorically excludes aliens detained in military custody outside the United States from the "'privilege of litigation'" in U.S. courts. 321 F.3d, at 1139. The courts of the United States have traditionally been open to nonresident aliens. And indeed, 28 U.S.C. §1350 explicitly confers the privilege of suing for an actionable "tort... committed in violation of the law of nations or a treaty of the United States" on aliens alone. The fact that petitioners in

---

15. Petitioners' allegations – that, although they have engaged neither in combat nor in acts of terrorism against the United States, they have been held in Executive detention for more than two years in territory subject to the long-term, exclusive jurisdiction and control of the United States, without access to counsel and without being charged with any wrongdoing – unquestionably describe "custody in violation of the Constitution or laws or treaties of the United States." 28 U.S.C. §2241(c)(3).

these cases are being held in military custody is immaterial to the question of the District Court's jurisdiction over their nonhabeas statutory claims.

VI

Whether and what further proceedings may become necessary after respondents make their response to the merits of petitioners' claims are matters that we need not address now. What is presently at stake is only whether the federal courts have jurisdiction to determine the legality of the Executive's potentially indefinite detention of individuals who claim to be wholly innocent of wrongdoing. Answering that question in the affirmative, we reverse the judgment of the Court of Appeals and remand for the District Court to consider in the first instance the merits of petitioners' claims.

It is so ordered.

Justice KENNEDY, concurring in the judgment. The Court is correct, in my view, to conclude that federal courts have jurisdiction to consider challenges to the legality of the detention of foreign nationals held at the Guantanamo Bay Naval Base in Cuba. While I reach the same conclusion, my analysis follows a different course. . . . In my view, the correct course is to follow the framework of *Eisentrager.*

Eisentrager considered the scope of the right to petition for a writ of habeas corpus against the backdrop of the constitutional command of the separation of powers. . . .

. . . Because the prisoners in *Eisentrager* were proven enemy aliens found and detained outside the United States, and because the existence of jurisdiction would have had a clear harmful effect on the Nation's military affairs, the matter was appropriately left to the Executive Branch and there was no jurisdiction for the courts to hear the prisoner's claims.

The decision in *Eisentrager* indicates that there is a realm of political authority over military affairs where the judicial power may not enter. The existence of this realm acknowledges the power of the President as Commander in Chief, and the joint role of the President and the Congress, in the conduct of military affairs. A faithful application of *Eisentrager,* then, requires an initial inquiry into the general circumstances of the detention to determine whether the Court has the authority to entertain the petition and to grant relief after considering all of the facts presented. A necessary corollary of *Eisentrager* is that there are circumstances in which the courts maintain the power and the responsibility to protect persons from

Chapter 13. Consequence Management: When the Worst Happens

unlawful detention even where military affairs are implicated. See also *Ex parte Milligan,* 4 Wall. 2 (1866).

The facts here are distinguishable from those in *Eisentrager* in two critical ways, leading to the conclusion that a federal court may entertain the petitions. First, Guantanamo Bay is in every practical respect a United States territory, and it is one far removed from any hostilities. . . .

The second critical set of facts is that the detainees at Guantanamo Bay are being held indefinitely, and without benefit of any legal proceeding to determine their status. In *Eisentrager,* the prisoners were tried and convicted by a military commission of violating the laws of war and were sentenced to prison terms. Having already been subject to procedures establishing their status, they could not justify "a limited opening of our courts" to show that they were "of friendly personal disposition" and not enemy aliens. 339 U.S., at 778. Indefinite detention without trial or other proceeding presents altogether different considerations. It allows friends and foes alike to remain in detention. It suggests a weaker case of military necessity and much greater alignment with the traditional function of habeas corpus. Perhaps, where detainees are taken from a zone of hostilities, detention without proceedings or trial would be justified by military necessity for a matter of weeks; but as the period of detention stretches from months to years, the case for continued detention to meet military exigencies becomes weaker.

In light of the status of Guantanamo Bay and the indefinite pretrial detention of the detainees, I would hold that federal-court jurisdiction is permitted in these cases. This approach would avoid creating automatic statutory authority to adjudicate the claims of persons located outside the United States, and remains true to the reasoning of *Eisentrager.* For these reasons, I concur in the judgment of the Court.

Justice SCALIA, with whom THE CHIEF JUSTICE and Justice THOMAS join, dissenting. The Court today holds that the habeas statute, 28 U.S.C. §2241, extends to aliens detained by the United States military overseas, outside the sovereign borders of the United States and beyond the territorial jurisdictions of all its courts. This is not only a novel holding; it contradicts a half-century-old precedent on which the military undoubtedly relied, *Johnson v. Eisentrager,* 339 U.S. 763 (1950). The Court's contention that *Eisentrager* was somehow negated by *Braden v. 30th Judicial Circuit Court of Ky.*, 410 U.S. 484 (1973) – a decision that dealt with a different issue and did not so much as mention *Eisentrager* – is implausible in the extreme. This is an irresponsible overturning of settled law in a matter of extreme importance to our forces currently in the field. I would leave it to Congress to change §2241, and dissent from the Court's unprecedented holding.

I . . .

Eisentrager's directly-on-point statutory holding makes it exceedingly difficult for the Court to reach the result it desires today. . . .

The reality is this: Today's opinion, and today's opinion alone, overrules *Eisentrager;* today's opinion, and today's opinion alone, extends the habeas statute, for the first time, to aliens held beyond the sovereign territory of the United States and beyond the territorial jurisdiction of its courts. No reasons are given for this result; no acknowledgment of its consequences made. By spurious reliance on *Braden* the Court evades explaining why *stare decisis* can be disregarded, *and why Eisentrager was wrong.* Normally, we consider the interests of those who have relied on our decisions. Today, the Court springs a trap on the Executive, subjecting Guantanamo Bay to the oversight of the federal courts even though it has never before been thought to be within their jurisdiction – and thus making it a foolish place to have housed alien wartime detainees.

II

In abandoning the venerable statutory line drawn in *Eisentrager,* the Court boldly extends the scope of the habeas statute to the four corners of the earth. Part III of its opinion asserts that *Braden* stands for the proposition that "a district court acts 'within [its] respective jurisdiction' within the meaning of §2241 as long as 'the custodian can be reached by service of process.'" Endorsement of that proposition is repeated in Part IV. ("Section 2241, by its terms, requires nothing more [than the District Court's jurisdiction over petitioners' custodians]").

The consequence of this holding, as applied to aliens outside the country, is breathtaking. It permits an alien captured in a foreign theater of active combat to bring a §2241 petition against the Secretary of Defense. Over the course of the last century, the United States has held millions of alien prisoners abroad. See, *e.g.,* Department of Army, G. Lewis & J. Mewha, History of Prisoner of War Utilization by the United States Army 1776-1945, Pamphlet No. 20-213, p. 244 (1955) (noting that, "[b]y the end of hostilities [in World War II], U.S. forces had in custody approximately two million enemy soldiers"). A great many of these prisoners would no doubt have complained about the circumstances of their capture and the terms of their confinement. The military is currently detaining over 600 prisoners at Guantanamo Bay alone; each detainee undoubtedly has complaints – real or contrived – about those terms and circumstances. The Court's unheralded expansion of federal-court jurisdiction is not even mitigated by a comforting assurance that the legion of ensuing claims will

Chapter 13. Consequence Management: When the Worst Happens

be easily resolved on the merits. To the contrary, the Court says that the "[p]etitioners' allegations . . . unquestionably describe 'custody in violation of the Constitution or laws or treaties of the United States.'" From this point forward, federal courts will entertain petitions from these prisoners, and others like them around the world, challenging actions and events far away, and forcing the courts to oversee one aspect of the Executive's conduct of a foreign war.

Today's carefree Court disregards, without a word of acknowledgment, the dire warning of a more circumspect Court in *Eisentrager:*

> "To grant the writ to these prisoners might mean that our army must transport them across the seas for hearing. This would require allocation for shipping space, guarding personnel, billeting and rations. It might also require transportation for whatever witnesses the prisoners desired to call as well as transportation for those necessary to defend legality of the sentence. The writ, since it is held to be a matter of right, would be equally available to enemies during active hostilities as in the present twilight between war and peace. Such trials would hamper the war effort and bring aid and comfort to the enemy. They would diminish the prestige of our commanders, not only with enemies but with wavering neutrals. It would be difficult to devise more effective fettering of a field commander than to allow the very enemies he is ordered to reduce to submission to call him to account in his own civil courts and divert his efforts and attention from the military offensive abroad to the legal defensive at home. Nor is it unlikely that the result of such enemy litigiousness would be conflict between judicial and military opinion highly comforting to enemies of the United States." 339 U.S., at 778-779.

These results should not be brought about lightly, and certainly not without a textual basis in the statute and on the strength of nothing more than a decision dealing with an Alabama prisoner's ability to seek habeas in Kentucky.

III

Part IV of the Court's opinion, dealing with the status of Guantanamo Bay, is a puzzlement. . . .

The Court gives only two reasons why the presumption against extraterritorial effect does not apply to Guantanamo Bay. First, the Court says (without any further elaboration) that "the United States exercises 'complete jurisdiction and control' over the Guantanamo Bay Naval Base [under the terms of a 1903 lease agreement], and may continue to exercise such control permanently if it so chooses [under the terms of a 1934

Treaty]." But that lease agreement explicitly recognized "the continuance of the ultimate sovereignty of the Republic of Cuba over the [leased areas]," Lease of Lands for Coaling and Naval Stations, Feb. 23, 1903, U.S.-Cuba, Art. III, T.S. No. 418, and the Executive Branch – whose head is "exclusively responsible" for the "conduct of diplomatic and foreign affairs," *Eisentrager, supra*, at 789 – affirms that the lease and treaty do not render Guantanamo Bay the sovereign territory of the United States.

The Court does not explain how "complete jurisdiction and control" without sovereignty causes an enclave to be part of the United States for purposes of its domestic laws. Since "jurisdiction and control" obtained through a lease is no different in effect from "jurisdiction and control" acquired by lawful force of arms, parts of Afghanistan and Iraq should logically be regarded as subject to our domestic laws. Indeed, if "jurisdiction and control" rather than sovereignty were the test, so should the Landsberg Prison in Germany, where the United States held the *Eisentrager* detainees.

The second and last reason the Court gives for the proposition that domestic law applies to Guantanamo Bay is the Solicitor General's concession that there would be habeas jurisdiction over a United States citizen in Guantanamo Bay. "Considering that the statute draws no distinction between Americans and aliens held in federal custody, there is little reason to think that Congress intended the geographical coverage of the statute to vary depending on the detainee's citizenship." But the reason the Solicitor General conceded there would be jurisdiction over a detainee who was a United States citizen had *nothing to do* with the special status of Guantanamo Bay: "Our answer to that question, Justice Souter, is that citizens of the United States, because of their constitutional circumstances, may have greater rights with respect to the scope and reach of the Habeas Statute as the Court has or would interpret it." And *that* position – the position that United States citizens throughout the world may be entitled to habeas corpus rights – is precisely the position that this Court adopted in *Eisentrager*, see 339 U.S., at 769-770, even while holding that aliens abroad *did not have* habeas corpus rights. Quite obviously, the Court's second reason has no force whatever....

In sum, the Court's treatment of Guantanamo Bay, like its treatment of §2241, is a wrenching departure from precedent....

Departure from our rule of *stare decisis* in statutory cases is always extraordinary; it ought to be unthinkable when the departure has a potentially harmful effect upon the Nation's conduct of a war. The Commander in Chief and his subordinates had every reason to expect that the internment of combatants at Guantanamo Bay would not have the consequence of bringing the cumbersome machinery of our domestic courts into military affairs. Congress is in session. If it wished to change federal judges' habeas jurisdiction from what this Court had previously held that to be, it could have done so. And it could have done so by intelligent revision of the statute, instead of by today's clumsy, countertextual reinterpretation that confers upon wartime prisoners greater habeas rights than domestic detainees. The latter must challenge their present physical confinement in the district of their confinement, see *Rumsfeld v. Padilla*, [2004 WL 1432135 (U.S. June 28, 2004), noted at p. 186 in this Supplement], whereas under today's strange holding Guantanamo Bay detainees can petition in any of the 94 federal judicial districts. The fact that extraterritorially located detainees lack the district of detention that the statute requires has been converted from a factor that precludes their ability to bring a petition at all into a factor that frees them to petition wherever they wish – and, as a result, to forum shop. For this Court to create such a monstrous scheme in time of war, and in frustration of our military commanders' reliance upon clearly stated prior law, is judicial adventurism of the worst sort. I dissent.

NOTES AND QUESTIONS

1. *Jurisdiction Over the Custodian.* In Rumsfeld v. Padilla, 542 U.S. 426 (2004) (noted at p. 246 in this Supplement), decided the same day as *Rasul*, the Supreme Court ruled that its earlier decision in *Ahrens* prevented a federal district court in New York from exercising jurisdiction over the habeas petition of a detainee in South Carolina, since the immediate custodian of the petitioner was the warden of the Navy brig in Charleston. Can the holdings on this point in *Padilla* and *Rasul* possibly be reconciled?

2. *Eisentrager's "Dire Warning."* Justice Scalia quotes *Eisentrager's* "dire warning" to suggest that the Court's ruling in *Rasul* will open the floodgates to habeas petitions by enemy aliens after we capture large numbers in battle. Indeed, alien detainees at Guantánamo quickly pressed habcas petitions in U.S. courts. See In re Guantanamo Detainee Cases, 355 F. Supp. 2d 443 (D.D.C. 2005) (excerpted *infra* p. 265) (reporting that thirteen cases involving more than sixty detainees had been filed as of July 2004).

Does the Court have any answer to this concern? *Milligan* and the statute it applied in 1866 supply one answer. What is it? Another is suggested by the first sentence of part VI of the opinion for the Court. What is it? How might the "further proceedings" in the habeas court, or prior proceedings by the military itself, affect the floodgates claim?

In an apparent effort to control the floodgates, the Pentagon announced shortly after the Supreme Court's decision in *Rasul* that it was creating a Combatant Status Review Tribunal (CSRT), to be staffed by military officers, before which detainees could contest their combatant status. Memorandum from the Deputy Secretary of Defense to the Secretary of the Navy, *Order Establishing Combatant Status Review Tribunal,* July 7, 2004, available at http://www.defenselink.mil/news/July2004/d20040707 review.pdf. Detainees would have the assistance of a "personal representative" assigned by the government, but not a lawyer, and they would have to overcome a "rebuttable presumption in favor of the government's evidence." *Id.* ¶¶c. and g.(12). Do you think this program will satisfy Justice Stevens' concerns? Justice Scalia's?

Another way to close the floodgates would be to hear an alien detainee's habeas petition, but then simply deny it on the grounds that the detainees have no cognizable constitutional or international rights. Would such an approach be consistent with *Rasul? See* footnote 15 therein.

3. *The Inner Realm of Military Affairs: What's Left of Eisentrager?* Judge Kennedy joined in the judgment by preserving part of *Eisentrager.* He found that it approved of "a realm of political authority over military affairs where the judicial power may not enter," but also that the Guantánamo Bay detentions, far removed from hostilities and attended by no status-determining procedures, even by the military, fell outside that realm. How does he define that realm? What detainees from the U.S. military operations in Afghanistan would fall within it? More generally, reading the opinion for the Court and Justice Kennedy's opinion together, what is left of *Eisentrager*?

4. *Contextual Influences.* Even if you are unconvinced or unmoved by Justice Scalia's floodgates concern, would you agree that the Court eviscerated *Eisentrager*? Did it not also ignore the executive's reliance interest and thus upset calculated military and intelligence policy (the prisoners at Guantánamo Bay are being detained partly for interrogation)? Speculation about the Court's motives is always treacherous. Yet between the oral arguments in *Rasul,* in which the government assured the Court that the detainees were being treated in compliance with basic international human rights principles, and the Court's decision, the press broke the scandal about abuse of prisoners in Iraq and possible use of torture by the United States in the interrogation of detainees. See pp. 39-94 in this Supplement. Might the reports of mistreatment and of possible violations of international laws against torture have influenced the Court's decision on opening access to Article III courts?

In re Guantanamo Detainee Cases
United States District Court, District of Columbia, 2005
355 F. Supp. 2d 443

JOYCE HENS GREEN, J. These eleven coordinated *habeas* cases were filed by detainees held as "enemy combatants" at the United States Naval Base at Guantanamo Bay, Cuba. . . . [T]he Court concludes that the petitioners have stated valid claims under the Fifth Amendment to the United States Constitution and that the procedures implemented by the government to confirm that the petitioners are "enemy combatants" subject to indefinite detention violate the petitioners' rights to due process of law. The Court also holds that at least some of the petitioners have stated valid claims under the Third Geneva Convention. . . .

[The more than 60 detainees who filed these petitions were taken into custody in Afghanistan, Gambia, Zambia, Bosnia, and Thailand and transferred to military custody at Guantánamo Bay after being deemed "enemy combatants" by military authorities. The court recited the procedural history of the detainees' cases and the Supreme Court decision in Rasul v. Bush, 542 U.S. 466 (2004) (p. 252 *supra*).]

On July 7, 2004, nine days after the issuance of the *Rasul* decision, Deputy Secretary of Defense Paul Wolfowitz issued an Order creating a military tribunal called the Combatant Status Review Tribunal (hereinafter "CSRT") to review the status of each detainee at Guantanamo Bay as an "enemy combatant." It appears that this is the first formal document to officially define the term "enemy combatant" as used by the respondents. That definition is as follows:

> [T]he term "enemy combatant" shall mean an individual who was part of or supporting Taliban or al Qaeda forces, or associated forces that are engaged in hostilities against the United States or its coalition partners. This includes any person who has committed a belligerent act or has directly supported hostilities in aid of enemy armed forces.

. . . The Order sets forth procedures by which detainees can contest this status before a panel of three commissioned military officers.

. . . [D]etainees for the first time have the right to hear the factual bases for their detention, at least to the extent that those facts do not involve information deemed classified by the administration. Detainees also have the right to testify why they contend they should not be considered "enemy combatants" and may present additional evidence they believe might exculpate them, at least to the extent the tribunal finds such evidence relevant and "reasonably available." The detainees do not have a right to counsel in the proceedings, although each is assigned a military officer who serves as a "Personal Representative" to assist the detainee in understanding the process and presenting his case. Formal rules of evidence do not apply, and there is a presumption in favor of the government's conclusion that a detainee is in fact an "enemy combatant." Although the tribunal is free to consider classified evidence supporting a contention that an individual is an "enemy combatant," that individual is not entitled to have access to or know the details of that classified evidence.

The record of the CSRT proceedings, including the tribunal's decision regarding "enemy combatant" status, is reviewed for legal sufficiency by the Staff Judge Advocate for the Convening Authority, the body designated by the Secretary of the Navy to appoint tribunal members and Personal Representatives. After that review, the Staff Judge Advocate makes a recommendation to the Convening Authority, which is then required either to approve the panel's decision or to send the decision back to the panel for further proceedings. It is the government's position that in the event a conclusion by the tribunal that a detainee is an "enemy combatant" is affirmed, it is legal to hold the detainee in custody until the war on terrorism has been declared by the President to have concluded or until the President or his designees have determined that the detainee is no longer a threat to national security. . . .

II. ANALYSIS . . .

A. Extraterritorial Application of the Constitution to Aliens

[The court first disposed of the claim that as aliens, the detainees possessed no constitutional rights to assert by habeas petition. After exhaustively reviewing case law concerning the extraterritorial application of constitutional rights, including Reid v. Covert, 354 U.S. 1 (1957) (casebook p. 639), and United States v. Verdugo-Urquidez, 494 U.S. 259 (1990) (casebook p. 642), the court turned back to *Rasul*.] . . .

. . . But perhaps the strongest basis for recognizing that the detainees have fundamental rights to due process rests at the conclusion of the *Rasul* majority opinion. In summarizing the nature of these actions, the Court recognized:

> Petitioners' allegations – that, although they have engaged neither in combat nor in acts of terrorism against the United States, they have been held in Executive detention for more than two years in territory subject to the long-term, exclusive jurisdiction and control of the United States, without access to counsel and without being charged with any wrongdoing

Chapter 13. Consequence Management: When the Worst Happens

– unquestionably describe "custody in violation of the Constitution or laws or treaties of the United States." 28 U.S.C. §2241(c)(3). Cf. *United States v. Verdugo-Urquidez,* 494 U.S. 259, 277-278 (1990) (Kennedy, J., concurring), and cases cited therein.

124 S. Ct. at 2698 n.15. This comment stands in sharp contrast to the declaration in *Verdugo-Urquidez* relied upon by the D.C. Circuit . . . [below] that the Supreme Court's "rejection of extraterritorial application of the Fifth Amendment [has been] emphatic." 494 U.S. at 269. Given the *Rasul* majority's careful scrutiny of *Eisentrager* [*v. Johnson*, 339 U.S. 763 (1950)], it is difficult to imagine that the Justices would have remarked that the petitions "unquestionably describe 'custody in violation of the Constitution or laws or treaties of the United States'" unless they considered the petitioners to be within a territory in which constitutional rights are guaranteed. Indeed, had the Supreme Court intended to uphold the D.C. Circuit's rejection . . . [below] of underlying constitutional rights, it is reasonable to assume that the majority would have included in its opinion at least a brief statement to that effect, rather than delay the ultimate resolution of this litigation and require the expenditure of additional judicial resources in the lower courts. To the contrary, rather than citing *Eisentrager* or even the portion of *Verdugo-Urquidez* that referenced the "emphatic" inapplicability of the Fifth Amendment to aliens outside U.S. territory, the *Rasul* Court specifically referenced the portion of Justice Kennedy's concurring opinion in *Verdugo-Urquidez* that discussed . . . Justice Harlan's concurring opinion in *Reid v. Covert* and Justice Kennedy's own consideration of whether requiring adherence to constitutional rights outside of the United States would be "impracticable and anomalous." This Court therefore interprets that portion of the [*Rasul*] opinion to require consideration of that precedent in the determination of the underlying rights of the detainees.

There would be nothing impracticable and anomalous in recognizing that the detainees at Guantanamo Bay have the fundamental right to due process of law under the Fifth Amendment. Recognizing the existence of that right at the Naval Base would not cause the United States government any more hardship than would recognizing the existence of constitutional rights of the detainees had they been held within the continental United States. American authorities are in full control at Guantanamo Bay, their activities are immune from Cuban law, and there are few or no significant remnants of native Cuban culture or tradition remaining that can interfere with the implementation of an American system of justice. The situation in these cases is very different from the circumstances in *Verdugo-Urquidez,* where the defendant claimed the United States government was required to get a warrant to perform a search in Mexico, a sovereign country that employs an entirely different legal system, lacks officials to issue warrants, and has potentially different concepts of privacy. Similarly, the imposition of constitutional rights would be less difficult at Guantanamo Bay than it was in any of the Insular Cases [in an omitted part of the opinion, the court refers to one of the earliest of these, Downes v. Bidwell, 182 U.S. 244 (1901)], where the courts were required to determine whether imposition of American rights such as the right to trial by jury and indictment by grand jury were even possible in places such as the Philippines and Puerto Rico with native legal systems and populations previously unexposed to American jurisprudence.

Of course, it would be far easier for the government to prosecute the war on terrorism if it could imprison all suspected "enemy combatants" at Guantanamo Bay without having to acknowledge and respect any constitutional rights of detainees. That, however, is not the relevant legal test. By definition, constitutional limitations often, if not always, burden the abilities of government officials to serve their constituencies. Although this nation unquestionably must take strong action under the leadership of the Commander in Chief to protect itself against enormous and unprecedented threats, that necessity cannot negate the existence of the most basic fundamental rights for which the people of this country have fought and died for well over two hundred years. . . .

In sum, there can be no question that the Fifth Amendment right asserted by the Guantanamo detainees in this litigation – the right not to be deprived of liberty without due process of law – is one of the most fundamental rights recognized by the U.S. Constitution. In light of the Supreme Court's decision in *Rasul*, it is clear that Guantanamo Bay must be considered the equivalent of a U.S. territory in which fundamental constitutional rights apply. Accordingly, and under the precedent set forth in *Verdugo-Urquidez* . . . the respondents' contention that the Guantanamo detainees have no constitutional rights is rejected, and the Court recognizes the detainees' rights under the Due Process Clause of the Fifth Amendment.

B. Specific Requirements of the Fifth Amendment's Due Process Clause

Having found that the Guantanamo detainees are entitled to due process under the Fifth Amendment to the United States Constitution, the Court must now address the exact contours of that right as it applies to the government's determinations that they are "enemy combatants." Due process is an inherently flexible concept, and the specific process due in a particular circumstance depends upon the context in which the right is asserted. *Morrissey v. Brewer,* 408 U.S. 471, 481 (1972). Resolution of a due process challenge requires the consideration and weighing of three factors: the private interest of the person asserting the lack of due process; the risk of erroneous deprivation of that interest through use of existing procedures and the probable value of additional or substitute procedural safeguards; and the competing interests of the government, including the financial, administrative, and other burdens that would be incurred were additional safeguards to be provided. *Mathews v. Eldridge,* 424 U.S. 319, 335 (1976). . . .

In addressing the detainee's private interest in *Hamdi* [v. Rumsfeld, 124 S. Ct. 2633 (2004)] [p. 208 *supra*] for purposes of the *Mathews v. Eldridge* analysis, the plurality opinion called it "the most elemental of liberty interests – the interest in being free from physical detention by one's own government." 124 S. Ct. at 2646. . . .

As was the case in *Hamdi,* the potential length of incarceration is highly relevant to the weighing of the individual interests at stake here. The government asserts the right to detain an "enemy combatant" until the war on terrorism has concluded or until the Executive, in its sole discretion, has determined that the individual no longer poses a threat to national security. The government, however, has been unable to inform the Court how long it believes the war on terrorism will last. Indeed, the government cannot even articulate at this moment how it will determine when the war on terrorism has ended. At a minimum, the government has conceded that the war could last several generations, thereby making it possible, if not likely, that "enemy combatants" will be subject to terms of life imprisonment at Guantanamo Bay. Short of the death penalty, life imprisonment is the ultimate deprivation of liberty, and the uncertainty of whether the war on terror – and thus the period of incarceration – will last a lifetime may be even worse than if the detainees had been tried, convicted, and definitively sentenced to a fixed term.

It must be added that the liberty interests of the detainees cannot be minimized for purposes of applying the *Mathews v. Eldridge* balancing test by the government's allegations that they are in fact terrorists or are affiliated with terrorist organizations. The purpose of imposing a due process requirement is to prevent mistaken characterizations and erroneous detentions, and the government is not entitled to short circuit this inquiry by claiming *ab initio* that the individuals are alleged to have committed bad acts. Moreover, all petitioners in these cases have asserted that they are not terrorists and have not been involved in terrorist activities, and under the standards provided by the applicable rules of procedure, those allegations must be accepted as true for purposes of resolving the government's motion to dismiss.

On the other side of the *Mathews v. Eldridge* analysis is the government's significant interest in safeguarding national security. . . . Congress itself expressly recognized this when it enacted the AUMF authorizing the President to use all necessary and appropriate force against those responsible for the September 11 attacks. . . .

Given the existence of competing, highly significant interests on both sides of the equation – the liberty of individuals asserting complete innocence of any terrorist activity versus the obligation of the government to protect this country against terrorist attacks – the question becomes what procedures will help ensure that innocents are not indefinitely held as "enemy combatants" without imposing undue burdens on the military to ensure the security of this nation and its citizens. The four member *Hamdi* plurality answered this question in some detail, and although the two concurring members of the Court, Justice Souter and Justice Ginsburg, emphasized a different basis for ruling in favor of Mr. Hamdi, they indicated their agreement that, at a minimum, he was entitled to the procedural protections set forth by the plurality. . . .

Hamdi was decided before the creation of the Combatant Status Review Tribunal, and the respondents contend in their motion to dismiss that were this Court to conclude that the detainees are entitled to due process under the Fifth Amendment, the CSRT proceedings would fully comply with all constitutional requirements. . . . Notwithstanding the procedures cited by the respondents, the Court finds that the procedures provided in the CSRT regulations fail to satisfy constitutional due process requirements in several respects.

C. Specific Constitutional Defects in the CSRT Process as Written in the Regulations and as Applied to the Detainees

The constitutional defects in the CSRT procedures can be separated into two categories. The first category consists of defects which apply across the board to all detainees in the cases before this Judge. Specifically, those deficiencies are the CSRT's failure to provide the detainees with access to material evidence upon which the tribunal affirmed their "enemy combatant" status and the failure to permit the assistance of counsel to compensate for the government's refusal to disclose classified information directly to the detainees. The second category of defects involves those which are detainee specific and may or may not apply to every petitioner in this litigation. Those defects include the manner in which the CSRT handled accusations of torture and the vague and potentially overbroad definition of "enemy combatant" in the CSRT regulations. . . .

1. General Defects Existing in All Cases Before the Court: Failure to Provide Detainees Access to Material Evidence Upon Which the CSRT Affirmed "Enemy Combatant" Status and Failure to Permit the Assistance of Counsel

The CSRT reviewed classified information when considering whether each detainee presently before this Court should be considered an "enemy combatant," and it appears that all of the CSRT's decisions substantially relied upon classified evidence. No detainee, however, was ever permitted access to any classified information nor was any detainee permitted to have an advocate review and challenge the classified evidence on his behalf. Accordingly, the CSRT failed to provide any detainee with sufficient notice of the factual basis for which he is being detained and with a fair opportunity to rebut the government's evidence supporting the determination that he is an "enemy combatant."

The inherent lack of fairness of the CSRT's consideration of classified information not disclosed to the detainees is perhaps most vividly illustrated in the following unclassified colloquy, which, though taken from a case not presently before this Judge, exemplifies the practical and severe disadvantages faced by all Guantanamo prisoners. In reading a list of allegations forming the basis for the detention of Mustafa Ait Idr, the Recorder of the CSRT asserted, "While living in Bosnia, the Detainee associated with a known Al Qaida operative." In response, the following exchange occurred:

Detainee: Give me his name.
Tribunal President: I do not know.
Detainee: How can I respond to this?
Tribunal President: Did you know of anybody that was a member of Al Qaida?
Detainee: No, no.
Tribunal President: I'm sorry, what was your response?
Detainee: No.
Tribunal President: No?
Detainee: No. This is something the interrogators told me a long while ago. I asked the interrogators to tell me who this person was. Then I could tell you if I might have known this person, but not if this person is a terrorist. Maybe I knew this person as a friend. Maybe it was a person that worked with me. Maybe it was a person that was on my team. But I do not know if this person is Bosnian, Indian or whatever. If you tell me the name, then I can respond and defend myself against this accusation.
Tribunal President: We are asking you the questions and we need you to respond to what is on the unclassified summary.

Subsequently, after the Recorder read the allegation that the detainee was arrested because of his alleged involvement in a plan to attack the U.S. Embassy in Sarajevo, the detainee expressly asked in the following colloquy to see the evidence upon which the government's assertion relied:

> Detainee: ... The only thing I can tell you is I did not plan or even think of [attacking the Embassy]. Did you find any explosives with me? Any weapons? Did you find me in front of the embassy? Did you find me in contact with the Americans? Did I threaten anyone? I am prepared now to tell you, if you have anything or any evidence, even if it is just very little, that proves I went to the embassy and looked like that [Detainee made a gesture with his head and neck as if he were looking into a building or a window] at the embassy, then I am ready to be punished. I can just tell you that I did not plan anything. Point by point, when we get to the point that I am associated with Al Qaida, but we already did that one.
> Recorder: It was [the] statement that preceded the first point.
> Detainee: If it is the same point, but I do not want to repeat myself. These accusations, my answer to all of them is I did not do these things. But I do not have anything to prove this. The only thing is the citizenship. I can tell you where I was and I had the papers to prove so. But to tell me I planned to bomb, I can only tell you that I did not plan.
> Tribunal President: Mustafa, does that conclude your statement?
> Detainee: That is it, but I was hoping you had evidence that you can give me. If I was in your place – and I apologize in advance for these words – but if a supervisor came to me and showed me accusations like these, I would take these accusations and I would hit him in the face with them. Sorry about that.
> [Everyone in the Tribunal room laughs.]
> Tribunal President: We had to laugh, but it is okay.
> Detainee: Why? Because these are accusations that I can't even answer. I am not able to answer them. You tell me I am from Al Qaida, but I am not an Al Qaida. I don't have any proof to give you except to ask you to catch Bin Laden and ask him if I am a part of Al Qaida. To tell me that I thought, I'll just tell you that I did not. I don't have proof regarding this. What should be done is you should give me evidence regarding these accusations because I am not able to give you any evidence. I can just tell you no, and that is it.

The laughter reflected in the transcript is understandable, and this exchange might have been truly humorous had the consequences of the detainee's "enemy combatant" status not been so terribly serious and had the detainee's criticism of the process not been so piercingly accurate. . . .

The Court fully appreciates the strong governmental interest in not disclosing classified evidence to individuals believed to be terrorists intent on causing great harm to the United States. Indeed, this Court's protective order prohibits the disclosure of any classified information to any of the petitioners in these *habeas* cases. To compensate for the resulting hardship to the petitioners and to ensure due process in the litigation of these cases, however, the protective order requires the disclosure of all relevant classified information to the petitioners' counsel who have the appropriate security clearances. . . . In a similar fashion, the rules regulating the military commission proceedings for aliens – rules which the government so vigorously defended in *Hamdan v. Rumsfeld* – expressly provide that although classified evidence may be withheld from the defendant, it may not be withheld from defense counsel. Procedures for Trials by Military Commissions of Certain Non-United States Citizens in the War Against Terrorism, 32 C.F.R. §9.6(b)(3) ("A decision to close a proceeding or portion thereof may include a decision to exclude the Accused, Civilian Defense Counsel, or any other person, but Detailed Defense Counsel may not be excluded from any trial proceeding or portion thereof."). In contrast, the CSRT regulations do not properly balance the detainees' need for access to material evidence considered by the tribunal against the government's interest in protecting classified information. . . .

[The court noted that the CSRT procedures do assign a "Personal Representative" to the detainee who could review classified information, but noted that this representative is neither a lawyer nor an advocate and has no confidential relationship with the detainee, and therefore cannot act as effective surrogate for a lawyer.]

In sum, the CSRT's extensive reliance on classified information in its resolution of "enemy combatant" status, the detainees' inability to review that information, and the prohibition of assistance by counsel jointly deprive the detainees of sufficient notice of the factual bases for their detention and deny them a fair opportunity to challenge their incarceration. These grounds alone are sufficient to find a violation of due process rights and to require the denial of the respondents' motion to dismiss these cases.

2. Specific Defects That May Exist in Individual Cases: Reliance on Statements Possibly Obtained Through Torture or Other Coercion and a Vague and Overly Broad Definition of "Enemy Combatant" . . .

a. Reliance on Statements Possibly Obtained Through Torture or Other Coercion

The first of these specific grounds involves the CSRT's reliance on statements allegedly obtained through torture or otherwise alleged to have been provided by some detainees involuntarily. The Supreme Court has long held that due process prohibits the government's use of involuntary statements obtained through torture or other mistreatment. In the landmark case of *Jackson v. Denno,* 378 U.S. 368 (1964), the Court gave two rationales for this rule: first, "because of the probable unreliability of confessions that are obtained in a manner deemed coercive," and second "because of the 'strongly felt attitude of our society that important human values are sacrificed where an agency of the government, in the course of securing a conviction, wrings a confession out of an accused against his will.'" 378 U.S. at 386 (*quoting Blackburn v. Alabama,* 361 U.S. 199 (1960)). Arguably, the second rationale may not be as relevant to these *habeas* cases as it is to criminal prosecutions in U.S. courts, given that the judiciary clearly does not have the supervisory powers over the U.S. military as it does over prosecutors, who are officers of the court. *Cf. United States v. Toscanino,* 500 F.2d 267, 276 (2d Cir. 1974) (the supervisory power of the district courts "may legitimately be used to prevent [them] from themselves becoming 'accomplices in willful disobedience of law'") (*quoting McNabb v. United States,* 318 U.S. 332, 345 (1943)). At a minimum, however, due process requires a thorough inquiry into the accuracy and reliability of statements alleged to have been obtained through torture.

Interpreting the evidence in a light most favorable to the petitioners as the Court must when considering the respondents' motion to dismiss, it can be reasonably inferred that the CSRT did not sufficiently consider whether the evidence upon which the tribunal relied in making its "enemy combatant" determinations was coerced from the detainees. The allegations and factual return of Mamdouh Habib are illustrative in this regard. Mr. Habib has alleged that after his capture by allied forces in Pakistan, he was sent to Egypt for interrogation and was subjected to torture there, including routine beatings to the point of unconsciousness. Additionally, the petitioner contends that he was locked in a room that would gradually be filled with water to a level just below his chin as he stood for hours on the tips of his toes. He further claims that he was suspended from a wall with his feet resting on the side of a large electrified cylindrical drum, which forced him either to suffer pain from hanging from his arms or pain from electric shocks to his feet. The petitioner asserts that as a result of this treatment, he made numerous "confessions" that can be proven false. According to the classified factual return for Mr. Habib, [Material redacted by court] and the CSRT found the allegations of torture serious enough to refer the matter on September 22, 2004 to the Criminal Investigation Task Force. [Material redacted by court] Examined in the light most favorable to the petitioner, this reliance cannot be viewed to have satisfied the requirements of due process.

Mr. Habib is not the only detainee before this Court to have alleged making confessions to interrogators as a result of torture. [Material redacted by court] . . . .

. . . [A]t this stage of the litigation it is premature to make any final determination as to whether any information acquired during interrogations of any petitioner in these cases and relied upon by the CSRT was in fact the result of torture or other mistreatment. What this Court needs to resolve at this juncture, however, is whether the petitioners have made sufficient allegations to allow their claims to survive the respondents' motion to dismiss. On that count, the Court concludes that the petitioners have done so.

b. Vague and Overly Broad Definition of "Enemy Combatant"

Although the government has been detaining individuals as "enemy combatants" since the issuance of the AUMF [Authorization for Use of Military Force, Pub. L. No. 107-40 115 Stat. 224 (2001) (casebook p. 262)] in 2001, it apparently did not formally define the term until the July 7, 2004 Order creating the CSRT. . . .

The definition of "enemy combatant" contained in the Order creating the CSRT is significantly broader than the definition considered in *Hamdi*. According to the definition currently applied by the government, an "enemy combatant" "shall mean an individual who was part of or supporting Taliban or al Qaeda forces, or associated forces that are engaged in hostilities against the United States or its coalition partners. This *includes* any person who has committed a belligerent act or has directly supported hostilities in aid of enemy armed forces." July 7, 2004 Order at 1 (emphasis added). Use of the word "includes" indicates that the government interprets the AUMF to permit the indefinite detention of individuals who never committed a belligerent act or who never directly supported hostilities against the U.S. or its allies. This Court explored the government's position on the matter by posing a series of hypothetical questions to counsel at the December 1, 2004 hearing on the motion to dismiss. In response to the hypotheticals, counsel for the respondents argued that the Executive has the authority to detain the following individuals until the conclusion of the war on terrorism: "[a] little old lady in Switzerland who writes checks to what she thinks is a charity that helps orphans in Afghanistan but [what] really is a front to finance al-Qaeda activities," a person who teaches English to the son of an al Qaeda member, and a journalist who knows the location of Osama Bin Laden but refuses to disclose it to protect her source. . . .

As already discussed above, the unclassified evidence upon which the CSRT relied in determining Murat Kurnaz's "enemy combatant" status consisted of findings that he was "associated" with an Islamic missionary group named Jama'at-Al-Tabliq, that he was an "associate" of and planned to travel to Pakistan with an individual who later engaged in a suicide bombing, and that he accepted free food, lodging, and schooling in Pakistan from an organization known to support terrorist acts. While these facts may be probative and could be used to bolster the credibility of other evidence, if any, establishing actual activities undertaken to harm American interests, by themselves they fall short of establishing that the detainee took any action or provided any direct support for terrorist actions against the U.S. or its allies. Nowhere does any unclassified evidence reveal that the detainee even had knowledge of his associate's planned suicide bombing, let alone establish that the detainee assisted in the bombing in any way. In fact, the detainee expressly denied knowledge of a bombing plan when he was informed of it by the American authorities. [Material redacted by court.] Absent other evidence, it would appear that the government is indefinitely holding the detainee – possibly for life – solely because of his contacts with individuals or organizations tied to terrorism and not because of any terrorist activities that the detainee aided, abetted, or undertook himself. Such detention, even if found to be authorized by the AUMF, would be a violation of due process. Accordingly, the detainee is entitled to fully litigate the factual basis for his detention in these *habeas* proceedings and to have a fair opportunity to prove that he is being detained on improper grounds. . . .

D. Claims Based on the Geneva Conventions

The petitioners in all of the above captioned cases except *Al Odah v. United States,* 02-CV-0828, have also asserted claims based on the Geneva Conventions, which regulate the treatment of certain prisoners of war and civilians. The respondents contend that all Geneva Convention claims filed by the petitioners must be dismissed because Congress has not enacted any separate legislation specifically granting individuals the right to file private lawsuits based on the Conventions and because the Conventions are not "self-executing," meaning they do not by themselves create such a private right of action. In the alternative, the respondents argue that even if the Geneva Conventions are self-executing, they do not apply to members of al Qaeda because that international terrorist organization is not a state party to the Conventions. Finally, although respondents concede that Afghanistan is a state party to the Conventions and admit that the Geneva Conventions apply to Taliban detainees, they emphasize that President Bush has determined that Taliban fighters are not entitled to prisoner of war status under the Third Geneva Convention and contend that this decision is the final word on the matter. . . .

After reviewing [Hamdan v. Rumsfeld, 344 F. Supp. 2d 152 (D.D.C. 2004) (Robertson, J.), *rev'd*, No. 04-5393, 2005 WL 1653046 (D.C. Cir. July 15, 2005) (p. 334 *infra*)] . . . , the Court concludes that the Conventions are self-executing and adopts the following reasoning provided by Judge Robertson:

> Because the Geneva Conventions were written to protect individuals, because the Executive Branch of our government has implemented the Geneva Conventions for fifty years without questioning the absence of implementing legislation, because Congress clearly understood that the Conventions did not require implementing legislation except in a few specific areas, and because nothing in the Third Geneva Convention itself manifests the contracting parties' intention that it not become effective as domestic law without the enactment of implementing legislation, I conclude that, insofar as it is pertinent here, the Third Geneva Convention is a self-executing treaty.

[344 F. Supp. 2d] at 165. . . .

[The court concluded that while the Geneva Convention did not apply to members of al Qaeda, it did apply to fighters for the Taliban.]

Nothing in the Convention itself or in Army Regulation 190-8 authorizes the President of the United States to rule by fiat that an entire group of fighters covered by the Third Geneva Convention falls outside of the Article 4 definitions of "prisoners of war." To the contrary, . . . the President's broad characterization of how the Taliban generally fought the war in Afghanistan cannot substitute for an Article 5 tribunal's determination on an individualized basis of whether a particular fighter complied with the laws of war or otherwise falls within an exception denying him prisoner of war status. Clearly, had an appropriate determination been properly made by an Article 5 tribunal that a petitioner was not a prisoner of war, that petitioner's claims based on the Third Geneva Convention could not survive the respondents' motion to dismiss. But although numerous petitioners in the above-captioned cases were found by the CSRT to have been Taliban fighters, nowhere do the CSRT records for many of those petitioners reveal specific findings that they committed some particular act or failed to satisfy some defined prerequisite entitling the respondents to deprive them of prisoner of war status. Accordingly, the Court denies that portion of the respondents' motion to dismiss addressing the Geneva Convention claims of those petitioners who were found to be Taliban fighters but who were not specifically determined to be excluded from prisoner of war status by a competent Article 5 tribunal. . . .

III. CONCLUSION

For the reasons provided above, the Court holds that the petitioners have stated valid claims under the Fifth Amendment and that the CSRT procedures are unconstitutional for failing to comport with the requirements of due process. Additionally, the Court holds that Taliban fighters who have not been specifically determined to be excluded from prisoner of war status by a competent Article 5 tribunal have also stated valid claims under the Third Geneva Convention. Finally, the Court concludes that the remaining claims of the petitioners must be denied. Accordingly, this Memorandum Opinion is accompanied by a separate Order denying in part and granting in part the respondents' Motion to Dismiss or for Judgment as a Matter of Law. . . .

Khalid v. Bush
United States District Court, District of Columbia, 2005
355 F. Supp. 2d 311

LEON, J. Petitioners are seven foreign nationals who were seized by United States forces and have been detained at the United States naval base at Guantanamo Bay, Cuba ("Guantanamo") pursuant to military orders arising out of the ongoing war against terror initiated in the aftermath of September 11, 2001 ("9/11"). Based on the Supreme Court's decision in *Rasul v. Bush,* ___ U.S. ___, 124 S. Ct. 2686 (2004) [*supra* p. 252], each detainee has filed a petition for a writ of habeas corpus with this Court seeking to challenge the lawfulness of his continued detention. . . .

. . . [T]hese cases pose the novel issue of whether there is any viable legal theory under which a federal court could issue a writ of habeas corpus challenging the legality of the detention of non-resident aliens captured abroad and detained outside the territorial sovereignty of the United States, pursuant to lawful military orders, during a Congressionally authorized conflict. . . .

I. BACKGROUND . . .

Pursuant to [the Military Order of November 13, 2001 (casebook p. 897)], the United States has targeted and captured, to-date, a large number of foreign nationals both on and off the battlefields of Afghanistan and transported them for detention to Guantanamo Bay, Cuba. In addition, the military has determined that many of these individuals should be detained for the duration of the conflict as "enemy combatants." At present, the Department of Defense ("DoD") is holding nearly 550 of these foreign nationals at Guantanamo, although recent media reports indicate that the DoD intends to release or transfer hundreds in the near future.

Seven of these foreign nationals are the petitioners in this case. None are United States citizens or have any connection to the United States, other than their current status as detainees at a U.S. military base. To the contrary, the petitioners are non-resident aliens captured outside of Afghanistan. They include five Algerian-Bosnian citizens; one Algerian citizen with permanent Bosnian residency; and one French citizen. All, with the exception of Khalid, were captured in Bosnia around October 2001. Khalid was seized in Pakistan sometime during the early fall of 2001. In January 2001, shortly after they were captured and transferred to United States military authorities, the petitioners were transported to Guantanamo, where they currently remain. . . .

III. ANALYSIS . . .

A. Congress Authorized the President to Capture and Detain Enemy Combatants . . .

In drafting the Constitution, the Founding Fathers chose to allocate the rights and duties for securing the Nation's "common defence" between Congress and the President (the political branches). . . . And, in *Ex parte Quirin*, the Supreme Court clearly articulated the relationship between Congress and the President in declaring and prosecuting armed conflict:

> The Constitution thus invests the President as Commander in Chief with the power to wage war which Congress has declared, *and to carry into effect all laws passed by Congress* for the conduct of war and for the government and regulation of the Armed Forces, and all laws defining and punishing offences against the law of nations, including those which pertain to the conduct of war.

Ex parte Quirin, 317 U.S. 1, 26 (1942) (emphasis added). . . .

Thus, when Congress, through the AUMF [Authorization for Use of Military Force, Pub. L. No. 107-40 115 Stat. 224 (2001) (casebook p. 262)], authorized the President "to use all necessary and appropriate force against those . . . persons he determines planned, authorized, committed, or aided the terrorist attacks [of 9/11]" "to prevent any future acts of international terrorism against the United States by such . . . persons[,]" *see* AUMF §2, it, in effect, gave the President the power to capture and detain those who the military determined were either responsible for the 9/11 attacks or posed a threat of future terrorist attacks. Indeed, the President's war powers could not be reasonably interpreted otherwise.

The history of armed conflict in which this Nation has engaged since our inception has firmly established that the President's "war power" *must* include the power to capture and detain our enemies. Indeed, the Supreme Court acknowledged as much in its recent decision in *Hamdi v. Rumsfeld*, 124 S. Ct. 2633, 2640 (2004) ("The capture and detention of lawful combatants and the capture, detention, and trial of unlawful combatants, by universal agreement and practice, are important incident[s] of war.") (internal quotations omitted); *see also, e.g., Fleming v. Page*, 50 U.S. (9 How.) 603, 615 (1850) ("As commander-in-chief, [the President] is authorized to direct the movements of the naval and military forces placed by law at his command, and to employ them in the manner he may deem most effectual to harass and *conquer and subdue* the enemy.") (emphasis added).

Moreover, the petitioners' contention, in effect, that the President's conduct is illegally excessive because Congress did not *expressly* authorize the detention of enemy combatants not captured on or near the battlefields of Afghanistan is fanciful, at best.

The Supreme Court, in *Hamdi,* made clear that specific Congressional authorization of detention is unnecessary "[b]ecause detention to prevent a combatant's return to the battlefield is a fundamental incident of waging war" and, thus, permitted by Congress under the clause of the AUMF authorizing the President to use "necessary and appropriate force." *Hamdi,* 124 S. Ct. at 2641; *see also Dames & Moore v. Regan,* 453 U.S. 654, 678 (1981) ("Congress cannot anticipate and legislate with regard to every possible action the President may find it necessary to take or every possible situation in which he might act[.]"). In addition, with respect to the duration of detention, the Supreme Court found that it is an equally clear and well-established principle of the law of war that detention may last for the duration of active hostilities, and, thus, the Supreme Court interpreted the AUMF to mean that Congress has granted the President the authority to detain enemy combatants for the duration of the current conflict, *id.* ("[W]e understand Congress' grant of authority for the use of 'necessary and appropriate force' to include the authority to detain for the duration of the relevant conflict[.]").[10]

The fact that the petitioners in this case were not captured on or near the battlefields of Afghanistan, unlike the petitioner in *Hamdi*, is of no legal significance to this conclusion because the AUMF does not place geographic parameters on the President's authority to wage this war against terrorists. Thus it is unmistakable that Congress, like the Supreme Court in *Quirin*, concluded that enemies who have committed or attempted to commit acts of violence outside of the "theatre or zone of active military operations" are equally as "belligerent" as those captured on the battlefield. *See Quirin*, 317 U.S. at 38. As the respondents aptly observe, the 9/11 attacks were orchestrated by a global force operating in such far-flung locations as Malaysia, Germany, and the United Arab Emirates. Any interpretation of the AUMF that would require the President and the military to restrict their search, capture, and detention to the battlefields of Afghanistan would contradict Congress's clear intention, and unduly hinder both the President's ability to protect our country from future acts of terrorism and his ability to gather vital intelligence regarding the capability, operations, and intentions of this elusive and cunning adversary. Indeed, if nothing else, the attacks on 9/11 exposed the weaknesses in, and the importance of, our intelligence gathering capabilities in preventing future terrorist attacks against our country. For this Court to interpret the AUMF as the petitioners contend, would make a mockery of Congress's intent, contradict the President's necessary and natural war powers, and improperly narrow the Supreme Court's ruling in *Hamdi*.

Thus, for all of these reasons, the Court finds that the President's Detention Order was lawful under the AUMF and consistent with his war powers under the Constitution. . . .

B. Non-Resident Aliens Captured and Detained Outside the United States Have No Cognizable Constitutional Rights

Petitioners' next theoretical basis for challenging the lawfulness of their

---

10. Notwithstanding the foregoing, the Court recognizes petitioners' concern at the prospect of indefinite or perpetual detention. However, as noted, the law of war, as it has been adopted over the years by the political branches, permits detention for the duration of the hostilities. If the current conflict continues for an unacceptable duration, inadequacies in the law of "traditional" warfare may be exposed, *see Hamdi*, 124 S. Ct. at 2641-42 ("If the practical circumstances of a given conflict are entirely unlike those of the conflicts that informed the development of the law of war, that understanding may unravel."), requiring a reevaluation of the laws by the *political branches*, not the judiciary.

continued detention under the habeas statute is their contention that it violates their substantive rights under the United States Constitution (e.g., due process, right to confrontation, right to counsel, and protection against cruel and unusual punishment). . . .

The petitioners in this case are neither United States citizens nor aliens located within sovereign United States territory. To the contrary, they are non-resident aliens, captured in foreign territory, and held at a naval base, which is located on land subject to the "ultimate sovereignty" of Cuba. *See* Lease of Lands for Coaling and Naval Stations, Feb. 23, 1903, U.S.-Cuba, Art. III, T.S. No. 418. Due to their status as aliens outside sovereign United States territory with no connection to the United States, it was well established prior to *Rasul* that the petitioners possess no cognizable constitutional rights. *See Johnson v. Eisentrager,* 339 U.S. 763, 783-85 (1950); *United States v. Curtiss-Wright Export Corp.,* 299 U.S. 304, 318 (1936) ("Neither the Constitution nor the laws passed in pursuance of it have any force in foreign territory unless in respect of our own citizens."). . . .

Petitioners contend, however, that the *Rasul* majority overruled *Eisentrager* when it permitted non-resident aliens detained at Guantanamo to file these petitions for a writ of habeas corpus. In short, the petitioners contend also that *Rasul* holds that such non-resident aliens possess substantive due process rights cognizable in habeas, because such rights are inextricably linked to the right to file a petition. The Court disagrees.

Nothing in *Rasul* alters the holding articulated in *Eisentrager* and its progeny. The Supreme Court majority in *Rasul* expressly limited its inquiry to whether non-resident aliens detained at Guantanamo have a right to a judicial review of the legality of their detention under the habeas statute, *Rasul,* 124 S. Ct. at 2693 ("The question now before us is whether the *habeas statute* confers a right to judicial review of the legality of Executive detention of aliens in a territory over which the United States exercises plenary and exclusive jurisdiction, but not 'ultimate sovereignty.'") (emphasis added), and, therefore, did not concern itself with whether the petitioners had any independent constitutional rights. . . .

Finally, petitioners' expansive reliance upon *Rasul*'s "footnote 15" for the proposition that the *Rasul* majority intended to overrule, *sub silentio, Eisentrager* and its progeny is equally misplaced and unpersuasive. *See Rasul,* 124 S. Ct. at 2698 n.15 [*supra* p. 257]. Stated simply, footnote 15 must be read in light of the context of the paragraph and opinion in which it is embedded. The paragraph in which it is included specifically focuses on the "question presented" in the case. The "question presented" in the case was unequivocally limited to: "the narrow . . . question whether the United States courts lack *jurisdiction* to consider challenges to the legality of the detention of foreign nationals captured abroad . . . and incarcerated

Chapter 13. Consequence Management: When the Worst Happens

at Guantanamo . . . ." *Rasul,* 124 S. Ct. at 2690 (emphasis added). The *Rasul* majority thereafter further emphasized the limitations on its holding in the concluding paragraph of the opinion by stating "[w]hat is presently at stake is only whether the federal courts have *jurisdiction* to determine the legality of the Executive's potentially indefinite detention of individuals who claim to be wholly innocent of wrongdoing." *Id.* at 2699. Thus, in its own words, the Supreme Court chose to only answer the question of jurisdiction, and not the question of whether these same individuals possess any substantive rights on the merits of their claims. Indeed, the *Rasul* Court expressly acknowledged that it expected that its decision would cause "further proceedings" among the lower courts to consider the very issue that it had not: the "merits of petitioners' claims."

Accordingly, for all of these reasons the Court concludes that the petitioners lack any viable theory under the United States Constitution to challenge the lawfulness of their continued detention at Guantanamo.

C. Petitioners Have Failed to Identify any United States Law or Treaty the Violation of Which Would Provide a Viable Basis to Grant a Habeas Petition

Having no constitutional rights upon which to base the issuance of a habeas petition, petitioners next seek to rely upon alleged violations of certain legal statutes and treaties as the basis for the issuance of a writ. In doing so, of course, they must demonstrate that the violation of that law or treaty would in turn render the petitioners' *custody* unlawful. *See* 28 U.S.C. §2241(c)(3) ("The writ of habeas corpus shall not extend to a prisoner unless . . . [h]e is in *custody* in violation of the Constitution or laws or treaties of the United States[.]") (emphasis added).

The petitioners, however, have not offered any viable theory relating to any existing federal laws or treaties that could serve as the basis for the issuance of a writ. By and large, their petitions do not contain detainee-specific allegations of mistreatment at the hands of the respondents. Instead, the petitioners have essentially cast their grievances in generalized terms. The crux of the petitioners' allegations is the amorphous contention that their detention somehow violates certain federal laws (e.g., the War Crimes Act, 18 U.S.C. §2441(a), (c)(1); Alien Tort Claims Act, 28 U.S.C. §1350), because they: (1) have been held "virtually incommunicado," (2) "have been or will be interrogated repeatedly . . . though they have not been charged with an offense," and (3) have been held "in accommodation[s] that fail[ ] to satisfy both domestic and internationally accepted standards of accommodation for any person subject to detention." . . .

Moreover, the petitioners have chosen to assert claims under federal laws the violation of which do not create a private right of action and, therefore, are not cognizable in habeas. Specifically, they contend their detention violates certain Army Regulations, which provide the "policy, procedures, and responsibilities" for the military with respect to detainment situations, *see* Army Regulation 190-8 §1-1.a ("Army Reg."), and the War Crimes Act, which criminalizes "grave breach[es] in any of the international conventions signed at Geneva 12 August 1949" committed by United States military personnel, *see* 18 U.S.C. §2441(c)(1). Neither of these statutes, however, create[s] a private right of action for a detainee to challenge the legality of their custody in an habeas proceeding. . . .

Similarly, petitioners have offered no viable theory regarding any treaty that could serve as the basis for the issuance of a writ. Although the petitioners assert that their continued detention violates the Geneva Convention, they subsequently conceded at oral argument that that Convention does not apply because these petitioners were not captured in the "zone of hostilities . . . in and around Afghanistan." As a result, petitioners are left contending that their detention unlawfully violates other United States treaties because their living conditions, in effect, constitute "torture" as that term is defined in the Convention Against Torture and Other Cruel, Inhuman or Degrading Treatment or Punishment, G.A. Res. 46, U.N. GAOR, 39th Sess., Supp. No. 51, at 197, U.N. Doc. A/RES/39/708 (1984), *reprinted in* 23 I.L.M. 1027 (1984) ("CAT") and the International Covenant on Civil and Political Rights, G.A. Res. 2200A (XXI), U.N. GAOR, 21st Sess., Supp. No. 16, at 52, U.N. Doc. A/6316 (1966) ("ICCPR"). For the following reasons, however, these claims are not a viable basis in a habeas proceeding to evaluate the legality of the petitioners' detention.

Treaties, as a general rule, are not privately enforceable. Indeed, enforcement in the final analysis is reserved to the executive authority of the governments who are parties to the treaties. *See, e.g., Comm. of the U.S. Citizens Living in Nicaragua v. Reagan,* 859 F.2d 929, 937-38 (D.C. Cir.1988) [casebook p. 218]. Where a treaty is not self-executing, its terms give rise to a private cause of action *only* if Congress enacts authorizing legislation. In the absence of a self-executing treaty and Congressional implementation, the individual does not have standing to assert the alleged violation in federal court.

In this case, neither the CAT nor the ICCPR is a self-executing treaty. Indeed, in giving its advice and consent to ratification of both treaties, the Senate expressly declared that the provisions of both would *not* be privately enforceable. *See* 136 Cong. Rec. S36,198 (Oct. 27, 1990) (dealing with the CAT); 138 Cong. Rec. S4781-01 (April 2, 1992) (dealing with the ICCPR).

Furthermore, Congress has not enacted any implementing legislation, with respect to either convention, that would authorize the petitioners to challenge the legality of their detention in federal court. As a result, the petitioners cannot rely on either the CAT or the ICCPR as a viable legal basis to support the issuance of a writ of habeas corpus. Accordingly, the Court finds no viable theory based on United States treaties upon which a writ could be issued.

D. There Is No Viable Legal Theory Under International Law Upon Which This Court Could Issue a Writ of Habeas Corpus

Because the petitioners' claims under the aforementioned treaties fail, they are left to rely in the final analysis on principles of international law for a viable theory by which to challenge the lawfulness of their detention. This effort, similarly, is to no avail. . . .

However, having concluded that Congress, through the AUMF, has conferred authority on the President to detain the petitioners, it would be impermissible, for the following reasons, under our constitutional system of separation of powers for the judiciary to engage in a substantive evaluation of the conditions of their detention. Simply stated, it is the province of the Executive branch and Congress, should it choose to enact legislation relating thereto, to define the conditions of detention and ensure that United States laws and treaties are being complied therewith. . . .

In the final analysis, the Court's role in reviewing the military's decision to capture and detain a non-resident alien is, and must be, highly circumscribed. The Court is well aware of the measures that have been adopted by the political branches – Congress and the Executive – to ensure that abuse does not occur and to ensure these petitioners are given the treatment that they are deserved. Indeed, Congress recently enacted the Reagan Act [Pub. L. No. 108-375, 118 Stat. 1811 (2004)] to ensure that all United States personnel clearly understand their obligations with respect to the treatment of detainees. *See* Reagan Act, §1091(b)(3). Conspicuous in its absence in the Reagan Act is any reference by Congress to federal court review where United States personnel engage[] in impermissible treatment of a detainee. Indeed, any enforcement and/or punishment for impermissible conduct under the Act remains, as it always has, with the Department of Defense and appropriate military authorities. In fact, the Act will soon be codified in Title 10 of the United States Code, which is the Title governing the Armed Forces. . . .

Thus, to the extent these non-resident detainees have rights, they are subject to both the military review process already in place and the laws Congress has passed defining the appropriate scope of military conduct towards these detainees. The extent to which these rights and conditions should be modified or extended is a matter for the political branches to determine and effectuate through either Constitutional amendments, appropriate international entities. Thus, until Congress and the President act further, there is similarly no viable legal theory under international law by which a federal court could issue a writ.

Accordingly, for this and all the reasons stated above, the respondents' motion to dismiss must be GRANTED. . . .

NOTES AND QUESTIONS

1. *Hamdan v. Rumsfeld.* The case law generated by the Guantánamo Bay detainees continues to metastasize, making it difficult to assert what the law of the circuit is, let alone the law more generally. At this writing, both In re Guantanamo Detainee Cases and Khalid v. Bush are being appealed. In Hamdan v. Rumsfeld, No. 04-5393, 2005 WL 1653046 (D.C. Cir. July 15, 2005), a D.C. Circuit Court of Appeals panel reversed Judge Robertson, whose reasoning about the applicability of the Geneva Conventions had been adopted by Judge Green in In re Guantanamo Detainee Cases. Arguably, that part of Judge Green's opinion is no longer good law in the D.C. Circuit, unless the panel on appeal of her decision departs from *Hamdan*'s reasoning on this question. However, *Hamdan* involves a challenge to trial of a detainee by military commission and its procedures, rather than a challenge to a status determination by a CSRT and *its* procedures, and it did not rule on the question of the applicability of the Constitution. (If this is Tuesday, we must be in Belgium.) We therefore discuss *Hamdan* below in Chapter 14D (p. 334 *infra*).

2. *CSRTs.* Reread the final paragraph of part III of the Supreme Court's opinion in Hamdi v. Rumsfeld, *supra* p. 218. Can you see why the CSRT was created? Between August 2004 and March 2005, CSRTs reviewed the status of 558 detainees, deeming 520 to be enemy combatants. *See Combatant Status Review Summary*, Mar. 29, 2005 (reporting review by Convening Authority Rear Adm. James M. McGarrah), *available at* http://www.dod.mil/news/Mar2005/d20050329csrt.pdf.

3. *The Constitutional Rights of Aliens.* Recall, and, if necessary, reread *Verdugo-Urquidez* (casebook p. 642). It held that alien Verdugo-Urquidez had no constitutional protection under the Fourth Amendment from a warrantless search of his property in Mexico. Why did it not resolve the question of the constitutional rights of aliens generally? If that question was left open, does *Rasul* shed light on the substantive constitutional rights

of the alien detainees, or is it just a jurisdictional ruling on their access to habeas corpus? If they have no substantive rights, is such a procedural right a cruel hoax? *See* Amnesty International, *Guantánamo and Beyond: The Continuing Pursuit of Unchecked Executive Power* 22, May 13, 2005, available at *http://web.amnesty.org/library/Index/ENGAMR510632005? open&of=ENG-USA* (characterizing the government's claim that *Rasul* conferred only "procedural rights" on alien detainees as an argument that "the detainees could file *habeas corpus* petitions, but only in order to have them necessarily dismissed"). What other rights could they assert in their petition?

Al-Marri v. Hanft, No. 2:04-2257-HFF-RSC, 2005 WL 1719110 (D.S.C. July 8, 2005), may help put some of these questions into sharper relief. Al-Marri is a Qatari national who earned a bachelor's degree during the 1990s from Bradley University in Illinois, and who legally returned to the United States with his family to pursue a master's degree from the same university. Unfortunately for him, he returned on September 10, 2001, and he was subsequently arrested on December 12 as a material witness and later indicted for making false statements and for credit card fraud, before being designated an enemy combatant by President Bush on June 23, 2003. The criminal case was dismissed with prejudice and al-Marri was transferred to military detention at the Naval Consolidated Brig in South Carolina, where, at this writing, he continues to be held.

Does al-Marri have any constitutional rights that he can assert to challenge his military detention? Is he differently situated from the Guantánamo detainees or Khalid? The court that rejected his petition cited *Eisentrager* in concluding that the Supreme Court had limited "a resident alien enemy's use of our courts . . . 'as necessary to prevent use of the courts to accomplish a purpose which might hamper our own war efforts or to give aid to the enemy.'" *Id.* at *5 (quoting *Eisentrager*, 339 U.S. at 776 [internal citation omitted]). Should the court have discussed *Verdugo-Urquidez*?

The *Al-Marri* court also reasoned that the Alien Enemy Act (p. 204 *supra*) confirmed that even resident enemy aliens receive different protections from citizens during war, although the court also conceded that the act had no direct application absent a declared war against a foreign nation or government. 2005 WL 1719110 at *5-6. What contrary argument could you make based upon the existence of that act?

4. *The Value of Due Process Rights.* The report cited in Note 2, above, indicates that in 520 of 538 cases the CSRT upheld the designations of detainees as "enemy combatants." Thirty-two of the 38 cases that rejected that designation were decided *after* Judge Green's decision in In re

Guantanamo Detainee Cases. Amnesty International, *supra* Note 3, at 24. However, it is not clear whether these results reflect a change in procedures or the way in which procedures were applied.

Interestingly, the case of Mustafa Ait Idr, whose testimony drew laughter in the CSRT excerpt quoted by Judge Green, was one of those that Judge Leon declined to probe, finding the CSRT process constitutionally adequate. In another case, which Judge Green used to illustrate what she found to be a vague and overly broad definition of "enemy combatant," previously classified evidence in the military file on Murat Kurnaz that was released after her decision states that "CTIF [Command Information Task Force] has no definite link/evidence of detainee having an association with al-Qaida or making any specific threat toward the US," that "the Germans confirmed that this detainee has no connection to an al-Qaida cell in Germany," and that CTIF had no evidence that Kurnaz harbored any al-Queda member or other person involved in terrorism against the United States. *See* Amnesty International, *supra*, at 28. German prosecutors have reportedly closed their investigative file for lack of evidence against the "suicide bomber" with whom Kurnaz allegedly associated. Amnesty International concludes that "it would appear that Murat Kurnaz has been held for more than three years without charge or trial on the basis of his association with a friend who he did know was involved in 'terrorism' because, it seems, he was not." *Id*. at 28-29. Amnesty International does not indicate either the information on which Kurnaz was originally detained or when the allegedly exculpatory information became available.

5. *AUMF vs. Treaty.* Does it really matter whether the Geneva Conventions are self-executing or whether they apply? They preceded in time the AUMF passed by Congress after 9/11. Why is not the AUMF simply *lex posterior* – a last-in-time controlling statute? *See* casebook pp. 219-220, 224 Note 6.

6. *Synthesis?* The cases in this sub-chapter present the following variables, among others: citizen or alien; detention in the mainland United States or Guantánamo Bay; capture on the Afghan battlefield or in the United States; member of al Queda or fighter for the Taliban. Can you distinguish their outcomes using these variables or others? Recognizing that you would have to choose between the reasoning of In re Guantanamo Detainee Cases and *Khalid* on some issues, can you synthesize your choice with the other cases to state the present law of military detention in the war on terrorism? If not, does it raise a question whether this is an appropriate issue for resolution by the courts? On the other hand, do the courts have a choice?

14

Trying International Terrorists

A. CRIMINALIZING SEDITION, TERRORISM, AND SUPPORT FOR TERRORISM

Page 832. Add the following material at the end of *United States v. Rahman.*

NOTES AND QUESTIONS

1. *Treason.* Why does Abdel Rahman argue that he has effectively been convicted of treason? Why does the Constitution single out treason among all crimes (it is the only crime expressly identified by the Constitution), not only defining it but specifying the evidence needed for a conviction? Do you see why the reasons you identify sound a general cautionary note about criminalizing sedition, party or group membership, advocacy of violence, conspiracy, or assisting terrorism?

2. *Inciting Imminent Harm.* The *Rahman* court's synopsis of the constitutional law governing advocacy of lawless action makes it sound more consistent than it is. In a World War I case under the 1918 Sedition Act, the Supreme Court declared that the government could constitutionally criminalize the utterance of "words . . . used in such circumstances . . . as to create a clear and present danger that they will bring about the substantive evils that Congress has a right to prevent." Schenck v. United States, 249 U.S. 47, 52 (1919). The Court seemed to relax the clear-and-present-danger test in Dennis v. United States, 341 U.S. 494 (1951), by finding that the harm from an overthrow of the government would be so grave that the government need not show its imminence or probability in order to punish advocacy of the overthrow. Dennis and his co-defendants were convicted and sentenced to long prison terms for violating the Smith

Act, which made it unlawful "to knowingly or willfully advocate, abet, advise, or teach the duty, necessity, desirability, or propriety of overthrowing or destroying any government in the United States by force or violence. . . ." Act of June 28, 1940, 54 Stat. 670, 671 (1940). What were their criminal acts? Apparently, according to the evidence adduced by the government, assembling to discuss and plan future teaching of books by Stalin, Marx and Engels, and Lenin. Finally, without disavowing these chilling precedents, the Court reversed a conviction for "criminal syndicalism" in Brandenberg v. Ohio, 395 U.S. 444 (1969). There, the defendant had given a racist and anti-Semitic speech at a Ku Klux Klan rally. The Court held that the a State could not criminalize "advocacy of the use of force or violation of law except where such advocacy is directed to inciting or producing imminent lawless action *and* is likely to incite or produce such action." *Id.* at 447 (emphasis added).

How does Section 2384 fare under these tests? Did the *Rahman* court apply them correctly?

3. *Expression as Evidence.* Are not Rahman's religious expressions, quoted in the case, quintessential protected speech? Why was it constitutional to base his criminal prosecution in part on them? *See generally* John Alan Cohen, *Seditious Conspiracy, The Smith Act, and Prosecution for Religious Speech Advocating the Violent Overthrow of Government*, 17 St. John's J. Legal Comment. 199 (2003).

Pages 832-840. Substitute the following material for *Humanitarian Law Project* and the Notes and Questions that follow it.

18 U.S.C. §2339A. Providing material support to terrorists

(a) Offense. – Whoever provides material support or resources or conceals or disguises the nature, location, source, or ownership of material support or resources, knowing or intending that they are to be used in preparation for, or in carrying out, a violation of [various specific terrorist crimes] or in preparation for, or in carrying out, the concealment of an escape from the commission of any such violation, or attempts or conspires to do such an act, shall be fined under this title, imprisoned not more than 15 years, or both, and, if the death of any person results, shall be imprisoned for any term of years or for life. A violation of this section may be prosecuted in any Federal judicial district in which the underlying offense was committed, or in any other Federal judicial district as provided by law.

(b) Definition. – In this section, the term "material support or resources" means currency or monetary instruments or financial securities,

Chapter 14. Trying International Terrorists

financial services, lodging, training, expert advice or assistance, safehouses, false documentation or identification, communications equipment, facilities, weapons, lethal substances, explosives, personnel, transportation, and other physical assets, except medicine or religious materials.

18 U.S.C. §2339B. Providing material support or resources to designated foreign terrorist organizations

(a) (1) Unlawful conduct. – Whoever knowingly provides material support or resources to a foreign terrorist organization, or attempts or conspires to do so, shall be fined under this title or imprisoned not more than 15 years, or both, and, if the death of any person results, shall be imprisoned for any term of years or for life. *To violate this paragraph, a person must have knowledge that the organization is a designated terrorist organization . . . , that the organization has engaged or engages in terrorist activity . . . , or that the organization has engaged or engages in terrorism . . . .*[1]

(g) Definitions – As used in this section – . . . (4) the term "material support or resources" has the same meaning as in section 2339A; . . . .

18 U.S.C. §2339C. Prohibitions against the financing of terrorism

(a) Offenses. – (1) In general. – Whoever, in a circumstance described in subsection (b) [prescribing jurisdictional attributes of crime], by any means, directly or indirectly, unlawfully and willfully provides or collects funds with the intention that such funds be used, or with the knowledge that such funds are to be used, in full or in part, in order to carry out . . . (B) any . . . act intended to cause death or serious bodily injury to a civilian, or to any other person not taking an active part in the hostilities in a situation of armed conflict, when the purpose of such act, by its nature or context, is to intimidate a population, or to compel a government or an international organization to do or to abstain from doing any act, shall be punished as prescribed in subsection (d)(1). . . .

(e) Definitions. – In this section – (1) the term "funds" means assets of every kind, whether tangible or intangible, movable or immovable, however acquired, and legal documents or instruments in any form, including electronic or digital, evidencing title to, or interest in, such assets,

---

[1. The italicized sentence was added by the Intelligence Reform and Terrorism Prevention Act of 2004, Pub. L. No. 108-458, §6603(c)(2), 118 Stat. 3638, 3763, after the following case was decided.]

including coin, currency, bank credits, travelers checks, bank checks, money orders, shares, securities, bonds, drafts, and letters of credit; . . .

(3) the term "proceeds" means any funds derived from or obtained, directly or indirectly, through the commission of an offense set forth in subsection (a);

(4) the term "provides" includes giving, donating, and transmitting;

(5) the term "collects" includes raising and receiving; . . .

United States v. Al-Arian
United States District Court, Middle District of Florida, 2004
308 F. Supp. 2d 1322

MOODY, J. . . .

I. BACKGROUND

A. Factual and Procedural Background

This is a criminal action against alleged members of the Palestinian Islamic Jihad-Shiqaqi Faction (the "PIJ") who purportedly operated and directed fundraising and other organizational activities in the United States for almost twenty years. The PIJ is a foreign organization that uses violence, principally suicide bombings, and threats of violence to pressure Israel to cede territory to the Palestinian people. On February 19, 2003, the government indicted the Defendants in a 50 count indictment that included counts for . . . (3) conspiracy to provide material support to or for the benefit of foreign terrorists (Counts 3 and 4) . . . .

Count 1 of the Indictment alleges a wide ranging pattern of racketeering activity beginning in 1984 lasting through February 2003, including murder, extortion, and money laundering. The Indictment details some 256 overt acts, ranging from soliciting and raising funds to providing management, organizational, and logistical support for the PIJ. The overt act section of the Indictment details numerous suicide bombings and attacks by PIJ members causing the deaths of over 100 people, including 2 American citizens, and injuries to over 350 people, including 7 American citizens. . . .

Each of the Defendants filed numerous pretrial motions primarily seeking the dismissal of Counts 1 through 4 of the Indictment and the striking of various overt acts or parts of overt acts as surplusage. . . .

Chapter 14. Trying International Terrorists

B. Statutory Background

Center stage in the motions are two statutes (along with the regulations, administrative designations, and executive orders associated with each): (1) the Antiterrorism and Effective Death Penalty Act of 1996, Pub. L. No. 104-132 ("AEDPA"); and (2) the International Emergency Economic Powers Act, 50 U.S.C. §1701, *et seq.* ("IEEPA").

1. AEDPA

AEDPA authorizes the Secretary of State (the "Secretary"), in consultation with the Attorney General and the Secretary of the Treasury, to designate an organization as a Foreign Terrorist Organization ("FTO"). *See* 8 U.S.C. §1189(a). . . .

In passing AEDPA, Congress sought to prevent persons within the United States or subject to United States' jurisdiction from providing material support to foreign organizations engaged in terrorist activities "to the fullest possible basis, consistent with the Constitution." AEDPA, Pub. L. No. 104-132, §301(b). Under Section 2339B(a)(1), a person who:

> knowingly provides material support or resources to a foreign terrorist organization, or attempts or conspires to do so, shall be fined under this title or imprisoned not more than 15 years, or both, and if the death of any person results, shall be imprisoned for any term of years or for life.

18 U.S.C. §2339B(a)(1). The term "material support"[8] is broadly defined in AEDPA to mean "currency or other financial securities, financial services, lodging, training, safehouses, false documentation or identification, communications equipment, facilities, weapons, lethal substances, explosives, personnel, transportation, and other physical assets, except medicine or religious materials." *Id.* §2339A(b); *id.* §2239B(g)(4). In passing such a broad prohibition, Congress found that FTOs "are so tainted by their criminal conduct that any contribution to such an organization facilitates that conduct." Pub. L. No. 104-132, §301(a)(7). . . .

[Here the court explained the process for designating an FTO, which is described in the casebook at pp. 566-569 and in this Supplement at pp. 34-38.]

---

8. The definition of "material support" was expanded by the Patriot Act to add "monetary instruments" and "expert advice or assistance." Pub. L. No. 107-56, §805(a)(2).

AEDPA limits the right, scope, basis and time period for judicial review by a FTO. *See id.* §1189(b) (limiting judicial review to 30 days after designation based solely on the administrative record, unless the government wants to submit additional classified evidence *ex parte,* and limiting the scope of review that the United States Court of Appeals for the District of Columbia Circuit takes of a designation). Further, AEDPA precludes a criminal defendant's right to "raise any question concerning the validity of the issuance of such designation as a defense or objection at any trial or hearing." *Id.* §1189(a)(8).

On October 8, 1997, the Secretary designated PIJ as a FTO under AEDPA. *See* 62 Fed. Reg. 52,650 (1997). The Secretary's designation of PIJ as a FTO was renewed in 1999, 2001, and 2003. Neither Congress nor the Secretary revoked the PIJ's designation at any time, and the PIJ has not sought judicial review of its designations as a FTO.

2. IEEPA . . .

[The Court explained the President's authority under the IEEPA when he declares a national emergency, described in the casebook at p. 115 nn. 1 and 2, and p. 122, Note 4. In 1995, President Clinton declared a national emergency with respect to the Middle East peace process and, in that connection, prohibited financial transactions with any specially designated terrorist ("SDT"). Exec. Order No. 12,947, 60 Fed. Reg. 5079 (1995). Defendants were charged with criminally violating regulations implementing this ban. The IEEPA does not explicitly provide for judicial review of an executive order, but the courts have held that an SDT designation under the IEEPA or its regulations is subject to judicial review under the Administrative Procedure Act. *See, e.g.,* Holy Land Foundation for Relief and Development v. Ashcroft, 333 F.3d 156 (D.C. Cir. 2003), *cert. denied,* 124 S. Ct. 1506 (2004). Thus, the counts charging violations of the IEEPA presented essentially the same legal issues as those charging violations of the AEDPA.]

II. DISCUSSION . . .

A. Statutory Construction and Constitutional Issues

1. Statutory Construction of AEDPA AND IEEPA

a. First Amendment, Overbreadth, and Vagueness Background

Chapter 14. Trying International Terrorists

Before reaching the statutory construction issues, it is helpful, if not necessary, to understand certain constitutional arguments raised by the parties that affect this Court's construction of AEDPA and IEEPA. Defendants have moved to dismiss Counts 1 through 4 of the Indictment, arguing that the Indictment attempts to criminalize their First Amendment rights of speech in support of and association with the PIJ. Defendants assert that Counts 1 through 4 are unconstitutional because they do not require either: (a) a specific intent to further the unlawful activities of the PIJ; or (b) an intent to incite and a likelihood of imminent disorder. Alternatively, Defendants argue that Counts 1 through 4 are not content neutral and are subject to analysis under strict scrutiny, which is rarely, if ever, met and is not met in this case.

As a corollary to their First Amendment argument, Defendants also claim that the doctrines of overbreadth and vagueness invalidate AEDPA or IEEPA in whole or in part. Defendants assert that the statutes sweep so broadly that they include substantial amounts of constitutionally protected advocacy within their prohibitions. Similarly, Defendants argue that the material terms of each statute are so broadly defined that a person is incapable of knowing when otherwise protected activity becomes criminal. In support of Defendants' position, Defendants cite to two Ninth Circuit opinions where that court twice concluded that portions of AEDPA are unconstitutionally vague as applied to the plaintiffs in that case.[20] Defendants argue that the same hypothetical utilized by the Ninth Circuit indicates that other sections of AEDPA and IEEPA are similarly vague and unconstitutional. . . .

While it may not be apparent from either parties' [sic] arguments, the dispute between the parties on what analysis applies and the constitutionality of Counts 3 and 4 of the Indictment actually turns on how this Court interprets AEDPA and IEEPA. The broader this Court interprets AEDPA and IEEPA, the more likely that the statutes receive a higher standard of review and are unconstitutional. For example, if this Court interprets AEDPA and IEEPA as requiring a specific intent to further the illegal activities of the FTO or SDT, then no constitutional problems exist. Similarly, if this Court interprets AEDPA's and IEEPA's prohibitions

---

20. *See Humanitarian Law Project v. United States Dep't of Justice*, 352 F.3d 382, 403-05 (9th Cir. 2003) (hereinafter referred to as "*Humanitarian II*"); *Humanitarian Law Project v. Reno*, 205 F.3d 1130, 1137-38 (9th Cir. 2000), *cert. den. sub nom., Humanitarian Law Project v. Ashcroft*, 532 U.S. 904 (2001) (hereinafter referred to as "*Humanitarian I*") (collectively *Humanitarian I* and *Humanitarian II* are referred to as "*Humanitarian*").

broadly and does not impose a specific intent *mens rea* requirement, it will likely be forced to perform a vagueness analysis and find portions of AEDPA and IEEPA unconstitutional, as did the Ninth Circuit in the *Humanitarian* cases.

b. Standards for interpreting a statute . . .

In [*United States v.*] *X-Citement Video* [513 U.S. 64 (1994)], the Supreme Court faced almost the same statutory interpretation issues faced in this case. There, the Supreme Court considered the Protection of Children Against Sexual Exploitation Act, 18 U.S.C. §2252. 513 U.S. at 65-66. Section 2252 of that Act made it unlawful for any person to "knowingly" transport, ship, receive, distribute, or reproduce a visual depiction involving a "minor engaging in sexually explicit conduct." *Id.* at 68. The Ninth Circuit had interpreted "knowingly" to only modify the surrounding verbs, like transport or ship. *See id.* Under this construction, whether a defendant knew the minority of the performer(s) or even knew whether the material was sexually explicit was inconsequential. *See id.* at 68-69. The Supreme Court reversed, concluding that, while the Ninth Circuit's construction of Section 2252 complied with the plain meaning rule, the construction caused absurd results. *See id.* at 69. Under the Ninth Circuit's construction, the Court noted that a Federal Express courier who knew that there was film in a package could be convicted even though the courier had no knowledge that the film contained child pornography. *See id.* To avoid such results, the Court utilized the cannons of statutory construction to imply a "knowing" requirement to each element, including the age of the performers and the sexually explicit nature of the material. *See id.* at 70-78. The Court stated that in criminal statutes "the presumption in favor of a scienter requirement should apply to each of the statutory elements that criminalize otherwise innocent conduct." *Id.* at 72.

c. Statutory Construction of AEDPA

Turning now to AEDPA, Section 2339B(a)(1) makes it unlawful for a person to "knowingly provide[ ] material support or resources to a foreign terrorist organization, or attempts or conspires to do so . . . ." 18 U.S.C. §2339B(a)(1). The Ninth Circuit has twice in a single case interpreted Section 2339B and found portions to be unconstitutionally vague as applied to the plaintiffs in that case. *See Humanitarian II,* 352 F.3d at 385, 393; *Humanitarian I,* 205 F.3d at 1133-36. *Humanitarian* involved a civil action for declaratory and injunctive relief brought by six organizations and two United States citizens who wished to provide the Kurdistan Workers' Party (the "PKK") and the Liberation Tigers of Tamil Eelam (the "LTTE") with support for the political and nonviolent humanitarian activities of each organization.

In *Humanitarian I,* the Ninth Circuit faced head on a challenge to Section 2339B on freedom of association, freedom of speech, and vagueness grounds. *See id.* at 1133-38. The Ninth Circuit affirmed the district court's determination that AEDPA did not impinge upon the plaintiffs' associational or speech rights. *See id.* at 133-36. However, the Ninth Circuit also affirmed the district court's determination that the terms "personnel" and "training" (specified elements of "material support") were unconstitutionally vague because those terms could impinge on a person's advocacy rights. *See id.* at 1137-38. The Ninth Circuit commented that:

> Someone who advocates the cause of PKK could be seen as supplying them with personnel; it even fits under the government's rubric of freeing up resources, since having an independent advocate frees up members to engage in terrorist activities instead of advocacy. But advocacy is pure speech protected by the First Amendment.

Id. at 1137.[27]

Similarly, the Ninth Circuit stated that training was also vague because it could include "a plaintiff who wishes to instruct members of a designated group on how to petition the United Nations to give aid to their group . . . ." *Id.* at 1138. The government "invite[d]" the Ninth Circuit to cure these vagueness problems by implying "knowingly," which occurs earlier in the statute, to the material support requirement. The Ninth Circuit rejected this construction, reasoning that such a construction would be judicially rewriting the statute. *See id.* at 1138. The Ninth Circuit construed "knowingly" as modifying only "provides," which meant that the scienter requirement was met when the accused had knowledge that he provided something, rather than "knowledge . . . that what is provided in fact constitutes material support." *See id.* at 1138 n. 5.

On subsequent appeal in *Humanitarian II,* the Ninth Circuit reaffirmed its prior rulings on the plaintiffs' First Amendment arguments. 352 F.3d at 385, 393. However, the *Humanitarian II* panel faced a new Fifth Amendment challenge by the plaintiffs, who argued that the lack of personal guilt requirement in Section 2339B rendered it unconstitutional.

---

27. The *Humanitarian II* panel provided an illustration of how an advocate could free up members to engage in terrorism. *See* 352 F.3d at 404. The Ninth Circuit stated that "personnel" could include "efforts to urge members of Congress to support the release of Kurdish political prisoners in Turkey." *Id.*

See id. at 385. Therefore, the Ninth Circuit reconsidered its interpretation of the *mens rea* requirement in *Humanitarian I. See id.* Under its new interpretation, the Ninth Circuit concluded that Section 2339B also required proof that a person either knew: (a) that an organization was a FTO; or (b) of an organization's unlawful activities that caused it to be designated as a FTO. *See id.* at 400. The Ninth Circuit then reaffirmed its prior holding on the vagueness of "personnel" and "training" without analyzing how the change in the *mens rea* requirement affected its prior vagueness analysis. *See id.* at 403-05.

This Court agrees with the Ninth Circuit in *Humanitarian I* that a purely grammatical reading of the plain language of Section 2339B(a)(1) makes it unlawful for any person to knowingly furnish any item contained in the material support categories to an organization that has been designated a FTO. And like *Humanitarian II,* this Court agrees that this construction renders odd results and raises serious constitutional concerns. For example, under *Humanitarian I,* a donor could be convicted for giving money to a FTO without knowledge that an organization was a FTO or that it committed unlawful activities, and without an intent that the money be used to commit future unlawful activities.[28]

Humanitarian II attempted to correct this odd result and accompanying constitutional concerns by interpreting "knowingly" to mean that a person knew: (a) an organization was a FTO; or (b) an organization committed unlawful activities, which caused it to be designated a FTO. *See* 352 F.3d at 400. But, *Humanitarian II*'s construction of Section 2339B only cures some of the Fifth Amendment concerns. First, *Humanitarian II* fails to comply with *X-Citement Video*'s holding that a *mens rea* requirement "should apply to each of the statutory elements that criminalize otherwise innocent conduct." 513 U.S. at 72. *Humanitarian II* implies only a *mens rea* requirement to the FTO element of Section 2339B(a)(1) and not to the material support element. Under *Humanitarian II*'s construction, a cab driver could be guilty for giving a ride to a FTO member to the UN, if he knows that the person is a member of a FTO or the member or his organization at some time conducted an unlawful activity in a foreign country. Similarly, a hotel clerk in New York could be committing a crime by providing lodging to that same FTO member under similar circumstances as the cab driver. Because the *Humanitarian II*'s construction fails to avoid potential Fifth Amendment concerns, this Court rejects its construction of Section 2339B.

---

28. Similarly, a bank teller who cashes the donor's check for a FTO could also be guilty despite a similar lack of knowledge.

Chapter 14. Trying International Terrorists

Second, the *Humanitarian II* construction does not solve the constitutional vagueness concerns of Section 2339B(a)(1), which can be avoided by implying a *mens rea* requirement to the "material support or resources" element of Section 2339(B)(a)(1). If this Court accepted the *Humanitarian II* construction, it would likely have to declare many more categories of "material support" (in addition to "training" and "personnel" determined to be unconstitutionally vague in the *Humanitarian* cases) unconstitutionally vague for impinging on advocacy rights, including "financial services," "lodging," "safe houses," "communications equipment," "facilities," "transportation" and "other physical assets." Using the Ninth Circuit's vagueness example on "training,"[30] the statute could likewise punish other innocent conduct, such as where a person in New York City (where the United Nations is located) gave a FTO member a ride from the airport to the United Nations before the member petitioned the United Nations. Such conduct could be punished as providing "transportation" to a FTO under Section 2339B.[31] The end result of the Ninth Circuit's statutory construction in *Humanitarian II* is to render a substantial portion of Section 2339B unconstitutionally vague.

But, it is not necessary to do such serious damage to the statute if one follows the analysis used by the United States Supreme Court in *X-Citement Video*.[32] This Court concludes that it is more consistent with Congress's intent, which was to prohibit material support from FTOs to the "fullest possible basis," to imply a *mens rea* requirement to the "material support" element of Section 2339B(a)(1). Therefore, this Court concludes that to convict a defendant under Section 2339B(a)(1) the government must prove

---

30. The Ninth Circuit utilized the example of "a plaintiff who wishes to instruct members of a designated group on how to petition the United Nations to give aid to their group . . . ." *Humanitarian I*, 205 F.3d at 1138.

31. Other examples of innocent conduct that could be prohibited include the same person allowing the FTO member to spend the night at his house, cashing a check, loaning the member a cell phone for use during the stay, or allowing the member to use the fax machine or laptop computer in preparing the petition. And, the additional phrase "expert advice or assistance" added by the Patriot Act in 2002 could also fail as unconstitutionally vague. *See, e.g., Humanitarian Law Project v. Ashcroft*, 2004 WL 112760, at *12-14 (C.D. Cal. Jan. 22, 2004) (holding that "expert advice or assistance" added by the Patriot Act to definition of "material support" was unconstitutionally vague).

32. The Supreme Court has repeatedly recognized that a *scienter* or *mens rea* requirement may mitigate a law's vagueness. *See, e.g., Posters 'N' Things, Ltd. v. United States*, 511 U.S. 513, 526 (1994).

beyond a reasonable doubt that the defendant knew that: (a) the organization was a FTO or had committed unlawful activities that caused it to be so designated; and (b) what he was furnishing was "material support." To avoid Fifth Amendment personal guilt problems, this Court concludes that the government must show more than a defendant knew something was within a category of "material support" in order to meet (b). In order to meet (b), the government must show that the defendant knew (had a specific intent) that the support would further the illegal activities of a FTO.

This Court does not believe this burden is that great in the typical case.[34] Often, such an intent will be easily inferred. For example, a jury could infer a specific intent to further the illegal activities of a FTO when a defendant knowingly provides weapons, explosives, or lethal substances to an organization that he knows is a FTO because of the nature of the support. Likewise, a jury could infer a specific intent when a defendant knows that the organization continues to commit illegal acts and the defendant provides funds to that organization knowing that money is fungible and, once received, the donee can use the funds for any purpose it chooses. That is, by its nature, money carries an inherent danger for furthering the illegal aims of an organization. Congress said as much when it found that FTOs were "so tainted by their criminal conduct that any contribution to such an organization facilitates that conduct." Pub.L. No. 104-132, §301(a)(7).

This opinion in no way creates a safe harbor for terrorists or their supporters to try and avoid prosecution through utilization of shell "charitable organizations" or by directing money through the memo line of a check towards lawful activities.[35] This Court believes that a jury can quickly peer through such facades when appropriate. This is especially true if other facts indicate a defendant's true intent, like where defendants or conspirators utilize codes or unusual transaction practices to transfer funds. Instead, this Court's holding works to avoid potential constitutional problems and fully accomplish congressional intent.

---

34. Indeed, Congress recently added 18 U.S.C. §2339C, which criminalized raising funds with the specific intent that the funds will be or are used to cause the death or serious bodily injury of a civilian with the purpose of intimidating the population or compelling a government to do or abstain from doing any act. *See* 18 U.S.C. §2339C.

35. For example, a donation to a suicide bomber's family given with the intent to encourage others to engage in such activities or support such activities would satisfy this specific intent requirement.

d. Construction of IEEPA, the Executive Order, and the Regulations

[The court applied the same analysis to IEEPA and its implementing regulations as it had to AEDPA and concluded that IEEPA's criminal provision must be read to require the government to prove defendant's specific intent to further the illegal activities of the SDT.] . . .

2. First Amendment

Given this Court's construction of the *mens rea* requirements of AEDPA and IEEPA, little remains to be said of Defendants' First Amendment challenges to Counts 3 and 4. This Court will address two points raised by Defendants as to the Indictment in general.

First, this Court agrees with the government that the Indictment does not criminalize "pure speech." Instead, the overt acts section of the Indictment utilizes the speech of Defendants to show the existence of the conspiracies, the Defendants' agreement to participate in them, their level of participation or role in them, and the Defendants' criminal intent. It is well established that the government can use speech to prove elements of crimes such as motive or intent. As Associate Justice Jackson eloquently stated concurring in *Dennis v. United States:*

> The defense of freedom of speech or press has often been raised in conspiracy cases, because, whether committed by Communists, by businessmen, or by common criminals, it usually consists of words written or spoken, evidenced by letters, conversations, speeches or documents. Communication is the essence of every conspiracy, for only by it can common purpose and concert of action be brought about or be proved. . . . "But it has never been deemed an abridgement of freedom of speech . . . merely because the conduct was in part initiated, evidenced, or carried out by means of language . . . . Such an expansive interpretation of the constitutional guaranties of speech and press would make it practically impossible ever to enforce laws against agreements . . . and conspiracies deemed injurious to society."

341 U.S. 494, 575-76 (1951) (quoting *Giboney v. Empire Storage & Ice Co.,* 336 U.S. 490, 498 (1949)) (Jackson, J., concurring).

Such words are equally applicable to the conspiracies charged in this case. The fact that Defendants' speech is contained in the overt act section of the Indictment is of little consequence. As the Eleventh Circuit stated in *United States v. Lanier,* "an overt act need not be criminal, and may indeed be otherwise innocent . . . ." 920 F.2d 887, 893 (11th Cir. 1991). . . . The reason that an overt act can include even protected speech is that it is the agreement that is punishable in a conspiracy charge and not the overt act itself. Therefore, this Court denies Defendants' motion to dismiss on "pure speech" grounds.

Second, this Court declines Defendants' invitation to heighten the level of First Amendment protection given to seeking and donating funds. The Supreme Court has repeatedly considered the issue and determined that such activities are more like expressive conduct than pure speech. *See, e.g., McConnell v. Fed'l Election Comm'n,* ___ U.S. ___, 124 S. Ct. 619, 654-56 (2003); *Nixon v. Shrink Missouri Gov't PAC,* 528 U.S. 377, 386-88 (2000); *Buckley v. Valeo,* 424 U.S. 1, 20-21 (1976).

This Court agrees with the Seventh Circuit in *Boim v. Quranic Literacy Institute and Holy Land Foundation for Relief and Development* that the *Buckley* standard applies to determine the constitutionality of a regulation prohibiting contributions to foreign organizations. 291 F.3d 1000, 1026-27 (7th Cir. 2002). . . .

Under *Buckley* and its progeny, a regulation of fundraising is constitutional if it is closely drawn to further a sufficiently important government interest. *See McConnell,* ___ U.S. at ___, 124 S. Ct. at 654-56; *Shrink Missouri Gov't PAC,* 528 U.S. at 387-88; *Buckley,* 424 U.S. at 30. This Court concludes that AEDPA, IEEPA, and the other statutes at issue in this case easily meet this analysis.

The Supreme Court has termed the protection of the foreign policy interests of the United States to be of great importance. *See, e.g., Haig v. Agee,* 453 U.S. 280, 307 (1981). Likewise, other courts have concluded that the government's interest in stopping the spread of global terrorism is "paramount" or "substantial." *Boim,* 291 F.3d at 1027; *Humanitarian I,* 205 F.3d at 1135. This Court agrees and would conclude that stopping the spread of terrorism is not just a sufficiently important governmental interest, but is a compelling governmental interest.

Similarly, a congressional decision to stop the spread of global terrorism by preventing fundraising and prohibiting support is closely drawn to further this interest. This Court's construction of AEDPA and IEEPA (requiring proof of a specific intent to further the unlawful activities of a SDT or FTO) reinforces this Court's conclusion that the prohibitions in AEDPA and IEEPA are closely drawn to further the governmental interest. Therefore, this Court denies Defendants' motion to dismiss on First Amendment grounds.

3. Procedural Due Process: PIJ'S FTO Designation Under AEDPA and SDT Designation Under IEEPA

Defendants argue that Counts 3 and 4 of the Indictment should be dismissed because the PIJ was denied due process under AEDPA and IEEPA when it was designated, respectively, a FTO and a SDT. Defendants rely primarily on the Supreme Court's opinion in *United States v. Mendoza-Lopez* [481 U.S. 828 (1987)], and a district court decision in . . . *United States v. Rahmani*,[46] in support of their argument. The government argues that *Mendoza-Lopez* is inapplicable to this case because these Defendants lack standing to challenge the PIJ's designation and that *Rahmani* is seriously flawed. This Court concludes for those and additional reasons Defendants may not collaterally attack the designations of the PIJ under AEDPA or IEEPA.

In *Mendoza-Lopez*, the Supreme Court broadly held that "[o]ur cases establish that where a determination made in an administrative proceeding is to play a critical role in the subsequent imposition of a criminal sanction, there must be *some* meaningful review of the administrative proceeding." 481 U.S. at 837-38 (emphasis in original). The Court continued that where defects in the original proceeding foreclosed judicial review, collateral attack of a prior administrative decision in a subsequent criminal proceeding was allowable. *See id.* at 838-42. *Mendoza-Lopez* involved a criminal prosecution for illegal re-entry in which the defendant had been deprived of his right to appeal in the underlying deportation proceeding. *See id.* at 842. The Court affirmed the dismissal of an indictment and concluded that in such circumstances a prior deportation determination could not be used in a subsequent criminal proceeding. *See id.* In reaching its decision in *Mendoza-Lopez*, the Court distinguished two of its prior cases, *Yakus v. United States*[48] and *Lewis v. United States*,[49] which provide this Court with additional guidance in this case.

---

46. 209 F. Supp. 2d 1045 (C.D. Cal. 2002). The district court in *Rahmani* dismissed an indictment charging a violation of AEDPA based on a denial of due process to an FTO in its designation. *See id.* at 1058-59. The Court held AEDPA's designation procedure was facially unconstitutional. *See id.*

48. 321 U.S. 414 (1944). The Court in *Mendoza-Lopez* distinguished *Yakus* on the grounds that *Yakus* involved the "exigencies of wartime," dealt with regulations and not an adjudication, and adequate judicial review was available in another forum. 481 U.S. at 838 n. 15.

49. 445 U.S. 55 (1980).

In *Yakus*, the Supreme Court dealt with the conviction of three defendants for violating the Emergency Price Control Act (the "EPCA") by selling beef at prices above the maximum prices allowable under a regulation. 321 U.S. at 418-19. The EPCA delegated to a price administrator the authority to make regulations setting maximum prices of certain goods. *See id.* at 423. The EPCA required someone challenging a regulation to seek administrative review within 60 days. The EPCA limited judicial review of that administrative review to a specially established court, with a short statute of limitations period (30 days). *See id.* at 428-29. The EPCA allowed criminal liability to attach prior to the expiration of the time periods for administrative review or judicial determination. *See id.* at 438-39. The Court concluded that the EPCA did not violate the defendant's due process rights by not allowing a defendant to challenge the regulation in a criminal prosecution because the defendants had the right to challenge the designation elsewhere. *See id.* at 447.

In *Lewis,* the Supreme Court dealt with whether a defendant could challenge the constitutionality of a prior felony conviction in a subsequent federal prosecution for possession of a firearm. 445 U.S. at 57-58. The Court held that it was constitutional to not allow a defendant to challenge a prior felony conviction in a subsequent federal prosecution because the defendant could challenge the validity of the conviction in another proceeding or otherwise seek removal of the disability before obtaining a firearm. *See id.* at 65-67.

Neither *Mendoza-Lopez, Yakus,* nor *Lewis* is exactly apposite to the case at hand. However, this Court concludes that this case is closer to *Yakus* and *Lewis* than *Mendoza-Lopez.* Unlike *Mendoza-Lopez* and like *Yakus,* AEDPA and IEEPA are measures taken to protect the national security of the United States. Similar to *Yakus* and *Lewis,* under either AEDPA or IEEPA, a designated organization can seek some judicial review of its designation. Additionally, like in the *Humanitarian* cases, Defendants could have challenged AEDPA and IEEPA in a civil action. In such circumstances, this Court concludes that Defendants, like the defendants in *Yakus* and *Lewis,* cannot collaterally challenge the designation procedure utilized to designate the PIJ.

Additionally, a FTO designation is a designation of a third party and not a designation of Defendants themselves. This Court views that distinction as a critical distinction to the cases under *Mendoza-Lopez.* Except in rare cases, third parties do not have standing to assert the legal rights or interests of others. . . .

This Court concludes that the PIJ has suffered no disincentive to assert its rights, . . . and third-party standing does not exist in this case. Indeed, the PIJ had every incentive to assert any due process rights that it might

Chapter 14. Trying International Terrorists

possess, so that it could resume fundraising and other activities in the United States. The existence of this incentive is demonstrated by the numerous groups that have challenged their designations under AEDPA. Therefore, this Court concludes that Defendants lack standing to collaterally attack the procedure utilized to designate the PIJ.

Even if this Court concluded that Defendants could challenge the procedure employed in designating the PIJ, this Court would conclude that AEDPA's and IEEPA's designation procedure is facially constitutional. The Supreme Court has stated that "[a] facial challenge to a legislative Act is, of course, the most difficult challenge to mount successfully, since the challenger must establish that no set of circumstances exists under which the Act would be valid." *United States v. Salerno,* 481 U.S. 739, 745 (1987). The Supreme Court has also held that aliens are generally not entitled to constitutional rights until they are within the United States' territory and develop a substantial connection to the United States. *See Zadvydas v. Davis,* 533 U.S. 678, 693 (2001) (distinguishing the constitutional rights of an alien who entered the United States with the lack of constitutional rights for an alien who has not entered the United States); *United States v. Verdugo-Urquidez,* 494 U.S. 259, 269 (1990) (holding Fifth Amendment protections do not extend to aliens outside the territorial boundaries of the United States).

AEDPA's and IEEPA's designation procedures are constitutional when they apply to foreign organizations and individuals without a substantial connection to the United States. Therefore, Defendants' facial challenge fails. By AEDPA's and IEEPA's very terms, the acts' designation procedures primarily apply to foreign organizations and individuals. In such limited and exceptional circumstances, this Court holds that the facial analysis of a statute, like AEDPA or IEEPA, should include application to foreign organizations and individuals without a substantial connection to the United States. This Court disagrees with the *Rahmani* court that such an analysis would "effectively eviscerate the doctrine of facial invalidity." 209 F. Supp. 2d at 1056. Instead, this Court concludes that such an analysis prevents this Court from intruding into an area that "the Judiciary has neither aptitude, facilities nor responsibility [, which] . . . belong[s] to the domain of political power not subject to judicial intrusion or inquiry." *Chicago & Southern Air Lines v. Waterman S. S. Corp.,* 333 U.S. 103, 111 (1948); *see also Zadvydas v. Davis,* 533 U.S. at 696 (stating that "heightened deference [is due] to the judgments of political branches with respect to matters of national security.")

Finally, even if Defendants could challenge the designation procedures as applied to the PIJ, this Court would conclude that AEDPA's and IEEPA's designation procedures did not violate the due process rights of the

PIJ. None of the Defendants argue that the PIJ has property in or a substantial connection to the United States. At best, it appears that the PIJ has members in the United States who themselves own property in the United States. The United States Court of Appeals for the District of Columbia has twice concluded that a foreign organization's due process rights were not violated by AEDPA's designation procedure in such circumstances. *See 32 County Sovereignty Committee v. Dep't of State*, 292 F.3d 797, 799-800 (D.C. Cir. 2002); *People's Mojahedin Org. of Iran v. U.S. Dep't of State*, 182 F.3d 17, 22 (D.C. Cir. 1999) [see p. 34 in this Supplement]. Without any compelling reason why the PIJ should be treated differently, this Court concludes that the PIJ had no right to due process under the Constitution because it has no substantial connection to the United States. Therefore, this Court denies Defendants' motions to dismiss the Indictment for alleged due process violations of the PIJ's rights. . . .

[The court denied defendants' motions to dismiss particular counts insofar as they were based on the aforementioned constitutional grounds and dismissed some other counts on other grounds.]

NOTES AND QUESTIONS

1. *The Anti-Terrorist Prosecutor's Weapon of Choice?* The terrorists who perpetrated the 1993 bombing of the World Trade Center (casebook p. 605) and the 1995 bombing of the Alfred P. Murrah Building in Oklahoma City (casebook p. 607) survived the attacks. If such terrorists can be apprehended, they can be prosecuted for actually conducting the attack and possibly for conspiring to conduct further attacks. In recent years, however, suicide terrorism appears to be on the rise. When terrorists die in the attack, like the 9/11 terrorists, they obviously escape prosecution. To use the criminal law against would-be suicide terrorists, the government must stop them before they attack and prosecute them for inchoate crimes.

But the apparent expansion of the suicide terrorist threat in the nineties, and the difficulty of identifying and arresting would-be suicide terrorists in time, has caused the government to begin searching more vigorously up the chain of causation not only for those who plan, but also those who support, acts of terrorism. Abdel Rahman's prosecution was a way station in this shift in prosecutorial focus, because he was prosecuted for "overall supervision and direction of the membership," as the *Rahman* court put it, and not for involvement in "individual operations." But the hoary "seditious conspiracy" crime that the government there charged was anachronistic, notwithstanding the eventual success of the prosecution. Prosecutors needed a tool better suited to interdicting material support and, thereby, suicide terrorism.

Congress responded by enacting the material support provision of AEDPA in 1996 and expanding material support liability in subsequent legislation. Prosecutors, in turn, took up their new weapon enthusiastically. The material support charge is increasingly the government's weapon of choice against suspected terrorists. Between 9/11 and May 2004, at least 58 persons were indicted under the material support provisions, according to the media. *See Broader Law on 'Material Support' to Terrorists Needed, Justice Says,* AP, May 6, 2004, *available at http://www.signonsandiego. com/uniontrib/20040506/news_1n6terror.html.* By the end of 2003, at least eight had been convicted. *See* Siobhan Roth, *Drawing the Line: Judges Have Started Shutting Down Some of the Administration's Tools Against Terror,* Legal Times, Dec. 22, 2003, at 27. *See also* Laurie L. Levinson, *Prosecuting Terrorists,* Natl. L.J., Feb. 23, 2004, at 12. More-over, prosecutors are apparently successfully using the threat of a 15-year prison term for material support to pressure defendants to plead out. *See* Siobhan Roth, *Material Support Law: Weapon in War on Terror,* Legal Times, May 5, 2003, at 11. *See generally* Norman Abrams, *The Material Support Terrorism Offenses: Perspectives Derived from the (Early) Model Penal Code,* 1 J. Natl. Security L. & Poly. 5 (2005).

More recent data indicate that material support charges rank second only to document fraud in numbers charged in the war on terrorism and in convictions. Center on Law and Security, *Terrorist Trials: A Report Card* 6-7, Feb. 2005, *available at http://www.law.nyu.edu/centers/lawsecurity/ publications/terroristtrialreportcard.pdf.* Critics charge that "'[m]aterial support' has been used as a catch-all category in terrorism cases . . . and has failed to provide clarity or consistency as to the use of these statutes." *Id.* at 2. (In Note 4, *infra,* we consider whether the italicized sentence at p. 291 in this Supplement meets this criticism.)

2. *Constitutional Issues in Criminalizing Material Support: An Overview.* When the government targets support it risks hitting advocacy and association. The *Rahman* case foreshadowed the resulting constitutional issues, but they have since surfaced more fully in material support prosecutions.

Vagueness is one issue: does the law give fair notice of the conduct it prohibits? Overbreadth is a related issue: does the law sweep so broadly that it may reach or at least chill activity that is protected by the First Amendment? Note that the material support statutes seem to pose different scienter requirements. This raises the further question whether they comport with the Fifth Amendment's implicit insistence on personal guilt for a criminal prosecution. These issues are complicated by their interaction, as *Al-Arian* suggests: a vague or overbroad statute may be saved by a narrow scienter requirement.

Of course, the material support provisions are *intended* to reach some activities usually protected by the First Amendment, such as fundraising, in order to achieve the government purpose of preventing terrorism. This poses an issue about the level of First Amendment protection to which such activity is entitled and the corresponding level of judicial scrutiny of governmental regulation of the activity.

Finally, 18 U.S.C. §2339B poses its own due process issue by criminalizing material support for an entity that has been designated an FTO. Does a criminal defendant have the right to challenge the FTO designation in his criminal case?

Keeping in mind the interrelation of many of these problems, we treat them separately in the following notes.

3. *Vagueness and Overbreadth.* "Because First Amendment freedoms need breathing space to survive, government may regulate in the area only with narrow specificity." NAACP v. Button, 371 U.S. 415, 433 (1963). Criminal laws that impact such freedoms are therefore always subject to attack for vagueness or overbreadth. A law is unconstitutionally vague if a reasonable person cannot tell what expression is prohibited and what is permitted. A law is unconstitutionally overbroad if it "regulates substantially more speech than the Constitution allows to be regulated and a person to whom the law constitutionally can be applied can argue that it would be unconstitutional as applied to others." Erwin Chemerinsky, *Constitutional Law* 912 (2d ed. 2002). Because the overbreadth doctrine creates substantial social costs, by prohibiting enforcement of a criminal statute even for behavior that it could otherwise constitutionally reach, the Supreme Court has "insisted that the law's application to protected speech be 'substantial,' not only in an absolute sense, but also relative to the scope of the law's plainly legitimate applications" for the statute to be struck down for overbreadth. Virginia v. Hicks, 539 U.S. 113, 119-120 (2003).

Applying just these principles for the moment, which, if any, of the following terms of §2339A(b), defining "material support," would you find unconstitutionally vague or overbroad?

a. "Personnel." Consider the case of a lawyer for a convicted terrorist who meets periodically with her client in prison and secretly conveys messages between him and his associates (including members of an FTO) outside of prison. Is this term unconstitutionally vague as applied to prosecute that lawyer for providing *herself* as "personnel" to a terrorist or FTO? *See* United States v. Sattar, 272 F. Supp. 2d 348 (S.D.N.Y. 2003)

Chapter 14. Trying International Terrorists

(*Sattar I*) (yes; government's assertion in oral argument that "you know it when you see it" is an "insufficient guide by which a person can predict the legality of that person's conduct," whatever merit it may have as a way to identify obscenity).

Is it too vague for prosecuting the lawyer for supplying *her client* as "personnel" to the FTO, by making him "available" through communications that she conveys? *See* United States v. Sattar, 314 F. Supp. 2d 279, 300 (S.D.N.Y. 2004) (*Sattar II*) (no; "the 'provision' of 'personnel' – in this case, by making Sheik Abdel Rahman available as a co-conspirator in a conspiracy to kill and kidnap persons in a foreign country – is conduct that plainly is prohibited by the statute" with sufficient definiteness).

Is it too vague as applied to the U.S. citizen who joins the Taliban to fight alongside al Qaeda fighters against U.S. armed forces in Afghanistan? *See* United States v. Lindh, 212 F. Supp. 2d 541, 574 (E.D. Va. 2002) (no; "personnel" is not unconstitutionally vague as applied to "employees" or "employee-like operatives" who were under the "direction and control" of an FTO).

b. "Communications equipment." Consider the lawyer hypothetical again. If the lawyer uses her phone to convey messages to or from her client in prison, can she be prosecuted for providing "communications equipment" to a terrorist or FTO? *See Sattar I*, 272 F. Supp. 2d at 358 (no; "by criminalizing the mere use of phones and other means of communication the statute provides neither notice nor standards for its application such that it is unconstitutionally vague as applied"). What application of this term would *not* be unconstitutionally vague?

c. "Training." In footnote 30, the court in *Al-Arian* quotes the Ninth Circuit's example of how this term would be unconstitutional as applied to "a plaintiff who wishes to instruct members of a designated group on how to petition the United Nations to give aid to their group." But suppose this person styled himself a "trainer" in lobbying and called the instruction "Training in Dealing with the UN"? Has the vagueness problem been cured? Is it still vague if applied to a person who is training members of an FTO in car bomb assembly? In either case, is the problem vagueness or overbreadth? *See Humanitarian I*, 205 F.3d at 1138.

d. "Expert advice or assistance." Is this term unconstitutionally vague as applied to the person who is advising FTO members on petitioning the United Nations? *See* Humanitarian Law Project v. Ashcroft, 2004 WL 112760, at *12-14 (C.D. Cal. Jan. 22, 2004) (yes). Overbroad? *Id.* (no). Is the term unconstitutionally vague as applied to a lawyer who represents a terrorist or member of an FTO or to the FTO itself? If not, what is the constitutional obstacle to indicting the lawyer for violating the material support statute?

4. *Scienter and Guilt by Association?* Congress has not made it a crime to be a member of an FTO. What legal reasons might explain why it has not?

In the Smith Act, Congress criminalized knowing membership in any organization that advocates the overthrow of the government by force or violence. 18 U.S.C. §2385 (2000). The act came before the Supreme Court in Scales v. United States, 367 U.S. 203 (1961), in which the Court upheld a conviction for membership on proof of *knowing* membership or affiliation and *specific intent* to further the group's unlawful goals. The Court explained its insistence on these elements of proof by rejecting the concept of guilt by association:

> In our jurisprudence guilt is personal, and when the imposition of punishment on a status or on conduct can only be justified by reference to the relationship of that status or conduct to other concededly criminal activity (here advocacy of violent overthrow), that relationship must be sufficiently substantial to satisfy the concept of personal guilt in order to withstand attack under the Due Process Clause of the Fifth Amendment. [*Id.* at 224-225.]

Specific intent implements the requirement of personal guilt by "tying the imposition of guilt to an individually culpable act." *See* David Cole, *Hanging With the Wrong Crowd: Of Gangs, Terrorists, and the Right of Association*, 1999 Sup. Ct. Rev. 203, 217. In First Amendment terms, the specific intent requirement "identifies the only narrowly tailored way to punish individuals for group wrongdoing (essentially by requiring evidence of individual wrongdoing), just as the *Brandenburg* test [casebook at p. 838] sets forth the narrowly tailored way to respond to advocacy of illegal conduct." Cole, *supra*, at 218.

But the material support statute does not criminalize membership in, or even support for the political goals of, an FTO. It criminalizes

> the act of giving material support, and there is no constitutional right to facilitate terrorism by giving terrorists the weapons and explosives with which to carry out their grisly mission . . . [or] to provide resources with which terrorists can buy weapons and explosives. [*Humanitarian I*, 205 F.3d at 1133.]

The Ninth Circuit therefore decided in *Humanitarian II*, 352 F.3d 382, that in a prosecution for violation of 28 U.S.C. §2339B, the government had only to prove that a defendant knowingly gave material support to a group he knew to have been designated an FTO or to have engaged in terrorist activities qualifying for such designation, not that he had any specific intent to further the FTO's illegal aims.

Would applying the Ninth Circuit analysis to the hypotheticals set out by the court in *Al-Arian* in footnote 31 and the related text be consistent with "the concept of personal guilt" mentioned in *Scales* or the "presumption in favor of a scienter requirement" declared in *X-Citement Video*? In that regard, consider the assertion that some FTOs engage in both terrorism and social work. *Cf.* Michael Whidden, Note, *Unequal Justice: Arabs in America and United States Antiterrorism in Legislation*, 69 Fordham L. Rev. 2825, 2873 (2001) (asserting that FTOs Hamas and Hezbollah operate orphanages, hospitals, schools, and medical clinics for indigent Palestinians, in addition to conducting terrorist activities).

On the other hand, does not the court's solution in *Al-Arian* undercut congressional intent? *See Aiding Terrorists – An Examination of the Material Support Statute: Hearing Before the Senate Judiciary Comm.*, 108th Cong. (May 5, 2004) (statement of Asst. Prof. Robert Chesney, Wake Forest Univ. School of Law), *available at http://judiciary.senate.gov/print_testimony.cfm?id=1172&wit_id=3394* ("By interpreting the statute to require proof of specific intent to further the illegal ends of the recipient organization in all its applications, the district court in effect rejected the Congressional determination that all forms of support for a foreign terrorist organization, however well-intentioned, enhance the overall capacity of the organization to engage in activities harmful to U.S. national security and foreign policy"). Congress apparently thought so, because it amended the statute after *Al-Arian* to add the italicized sentence at page 291. Intelligence Reform and Terrorism Prevention Act of 2004, Pub. L. No. 108-458, §6603(c)(2), 118 Stat. 3638, 3763. Does this solve the problem that *Al-Arian* identified?

Why are not the same scienter concerns present in 2339A? (Hint: compare the language of the two provisions.) *See Sattar II*, 314 F. Supp. 2d at 301.

5. *Scienter and Vagueness.* Note that the court in *Al-Arian* treats these concepts as reciprocals – reading a heightened scienter requirement into vague terms cures their constitutional infirmity. Other courts disagree. "The statute's vagueness as applied to the allegations in the Indictment concerning the provision of personnel is a fatal flaw that the Court cannot cure by reading into the statute a stricter definition of the material support provision than the statute itself provides." *Sattar I*, 272 F. Supp. 2d at 360.

Is there anything about 18 U.S.C. §§2339A, 2339B, and 2339C, when read together, that should have given the court in *Al-Arian* pause about its construction of §2339B?

6. *Donating Money as Protected Expression.* Donating money is not membership, but it is also unlike donating weapons, safe houses, or transportation. "The right to join together 'for the advancement of beliefs and ideas' is diluted," the Supreme Court explained, "if it does not include the right to pool money through contributions, for funds are often essential if 'advocacy' is to be truly or optimally 'effective.'" Buckley v. Valeo, 424 U.S. 1, 65-66 (1974) (quoting NAACP v. Alabama ex rel. Patterson, 357 U.S. 449, 460 (1958)). Why is donating money to an FTO not protected political expression?

One answer is that it *is* protected expression but that the protection is not absolute. What degree of scrutiny should a court then give to its regulation? *Compare* Cole, *supra*, at 237-238 (urging strict scrutiny – requiring a close relationship to a compelling government interest – when government's purpose is to regulate association as such) *with Al-Arian, supra* (apparently applying intermediate scrutiny – requiring a "sufficiently important government interest"). Does it matter, given the government interest in regulating material support? *See generally* Nina J. Crimm, *High Alert: The Government's War on the Financing of Terrorism and Implications for Donors, Domestic Charitable Organizations, and Global Philanthropy*, 45 Wm. & Mary L. Rev. 1341 (2004); David Cole, *The New McCarthyism: Repeating History in the War on Terrorism*, 38 Harv. C.R.-C.L. L. Rev. 1, 11 (2003).

7. *Challenging the FTO Designation.* We have seen that the D.C. Circuit has held that some FTOs have a due process right, in connection with their designation as FTOs, to notice, disclosure of at least unclassified parts of the administrative record underlying their designation, and an opportunity to be heard. See this Supplement at p. 34. *See generally* Sahar Aziz, *The Laws on Providing Material Support to Terrorist Organizations: Erosion of Constitutional Rights or a Legitimate Tool for Preventing Terrorism?*, 9 Tex. J. on C.L. & C.R. 45 (2003). Is Al-Arian bound by the designation when he is prosecuted for violating 2339B? Why? Would it have made any difference to Al-Arian's challenge to the designation of PIJ as an FTO and SDT if PIJ had some U.S. citizens as members? An office in the United States? No notice or opportunity to defend against its designation? Which court is right about a 2339B defendant's right to challenge the designation of the FTO he is alleged to have given material support, the court in *Al-Arian* or the court in *Rahmani*?

Chapter 14. Trying International Terrorists

8. *Terrorist Web Sites?* What arguments would you make about the legality of a material support prosecution for maintaining a Web site that urges "jihad" against the United States, "fight[ing] the idolator with your money, your selves, your tongues and your prayers, financial donations to jihadists, and 'struggle' against U.S. troops and facilities in Muslim lands to 'make them leave the holy lands'"? The government indicted a Saudi student in Idaho in part for giving material support to al Qaeda by maintaining such a Web site. *See* Susan Schmidt, *U.S. Indicts Saudi Student*, Wash. Post, Jan. 10, 2004, at A10. The jury subsequently acquitted him on these charges, finding insufficient evidence. *See* Patrick Orr, *Sami Al-Hussayen Not Guilty of Aiding Terrorist Groups*, Idaho Statesman, June 11, 2004. "Material support . . . is a difficult charge to prove," the prosecutor said. "It isn't like a case where you find fingerprints on a bomb." *Id.*

C. BRINGING THEM BACK ALIVE: EXTRADITION AND OTHER RENDITION

Page 867. Add the following material to the end of Note 4.

The Supreme Court had a chance to consider the propriety of Alvarez-Machain's abduction a dozen years later. In Sosa v. Alvarez-Machain, 542 U.S. 692, 124 S. Ct. 2739 (2004), the Mexican doctor sued his Mexican captors for damages under the Alien Tort Claims Act, 28 U.S.C. §1350 (2000). That statute creates jurisdiction in federal courts for "a "civil action by an alien for a tort only, committed in violation of the law of nations or a treaty of the United States." The Court declared that it could grant relief for violation of a customary international norm, provided the "content and acceptance among civilized nations" of that norm are clearly defined. 124 S. Ct. at 2765. But the Court went on to rule that the norms asserted by Alvarez-Machain failed to meet the Court's test of clear definition. While arbitrary arrest is condemned by both the Universal Declaration of Human Rights and the International Covenant on Civil and Political Rights, the Court noted, the first of these principles is not binding on the United States, while the second is non-self-executing and thus not enforceable in U.S. courts. *Id.* at 2767. The Court also rejected Alvarez-Machain's claim that because arbitrary arrest is not authorized by any applicable law, it is therefore forbidden by international law. *Id.* at 2768. Finally, the Court decided that while "prolonged arbitrary detention" is described as a violation of international law by §702 of the Restatement (Third) of Foreign Relations Law, Alvarez-Machain's prayer for relief based on such a "relatively brief detention" – less than a day – "expresses an aspiration that exceeds any binding customary rule having the specificity we require." *Id.* at 2769.

D. TRYING TERRORISTS AND OTHER INTERNATIONAL CRIMINALS

1. Secret Information in Proceedings Against Terrorists

Page 878. Add this material at the end of Note 3.

The risk of inaccuracy from using secret evidence may also be illustrated by a case described by the Washington Post as "the only criminal case since the Sept. 11 attacks in which secret evidence was presented against the defendant." *See* Dale Russakoff, *N.J. Judge Unseals Transcript in Controversial Terror Case*, Wash. Post, June 25, 2003, at A3. Reportedly local (non-federal) prosecutors convinced a state judge during a bail hearing that evidence against a defendant whom they alleged had ties to terrorists was so sensitive that the defendant could not be allowed to see it. Months later, an appellate judge ruled that prosecutors had not shown the defendant to be a security risk, and the trial judge then unsealed the bail hearing transcript. *Id.*; Robert Hanley & Jonathan Miller, *4 Transcripts Are Released in Case Tied to 9/11 Hijackers*, N.Y. Times, June 25, 2003, at B5; Jennifer V. Hughes, *Supposed Links to Terrorism Revealed,* The Record, June 25, 2003, at A01. Most of the evidence consisted of testimony by a detective about what he had heard from FBI agents about the defendant. Federal authorities, however, contradicted or denied knowledge of some of this information after release of the transcripts, and the defendant's attorney dismissed it as "slanderous, hearsay, double- and triple-hearsay, evidence which he claimed he could have rebutted if only he and the defendant had been allowed to see it." Russakoff, *supra.* "To think that they kept me in jail on this," the defendant said, after being held for six months as a suspected terrorist. *Id.* The state dropped all but one of 25 counts of selling fraudulent documents to Hispanic immigrants (none tied to terrorism).

Page 885. Add this material to the end of Note 1.

The decision to prosecute and the government's conduct of the trial of Wen Ho Lee are dealt with extensively in Dan Stober & Ian Hoffman, *A Convenient Spy: Wen Ho Lee and the Politics of Nuclear Espionage* (2001).

Chapter 14. Trying International Terrorists

Page 888. Add this material after Note 8.

9. *Another Option: Lying?* In 1983, a former CIA officer named Edwin P. Wilson was tried and convicted for illegally exporting explosives to Libya. He claimed that he was still working for the Agency and acting on its authority. During Wilson's trial, the government introduced an affidavit from a high-ranking CIA official denying Wilson's continued employment. The affidavit was a deliberate falsehood. Before Wilson was sentenced, attorneys at the CIA and the Justice Department learned of the fabrication, yet they failed to inform either the trial or appellate court. When the truth came to light 20 years later, Wilson's conviction was vacated. United States v. Wilson, 289 F. Supp. 2d 801 (S.D. Tex. 2003). A clearly incensed judge wrote, "Honesty comes hard to the government." *Id.* at 809.

United States v. Moussaoui
United States Court of Appeals, 4th Circuit, 2004
365 F.3d 292, *amended on reh'g,* 382 F.3d 453,
cert. denied, 125 S. Ct. 1670 (2005)

WILLIAM W. WILKINS, Chief Judge: The Government appeals a series of rulings by the district court granting Appellee Zacarias Moussaoui access to certain individuals[1] ("the enemy combatant witnesses" or "the witnesses") for the purpose of deposing them pursuant to Federal Rule of Criminal Procedure 15; rejecting the Government's proposed substitutions for the depositions; and imposing sanctions for the Government's refusal to produce the witnesses. We are presented with questions of grave significance – questions that test the commitment of this nation to an independent judiciary, to the constitutional guarantee of a fair trial even to one accused of the most heinous of crimes, and to the protection of our citizens against additional terrorist attacks. These questions do not admit of easy answers. . . .

---

1. The names of these individuals are classified, as is much of the information pertinent to this appeal. We have avoided reference to classified material to the greatest extent possible. Where classified information has been redacted, it has been noted by "* * * *."

I.

A. *Background Information* . . .

Moussaoui was arrested for an immigration violation in mid-August 2001 and, in December of that year, was indicted on several charges of conspiracy related to the September 11 attacks. In July 2002, the Government filed a superseding indictment charging Moussaoui with six offenses: conspiracy to commit acts of terrorism transcending national boundaries; conspiracy to commit aircraft piracy; conspiracy to destroy aircraft; conspiracy to use weapons of mass destruction; conspiracy to murder United States employees; and conspiracy to destroy property. The Government seeks the death penalty on the first four of these charges.

According to the allegations of the indictment, Moussaoui was present at an al Qaeda training camp in April 1998. The indictment further alleges that Moussaoui arrived in the United States in late February 2001 and thereafter began flight lessons in Norman, Oklahoma. Other allegations in the indictment highlight similarities between Moussaoui's conduct and the conduct of the September 11 hijackers. Each of the four death-eligible counts of the indictment alleges that the actions of Moussaoui and his coconspirators "result[ed] in the deaths of thousands of persons on September 11, 2001."

B. *Events Leading to This Appeal*

Simultaneously with its prosecution of Moussaoui, the Executive Branch has been engaged in ongoing efforts to eradicate al Qaeda and to capture its leader, Usama bin Laden. These efforts have resulted in the capture of numerous members of al Qaeda, including the witnesses at issue here: * * * *

Witness * * * * was captured * * * *. * * * *, Moussaoui (who at that time was representing himself in the district court) moved for access to Witness * * * *, asserting that the witness would be an important part of his defense. * * * * The Government opposed this request. . . .

[The district court found that * * * * was a material witness who might support Moussaoui's claim that he was not involved in the 9/11 attacks and that he should not receive the death penalty if convicted. The court ordered the witness's deposition by remote video, but the government appealed. The court of appeals remanded for the district court to determine whether any substitution existed which would place Moussaoui in substantially the same position as would a deposition. The district court rejected the government's proposed substitutions and again ordered deposition of the witness. When the government refused to comply with this order, the district court dismissed the death notice and prohibited the government] . . . "from making any argument, or offering any evidence, suggesting that the defendant had any involvement in, or knowledge of, the September 11 attacks." In conjunction with this ruling, the district court denied the Government's motions to admit into evidence cockpit voice recordings made on September 11; video footage of the collapse of the World Trade Center towers; and photographs of the victims of the attacks.

The Government now appeals, attacking multiple aspects of the rulings of the district court. . . .

III.

With respect to the merits, the Government first argues that the district court erred in ordering the production of the enemy combatant witnesses for the purpose of deposing them. Within the context of this argument, the Government makes two related claims. First, the Government asserts that because the witnesses are noncitizens outside the territorial boundaries of the United States, there is no means by which the district court can compel their appearance on Moussaoui's behalf. Second, the Government maintains that even if the district court has the power to reach the witnesses, its exercise of that power is curtailed by the reality that the witnesses are in military custody in time of war, and thus requiring them to be produced would violate constitutional principles of separation of powers. We address these arguments seriatim.

A. *Process Power*

The Sixth Amendment guarantees that "[i]n all criminal prosecutions, the accused shall enjoy the right . . . to have compulsory process for obtaining witnesses in his favor." U.S. Const. amend. VI. The compulsory process right is circumscribed, however, by the ability of the district court to obtain the presence of a witness through service of process. The Government maintains that because the enemy combatant witnesses are foreign nationals outside the boundaries of the United States, they are beyond the process power of the district court and, hence, unavailable to Moussaoui.

The Government's argument rests primarily on the well established and undisputed principle that the process power of the district court does not extend to foreign nationals abroad. . . .

The Government's argument overlooks the critical fact that the enemy combatant witnesses are in the custody of an official of the United States

Government. Therefore, we are concerned not with the ability of the district court to issue a subpoena to the witnesses, but rather with its power to issue a writ of habeas corpus *ad testificandum* ("testimonial writ") to the witnesses' custodian. . . .

. . . Therefore, the relevant question is not whether the district court can serve the *witnesses,* but rather whether the court can serve the *custodian.* . . .

[The court found that Secretary Rumsfeld was the proper custodian and that he was within the process power of the district court.]

IV.

The Government next argues that even if the district court would otherwise have the power to order the production of the witnesses, the January 30 and August 29 orders are improper because they infringe on the Executive's warmaking authority, in violation of separation of powers principles. . . .

B. *Governing Principles* . . .

Stated in its simplest terms, the separation of powers doctrine prohibits each branch of the government from "intru[ding] upon the central prerogatives of another." Such an intrusion occurs when one branch arrogates to itself powers constitutionally assigned to another branch or when the otherwise legitimate actions of one branch impair the functions of another.

This is not a case involving arrogation of the powers or duties of another branch. The district court orders requiring production of the enemy combatant witnesses involved the resolution of questions properly – indeed, exclusively – reserved to the judiciary. Therefore, if there is a separation of powers problem at all, it arises only from the burden the actions of the district court place on the Executive's performance of its duties.

The Supreme Court has explained on several occasions that determining whether a judicial act places impermissible burdens on another branch of government requires balancing the competing interests. *See, e.g., Nixon v. Admin'r of Gen. Servs.,* 433 U.S. 425, 443 (1977). . . .

C. Balancing

1. *The Burden on the Government*

The Constitution charges the Congress and the Executive with the making and conduct of war. It is not an exaggeration to state that the effective performance of these duties is essential to our continued existence as a sovereign nation. Indeed, "no governmental interest is more compelling than the security of the Nation." *Haig v. Agee,* 453 U.S. 280, 307 (1981). . . .

The Government alleges – and we accept as true – that * * * * the enemy combatant witnesses is critical to the ongoing effort to combat terrorism by al Qaeda. The witnesses are al Qaeda operatives * * * * Their value as intelligence sources can hardly be overstated. And, we must defer to the Government's assertion that interruption * * * * will have devastating effects on the ability to gather information from them. * * * *, it is not unreasonable to suppose that interruption * * * * could result in the loss of information that might prevent future terrorist attacks.

The Government also asserts that production of the witnesses would burden the Executive's ability to conduct foreign relations. The Government claims that if the Executive's assurances of confidentiality can be abrogated by the judiciary, the vital ability to obtain the cooperation of other governments will be devastated.

The Government also reminds us of the bolstering effect production of the witnesses might have on our enemies. . . . For example, al Qaeda operatives are trained to disrupt the legal process in whatever manner possible; indications that such techniques may be successful will only cause a redoubling of their efforts.

In summary, the burdens that would arise from production of the enemy combatant witnesses are substantial.

2. *Moussaoui's Interest*

The importance of the Sixth Amendment right to compulsory process is not subject to question – it is integral to our adversarial criminal justice system:

> The need to develop all relevant facts in the adversary system is both fundamental and comprehensive. The ends of criminal justice would be defeated if judgments were to be founded on a partial or speculative presentation of the facts. The very integrity of the judicial system and public confidence in the system depend on full disclosure of all the facts,

within the framework of the rules of evidence. To ensure that justice is done, it is imperative to the function of the courts that compulsory process be available for the production of evidence needed either by the prosecution or by the defense.

United States v. Nixon, 418 U.S. 683, 709 (1974).

The compulsory process right does not attach to any witness the defendant wishes to call, however. Rather, a defendant must demonstrate that the witness he desires to have produced would testify "in his favor." Thus, in order to assess Moussaoui's interest, we must determine whether the enemy combatant witnesses could provide testimony material to Moussaoui's defense.

In the CIPA context,[12] we have adopted the standard articulated by the Supreme Court in *Roviaro v. United States,* 353 U.S. 53 (1957), for determining whether the government's privilege in classified information must give way. Under that standard, a defendant becomes entitled to disclosure of classified information upon a showing that the information "'is relevant and helpful to the defense . . . or is essential to a fair determination of a cause.'" [United States v. Smith, 780 F.2d 1102 (4th Cir. 1985)], at 1107 (quoting *Roviaro,* 353 U.S. at 60-61).

Because Moussaoui has not had – and will not receive – direct access to any of the witnesses, he cannot be required to show materiality with the degree of specificity that applies in the ordinary case. Rather, it is sufficient if Moussaoui can make a "plausible showing" of materiality. However, in determining whether Moussaoui has made a plausible showing, we must bear in mind that Moussaoui *does* have access to the * * * * summaries.

Before considering whether Moussaoui has made the necessary showing with respect to each witness, we pause to consider some general arguments raised by the Government concerning materiality. First, the Government maintains that Moussaoui can demonstrate materiality only by relying on admissible evidence. We agree with the Government to a certain extent – Moussaoui should not be allowed to rely on obviously inadmissible

---

12. We adhere to our prior ruling that CIPA does not apply because the January 30 and August 29 orders of the district court are not covered by either of the potentially relevant provisions of CIPA: §4 (concerning deletion of classified information from *documents* to be turned over to the defendant during discovery) or §6 (concerning the disclosure of classified information by the defense during pretrial or trial proceedings). *See Moussaoui I,* 333 F.3d at 514-15. Like the district court, however, we believe that CIPA provides a useful framework for considering the questions raised by Moussaoui's request for access to the enemy combatant witnesses.

Chapter 14. Trying International Terrorists

statements (*e.g.*, statements resting on a witness' belief rather than his personal knowledge). However, because many rulings on admissibility – particularly those relating to relevance – can only be decided in the context of a trial, most of the witnesses' statements cannot meaningfully be assessed for admissibility at this time. Moreover, statements that may not be admissible at the guilt phase may be admissible during the penalty phase, with its more relaxed evidentiary standards.

Second, the Government maintains that Moussaoui cannot establish materiality unless he can prove that the witnesses would not invoke their Fifth Amendment rights against self-incrimination. We have previously indicated, however, that a court should not assume that a potential witness will invoke the Fifth Amendment. . . .

Additionally, the Government argues that even if the witnesses' testimony would tend to exonerate Moussaoui of involvement in the September 11 attacks, such testimony would not be material because the conspiracies with which Moussaoui is charged are broader than September 11. Thus, the Government argues, Moussaoui can be convicted even if he lacked any prior knowledge of September 11. This argument ignores the principle that the scope of an alleged conspiracy is a jury question, and the possibility that Moussaoui may assert that the conspiracy culminating in the September 11 attacks was distinct from any conspiracy in which he was involved. Moreover, even if the jury accepts the Government's claims regarding the scope of the charged conspiracy, testimony regarding Moussaoui's non-involvement in September 11 is critical to the penalty phase. If Moussaoui had no involvement in or knowledge of September 11, it is entirely possible that he would not be found eligible for the death penalty.

We now consider the rulings of the district court regarding the ability of each witness to provide material testimony in Moussaoui's favor.

* * * * * *

The district court did not err in concluding that Witness * * * * could offer material evidence on Moussaoui's behalf. * * * * Several statements by Witness * * * * tend to exculpate Moussaoui. For example, the * * * * summaries state that * * * * This statement tends to undermine the theory (which the Government may or may not intend to advance at trial) that Moussaoui was to pilot a fifth plane into the White House. Witness * * * * has also * * * * This statement is significant in light of other evidence * * * * indicating that Moussaoui had no contact with any of the hijackers. * * * * This is consistent with Moussaoui's claim that he was to be part of a post-September 11 operation. . . .

... On balance, however, Moussaoui has made a sufficient showing that evidence from Witness * * * * would be more helpful than hurtful, or at least that we cannot have confidence in the outcome of the trial without Witness * * * * evidence. ...

* * * * * *

The district court determined that Witness * * * * could provide material evidence because he could support Moussaoui's contention that he was not involved in the September 11 attacks. We agree with the district court that a jury might reasonably infer, from Witness * * * * that Moussaoui was not involved in September 11. We therefore conclude that Moussaoui has made a plausible showing that Witness * * * * would, if available, be a favorable witness.

3. *Balancing*

Having considered the burden alleged by the Government and the right claimed by Moussaoui, we now turn to the question of whether the district court should have refrained from acting in light of the national security interests asserted by the Government. The question is not unique; the Supreme Court has addressed similar matters on numerous occasions. In all cases of this type – cases falling into "what might loosely be called the area of constitutionally guaranteed access to evidence," *Arizona v. Youngblood,* 488 U.S. 51, 55 (1988) (internal quotation marks omitted) – the Supreme Court has held that the defendant's right to a trial that comports with the Fifth and Sixth Amendments prevails over the governmental privilege. Ultimately, as these cases make clear, the appropriate procedure is for the district court to order production of the evidence or witness and leave to the Government the choice of whether to comply with that order. If the government refuses to produce the information at issue – as it may properly do – the result is ordinarily dismissal. ...

In addition to the pronouncements of the Supreme Court in this area, we are also mindful of Congress' judgment, expressed in CIPA, that the Executive's interest in protecting classified information does not overcome a defendant's right to present his case. Under CIPA, once the district court determines that an item of classified information is relevant and material, that item must be admitted unless the government provides an adequate substitution. If no adequate substitution can be found, the government must decide whether it will prohibit the disclosure of the classified information; if it does so, the district court must impose a sanction, which is

Chapter 14. Trying International Terrorists

presumptively dismissal of the indictment.

In view of these authorities, it is clear that when an evidentiary privilege – even one that involves national security – is asserted by the Government in the context of its prosecution of a criminal offense, the "balancing" we must conduct is primarily, if not solely, an examination of whether the district court correctly determined that the information the Government seeks to withhold is material to the defense. We have determined that the enemy combatant witnesses can offer material testimony that is essential to Moussaoui's defense, and we therefore affirm the January 30 and August 29 orders. Thus, the choice is the Government's whether to comply with those orders or suffer a sanction.

V.

As noted previously, the Government has stated that it will not produce the enemy combatant witnesses for depositions (or, we presume, for any other purpose related to this litigation). We are thus left in the following situation: the district court has the power to order production of the enemy combatant witnesses and has properly determined that they could offer material testimony on Moussaoui's behalf, but the Government has refused to produce the witnesses. Under such circumstances, dismissal of the indictment is the usual course. Like the district court, however, we believe that a more measured approach is required. Additionally, we emphasize that no punitive sanction is warranted here because the Government has rightfully exercised its prerogative to protect national security interests by refusing to produce the witnesses.

Although, as explained above, this is not a CIPA case, that act nevertheless provides useful guidance in determining the nature of the remedies that may be available. Under CIPA, dismissal of an indictment is authorized only if the government has failed to produce an adequate substitute for the classified information, and the interests of justice would not be served by imposition of a lesser sanction. CIPA thus enjoins district courts to seek a solution that neither disadvantages the defendant nor penalizes the government (and the public) for protecting classified information that may be vital to national security.

A similar approach is appropriate here. Under such an approach, the first question is whether there is any appropriate substitution for the witnesses' testimony. Because we conclude, for the reasons set forth below, that appropriate substitutions are available, we need not consider any other remedy.

A. *Standard*

CIPA provides that the government may avoid the disclosure of classified information by proposing a substitute for the information, which the district court must accept if it "will provide the defendant with substantially the same ability to make his defense as would disclosure of the specific classified information." §6(c)(1). We believe that the standard set forth in CIPA adequately conveys the fundamental purpose of a substitution: to place the defendant, as nearly as possible, in the position he would be in if the classified information (here, the depositions of the witnesses) were available to him. Thus, a substitution is an appropriate remedy when it will not materially disadvantage the defendant. . . .

C. *Instructions*

For the reasons set forth above, we conclude that the district court erred in ruling that any substitution for the witnesses' testimony is inherently inadequate to the extent it is derived from the * * * * reports. To the contrary, we hold that the * * * * summaries (which, as the district court determined, accurately recapitulate the * * * * reports) provide an adequate basis for the creation of written statements that may be submitted to the jury in lieu of the witnesses' deposition testimony.

The crafting of substitutions is a task best suited to the district court, given its greater familiarity with the facts of the case and its authority to manage the presentation of evidence. Nevertheless, we think it is appropriate to provide some guidance to the court and the parties.

First, the circumstances of this case – most notably, the fact that the substitutions may very well support Moussaoui's defense – dictate that the crafting of substitutions be an interactive process among the parties and the district court. Second, we think that accuracy and fairness are best achieved by crafting substitutions that use the exact language of the * * * * summaries to the greatest extent possible. We believe that the best means of achieving both of these objectives is for defense counsel to identify particular portions of the * * * * summaries that Moussaoui may want to admit into evidence at trial. The Government may then argue that additional portions must be included in the interest of completeness. . . . If the substitutions are to be admitted at all (we leave open the possibility that Moussaoui may decide not to use the substitutions in his defense), they may be admitted only by Moussaoui. Based on defense counsel's submissions and the Government's objections, the district court could then create an appropriate set of substitutions. . . .

As previously indicated, the jury must be provided with certain information regarding the substitutions. While we leave the particulars of the instructions to the district court, the jury must be informed, at a minimum, that the substitutions are what the witnesses would say if called to testify; that the substitutions are derived from statements obtained under conditions that provide circumstantial guarantees of reliability: that the substitutions contain statements obtained * * * * ; and that neither the parties nor the district court has ever had access to the witnesses. . . .

Affirmed in part, vacated in part, and remanded.

[The opinions of WILLIAMS, Circuit Judge, and GREGORY, Circuit Judge, each concurring in part and dissenting in part, are omitted.]

NOTES AND QUESTIONS

1. *Moussaoui on Rehearing.* The Fourth Circuit reissued substantially the same opinion on rehearing. 382 F.3d 453 (4th Cir. 2004). This is how it explained the need for rehearing:

> On May 12, the Government submitted a letter to the court purporting to "clarify certain factual matters." In particular, the Government referred to pages 50-51 of the classified slip opinion, where the court stated: [Redacted] In response to the emphasized portion of the above quotation, the Government stated that members of the prosecution team, including FBI Special Agents assigned to the September 11 and other related investigations, [Redacted] have provided [Redacted] information [Redacted] consistent with the [Redacted] desire to maximize their own efforts to obtain actionable information [Redacted] The Government went on to note, however, that "[a]ny information or suggested areas of inquiry that have been shared [Redacted] have been used, like information from numerous other sources, at the sole discretion [Redacted]" *Id.* at 3. The Government asserted that [Redacted] *Id.*
>
> Based in part on the revelations in the May 12 letter, we directed the Government to file a response to the Petition. In particular, we directed the Government to provide answers to the following questions:
>
> (1) Why was the information in the May 12 Letter not provided to this court or the district court prior to May 12?
> (2) [Redacted]
> (3) [Redacted]
> (4) [Redacted] provided inculpatory of exculpatory information regarding Moussaoui?
> (5) In light of the information contained in the Letter and any other

pertinent developments, would it now be appropriate to submit written questions to any of the enemy combatant witnesses?
(6) What restrictions would apply to such a process and how should it be conducted?
(7) If access is granted by written questions, is the Compulsory Process Clause satisfied?
(8) If access is granted by written questions, what effect, if any, would *Crawford v. Washington,* 541 U.S. 36 (2004), have on such a process?
(9) If circumstances have changed such that submission of written questions is now possible, when did the circumstances change and why was neither this court nor the district court so informed at that time? [*Id.* at 460-461.]

Can you tell what was going on? *Should* we be able to tell, when the subject is not only Moussaoui's individual rights, but how the Sixth Amendment applies in a terrorism prosecution?

It does not help that the court explained that it then "conducted a sealed oral argument regarding the petition for rehearing" (*id.* at 461) in connection with which it received a joint appendix that is so heavily redacted in the amended opinion that we cannot tell what it includes. But perhaps you can guess from this excerpt:

[Redacted][12] [Redacted] the intelligence community is interested only in obtaining information that has foreign intelligence value; the intelligence community is not concerned with obtaining information to aid in the prosecution of Moussaoui. [Redacted] not create special [Redacted] reports for use by the prosecution, rather, the prosecution and the PESTTBOM team receive the same reports that are distributed to the intelligence community at large. Information is included in these reports only if [Redacted] the information to have foreign intelligence value.[14] [*Id.* at 461-462.]

---

12. After the Petition was filed, news articles indicated that the National Commission on Terrorist Attacks Upon the United States ("the 9/11 Commission") had submitted questions to be asked of unidentified al Qaeda detainees. *See* Philip Shenon, "Accord Near for 9/11 Panel to Question Qaeda Leaders," *N.Y. Times,* May 12, 2004, at A20 (reporting a statement by the 9/11 Commission that it was "close to an agreement with the Bush administration that would allow the panel to submit questions to captured Qaeda leaders who are believed to have been involved in planning the attacks") . . . .

14. The Government's submissions indicate that those responsible for [Redacted] the witnesses record and pass on only information [Redacted] to have foreign intelligence value. Consequently, it is at least possible, albeit unlikely, that one of the witnesses has imparted significant exculpatory information related to Moussaoui that has not been included [Redacted] If so, there may be a due process problem

Chapter 14. Trying International Terrorists

Then again, maybe not. If you represented the next accused terrorist, could you confidently ascertain the precedential value of *Moussaoui* in light of these opaque circumstances?

On rehearing, the Court of Appeals added this statement to the original opinion regarding CIPA:

> On rehearing, both parties acknowledged our holding that CIPA does not apply here but indicated their belief that once the district court has approved substitutions for the witnesses' testimony, CIPA comes into play, with the result that the Government may object to the disclosure of the classified information in the substitutions and request that the district court adopt an alternative form of evidence. *See* 18 U.S.C.A.App. 3 §6. We disagree.
>
> It must be remembered that the substitution process we here order is a *replacement* for the testimony of the enemy combatant witnesses. Because the Government will not allow Moussaoui to have contact with the witnesses, we must provide a remedy adequate to protect Moussaoui's constitutional rights. Here, that remedy is substitutions. Once Moussaoui has selected the portions of the [Redacted] summaries he wishes to submit to the jury and the Government has been given an opportunity to be heard, the district court will compile the substitutions, using such additional language as may be necessary to aid the understanding of the jury. Once this process is complete, the matter is at an end – there are to be no additional or supplementary proceedings under CIPA regarding the substitutions. [382 F.3d at 482.]

Is this another example of what Justice Scalia condemned in *Hamdi* as the "Mr. Fix-It Mentality" of federal courts? Judge Gregory, writing separately, found the majority's approach troubling, because "the majority has left the Government with no clear mechanism for mitigating the potential national security consequences of admission of Moussaoui's chosen portions of the summaries, other than the possibility of non-substantive changes to names, places, and the like." If CIPA is to be cut and pasted to deal with the issue in *Moussaoui*, why not leave the job to Congress?

---

under *Brady v. Maryland*, 373 U.S. 83 (1963). *See United States v. Perdomo*, 929 F.2d 967, 971 (3d Cir. 1991) (stating that prosecution is obligated under *Brady* to disclose all exculpatory information "in the possession of some arm of the state"). We need not consider this question, however, as there is no evidence before us that the Government possesses exculpatory material that has not been disclosed to the defense.

2. *Guilty Plea.* On April 22, 2005, Moussaoui surprised everyone by pleading guilty to the key charges against him, while at the same time denying having any intention to commit mass murder. As a result, he faces a possible death penalty going into the sentencing phase of his case, although the defense reportedly intends to argue that a death sentence would be unconstitutional and inappropriate in light of his mental condition. See *Moussaoui Pleads Guilty to Terror Charges,* CNN.com, Apr. 23, 2005, *at* http://www.cnn.com/2005/LAW/04/22/moussaoui/index.html.

3. *Deciding a Clash Between Branches: Formalism or Balancing?* The court concludes that the appropriate separation of powers analysis required by Moussaoui's insistence on access to * * * * is balancing as prescribed by Nixon v. Administrator of General Services, 433 U.S. 425, 443 (1977):

> [T]he proper inquiry focuses on the extent to which [the judicial act of ordering access, in this instance] prevents the Executive Branch from accomplishing its constitutionally assigned functions, . . . [and whether] that impact is justified by an overriding need to promote objectives within the constitutional authority of [the court].

See casebook p. 57. But in Public Citizen v. United States Department of Justice, 491 U.S. 440, 485 (1989) (casebook p. 56), Justice Kennedy noted that there is "a line of cases of equal weight and authority, . . . where the Constitution by explicit text commits the power at issue to the exclusive control of the President, . . . [and the Court has] refused to tolerate *any* intrusion by [the courts]." Why is not *Moussaoui* controlled by the latter line of cases? Does not the Commander in Chief Clause of Article II commit command of the armed forces in war to the President and is not the interrogation of enemy combatants in war part of that command? Does *Hamdi* (this Supplement p. 208) or *Padilla* (this Supplement p. 235) suggest any answer to this argument?

4. *A Wartime Exception?* What other cases would you rely on in making the formalist argument for the government, or, by a balancing analysis, in arguing the extent to which court-ordered access to * * * * would prevent the President from conducting the war? In this regard, consider *Keith* (casebook p. 615), *Korematsu* (casebook p. 796), and *Zadvydas* (casebook p. 732, Note 1). What other parts of Moussaoui's trial might again pose the question of a wartime exception to his rights? If the

Chapter 14. Trying International Terrorists 329

Moussaoui jury is the target of serious threats of harm, how would you balance his Sixth Amendment right to trial by jury against the government's interest in protecting them by empaneling them secretly in a secure location to hear the trial by video?

5. *Overriding Need?* The balancing test looks to whether the impact on the Commander in Chief is justified by an overriding need of the court to promote objectives within its constitutional authority. What is that need here? To judge its weight, should not the court consider whether there are alternatives that could also promote such objectives. What are the alternatives here to ordering summaries of * * * *'s evidence?

6. *CIPA by Analogy.* In deciding the alternatives, the court determined that the Classified Information Procedures Act (CIPA) (see casebook pp. 880-881) did not apply but relied upon it anyway for a "useful framework." Why did CIPA not apply? By what authority did the court undertake the relevance and balancing inquiries and order access to the summaries? Did the court, in effect, create a "wartime exception" to the Sixth Amendment after all?

Is this another example of what Justice Scalia condemned as the "Mr. Fix-It Mentality" of courts? If CIPA is to be amended to cover the *Moussaoui* problem, why not leave that job to Congress?

7. *Switching Fora?* The district court invited the government to "reconsider whether the civilian criminal courts are the appropriate fora" for trying someone like Moussaoui. The alternative is trial by military commission, which we explore at casebook pp. 889-906. Indeed, even Moussaoui's standby counsel appears to have invited this alternative, gratuitously conceding that the government's authority to try enemy combatants by military commission is "settled," and implying that the government can simply dismiss the criminal prosecution and proceed instead by a military commission to resolve the tension between Moussaoui's Sixth Amendment rights and the war powers. Brief of the Appellee at 3-4, United States v. Moussaoui, No. 03-4162 (4th Cir. May 13, 2003).

After you read the materials on military commissions, you can decide for yourself whether this is a wise concession. But do you agree with the apparent assumption upon which it and the district court's invitation rest – that the government can switch fora in midstream? Even assuming that the government could lawfully have tried Moussaoui by military commission *ab initio*, does it necessarily follow that it can start in a civilian court and then dismiss in favor of a military commission when it is unhappy with the civilian court's rulings? Would it matter how far the criminal prosecution had progressed beyond the indictment? If such a switch survived constitutional challenges, would it nevertheless violate the spirit of the law?

The government did, in fact, make a switch – actually a double-switch – in Al-Marri v. Hanft, No. 2:04-2257-HFF-RSC, 2005 WL 1719110 (D.S.C. July 8, 1005), noted *supra* p. 287. After al-Marri lawfully entered the United States with his family to obtain a master's degree, he was initially arrested as a material witness in the 9/11 investigation. In the first switch, he was then rearrested and indicted for making false statements and credit card fraud. More than two years later, President Bush interrupted the course of normal criminal proceedings (trial had not begun) by designating al-Marri an enemy combatant, after which he was transferred to military detention in South Carolina. The government then successfully moved to drop the criminal indictment with prejudice. At this writing, al-Marri remains in military detention without charges.

Al-Marri argued that his criminal detention was sufficient to thwart any terrorist acts and that there was no necessity for military detention. The district court rejected his argument in part on the reasoning that when a federal investigation of criminal charges pending in state court reveals a federal crime, the state charges can be dismissed and the matter can be transferred to federal jurisdiction. *Id.* at *7. Is the analogy sound?

Al-Marri also protested that while he might have been acquitted of the criminal charges, he had no opportunity to prove his innocence in military detention. The court rejected this claim as well, reasoning that the purpose of military detention is preventive.

> This Court recognizes the natural response to this reasoning that, when a defendant is acquitted of criminal charges, society should not assume that he ever did nor that he will, in the future, engage in the activities for which he was charged. In this case, however, Petitioner was not charged with crimes of terrorism, and thus, an acquittal of various fraud charges does not lead to the conclusion that he will not, in the future, engage in acts of terrorism as alleged by the government.

Id. *7 n.8.

2. Trial by Military Commission

Page 903. Add this material to Note 4.

On April 30, 2003, the Department of Defense issued an instruction defining crimes that could be tried by military commissions. The

Chapter 14. Trying International Terrorists

instruction purports to be "declarative of existing law" of armed conflict. Most of the listed crimes require a nexus with armed conflict – "in the context of and . . . associated with armed conflict" – which nevertheless

> does not require a declaration of war, ongoing mutual hostilities, or confrontation involving a regular national armed force. A single hostile act or attempted act may provide sufficient basis for the nexus so long as its magnitude or severity rises to the level of an "armed attack" or an "act of war," or the number, power, stated intent or organization of the force with which the actor is associated is such that the act or attempted act is tantamount to an attack by an armed force. [Department of Defense, *Military Commission Instruction No. 2*, at §5(C) (April 30, 2003).]

The instruction includes commonly recognized war crimes, such as willful killing of protected persons and attacking civilians, civilian objects, or protected property, as well as other offenses such as hijacking, terrorism, murder by an unprivileged belligerent, and aiding the enemy. "Terrorism" is defined as intentionally killing or harming one or more persons or engaging in an act that is inherently dangerous to another and evinces a wanton disregard of human life, to intimidate or coerce a civilian population, or to influence the policy of a government by intimidation or coercion, "in the context of and . . . associated with armed conflict." *Id.* §6(B)(2). Aiding and abetting, soliciting, conspiring to commit, or being an accessory after the fact to terrorism are also defined as crimes. Comments to the instructions state that solicitation of terrorism "may be by means other than speech and writing. Any act or conduct that reasonably may be construed as a serious request, order, inducement, advice, or offer of assistance to commit any offense triable by military commission may constitute solicitation." *Id.* at §6(C)(2)(b)(2). Do these instructions resolve the questions raised above? *If* the Constitution applies to prosecutions brought before military commissions, do you see any constitutional problems raised by the substantive offenses defined in the instructions?

Page 906. Add these materials at the end of Note 6.

The final military commission procedures have been issued and are mainly consistent with the draft procedures described in Note 6. Dept. of Defense, *Military Commission Order No. 1*, Mar. 21, 2002. The flow chart on page 333 depicts the military commission process.

7. *Restrictions on Defense Counsel.* One instruction caused particular controversy among members of the bar. *See* Office of the Secretary, Dept.

of Defense, *Qualification of Civilian Defense Counsel,* 68 Fed. Reg. 39391 (July 1, 2003) (to be codified at 32 C.F.R. pt. 14). This instruction required such counsel to take an oath that:

> I will not travel or transmit documents from the site of the proceedings without the approval of the Appointing Authority or the Presiding Officer. The Defense Team and I will otherwise perform all of our work relating to the proceedings, including any electronic or other research, at the site of the proceedings . . . .
>
> I will not discuss or otherwise communicate or share documents or information about the case with anyone except persons who have been designated as members of the Defense Team . . . .
>
> I understand that my communications with my client, even if traditionally covered by the attorney-client privilege, may be subject to monitoring or review by government officials, using any available means, for security and intelligence purposes. I understand that any such monitoring will only take place in limited circumstances when approved by proper authority, and that any evidence or information derived from such communications will not be used in proceedings against the Accused who made or received the relevant communication. . . . [*Id.* Annex B, ¶¶II(E)(1), (2), and (I).]

What issues, if any, do these requirements present for civilian lawyers subject to the Model Rules of Professional Responsibility? "An attorney would be committing malpractice by signing their affidavit," one lawyer is reported as asserting. *See* Vanessa Blum, *The Outlines of Justice,* Legal Times, May 26, 2003, at 1. Reportedly, the promulgation of these requirements discouraged civilian lawyers from applying. "Who's going to want to take a case where your conversations are going to be overheard, you are not going to be able to speak about the case to the press or anyone else, you are not going to be able to see classified evidence that's being used to convict your client, and your case is going to essentially take over your life – often without compensation?" asked one law professor and veteran lawyer for immigrant terrorist suspects. *See* Dan Christensen, *Veteran Attorneys Blast Rules for Military Trials,* Legal Intelligencer, May 15, 2003, at 4. "[T]he only thing more difficult than getting out of Guantánamo may be finding a lawyer willing to participate as civilian defense counsel in a military tribunal." David Cole, *Defending Show Trials,* The Nation, June 15, 2003, at 6.

In response to these comments, the Defense Department quietly and without notice or explanation changed its requirements in the instruction appearing on its Web site. *See* Peter Raven-Hansen, *Detaining Combatants by Law or by Order?,* 64 La. L. Rev. 831 (2004); Eugene R. Fidell, *Military*

Chapter 14. Trying International Terrorists

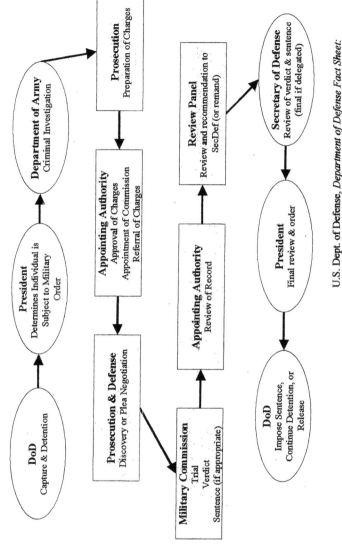

Commissions & Administrative Law, 6 Green Bag 379, 384 (2003).

Recall, on the other hand, that the military lawyers on the defense team have access to all proceedings and evidence. Does this compensate for the restrictions on civilian defense counsel? Do you think that it is accurate to call the anticipated military trials "show trials" or "kangaroo courts"? Are there less restrictive ways to address legitimate government interests in security during the trials?

8. *Detainees Designated for Trial.* At this writing, four detainees have been designated for trial, including Yemeni national Salim Ahmed Hamdan. *See* Josh White, *Long-Silent Detainees Talking,* Wash. Post, June 30, 2005, at A7. Hamdan successfully brought a petition for a writ of habeas corpus, which occasioned the following decision on appeal.

Hamdan v. Rumsfeld
United States Court of Appeals, D.C. Circuit, July 15, 2005
No. 04-5393, 2005 WL 1653046

RANDOLPH, Circuit Judge. Afghani militia forces captured Salim Ahmed Hamdan in Afghanistan in late November 2001. Hamdan's captors turned him over to the American military, which transported him to the Guantanamo Bay Naval Base in Cuba. The military initially kept him in the general detention facility, known as Camp Delta. On July 3, 2003, the President determined "that there is reason to believe that [Hamdan] was a member of al Qaeda or was otherwise involved in terrorism directed against the United States." This finding brought Hamdan within the compass of the President's November 13, 2001, Order concerning the Detention, Treatment, and Trial of Certain Non-Citizens in the War Against Terrorism, 66 Fed. Reg. 57,833. Accordingly, Hamdan was designated for trial before a military commission. . . .

[Hamdan filed a petition for habeas corpus. While the petition was pending, the government formally charged him with conspiracy to commit attacks on civilians and civilian objects, murder and destruction of property by an unprivileged belligerent, and terrorism. The charges alleged that Hamdan was Osama bin Laden's personal driver in Afghanistan between 1996 and November 2001 (an allegation Hamdan admitted in an affidavit) and that he served as bin Laden's personal bodyguard, delivered weapons to al Qaeda members, drove bin Laden to al Qaeda training camps and safe havens in Afghanistan, and trained at the al Qaeda-sponsored al Farouq camp.

In response to the Supreme Court's decision in Rasul v. Bush, 542 U.S.

466 (2004) (Supplement p. 252), Hamdan received a formal hearing before a Combatant Status Review Tribunal. The Tribunal affirmed his status as an enemy combatant, "either a member of or affiliated with Al Qaeda," for whom continued detention was required.

The district court granted Hamdan's petition in part, finding, *inter alia*, that he could not be tried by a military commission unless a competent tribunal determined that he was not a prisoner of war under the 1949 Geneva Convention governing the treatment of prisoners. It then enjoined the Secretary of Defense from conducting any further military commission proceedings against Hamdan. This appeal followed.]

I . . .

The government's initial argument is that the district court should have abstained from exercising jurisdiction over Hamdan's habeas corpus petition. . . .

. . . [T]here is an exception to abstention: "a person need not exhaust remedies in a military tribunal if the military court has no jurisdiction over him." [*New v. Cohen,* 129 F.3d 639, 644 (D.C. Cir. 1997).] . . . While . . . [Hamdan] does not deny the military's authority to try him, he does contend that a military commission has no jurisdiction over him and that any trial must be by court-martial. His claim, therefore, falls within the exception . . . .

II

In an argument distinct from his claims about the Geneva Convention, which we will discuss next, Hamdan maintains that the President violated the separation of powers inherent in the Constitution when he established military commissions. The argument is that Article I, §8, of the Constitution gives Congress the power "to constitute Tribunals inferior to the supreme Court," that Congress has not established military commissions, and that the President has no inherent authority to do so under Article II. . . .

The President's Military Order of November 13, 2001, stated that any person subject to the order, including members of al Qaeda, "shall, when tried, be tried by a military commission for any and all offenses triable by [a] military commission that such individual is alleged to have committed . . . ." 66 Fed. Reg. at 57,834. The President relied on four sources of authority: his authority as Commander in Chief of the Armed Forces, U.S. Const. art. II, §2; Congress's joint resolution authorizing the use of force; 10 U.S.C. §821; and 10 U.S.C. §836. The last three are, of course, actions of Congress.

In the joint resolution, passed in response to the attacks of September 11, 2001, Congress authorized the President "to use all necessary and appropriate force against those nations, organizations, or persons he determines planned, authorized, committed, or aided" the attacks and recognized the President's "authority under the Constitution to take action to deter and prevent acts of international terrorism against the United States." Authorization for Use of Military Force, Pub. L. No. 107-40, 115 Stat. 224, 224 (2001). *In re Yamashita,* 327 U.S. 1 (1946), which dealt with the validity of a military commission, held that an "important incident to the conduct of war is the adoption of measures by the military commander, not only to repel and defeat the enemy, but to seize and subject to disciplinary measures those enemies who, in their attempt to thwart or impede our military effort, have violated the law of war." *Id.* at 11. "The trial and punishment of enemy combatants," the Court further held, is thus part of the "conduct of war." *Id.* We think it no answer to say, as Hamdan does, that this case is different because Congress did not formally declare war. It has been suggested that only wars between sovereign nations would qualify for such a declaration. Even so, the joint resolution "went as far toward a declaration of war as it might, and as far or further than Congress went in the Civil War, the Philippine Insurrection, the Boxer Rebellion, the Punitive Expedition against Pancho Villa, the Korean War, the Vietnam War, the invasion of Panama, the Gulf War, and numerous other conflicts." The plurality in *Hamdi v. Rumsfeld,* in suggesting that a military commission could determine whether an American citizen was an enemy combatant in the current conflict, drew no distinction of the sort Hamdan urges upon us.

Ex parte Quirin also stands solidly against Hamdan's argument. The Court held that Congress had authorized military commissions through Article 15 of the Articles of War. The modern version of Article 15 is 10 U.S.C. §821, which the President invoked when he issued his military order. Section 821 states that court-martial jurisdiction does not "deprive military commissions . . . of concurrent jurisdiction with respect to offenders or offenses that by statute or by the law of war may be tried by military commissions." Congress also authorized the President, in another provision the military order cited, to establish procedures for military commissions. 10 U.S.C. §836(a). Given these provisions and *Quirin* and *Yamashita,* it is impossible to see any basis for Hamdan's claim that Congress has not authorized military commissions. He attempts to distinguish *Quirin* and *Yamashita* on the ground that the military commissions there were in "war zones" while Guantanamo is far removed from the battlefield. We are left to wonder why this should matter and, in any event, the distinction does not hold: the military commission in *Quirin* sat in Washington, D.C., in the Department of Justice building; the military commission in *Yamashita* sat in the Philippines after Japan had surrendered.

We therefore hold that through the joint resolution and the two statutes just mentioned, Congress authorized the military commission that will try Hamdan.

III

This brings us to Hamdan's argument, accepted by the district court, that the Geneva Convention Relative to the Treatment of Prisoners of War, Aug. 12, 1949, 6 U.S.T. 3316 ("1949 Geneva Convention"), ratified in 1955, may be enforced in federal court.

"Treaties made, or which shall be made, under the Authority of the United States, shall be the supreme Law of the Land." U.S. Const. art. VI, cl. 2. Even so, this country has traditionally negotiated treaties with the understanding that they do not create judicially enforceable individual rights. As a general matter, a "treaty is primarily a compact between independent nations," and "depends for the enforcement of its provisions on the interest and honor of the governments which are parties to it." *Head Money Cases,* 112 U.S. 580, 598 (1884). If a treaty is violated, this "becomes the subject of international negotiations and reclamation," not the subject of a lawsuit. *Id.*

Thus, "[i]nternational agreements, even those directly benefitting private persons, generally do not create private rights or provide for a private cause of action in domestic courts." Restatement (Third) of the Foreign Relations Law of the United States §907 cmt. a, at 395 (1987). The district court nevertheless concluded that the 1949 Geneva Convention conferred individual rights enforceable in federal court. We believe the court's conclusion disregards the principles just mentioned and is contrary to the Convention itself. To explain why, we must consider the Supreme Court's treatment of the Geneva Convention of 1929 in *Johnson v. Eisentrager,* 339 U.S. 763 (1950) . . . .

In *Eisentrager,* German nationals, convicted by a military commission in China of violating the laws of war and imprisoned in Germany, sought writs of habeas corpus in federal district court on the ground that the military commission violated their rights under the Constitution and their rights under the 1929 Geneva Convention. 339 U.S. at 767. The Supreme Court, speaking through Justice Jackson, wrote in an alternative holding that the Convention was not judicially enforceable: the Convention specifies rights of prisoners of war, but "responsibility for observance and enforcement of these rights is upon political and military authorities." *Id.* at 789 n.14. . . .

This aspect of *Eisentrager* is still good law and demands our adherence. *Rasul v. Bush,* 542 U.S. 466, 124 S. Ct. 2686 (2004), decided a different and "narrow" question: whether federal courts had jurisdiction under 28 U.S.C. §2241 "to consider challenges to the legality of the detention of foreign nationals" at Guantanamo Bay. *Id.* at 2690. The Court's decision in *Rasul* had nothing to say about enforcing any Geneva Convention. Its holding that federal courts had habeas corpus jurisdiction had no effect on *Eisentrager*'s interpretation of the 1929 Geneva Convention. That interpretation, we believe, leads to the conclusion that the 1949 Geneva Convention cannot be judicially enforced. . . .

[The court then compared the 1949 Convention to the 1929 Convention at issue in *Eisentrager*, and concluded that the essential provisions of both conventions contemplated enforcement by and among the signatory nations rather than judicial enforcement by private parties.]

Hamdan points out that the 1949 Geneva Convention protects individual rights. But so did the 1929 Geneva Convention, as the Court recognized in *Eisentrager,* 339 U.S. at 789-90. . . .

Eisentrager also answers Hamdan's argument that the habeas corpus statute, 28 U.S.C §2241, permits courts to enforce the "treaty-based individual rights" set forth in the Geneva Convention. The 1929 Convention specified individual rights[,] but as we have discussed, the Supreme Court ruled that these rights were to be enforced by means other than the writ of habeas corpus. The Supreme Court's *Rasul* decision did give district courts jurisdiction over habeas corpus petitions filed on behalf of Guantanamo detainees such as Hamdan. But *Rasul* did not render the Geneva Convention judicially enforceable. That a court has jurisdiction over a claim does not mean the claim is valid. The availability of habeas may obviate a petitioner's need to rely on a private right of action, *but* it does not render a treaty judicially enforceable.

We therefore hold that the 1949 Geneva Convention does not confer upon Hamdan a right to enforce its provisions in court.

IV

Even if the 1949 Geneva Convention could be enforced in court, this would not assist Hamdan. He contends that a military commission trial would violate his rights under Article 102, which provides that a "prisoner of war can be validly sentenced only if the sentence has been pronounced by the same courts according to the same procedure as in the case of members of the armed forces of the Detaining Power." One problem for Hamdan is that he does not fit the Article 4 definition of a "prisoner of war" entitled to the protection of the Convention. He does not purport to be a

Chapter 14. Trying International Terrorists 339

member of a group who displayed "a fixed distinctive sign recognizable at a distance" and who conducted "their operations in accordance with the laws and customs of war." *See* 1949 Convention, arts. 4A(2)(b), (c) & (d). If Hamdan were to claim prisoner of war status under Article 4A(4) as a person who accompanied "the armed forces without actually being [a] member[ ] thereof," he might raise that claim before the military commission under Army Regulation 190-8. (We note that Hamdan has not specifically made such a claim before this court.)

Another problem for Hamdan is that the 1949 Convention does not apply to al Qaeda and its members. The Convention appears to contemplate only two types of armed conflicts. The first is an international conflict. Under Common Article 2, the provisions of the Convention apply to "all cases of declared war or of any other armed conflict which may arise between two or more of the High Contracting Parties, even if the state of war is not recognized by one of them." Needless to say, al Qaeda is not a state and it was not a "High Contracting Party." There is an exception, set forth in the last paragraph of Common Article 2, when one of the "Powers" in a conflict is not a signatory but the other is. Then the signatory nation is bound to adhere to the Convention so long as the opposing Power "accepts and applies the provisions thereof." Even if al Qaeda could be considered a Power, which we doubt, no one claims that al Qaeda has accepted and applied the provisions of the Convention.

The second type of conflict, covered by Common Article 3, is a civil war – that is, an "armed conflict not of an international character occurring in the territory of one of the High Contracting Parties . . . ." In that situation, Common Article 3 prohibits "the passing of sentences and the carrying out of executions without previous judgment pronounced by a regularly constituted court affording all the judicial guarantees which are recognized as indispensable by a civilized people." Hamdan assumes that if Common Article 3 applies, a military commission could not try him. We will make the same assumption *arguendo,* which leaves the question whether Common Article 3 applies. Afghanistan is a "High Contracting Party." Hamdan was captured during hostilities there. But is the war against terrorism in general and the war against al Qaeda in particular, an "armed conflict not of an international character"? *See* Int'l Comm. Red Cross, Commentary: III Geneva Convention Relative to the Treatment of Prisoners of War 37 (1960) (Common Article 3 applies only to armed conflicts confined to "a single country"). President Bush determined, in a memorandum to the Vice President and others on February 7, 2002, that it did not fit that description because the conflict was "international in scope." The district court disagreed with the President's view of Common Article 3, apparently because the court thought we were not engaged in a separate conflict with al Qaeda, distinct from the conflict with the Taliban. We have difficulty understanding the court's rationale. Hamdan was captured in Afghanistan in November 2001, but the conflict with al Qaeda arose before then, in other regions, including this country on September 11, 2001. Under the Constitution, the President "has a degree of independent authority to act" in foreign affairs, *Am. Ins. Ass'n v. Garamendi,* 539 U.S. 396, 414 (2003), and, for this reason and others, his construction and application of treaty provisions is entitled to "great weight." *United States v. Stuart,* 489 U.S. 353, 369 (1989). While the district court determined that the actions in Afghanistan constituted a single conflict, the President's decision to treat our conflict with the Taliban separately from our conflict with al Qaeda is the sort of political-military decision constitutionally committed to him. To the extent there is ambiguity about the meaning of Common Article 3 as applied to al Qaeda and its members, the President's reasonable view of the provision must therefore prevail.

V

Suppose we are mistaken about Common Article 3. Suppose it does cover Hamdan. Even then we would abstain from testing the military commission against the requirement in Common Article 3(1)(d) that sentences must be pronounced "by a regularly constituted court affording all the judicial guarantees which are recognized as indispensable by civilized peoples." Unlike his arguments that the military commission lacked jurisdiction, his argument here is that the commission's procedures – particularly its alleged failure to require his presence at all stages of the proceedings – fall short of what Common Article 3 requires. The issue thus raised is not *whether* the commission may try him, but rather *how* the commission may try him. That is by no stretch a jurisdictional argument. No one would say that a criminal defendant's contention that a district court will not allow him to confront the witnesses against him raises a jurisdictional objection. Hamdan's claim therefore falls outside the recognized exception to the [exhaustion] doctrine. Accordingly, comity would dictate that we defer to the ongoing military proceedings. If Hamdan were convicted, and if Common Article 3 covered him, he could contest his conviction in federal court after he exhausted his military remedies.

VI

After determining that the 1949 Geneva Convention provided Hamdan a basis for judicial relief, the district court went on to consider the legitimacy of a military commission in the event Hamdan should eventually

Chapter 14. Trying International Terrorists

appear before one. In the district court's view, the principal constraint on the President's power to utilize such commissions is found in Article 36 of the Uniform Code of Military Justice, 10 U.S.C. §836, which provides:

> Pretrial, trial, and post-trial procedures, including modes of proof, for cases arising under this chapter triable in courts-martial, military commissions and other military tribunals . . . may be prescribed by the President by regulations which shall, so far as he considers practicable, apply the principles of law and the rules of evidence generally recognized in the trial of criminal cases in the United States district courts, *but which may not be contrary to or inconsistent with this chapter.*

(Emphasis added.) The district court interpreted the final qualifying clause to mean that military commissions must comply in all respects with the requirements of the Uniform Code of Military Justice (UCMJ). This was an error.

Throughout its Articles, the UCMJ takes care to distinguish between "courts-martial" and "military commissions." *See, e.g.,* 10 U.S.C. §821 (noting that "provisions of this chapter conferring jurisdiction upon courts-martial do not deprive military commissions . . . of concurrent jurisdiction"). The terms are not used interchangeably, and the majority of the UCMJ's procedural requirements refer only to courts-martial. The district court's approach would obliterate this distinction. A far more sensible reading is that in establishing military commissions, the President may not adopt procedures that are "contrary to or inconsistent with" the UCMJ's provisions governing military commissions. In particular, Article 39 requires that sessions of a "trial by *court-martial* . . . shall be conducted in the presence of the accused." Hamdan's trial before a *military commission* does not violate Article 36 if it omits this procedural guarantee.

The Supreme Court's opinion in *Madsen v. Kinsella,* 343 U.S. 341 (1952), provides further support for this reading of the UCMJ. There, the Court spoke of the place of military commissions in our history, referring to them as "our commonlaw war courts. . . . Neither their procedure nor their jurisdiction has been prescribed by statute." *Id.* at 346-48. The Court issued its opinion two years after enactment of the UCMJ, and it is difficult, if not impossible, to square the Court's language in *Madsen* with the sweeping effect with which the district court would invest Article 36. The UCMJ thus imposes only minimal restrictions upon the form and function of military commissions, *see, e.g.,* 10 U.S.C. §§828, 847(a)(1), 849(d), and Hamdan does not allege that the regulations establishing the present commission violate any of the pertinent provisions. . . .

For the reasons stated above, the judgment of the district court is reversed.

So ordered.

WILLIAMS, Senior Circuit Judge, concurring. I concur in all aspects of the court's opinion except for the conclusion that Common Article 3 does not apply to the United States's conduct toward al Qaeda personnel captured in the conflict in Afghanistan. Because I agree that the Geneva Convention is not enforceable in courts of the United States, and that any claims under Common Article 3 should be deferred until proceedings against Hamdan are finished, I fully agree with the court's judgment. . . .

There is, I believe, a fundamental logic to the Convention's provisions on its application. Article 2 (¶1) covers armed conflicts between two or more contracting parties. . . .

Non-state actors cannot sign an international treaty. Nor is such an actor even a "Power" that would be eligible under Article 2 (¶3) to secure protection by complying with the Convention's requirements. Common Article 3 fills the gap, providing some minimal protection for such non-eligibles in an "armed conflict not of an international character occurring in the territory of one of the High Contracting Parties." The gap being filled is the non-eligible party's failure to be a nation. Thus the words "not of an international character" are sensibly understood to refer to a conflict between a signatory nation and a non-state actor. The most obvious form of such a conflict is a civil war. But given the Convention's structure, the logical reading of "international character" is one that matches the basic derivation of the word "international," i.e., *between nations*. Thus, I think the context compels the view that a conflict between a signatory and a non-state actor is a conflict "not of an international character." In such a conflict, the signatory is bound to Common Article 3's modest requirements of "humane[ ]" treatment and "the judicial guarantees which are recognized as indispensable by civilized peoples."

I assume that our conflicts with the Taliban and al Qaeda are distinct, and I agree with the court that in reading the Convention we owe the President's construction "great weight." But I believe the Convention's language and structure compel the view that Common Article 3 covers the conflict with al Qaeda.

NOTES AND QUESTIONS

1. *After Hamdan.* Following the issuance of this decision, the Department of Defense promptly announced that it would proceed with the

Chapter 14. Trying International Terrorists

trials by military commission of four persons, including Hamdan, and continue to prepare charges against eight others. U.S. Dept. of Defense News Release, *Military Commissions to Resume*, July 18, 2005, *available at http://www.defenselink.mil/releases/2005/nr20050718-4063.html.*

2. *Torture Redux.* In *Hamdan*, the government in court made many of the same arguments against the application of the international law of war that its lawyers had made internally to authorize certain interrogation practices in Iraq and Afghanistan. *See* pp. 39-94 *supra*. First, the government argues, the President has inherent and paramount authority as Commander in Chief. Second, the Third Geneva Convention does not apply to the conflict with al Qaeda. Third, even if it did, it does not apply to Hamdan because he does not enjoy POW status. Assuming that the court of appeals correctly accepted these arguments, does its reasoning validate the earlier analysis of international law by lawyers at the OLC, the White House, and the Pentagon?

3. *Due Process in Military Commissions.* The lower court found it unnecessary to reach the question whether Hamdan has any constitutional rights, although it noted that the Supreme Court's decision in *Rasul* "may contain some hint that non-citizens held at Guantanamo Bay have some Constitutional protection." 355 F. Supp. 2d 152, 173 n.19 (D.D.C. 2004). The court of appeals therefore did not reach this question either.

Recall, however, that in In re Guantanamo Detainee Cases (p. 265 in this Supplement), Judge Joyce Hens Green found that the Due Process Clause applied to the procedures followed in Combatant Status Review Tribunals (CSRTs) for detainees held at the Guantánamo Bay Naval Base. *Contra, Khalid v. Bush*, 355 F. Supp. 2d 311 (D.D.C. 2005) (p. 278 in this Supplement). If she is right, would it apply also to military commission trials held at Guantánamo Bay? She noted that the military commission procedures, unlike the CSRT procedures, authorize withholding of classified information only from the defendant, not from defense counsel. *See* p. 273 in this Supplement. Would this difference save a commission hearing from a due process challenge, if due process applied to military commission proceedings? Presumably, military commissions may also use information obtained through torture or coercion, if it "would have probative value to a reasonable person." Military Order of November 13, 2001, §4(c)(3) (casebook p. 899). If a military commission relies on such evidence, would it violate due process?

15
Public Access to National Security Information

A. EXECUTIVE ORDER NO. 12,958 – CLASSIFIED NATIONAL SECURITY INFORMATION

Page 923. Add this material after Note 7.

8. *Readjusting the Balance: A New Executive Order.* On March 25, 2003, President Bush signed a new executive order on classification amending, rather than replacing, the 1995 Clinton order. Exec. Order No. 13,292, 68 Fed. Reg. 15, 315 (2003). The new order renumbers many sections and includes a variety of important substantive changes. Among them, the categories of information that may be classified have been increased to include "transnational terrorism," §§1.1(a)(4), 1.4(e), "vulnerabilities or capabilities of... infrastructures," §1.4(f), and "weapons of mass destruction." §1.4(h). No definitions are provided for any of these terms. In addition, information that has been declassified now may be reclassified under certain conditions. §1.7(c).

Significantly, the new order preserves the requirement of a determination that "the unauthorized disclosure of the information reasonably could be expected to result in damage to the national security ... and the original classification authority is able to identify or describe the damage." §1.1(4). On the other hand, the presumption against classification in §1.2(b) of the earlier order has been removed. And the new order provides that the "unauthorized disclosure of foreign government information is presumed to cause damage to the national security." §1.1(c).

How do you think these changes might affect agency practice in classifying records or the response of courts to FOIA suits challenging that practice?

B. THE FREEDOM OF INFORMATION ACT

1. The Statutory Text

Page 930. Add this material at the end of Note 4.

Until 2002, FOIA could be utilized by "any person" to obtain agency records. The Intelligence Authorization Act for FY 2003, however, amended 5 U.S.C. §552(a)(3) to bar requests from foreign governments, international governmental organizations, or their representatives for records held by elements of the intelligence community. Pub. L. No. 107-306, §312, 116 Stat. 2383, 2390-2391 (2002). *See* U.S. Department of Justice, *FOIA Amended by Intelligence Authorization Act,* FOIA Post, Dec. 23, 2002, *at http://www.usdoj.gov/oip/foiapost/2002foiapost38.htm.* This change was reportedly intended to prevent access to intelligence agency records by states that support terrorism. See H.R. Rep. No. 107-592, at 27 (2002). Can you think of any other reasons to adopt such a restriction?

Page 932. Add this material to Note 9.

The E-Government Act of 2002, Pub. L. No. 107-347, 116 Stat. 2899 (2002), furthers the goals of E-FOIA by pushing agencies to make better use of the Internet to provide information and services to citizens. It requires regulatory agencies to conduct rule-making online, for example, and to post everything on their Web sites that they publish in the Federal Register. It also calls for creation of an online directory of all government Web sites, so that a searcher can locate information on a given topic without having to know what agency holds it.

2. Statutory Exemptions and Judicial Review

Page 946. Add this material at the end of Note 7.

In recent years, business groups have argued that if companies learned of a security problem in their information systems, they were reluctant to forward the information to federal officials because they feared the information could later be accessed under FOIA. In response to these concerns, §214 of the Homeland Security Act amended FOIA to exempt

Chapter 15. Public Access to National Security Information 347

from disclosure "critical infrastructure information" that is "voluntarily" submitted to the federal government. Homeland Security Act of 2002, Pub. L. No. 107-296, §214, 116 Stat. 2135, 2151. The Act also bars the government from using any such submitted information "in any civil action arising under Federal or State law." *Id.* §214(a)(1)(c). Billed as an important component of information sharing after the September 11 attacks, the new FOIA exemption prompted opponents to argue that the provision permits companies to submit broad categories of information to the government, including company misdeeds, and deny any other agency or person access to the information. *See* Rena I. Steinzor, *"Democracies Die Behind Closed Doors": The Homeland Security Act and Corporate Accountability,* 12 Kan. J.L. & Pub. Poly. 641 (2003); *Homeland Security Act Will Affect Individual Privacy, Experts Say,* 71 U.S.L.W. 2387-2388 (Dec. 17, 2002). Recently published regulations to implement this section may not allay such concerns. *See* 69 Fed. Reg. 8074 (Feb. 20, 2004).

The Homeland Security Act also directed the President to develop procedures to "identify and safeguard homeland security information that is sensitive but unclassified." Pub. L. No. 107-296, §892(a)(1)(B), 116 Stat. 2135, 2253. Congress neglected, however, to define the term "sensitive" or to indicate how access to such information might be restricted. *See* Geneviev Knezo, *"Sensitive but Unclassified" and Other Federal Security Controls on Scientific and Technical Information: History and Current Controversy* (Cong. Res. Serv. RL31845), July 2, 2003.

Page 948. Add this material to Note 9.

Center for National Security Studies v. United States Dept. of Justice, 331 F.3d 918 (D.C. Cir. 2003), *cert. denied,* 124 S. Ct. 1041 (2004), concerned a request for information about persons detained and questioned after 9/11 – more than 700 for immigration law violations, 134 on criminal charges, and others as material witnesses. (See casebook pp. 728-736.) The FOIA plaintiffs sought the names of the detainees and their attorneys, dates of their arrest and release, and reasons for their detention. The court agreed with the government that this was "law enforcement" information, the production of which "could reasonably be expected to interfere with enforcement proceedings," within the meaning of Exemption 7(A). The terrorism investigation, said the court, concerned "a heinous violation of federal law as well as a breach of this nation's security." 331 F.3d at 926. The court also declared that "the judiciary is in an extremely poor position to second-guess the executive's judgment in this area of national security," *id.* at 928, and it relied on the same government arguments made and accepted in North Jersey Media v. Ashcroft, 308 F.3d 198 (3d Cir. 2002), *cert. denied,* 123 S. Ct. 2215 (2003) (p. 348 in this Supplement). Judge Tatel, dissenting, complained that the court had never before held that such heightened deference was appropriate in an Exemption 7 case, as it did in Exemption 1 cases. 331 F.3d at 939.

C. OTHER OPEN GOVERNMENT LAWS

1. Presidential Records Act

Page 952. Add the following material at the bottom of the page.

Two and a half years passed before the court reached a decision in the case, during which time all but 74 of some 68,000 pages of disputed materials were released. American Historical Assn. v. National Archives and Records Admin., 310 F. Supp. 2d 216 (D.D.C. 2004). The court avoided ruling on the propriety of the Bush executive order when it decided that the case was nonjusticiable. The plaintiffs lacked standing to sue, the court said, since it assumed (incorrectly, as it turned out) that they did not contest the withholding of the last 74 pages, concerning which President Bush had asserted the executive privilege. That assumption allowed the court to determine that plaintiffs could assert no imminent injury in fact that was redressable. The court also found that without the requisite impending injury, the case was not ripe for hearing. *See* National Security Archive, *Archive, Historians Ask Judge to Rethink Dismissal,* Apr. 30, 2004, *at* http://www.gwu.edu/~nsarchiv/news/20040430/index.htm; Stephen H. Yuhan, Note, *The Imperial Presidency Strikes Back: Executive Order 13,233, the National Archives, and the Capture of Presidential History,* 79 NYU L. Rev. 1570 (2004).

3. Open Meetings Laws

Page 954. Add the following material after the last full paragraph on the page.

A case involving the Federal Advisory Committee Act (FACA) came before the Supreme Court in 2004. Cheney v. United States District Court, 542 U.S. 367, 124 S. Ct. 2576 (2004). Public interest groups sought various records of the Vice President's energy policy task force, appointed by President Bush early in his administration. Suing under the Mandamus Act, 28 U.S.C. §1361, and the Administrative Procedure Act, 5 U.S.C. §706, to enforce the disclosure provisions of FACA, the plaintiffs asserted that individuals in the private sector worked so closely with the task force that they became *de facto* members of it, thereby making it an advisory

Chapter 15. Public Access to National Security Information 349

committee subject to FACA's requirements. To establish this factual predicate, the plaintiffs requested discovery that the Court called "overly broad," since the request covered more information than FACA itself would require to be disclosed. 124 S. Ct. at 2584. Distinguishing its holding in United States v. Nixon, 418 U.S. 683 (1974) [noted at casebook p. 89], the Court ruled that the Vice President (or the President) was not necessarily required to invoke executive privilege to avoid discovery, because of the burden that requirement would impose on the executive. "Special considerations" control discovery requests, said the Court, "when the Executive Branch's interests in maintaining the autonomy of its office and safeguarding the confidentiality of its communications are implicated." *Id.* at 2581. After all, the Court remarked, "[e]ven if FACA embodies important congressional objectives, the only consequence from [plaintiffs'] inability to obtain the discovery they seek is that it would be more difficult for private complainants to vindicate Congress' policy objectives under FACA." *Id.* at 2589. So saying, the Court remanded the case for reconsideration of the discovery request. Other aspects of the *Cheney* decision in the Supreme Court are discussed in this Supplement at p. 3.

On remand, the Court of Appeals reasoned that the alleged de facto private sector members of the Vice President's energy policy group were not members of an advisory committee covered by FACA, since they had no vote or veto over committee decisions, and the internal communications of the task force could therefore remain confidential. In re Cheney, 406 F.3d 723, 728 (D.C. Cir. 2005) (en banc).

In another recent development, in the Homeland Security Act of 2002 Congress decided that no communication of "voluntarily shared critical infrastructure information" to the Department of Homeland Security will be subject to FACA. Pub. L. No. 107-256, §214(b), 116 Stat. 2135, 2153. See also pp. 346-347 in this Supplement.

D. COMMON LAW RIGHT TO KNOW

Page 956. Add this material to Note 1.

In Center for National Security Studies v. United States Dept. of Justice, 331 F.3d 918 (D.C. Cir. 2003), plaintiffs asserted a common law right to information about more than 700 post-September 11 detainees held inside the United States. (The detentions are addressed in the casebook at pp. 728-736.) The government argued that the common law right is limited to judicial records and that, even if that right might otherwise apply to executive records, FOIA has displaced it. The court rejected the government's first argument but accepted the second one:

FOIA provides an extensive statutory regime for plaintiffs to request the information they seek. Not only is it uncontested that the requested information meets the general category of information for which FOIA mandates disclosure, but for the reasons set forth above, we have concluded that it falls within an express statutory exemption as well. It would make no sense for Congress to have enacted the balanced scheme of disclosure and exemption, and for the court to carefully apply that statutory scheme, and then to turn and determine that the statute had no effect on a preexisting common law right of access. Congress has provided a carefully calibrated statutory scheme, balancing the benefits and harms of disclosure. That scheme preempts any preexisting common law right. . . . [331 F.3d at 936-937.]

Can you reconcile the court's conclusion with the statement in *Schwartz* that "we can find no inconsistency or conflict between the Freedom of Information Act and the common law rule"? Do you think Congress intended for FOIA to provide the exclusive means for access to executive branch records?

E. CONSTITUTIONAL RIGHT TO KNOW

Page 969. Add this material to Note 6.

In late 2001, the publisher of Hustler magazine filed suit on First Amendment grounds when one of his journalists was denied, at least temporarily, the right not only to travel with U.S. troops in Afghanistan, but also "to be accommodated and otherwise facilitated by the military in their reporting efforts during combat, subject only to reasonable security and safety restrictions." Flynt v. Rumsfeld, 355 F.3d 697, 703 (D.C. Cir. 2004). Observing that neither the Supreme Court nor the D.C. Circuit had ever applied the *Richmond Newspapers* test of press access outside the context of criminal judicial proceedings, the court refused to do so in this case. *Id.* at 704. It also found no history of media access like that claimed, and it ruled that restrictions imposed by the military in Afghanistan were reasonable. *Id.* 704-705.

Page 969. Add this material to Note 7.

The Pentagon dramatically revised its rules for press access to the battlefield during the 2003 war in Iraq. It "embedded" some 775 print and broadcast journalists into a number of military units, although only about 50 or 60 had "front row seats" for combat. Embed "slots" were allocated

Chapter 15. Public Access to National Security Information 351

to media organizations, 80 percent of them domestic, rather than to individual journalists. *See Public Affairs Guidance on Embedding Media,* Feb. 10, 2003 (*Guidelines*), *http://www.defenselink.mil/news/Feb2003/d20030228pag.pdf.* This arrangement was intended, according to a DOD spokesman, to accommodate the wishes of the media, and also to refute any misinformation about, say, civilian casualties that might be disseminated by Saddam Hussein. *See Deputy Assistant Secretary Whitman Interview with BBC TV,* DOD News, Apr. 18, 2003, *at http://www.defenselink.mil/transcripts/2003/tr20030418-0142.html.* Live television coverage from the battlefield was extensive, yet apparently none of the reporting "compromised significantly anything that was occurring or endangered personnel out there." *Id.*

In return for this extensive access, reporters were obliged to follow broad guidelines about what could be covered (e.g., "military targets and objectives previously under attack") and what could not (e.g., "information regarding future operations"). *Guidelines* ¶4. Unit commanders could "impose temporary restrictions on electronic transmissions for operational security reasons," and reporters had to "seek approval to use electronic devices in a combat/hostile environment." ¶2.C.4. Disputes about coverage of particular events were left to be worked out between reporters and unit commanders. ¶6. Commanders were to "ensure that media are provided with every opportunity to observe actual combat operations," but reporters could be given "escorts." ¶¶3.F., 3.G. There was no general review process for media products, as there was during the 1991 Persian Gulf War, but embargoes could be imposed "to protect operational security." ¶¶3.R., 4.E. The guidelines also included this enigmatic instruction: "Use of lipstick and helmet-mounted cameras on combat sorties is approved and encouraged to the greatest extent possible." ¶7.C.

An even larger number of "unilateral" journalists operated without the limitations of embedding, but also without its physical protections or preferred access to information. They were free to move about independently of the troops, as well as to interview Iraqis and report on the Iraqi view of the war. They were, however, reportedly a "nightmare" for the military, which worried that they might be captured or killed by enemy forces or perhaps come under "friendly" fire.

A detailed description and critique of media coverage of the 2003 Iraq War may be found in Alicia C. Shepard, *Narrowing the Gap: Military, Media, and the Iraq War* (McCormick Tribune Fdn. 2004).

Page 970. Add these materials before Section F.

Detroit Free Press v. Ashcroft
United States Court of Appeals, Sixth Circuit, 2002
303 F.3d 681

KEITH, Circuit Judge. The primary issue on appeal in this case is whether the First Amendment to the United States Constitution confers a public right of access to deportation hearings. If it does, then the Government must make a showing to overcome that right.

No one will ever forget the egregious, deplorable, and despicable terrorist attacks of September 11, 2001. These were cowardly acts. In response, our government launched an extensive investigation into the attacks, future threats, conspiracies, and attempts to come. As part of this effort, immigration laws are prosecuted with increased vigor. The issue before us today involves these efforts.

The political branches of our government enjoy near-unrestrained ability to control our borders. "[T]hese are policy questions entrusted exclusively to the political branches of our government." Fiallo v. Bell, 430 U.S. 787, 798 (1977). Since the end of the 19th Century, our government has enacted immigration laws banishing, or deporting, non-citizens because of their race and their beliefs. While the Bill of Rights jealously protects citizens from such laws, it has never protected non-citizens facing deportation in the same way. In our democracy, based on checks and balances, neither the Bill of Rights nor the judiciary can second-guess government's choices. The only safeguard on this extraordinary governmental power is the public, deputizing the press as the guardians of their liberty. "An informed public is the most potent of all restraints upon misgovernment[.]" Grosjean v. Am. Press Co., 297 U.S. 233, 250 (1936). "[They] alone can here protect the values of democratic government." New York Times v. United States, 403 U.S. 713, 728 (1971) (per curiam) (Stewart, J., concurring).

Today, the Executive Branch seeks to take this safeguard away from the public by placing its actions beyond public scrutiny. Against non-citizens, it seeks the power to secretly deport a class if it unilaterally calls them "special interest" cases. The Executive Branch seeks to uproot people's lives, outside the public eye, and behind a closed door. Democracies die behind closed doors. The First Amendment, through a free press, protects the people's right to know that their government acts fairly, lawfully, and accurately in deportation proceedings. When government begins closing doors, it selectively controls information rightfully belonging to the people. Selective information is misinformation. The Framers of the First

Chapter 15. Public Access to National Security Information

Amendment "did not trust any government to separate the true from the false for us." Kleindienst v. Mandel, 408 U.S. 753, 773 (1972) (quoting Thomas v. Collins, 323 U.S. 516, 545 (Jackson, J., concurring)). They protected the people against secret government. . . .

I. Facts and Procedural History

On September 21, 2001, Chief Immigration Judge Michael Creppy issued a directive (the "Creppy directive") to all United States Immigration Judges requiring closure of special interest cases. The Creppy directive requires that all proceedings in such cases be closed to the press and public, including family members and friends. The Record of the Proceeding is not to be disclosed to anyone except a deportee's attorney or representative, "assuming the file does not contain classified information." "This restriction on information includes confirming or denying whether such a case is on the docket or scheduled for a hearing."

On December 19, 2002, Immigration Judge Elizabeth Hacker conducted a bond hearing for Rabih Haddad ("Haddad"), one such special interest case. Haddad was subject to deportation, having overstayed his tourist visa. The Government further suspects that the Islamic charity Haddad operates supplies funds to terrorist organizations. Haddad's family, members of the public, including Congressman John Conyers, and several newspapers sought to attend his deportation hearing. Without prior notice to the public, Haddad, or his attorney, courtroom security officers announced that the hearing was closed to the public and the press. Haddad was denied bail, detained, and has since been in the government's custody. Subsequent hearings, conducted on January 2 and 10, 2002, were also closed to the public and the press. Haddad has been transferred to Chicago for additional proceedings.

Haddad, several newspapers (the "Newspaper Plaintiffs"), and Congressman Conyers filed complaints for injunctive and declaratory relief, asserting claims under (1) the Administrative Procedures Act ("APA"), 5 U.S.C. §551 *et seq.;* (2) the Immigration and Nationality Act ("INA"), 8 U.S.C. §1101 *et seq.,* and the regulations promulgated thereunder, 8 C.F.R. §§3.27 & 240.10; and (3) the First and Fifth Amendments to the United States Constitution. . . .

III. Analysis

A. Likelihood of Success on the Merits

1. The Effect of the Government's Plenary Power Over Immigration

The Government argues that the district court erred in ruling that the government's plenary power over immigration did not warrant deferential review. We are unpersuaded by the Government's claim, which would require complete deference in all facets of immigration law, including non-substantive immigration laws that infringe upon the Constitution. We hold that the Constitution meaningfully limits non-substantive immigration laws and does not require special deference to the Government.

The Government's broad authority over immigration was first announced more than one-hundred years ago in The Chinese Exclusion Case, 130 U.S. 581 (1889).... This power was derived not from an express provision of the Constitution, but from powers incident to sovereignty....

Even The Chinese Exclusion Case, however, acknowledged that Congress's power over immigration matters was limited by "the constitution itself." *Id.* at 604. Were we to adopt the Government's position, one would wonder whether and how the Constitution could limit the political branches' power over immigration matters. Similarly, that position would undercut the force of the First Amendment. "The dominant purpose of the First Amendment was to prohibit the widespread practice of governmental suppression of embarrassing information." *New York Times*, 403 U.S. at 723-24 (Douglas, J., concurring) (citations omitted). It would be ironic, indeed, to allow the Government's assertion of plenary power to transform the First Amendment from the great instrument of open democracy to a safe harbor from public scrutiny. In the words of Justice Murphy, "[such a] conclusion would make our constitutional safeguards transitory and discriminatory in nature.... [We] cannot agree that the framers of the Constitution meant to make such an empty mockery of human freedom." Bridges v. Wixon, 326 U.S. 135, 162 (1945) (Murphy, J., concurring). As a result, the Government's stated position finds no authority in the Constitution and is untenable.

a. *The Government Interprets* Kleindienst *Too Broadly*

The Government's blanket reliance on *Kleindienst* ignores the varied aspects of immigration law. Immigration includes substantive laws over who may enter or remain in this country, laws governing procedural aspects

Chapter 15. Public Access to National Security Information

of immigration hearings, and regulations on the mechanics of deportation. Although acknowledging the political branches' plenary power over all substantive immigration laws and non-substantive immigration laws that do not implicate constitutional rights, the Supreme Court has repeatedly allowed for meaningful judicial review of non-substantive immigration laws where constitutional rights are involved. *Kleindienst* did not change these long-standing traditions.

In *Kleindienst,* Ernest Mandel, a self-proclaimed "revolutionary Marxist" and Belgian citizen, sought entry into the United States to speak at a conference at Stanford University. *Kleindienst,* 408 U.S. at 756-59. Mandel applied for and was denied a non-immigrant visa under a blanket provision of the Immigration and Nationality Act, §212(a)(28), prohibiting the entrance of "anarchists" or "persons advocating the overthrow of the government." *Id.* at 759. In excluding Mandel, the Attorney General declined to exercise his discretionary authority to waive this prohibition. *Id.*

Several professors brought suit alleging a violation of their First Amendment rights. . . . The Court, while acknowledging that the professors' First Amendment rights were implicated, affirmed the decision denying Mandel a visa. The Court stated:

> [p]lenary congressional power to make policies and rules for exclusion of aliens has long been firmly established. In the case of an alien excludable under §212(a)(28), Congress has delegated conditional exercise of this power to the Executive. We hold that when the Executive exercises this power negatively on the basis of a facially legitimate and bona fide reason, the courts will neither look behind the exercise of that discretion, *nor test it by balancing its justification against the First Amendment interests* of those who seek personal communication with the applicant.

Id. at 769-70 (emphasis added).

Kleindienst differs from the present case in two important, and related, ways. First, *Kleindienst* involved a substantive immigration decision. The law and decision at issue determined who entered the United States. Here, the Creppy directive has no effect on the eventual outcome of the deportation hearings. Second, *Kleindienst,* although recognizing a constitutional right, did not give any weight to that right. It specifically declined to balance the First Amendment right against the government's plenary power, because the law was a substantive immigration law. Therefore, if the First Amendment limits non-substantive immigration laws, *Kleindienst* offers no authority that the Government's actions are entitled to deferential review – *Kleindienst* ignored the existence of the professors' First Amendment rights altogether. Nor does it offer authority that the First Amendment does not limit non-substantive immigration laws – *Kleindienst* involved a substantive immigration law. In a case such as this, where a non-substantive immigration law involving a constitutional right is at issue, the Supreme Court has always recognized the importance of that constitutional right, never deferring to an assertion of plenary authority.

b. *The Constitution, Including the First Amendment, Meaningfully Limits Non-Substantive Immigration Laws*

The Supreme Court has always interpreted the Constitution meaningfully to limit non-substantive immigration laws, without granting the Government special deference. First, the Supreme Court has explicitly stated that non-citizens are afforded "the same constitutional protections of due process that we accord citizens." Hellenic Lines Ltd. v. Rhoditis, 398 U.S. 306, 309 (1970) (citing Kwong Hai Chew v. Colding, 344 U.S. 590, 596 (1953) (stating that "once an alien lawfully enters and resides in this country he becomes invested with the rights guaranteed by the Constitution to all people within our borders.")).

As old as the first immigration laws of this country is the recognition that non-citizens, even if illegally present in the United States, are "persons" entitled to the Fifth Amendment right of due process in deportation proceedings. *See* Wong Wing [v. United States, 163 U.S. 228 (1896)], at 238 (recognizing Fifth Amendment right in deportation proceedings). . . .

More recently, the Supreme Court has again applied non-deferential review to non-substantive immigration law. In Zadvydas v. Davis, 533 U.S. 678 (2001), two non-citizens were being held indefinitely beyond the normal statutory-removal period of ninety days, because no country would accept them. A post-removal-period statute authorized such detention. The issue, however, was whether the post-removal statute authorized a detention indefinitely, or for a period reasonably necessary to secure removal. The language of the statute set no such limit. The Court read an implicit reasonableness limit into the statute to avoid "serious constitutional problems." *Id.* at 690. Significantly, the Court dismissed the government's argument that Congress's plenary power to create immigration law required deference to the political branches' decision-making. *Id.* at 699-700. The Court repeated the mantra that the plenary power was "subject to important constitutional limitations." *Id.* at 695 (citing INS v. Chadha, 462 U.S. 919, 941-942 (1983); The Chinese Exclusion Case, 130 U.S. 581, 604 (1889)).

The Government correctly notes that the Court in *Zadvydas* twice indicated that it might be deferential in situations involving terrorism. *See id.* at 691, 696 ("noting that [t]he provision authorizing detention does not apply narrowly to 'a small segment of particularly dangerous individuals,' say suspected terrorists, but broadly to aliens ordered removed for many and various reasons, including tourist visa violations," and noting that "Neither do we consider terrorism or other special circumstances where special arguments might be made for forms of preventative detention and for heightened deference to the judgments of the political branches with respect to matters of national security."). However, nothing in *Zadvydas* indicates that given such a situation, the Court would defer to the political branches' determination of who belongs in that "small segment of particularly dangerous individuals" without judicial review of the individual circumstances of each case, something that the Creppy directive strikingly lacks. The Court repeated the importance of strong procedural protections when constitutional rights were involved . . . .

Importantly, the Creppy directive does not apply to "a small segment of particularly dangerous" information, but a broad, indiscriminate range of information, including information likely to be entirely innocuous. Similarly, no definable standards used to determine whether a case is of "special interest" have been articulated. Nothing in the Creppy directive counsels that it is limited to "a small segment of particularly dangerous individuals." In fact, the Government so much as argues that certain non-citizens known to have no links to terrorism will be designated "special interest" cases. Supposedly, closing a more targeted class would allow terrorists to draw inferences from which hearings are open and which are closed.

While we sympathize and share the Government's fear that dangerous information might be disclosed in some of these hearings, we feel that the ordinary process of determining whether closure is warranted on a case-by-case basis sufficiently addresses their concerns. Using this stricter standard does not mean that information helpful to terrorists will be disclosed, only that the Government must be more targeted and precise in its approach. Given the importance of the constitutional rights involved, such safeguards must be vigorously guarded, lest the First Amendment turn into another balancing test. In the words of Justice Black:

> The word "security" is a broad, vague generality whose contours should not be invoked to abrogate the fundamental law embodied in the First Amendment. The guarding of military and diplomatic secrets at the expense of informed representative government provides no real security for our Republic.

New York Times, 403 U.S. at 719 (Black, J., concurring). . . .

c. *The Government's Remaining Argument*

Finally, the Government argues that this distinction between substantive and non-substantive immigration laws "fails to acknowledge that procedural requirements often reflect, and encompass, substantive choices" and that it "makes no sense." This contention strikes us as profoundly undemocratic in that it ignores the basic concept of checks and balances. More fundamentally, though, were the political branches' decisions not subject to certain basic procedural requirements, the government could act arbitrarily and behind closed doors, leaving unsettled the lives of thousands of immigrants. Even though the political branches may have unfettered discretion to deport and exclude certain people, requiring the Government to account for their choices assures an informed public – a foundational principle of democracy. . . .

2. Applicability of *Richmond Newspapers*

We next consider whether the First Amendment affords the press and public a right of access to deportation hearings. The Newspaper Plaintiffs argue that the right of access should be governed by the standards set forth in Richmond Newspapers, Inc. v. Virginia, 448 U.S. 555 (1980), and its progeny. The Government, on the other hand, contends that *Richmond Newspapers* and its progeny are limited to judicial proceedings, and therefore, the standards articulated in these cases do not apply to deportation hearings, which are administrative proceedings. According to the Government, review of claims of access to administrative proceedings are governed by the more deferential standard articulated in Houchins v. KQED, Inc., 438 U.S. 1 (1978). The Government also argues that even if the standard articulated in *Richmond Newspapers* and its progeny is the appropriate test, the Newspaper Plaintiffs cannot demonstrate a right of access to deportation hearings by the standards articulated therein. . . .

a. Richmond Newspapers *Is a Test of General Applicability*

. . . [I]n repeatedly applying *Richmond Newspapers's* two-part "experience and logic" test to assess the merits of cases claiming First Amendment access rights to different government proceedings, it is clear that the Court has since moved away from its position in *Houchins* and recognizes that there is a limited constitutional right to some government information. . . .

The *Richmond Newspapers* two-part test has also been applied to particular proceedings outside the criminal judicial context, including administrative proceedings. . . . Thus, we reject the Government's assertion that a line has been drawn between judicial and administrative proceedings, with the First Amendment guaranteeing access to the former but not the latter. "[T]he First Amendment question cannot be resolved solely on the label we give the event, i.e., 'trial' or otherwise." [Press-Enterprise Co. v. Superior Court, 478 U.S. 1 (1986) (*Press-Enterprise II*)], at 7. Moreover, the Government cites no cases explicitly stating such a categorical distinction − that the political branches of government are completely immune from the First Amendment guarantee of access recognized in *Richmond Newspapers*. On the contrary, we believe that there is a limited First Amendment right of access to certain aspects of the executive and legislative branches. *See Richmond Newspapers*, 448 U.S. at 584 ("[T]he First Amendment protects the public and the press from abridgment of their rights of access to information about the operation of *their government, including the Judicial Branch.* . . .") (Stevens, J., concurring) (emphasis added). While the Government is free to argue that the particular historical and structural features of certain administrative proceedings do not satisfy the *Richmond Newspapers* two-part test, we find that there is no basis to argue that the test itself does not apply.

b. *If the Houchins Test Is Still Good Law, It Does Not Apply to Formal, Quasi-Judicial Proceedings, Like Deportation Proceedings*

Finally, to the extent that the standard in *Houchins* remains good law, we do not find *Houchins* applicable to the facts of the present case. Here, the Newspaper Plaintiffs seek access to a demonstrably quasi-judicial government administrative proceeding normally open to the public, as opposed to *Houchins*, where the plaintiffs sought access to a government facility normally restricted to the public. . . .

A deportation proceeding, although administrative, is an adversarial, adjudicative process, designed to expel non-citizens from this country. "[T]he ultimate individual stake in these proceedings is the same as or greater than in criminal or civil actions." *See N. Jersey Media Group, Inc. v. Ashcroft*, 205 F. Supp. 2d 288, 301 (D.N.J. 2002). . . .

. . . [T]he line of cases from *Richmond Newspapers* to *Press-Enterprise II* recognize that there is in fact a *limited* constitutional right to *some* government information and also provide a test of general applicability for making that determination. Accordingly, we must assess whether the Newspaper Plaintiffs enjoy a First Amendment right of access to deportation hearings under the two-part test of *Richmond Newspapers* and its progeny.

3. The Two-Part *Richmond Newspapers* Test

Under the two-part "experience and logic" test from *Richmond Newspapers*, we conclude that there is a First Amendment right of access to deportation proceedings. Deportation hearings, and similar proceedings, have traditionally been open to the public, and openness undoubtedly plays a significant positive role in this process.

a. Deportation Proceedings Have Traditionally Been Accessible to the Public

"[B]ecause a 'tradition of accessibility implies the favorable judgment of experience,' *Globe Newspaper* [Co. v. Superior Court, 457 U.S. 596 (1982)], at 605 (quoting *Richmond Newspapers*, 448 U.S. at 589 (Brennan, J., concurring)), we . . . consider . . . whether the place and process have historically been open to the press and general public." *Press-Enter. II*, 478 U.S. at 8.

The parties first dispute whether this inquiry requires a significantly long showing that the proceedings at issue were historically open, such as a common law tradition. The government cites *Richmond Newspapers* for the proposition that the tradition of open hearings must have existed from the time "when our organic laws were adopted," presumably at the adoption of the Bill of Rights. *See Richmond Newspapers*, 448 U.S. at 569. . . .

. . . [A]lthough historical context is important, a brief historical tradition might be sufficient to establish a First Amendment right of access where the beneficial effects of access to that process are overwhelming and uncontradicted. *See id.* Accordingly, the Supreme Court has called both prongs of the test "complimentary considerations." *Press-Enter. II*, 478 U.S. at 8. This comports with the Court's view that the First Amendment concerns "broad principles," *Globe Newspaper*, 457 U.S. at 604, applicable to contexts not known to the Framers. However, we are mindful that "[a] historical tradition of at least some duration is obviously necessary, . . . [or] nothing would separate the judicial task of constitutional interpretation from the political task of enacting laws currently deemed essential." In re The Reporters Comm. for Freedom of the Press, 773 F.2d 1325, 1332 (D.C. Cir. 1985) (Scalia, J.).

Nonetheless, deportation proceedings historically have been open. Although exceptions may have been allowed, the general policy has been one of openness. The first general immigration act was enacted in 1882. *See Kleindienst*, 408 U.S. at 761. Repeatedly, Congress has enacted statutes closing exclusion hearings. None of these statutes, however, has ever required closure of deportation hearings. Since 1965, INS regulations have explicitly required deportation proceedings to be presumptively open. *See* 8 C.F.R. §3.27. Since that time, Congress has revised the Immigration and Nationality Act at least 53 times without indicating that the INS had judged their intent incorrectly.

Moreover, the history of immigration law informs Congress's legislation. Open hearings, apart from their value to the community, have long been considered to advance fairness to the parties. *See generally Richmond Newspapers,* 448 U.S. 555. Additionally, Congress has long been aware that deportees are constitutionally guaranteed greater procedural rights than those excluded upon initial entry. Therefore, Congress likely legislated key differences between both procedures accordingly.

Next, relying on Capital Cities Media, Inc. [v. Chester, 797 F.2d 1164 (3d Cir. 1986)], the Government impermissibly expands the relevant inquiry by arguing that there was no common law right of access to administrative proceedings. First, this argument ignores the fact that the modern administrative state is an entity unknown to the Framers of the First Amendment. This argument also fails to recognize the evolving nature of our government. Administrative proceedings come in all shapes and sizes. To the extent that we look to similar proceedings, we should look to proceedings that are similar in form and substance. . . .

As stated earlier, to paraphrase the Supreme Court, deportation hearings "walk, talk, and squawk" very much like a judicial proceeding. Substantively, we look to other proceedings that have the same effect as deportation. Here, the only other federal court that can enter an order of removal is a United States District Court during sentencing in a criminal trial. *See* 8 U.S.C.A. §1228(c) (2002). At common law, beginning with the Transportation Act of 1718, the English criminal courts could enter an order of transportation or banishment as a sentence in a criminal trial. As *Richmond Newspapers* discussed in great length, these types of criminal proceedings have historically been open. *Richmond Newspapers,* 448 U.S. at 564-74. . . .

b. *Public Access Plays a Significant Positive Role in Deportation Hearings*

Next, we turn to the "logic" prong, which asks "whether public access plays a significant positive role in the functioning of the particular process in question." *Press-Enter. II,* 478 U.S. at 8-9. Public access undoubtedly enhances the quality of deportation proceedings. Much of the reasoning from *Richmond Newspapers* is also applicable to this context.

First, public access acts as a check on the actions of the Executive by assuring us that proceedings are conducted fairly and properly. *See*

Richmond Newspapers, 448 U.S. at 569 (noting that public access assures that proceedings are conducted fairly, including discouraging perjury, the misconduct of participants, and decisions based on secret bias or partiality). In an area such as immigration, where the government has nearly unlimited authority, the press and the public serve as perhaps the only check on abusive government practices.

Second, openness ensures that government does its job properly; that it does not make mistakes. "It is better that many [immigrants] should be improperly admitted than one natural born citizen of the United States should be permanently excluded from his country." *Kwock Jan Fat* [v. White, 253 U.S. 454 (1920)], at 464....

Third, after the devastation of September 11 and the massive investigation that followed, the cathartic effect of open deportations cannot be overstated. They serve a "therapeutic" purpose as outlets for "community concern, hostility, and emotions." *Richmond Newspapers,* 448 U.S. at 571....

Fourth, openness enhances the perception of integrity and fairness. "The value of openness lies in the fact that people not actually attending trials can have confidence that standards of fairness are being observed; the sure knowledge that *anyone* is free to attend gives assurance that established procedures are being followed and that deviations will become known." [Press-Enterprise Co. v. Superior Court, 464 U.S. 501 (1984)], at 508. The most stringent safeguards for a deportee "would be of limited worth if the public is not persuaded that the standards are being fairly enforced. Legitimacy rests in large part on public understanding." *See* First Amendment Coalition [v. Judicial Inquiry & Review Bd.], 784 F.2d [467 (3d Cir. 1986 (en banc)] at 486 (Adams, J., concurring in part, dissenting in part).

Fifth, public access helps ensure that "the individual citizen can effectively participate in and contribute to our republican system of self-government." *Globe Newspaper,* 457 U.S. at 604. "[A] major purpose of [the First Amendment] was to protect the free discussion of governmental affairs." *Id.* Public access to deportation proceedings helps inform the public of the affairs of the government. Direct knowledge of how their government is operating enhances the public's ability to affirm or protest government's efforts. When government selectively chooses what information it allows the public to see, it can become a powerful tool for deception....

Having found a First Amendment right of access to deportation hearings, we now determine whether the Government has made a sufficient showing to overcome that right.

4. Strict Scrutiny

Under the standard articulated in *Globe Newspaper,* government action that curtails a First Amendment right of access "in order to inhibit the disclosure of sensitive information" must be supported by a showing "that denial is necessitated by a compelling governmental interest, and is narrowly tailored to serve that interest." *Globe Newspaper Co.,* 457 U.S. at 606-07. Moreover, "[t]he interest is to be articulated along with findings specific enough that a reviewing court can determine whether the closure order was properly entered." *Press-Enter. II,* 478 U.S. at 10. The Government's ongoing anti-terrorism investigation certainly implicates a compelling interest. However, the Creppy directive is neither narrowly tailored, nor does it require particularized findings. Therefore, it impermissibly infringes on the Newspaper Plaintiffs' First Amendment right of access.

a. *The Government Cites Compelling Interests . . .*

Before the district court, the Government provided the affidavit of James S. Reynolds, Chief of the Terrorism and Violent Crimes Section of the Justice Department's Criminal Division, to explain the types of information that public access to removal proceedings would disclose. In his affidavit, Mr. Reynolds explained the rationale for prohibiting public access to the proceedings. . . .

The Government certainly has a compelling interest in preventing terrorism. In addition to Mr. Reynold's affidavit, other affidavits have been provided that justify the Government's interest in closure. According to the additional affidavits, public access to removal proceedings would disclose the following information that would impede the Government's investigation:

> "Bits and pieces of information that may appear innocuous in isolation," but used by terrorist groups to help form a "bigger picture" of the Government's terrorism investigation, would be disclosed. The Government describes this type of intelligence gathering as "akin to the construction of a mosaic," where an individual piece of information is not of obvious importance until pieced together with other pieces of information. J. Roderick MacArthur Found. v. F.B.I., 102 F.3d 600, 604 (D.C. Cir. 1996).

See Gov't Brief at 47-49.

Inasmuch as these agents' declarations establish that certain information revealed during removal proceedings could impede the ongoing anti-terrorism investigation, we defer to their judgment. These agents are certainly in a better position to understand the contours of the investigation and the intelligence capabilities of terrorist organizations.

b. *The Creppy Directive Does Not Require Particularized Findings*

Although the Government is able to demonstrate a compelling interest for closure, the immigration judge, Defendant Hacker, failed to make specific findings before closing Haddad's deportation proceedings. *Press-Enterprise II* instructs that in cases where partial or complete closure is warranted, there must be specific findings on the record so that a reviewing court can determine whether closure was proper and whether less restrictive alternatives exist. *Press-Enter. II,* 478 U.S. at 13. Similarly, the Creppy directive fails this requirement.

c. *The Creppy Directive Is Not Narrowly Tailored*

Finally, the blanket closure rule mandated by the Creppy directive is not narrowly tailored. The Government offers no persuasive argument as to why the Government's concerns cannot be addressed on a case-by-case basis. The Newspaper Plaintiffs argue, and the district court agreed, that the Creppy directive is ineffective in achieving its purported goals because the detainees and their lawyers are allowed to publicize the proceedings. According to the Newspaper Plaintiffs, to the extent that Haddad had discussed his proceedings (and disclosed documents) with family, friends and the media, the information that the Government seeks to protect is disclosed to the public anyway. We are not persuaded by the Government's argument in response that few detainees will disclose any information and that their disclosure will be less than complete public access. This contention is, at best, speculative and belies the Government's assertion that *any* information disclosed, even bits and pieces that seem innocuous, will be detrimental to the anti-terrorism investigation.

The recent interim rule promulgated by the Department of Justice ("DOJ") regarding protective orders and sealing of documents in these special interest cases does not fully address our concern that the Creppy directive is under-inclusive. The parties do not dispute that the rule is meant to work in tandem with the Creppy directive. The interim DOJ rule authorizes immigration judges to issue protective orders and seal documents relating to law enforcement or national security information in the course of immigration proceedings. *See* 67 Fed. Reg. 36799. Pursuant to the interim rules, the immigration judge is authorized to order that detainees and their attorneys refrain from disclosing certain confidential information.

. . . [W]e construe the orders to terminate when the deportation proceedings end. At this juncture, nothing precludes the deportee from disclosing this information. Thus, the interim rule does not remedy the under-inclusiveness of the Creppy directive.

The interim rule notwithstanding, the Creppy directive is also over-inclusive, being too broad and indiscriminate. The Government contends that the closure mandated by the Creppy directive is narrowly tailored because "no less restrictive alternative would serve the Government's purpose." *See* United States v. Playboy, 529 U.S. 803, 815 (2000) ("[I]f a less restrictive means is available for the Government to achieve its goals, the Government must use it.").

It is clear that certain types of information that the Government seeks to keep confidential could be kept from the public on a case-by-case basis through protective orders or in camera review – for example, the identification of investigative sources and witnesses. The Government, however, argues that it is impossible to keep some sensitive information confidential if any portion of a hearing is open or if the immigration court conducts a hearing to determine if closure is proper. Stated differently, the Government argues that there is sensitive information that would be disclosed if closure occurred on a case-by-case basis. First, the Government contends that the identities of the detainees would be revealed if closure occurred on a case-by-case basis, and such information would impede the anti-terrorism investigation. This information, however, is already being disclosed to the public through the detainees themselves or their counsel. Even if, as a result of the interim rule, a detainee remains silent, a terrorist group capable of sophisticated intelligence-gathering would certainly be made aware that one of its operatives, or someone connected to a particular terrorist plot, has disappeared into the Government's custody. Moreover, if a deportee does have links to terrorist organizations, there is nothing to stop that deportee from divulging the information learned from these proceedings once deported.

Next, the Government argues that open hearings would reveal the amount of intelligence that the Government does not possess. The Government argues that evidence concerning a particular detainee could be incomplete, and an incomplete presentation of evidence would permit terrorist groups to gauge how much the Government knows and does not know about their operations. The issue in a removal hearing is, however, narrowly focused, and the Government has enormous control over what evidence it introduces. "To deport an overstay, the INS must convince the immigration judge by clear and convincing evidence that the alien was admitted as a non-immigrant for a specific period, that the period has elapsed, and that the alien is still in this country." Shahla v. INS, 749 F.2d

561, 563 (9th Cir. 1984).

Here, the Government has detained Haddad and instituted removal proceedings based on his overstay of a tourist visa. Thus, the Government need only establish that Haddad obtained a visa, the visa has expired, and that he is still in the country. Very little information is required. The fact that the Government may have to contest the non-citizen's application for discretionary relief is similarly unavailing. At oral argument, it was brought to our attention that Haddad intends to apply for asylum, a form of discretionary relief available to non-citizens in deportation proceedings. We see no reason why, in making its case against the applicant's request for discretionary relief, the Government could not seek to keep confidential, pertinent information, as the need arises.

Finally, the Government seeks to protect from disclosure the bits and pieces of information that seem innocuous in isolation, but when pieced together with other bits and pieces aid in creating a bigger picture of the Government's anti-terrorism investigation, i.e., the "mosaic intelligence." Mindful of the Government's concerns, we must nevertheless conclude that the Creppy directive is over-inclusive. While the risk of "mosaic intelligence" may exist, we do not believe speculation should form the basis for such a drastic restriction of the public's First Amendment rights. *See Press-Enter. II,* 478 U.S. at 13 ("Since a qualified First Amendment right of access attaches . . ., the proceeding cannot be closed unless *specific, on the record findings are made* demonstrating that closure is *essential to preserve higher values* and is narrowly tailored to serve that interest."). Fittingly, in this case, the Government subsequently admitted that there was no information disclosed in any of Haddad's first three hearings that threatened "national security or the safety of the American people." U.S. Dept. of Justice, *Statement of Associate Attorney General Jay Stephens Regarding the Sixth Circuit Decision in the Haddad Case,* (last modified 8/20/02) <http://www.usdoj.gov/opa/pr/2002/April/02_ag_238.htm>. Yet, all these hearings were closed. The only reason offered for closing the hearings has been that the presiding immigration judge was told [to] do it by the chief immigration judge, who in turn was told to do it by the Attorney General.

Furthermore, there seems to be no limit to the Government's argument. The Government could use its "mosaic intelligence" argument as a justification to close any public hearing completely and categorically, including criminal proceedings. The Government could operate in virtual secrecy in all matters dealing, even remotely, with "national security," resulting in a wholesale suspension of First Amendment rights. By the simple assertion of "national security," the Government seeks a process where it may, without review, designate certain classes of cases as "special interest cases" and, behind closed doors, adjudicate the merits of these cases to deprive non-citizens of their fundamental liberty interests.

This, we simply may not countenance. A government operating in the shadow of secrecy stands in complete opposition to the society envisioned by the Framers of our Constitution. "[F]ully aware of both the need to defend a new nation and the abuses of the English and Colonial governments, [the Framers of the First Amendment] sought to give this new society strength and security by providing that freedom of speech, press, religion, and assembly should not be abridged." *See New York Times,* 403 U.S. at 719 (Black, J., concurring).

Moreover, we find unpersuasive the Government's argument that the closure of special interest hearings has been accomplished on a case-by-case basis. In its reply, the Government alleges that "[e]ach special interest detainee has been evaluated and designated on the basis of the government's ongoing investigative interest in him and his relationship to the ongoing anti-terrorism investigation." Assuming such an evaluation has occurred, we find that problems still remain. The task of designating a case special interest is performed in secret, without any established standards or procedures, and the process is, thus, not subject to any sort of review, either by another administrative entity or the courts. Therefore, no real safeguard on this exercise of authority exists. "Civil liberties, as guaranteed by the Constitution, imply the existence of an organized society maintaining public order without which liberty itself would be lost in the excesses of unrestrained abuses." *United States v. United States District Court,* 407 U.S. 297, 312 (1972) (quoting *Cox v. New Hampshire,* 312 U.S. 569, 574 (1941)). The Government states that special interest cases represent "a small, carefully chosen subset of the universe of aliens facing removal proceedings." Yet, to date, the Government has failed to disclose the actual number of special interest cases it has designated.

In sum, we find that the Government's attempt to establish a narrowly tailored restriction has failed. The Creppy directive is under-inclusive by permitting the disclosure of sensitive information while at the same time drastically restricting First Amendment rights. The directive is over-inclusive by categorically and completely closing all special interest hearings without demonstrating, beyond speculation, that such a closure is absolutely necessary. . . .

Lastly, the public's interests are best served by open proceedings. A true democracy is one that operates on faith – faith that government officials are forthcoming and honest, and faith that informed citizens will arrive at logical conclusions. This is a vital reciprocity that America should not discard in these troubling times. Without question, the events of September 11, 2001, left an indelible mark on our nation, but we as a people are united in the wake of the destruction to demonstrate to the world that we are a country deeply committed to preserving the rights and freedoms guaranteed by our democracy. Today, we reflect our commitment to those democratic values by ensuring that our government is held accountable to the people and that First Amendment rights are not impermissibly compromised. Open proceedings, with a vigorous and scrutinizing press, serve to ensure the durability of our democracy.

IV. Conclusion

For the foregoing reasons, we AFFIRM.

North Jersey Media Group, Inc. v. Ashcroft
United States Court of Appeals, Third Circuit, 2002
308 F.3d 198, *cert. denied,* 123 S. Ct. 2215 (2003)

BECKER, Chief Judge. This civil action was brought in the District Court for the District of New Jersey by a consortium of media groups seeking access to "special interest" deportation hearings involving persons whom the Attorney General has determined might have connections to or knowledge of the September 11, 2001 terrorist attacks. This category was created by a directive issued by Michael Creppy, the Chief United States Immigration Judge, outlining additional security measures to be applied in this class of cases, including closing hearings to the public and the press. Named as defendants in the suit were Attorney General John Ashcroft and Chief Judge Creppy. The District Court found for the media plaintiffs and issued an order enjoining the Attorney General from denying access, from which he now appeals. . . .

As we will now explain in detail, we find that the application of the *Richmond Newspapers* [Richmond Newspapers, Inc. v. Virginia, 448 U.S. 555 (1980)] experience and logic tests does not compel us to declare the Creppy Directive unconstitutional. We will therefore reverse the Order of the District Court.

Chapter 15. Public Access to National Security Information

I. BACKGROUND

A. *The Creppy Directive* ...

In closing special interest deportation hearings, the Government's stated purpose is to avoid disclosing potentially sensitive information to those who may pose an ongoing security threat to the United States and its interests. The Government represents that "if evidence is offered about a particular phone number link between a detainee and a number connected to a terrorist organization or member," the terrorists "will be on notice that the United States is now aware of the link" and "may even be able to determine what sources and methods the United States used to become aware of that link." (Watson Declaration) Equally important, however, is "information that might appear innocuous in isolation [but that] can be fit into a bigger picture by terrorist groups in order to thwart the Government's efforts to investigate and prevent terrorism." (*Id.*) For example, information about how and why special interest aliens were detained "would allow the terrorist organizations to discern patterns and methods of investigation"; information about how such aliens entered the country "would allow the terrorist organization to see patterns of entry, what works and what doesn't"; and information "about what evidence the United States has against members of a particular cell collectively" would reveal to the terrorist organization which of its cells have been significantly compromised. (*Id.*)

The Government offers a litany of harms that might flow from open hearings. Most obviously, terrorist organizations could alter future attack plans, or devise new, easier ways to enter the country through channels they learn are relatively unguarded by the Department of Justice. They might also obstruct or disrupt pending proceedings by destroying evidence, threatening potential witnesses, or targeting the hearings themselves. Finally, if the government cannot guarantee a closed hearing, aliens might be deterred from cooperating with the ongoing investigation. *See infra*. ...

II. APPLICABILITY OF *RICHMOND NEWSPAPERS* ...

While we agree with the District Court's conclusion that *Richmond Newspapers* analysis is proper in the administrative context, we disagree with its application and hold that under that test, there is no First Amendment right to attend deportation proceedings.

A. Applicability to Article III Proceedings

... The *Richmond Newspapers* First Amendment right of access to criminal trials ... stemmed from an "uncontradicted history, supported by reasons as valid today as in centuries past." *Id.* at 573. In his pragmatic concurrence, Justice Brennan concluded that:

> [T]wo helpful principles may be sketched. First, the case for a right of access has special force when drawn from an enduring and vital tradition of public entree to particular proceedings or information. Such a tradition commands respect in part because the Constitution carries the gloss of history. More importantly, a tradition of accessibility implies the favorable judgment of experience. Second, the value of access must be measured in specifics. Analysis is not advanced by rhetorical statements that all information bears upon public issues; what is crucial in individual cases is whether access to a particular government process is important in terms of that very process.

Id. at 589.

Despite Justice O'Connor's admonition that *Richmond Newspapers* does not have "any implications outside the context of criminal trials," *Globe Newspaper Co. v. Superior Court*, 457 U.S. 596, 611 (1982), a majority of the Court has since adopted Justice Brennan's language as a test of at least somewhat broader application. In *Press-Enterprise Co. v. Superior Court*, 478 U.S. [1 (1986)] (*Press-Enterprise II*), the Court held that there is a First Amendment right of access to preliminary hearings. *Id.* at 13. In so doing, it formalized what has come to be known as the *Richmond Newspapers* "experience and logic" test:

> First, because a tradition of accessibility implies the favorable judgment of experience, we have considered whether the place and process have historically been open to the press and general public. . . . Second, in this setting the Court has traditionally considered whether public access plays a significant positive role in the functioning of the particular process in question.

Id. at 8 (citations omitted). The Court recognized that "[t]hese considerations of experience and logic are, of course, related, for history and experience shape the functioning of governmental processes." *Id.* at 9. Nevertheless, it made clear that relation is not tantamount to equivalence, and it independently applied both prongs of the test to preliminary proceedings. . . .

B. Applicability of Richmond Newspapers to Administrative Proceedings

The Government contends that while *Richmond Newspapers* properly applies to civil and criminal proceedings under Article III, the Constitution's text militates against extending First Amendment rights to non-Article III proceedings such as deportation. Its premise is one of *expressio unius est exclusio alterius:* Article III is silent on the question of public access to judicial trials, but the Sixth Amendment expressly incorporates the common law tradition of public trials, thus supporting the notion that the First Amendment likewise incorporates that tradition for Article III purposes. Articles I and II, conversely, *do* address the question of access, and they *do not* provide for Executive or Legislative proceedings to be open to the public. To the Government, the absence of an explicit guarantee of access for Article I and II proceedings (as exists in Article III) gives rise to a distinction with a difference because, without an incorporating provision parallel to the Sixth Amendment, the Framers must have intended to deny the public access to political proceedings.

The Government's suggestion is ultimately that we should not apply *Richmond Newspapers* where the Constitution's structure dictates that no First Amendment right applies, and should instead let the political branches (here, the Executive, acting through the Justice Department) determine the proper degree of access to administrative proceedings.

Our own jurisprudence precludes this approach. In *Publicker* [Industries, Inc. v. Cohen, 733 F.2d 1059 (3d Cir. 1984)], for example, we found a First Amendment right to attend civil trials, proceedings to which the Sixth Amendment is entirely inapplicable. . . .

. . . [I]n this Court, *Richmond Newspapers* is a test broadly applicable to issues of access to government proceedings, including removal. In this one respect we note our agreement with the Sixth Circuit's conclusion in their nearly identical case. *See Detroit Free Press v. Ashcroft,* 303 F.3d 681 (6th Cir. 2002). We now employ that test to determine whether the press and public have a First Amendment right to attend deportation hearings.

III. UNDER *RICHMOND NEWSPAPERS*, IS THERE A FIRST AMENDMENT RIGHT TO ATTEND DEPORTATION HEARINGS? . . .

A. The "Experience" Test

1. Is there an historical right of access to government proceedings generally?

In *Richmond Newspapers,* 448 U.S. at 575, the Supreme Court acknowledged the State's argument that the Constitution nowhere explicitly guarantees the public's right to attend criminal trials, but it found that right implicit because the Framers drafted the Constitution against a backdrop of longstanding popular access to criminal trials. Likewise, in *Publicker,* 733 F.2d at 1059, we found a First Amendment right of access to civil trials because at common law, such access had been "beyond dispute."

The history of access to political branch proceedings is quite different. The Government correctly notes that the Framers themselves rejected any unqualified right of access to the political branches for, as we explained in *Capital Cities Media* [Inc. v. Chester, 797 F.2d 1164 (3d Cir. 1986], at 1168-1171, the evidence on this point is extensive and compelling. . . .

This tradition of closing sensitive proceedings extends to many hearings before administrative agencies. For example, although hearings on Social Security disability claims profoundly affect hundreds of thousands of people annually, and have great impact on expenditure of government funds, they are open only to "the parties and to other persons the administrative law judge considers necessary and proper." 20 C.F.R. §404.944. Likewise, administrative disbarment hearings are often presumptively closed. . . .

Faced with this litany of administrative hearings that are closed to the public, the Newspapers cannot claim a general First Amendment right of access to government proceedings without urging a judicially-imposed revolution in the administrative state. They wisely avoid that tactic, at least directly. Instead they submit that, despite frequent closures throughout the administrative realm, deportation proceedings in particular boast a history of openness sufficient to meet the *Richmond Newspapers* requirement. We now assess that claim, and find that we disagree.

2. Is the history of open deportation proceedings sufficient to satisfy the *Richmond Newspapers* "experience" prong?

For a First Amendment right of access to vest under *Richmond*

Chapter 15. Public Access to National Security Information

Newspapers, we must consider whether "the place and process have historically been open to the press and general public," because such a "tradition of accessibility implies the favorable judgment of experience." *Press-Enterprise II,* 478 U.S. at 8. Noting preliminarily that the question whether a proceeding has been "historically open" is only arguably an objective inquiry, we nonetheless find that based on both Supreme Court and Third Circuit precedents, the tradition of open deportation hearings is too recent and inconsistent to support a First Amendment right of access.

The strongest historical evidence of open deportation proceedings is that since the 1890s, when Congress first codified deportation procedures, "[t]he governing statutes have always expressly closed *exclusion* hearings, but have *never* closed deportation hearings." (Newspapers' Br. at 30-31.) In 1893, the Executive promulgated the first set of immigration regulations, which expressly stated that exclusion proceedings shall be conducted "separate from the public." *See* Treasury Dept., *Immigration Laws and Regulations* 4 (Washington D.C., Gov't Printing Office 1893). Congress codified those regulations in 1903 and, since that time, it has repeatedly reenacted provisions closing exclusion hearings. In contrast, although Congress codified the regulations governing deportation proceedings in 1904 and has reenacted them many times since, it has never authorized the general closure that has long existed in the exclusion context.

The Newspapers submit that under the rule of construction *expressio unius est exclusio alterius,* Congress's practice of closing exclusion proceedings while remaining silent on deportation proceedings creates a presumption that it intended deportation proceedings to be open. In support of this interpretation, they point out that the current Justice Department regulations provide explicitly that "[a]ll hearings, other than exclusion hearings, shall be open to the public except that . . . [f]or the purpose of protecting . . . the public interest, the Immigration Judge may limit attendance or hold a closed hearing." 8 C.F.R. §3.27. From this they conclude that the regulations state explicitly what the statutes had long said implicitly, namely that deportation hearings are to be open unless an individualized case is made for closure.

But there is also evidence that, in practice, deportation hearings have frequently been closed to the general public. From the early 1900s, the government has often conducted deportation hearings in prisons, hospitals, or private homes, places where there is no general right of public access. Even in recent times, the government has continued to hold thousands of deportation hearings each year in federal and state prisons. Moreover, hearings involving abused alien children are closed by regulation no matter where they are held, and those involving abused alien spouses are closed presumptively. *See* 8 C.F.R. §3.27(c).

We ultimately do not believe that deportation hearings boast a tradition of openness sufficient to satisfy *Richmond Newspapers*. In *Richmond Newspapers* itself, the Court noted an "unbroken, uncontradicted history" of public access to criminal trials in Anglo American law running from "before the Norman Conquest" to the present, and it emphasized that it had not found "a single instance of a criminal trial conducted in camera in any federal, state, or municipal court during the history of this country." 448 U.S. at 565, 572, 573 & n. 9. Likewise, in *Publicker,* 733 F.2d at 1059, we found that access to civil trials at common law was "beyond dispute."

The tradition of open deportation hearings is simply not comparable. While the *expressio unius* distinction between exclusion and deportation proceedings is a tempting road to travel, we are unwilling effectively to craft a constitutional right from mere Congressional silence, especially when faced with evidence that some deportation proceedings were, and are, explicitly closed to the public or conducted in places unlikely to allow general public access. Although the 1964 Department of Justice regulations did create a presumption of openness, a recent – and rebuttable – regulatory presumption is hardly the stuff of which Constitutional rights are forged. . . .

3. Relaxing the *Richmond Newspapers* experience requirement would lead to perverse consequences.

. . . [T]here is no fundamental right of access to administrative proceedings. Any such access, therefore, must initially be granted as a matter of executive grace. The Government contends that by relaxing the need for a "1000-year tradition of public access," (Gov't Br. at 35), we would permanently constitutionalize a right of access whenever an executive agency does not consistently bar all public access to a particular proceeding. We do not adopt this reasoning in its entirety, for as we have discussed *supra,* we have sometimes found a constitutional right of access to proceedings that did not exist at common law.

Nevertheless, we agree with the Government that a rigorous experience test is necessary to preserve the "basic tenet of administrative law that agencies should be free to fashion their own rules of procedure." *Vermont Yankee Nuclear Power Corp. v. Natural Resources Defense Council, Inc.,* 435 U.S. 519, 544 (1978). Were we to adopt the Newspapers' view that we can recognize a First Amendment right based solely on the logic prong if there is no history of closure, we would effectively compel the Executive to close its proceedings to the public *ab initio* or risk creating a constitutional right of access that would preclude it from closing them in the future. Under such a system, reserved powers of closure would be meaningless. It seems possible that, ironically, such a system would result in less public access than one in which a constitutional right of access is more difficult to create.

At all events, we would find this outcome incredible in an area of traditional procedural flexibility, and we are unwilling to reach it when a reasonable alternative is present. By insisting on a strong tradition of public access in the *Richmond Newspapers* test, we preserve administrative flexibility and avoid constitutionalizing ambiguous, and potentially unconsidered, executive decisions.

IV. DOES THE *RICHMOND NEWSPAPERS* "LOGIC" PRONG, PROPERLY APPLIED, SUPPORT A RIGHT OF ACCESS?

Even if we could find a right of access under the *Richmond Newspapers* logic prong, absent a strong showing of openness under the experience prong, a proposition we do not embrace, we would find no such right here. The logic test compels us to consider "whether public access plays a significant positive role in the functioning of the particular process in question." *Press-Enterprise II*, 478 U.S. at 8. . . .

In *Press-Enterprise II*, the case that formalized the *Richmond Newspapers* test, the Court identified several reasons that openness plays a significant positive role in preliminary hearings. It recognized that "[b]ecause of its extensive scope, the preliminary hearing is often the final and most important step in the criminal proceeding," and in many cases it "provides the sole occasion for public observation of the criminal justice system." *Id.* at 12 (citation omitted). Similarly, it found that "the absence of a jury, long recognized as an inestimable safeguard against the corrupt or overzealous prosecutor and against the compliant, biased, or eccentric judge, makes the importance of public access to a preliminary hearing even more significant." *Id.* at 12-13 (citations omitted). Summarizing that "[d]enying the transcript of a [ ] preliminary hearing would frustrate what we have characterized as the 'community therapeutic value' of openness," it concluded that a qualified First Amendment right of access attaches to preliminary hearings. *Id.* at 13. . . .

We agree with the District Court and the Sixth Circuit that openness in deportation hearings performs each of these salutary functions, but we are troubled by our sense that the logic inquiry, as currently conducted, does not do much work in the *Richmond Newspapers* test. We have not found a case in which a proceeding passed the experience test through its history of openness yet failed the logic test by not serving community values. Under the reported cases, whenever a court has found that openness serves community values, it has concluded that openness plays a "significant positive role" in that proceeding. But that cannot be the story's end, for to gauge accurately whether a role is positive, the calculus must perforce take account of the flip side – the extent to which openness impairs the public good. We note in this respect that, were the logic prong only to determine whether openness serves some good, it is difficult to conceive of a government proceeding to which the public would not have a First Amendment right of access. For example, public access to *any* government affair, even internal CIA deliberations, would "promote informed discussion" among the citizenry. It is unlikely the Supreme Court intended this result.

In this case the Government presented substantial evidence that open deportation hearings would threaten national security. Although the District Court discussed these concerns as part of its strict scrutiny analysis, they are equally applicable to the question whether openness, on balance, serves a positive role in removal hearings. We find that upon factoring them into the logic equation, it is doubtful that openness promotes the public good in this context.

The Government's security evidence is contained in the declaration of Dale Watson, the FBI's Executive Assistant Director for Counterterrorism and Counterintelligence. Watson presents a range of potential dangers, the most pressing of which we [d]escribe here.

First, public hearings would necessarily reveal sources and methods of investigation. That is information which, "when assimilated with other information the United States may or may not have in hand, allows a terrorist organization to build a picture of the investigation." (Watson Dec. at 4.) Even minor pieces of evidence that might appear innocuous to us would provide valuable clues to a person within the terrorist network, clues that may allow them to thwart the government's efforts to investigate and prevent future acts of violence. *Id.*

Second, "information about how any given individual entered the country (from where, when, and how) may not divulge significant information that would reveal sources and methods of investigation. However, putting entry information into the public realm regarding all 'special interest cases' would allow the terrorist organization to see patterns of entry, what works and what doesn't." *Id.* That information would allow it to tailor future entries to exploit weaknesses in the United States immigration system.

Third, "[i]nformation about what evidence the United States has against members of a particular cell collectively will inform the terrorist organization as to what cells to use and which not to use for further plots and attacks." *Id.* A related concern is that open hearings would reveal what evidence the government lacks. For example, the United States may disclose in a public hearing certain evidence it possesses about a member of a terrorist organization. If that detainee is actually involved in planning an attack, opening the hearing might allow the organization to know that the United States is not yet aware of the attack based on the evidence it presents at the open hearing. *Id.*

Fourth, if a terrorist organization discovers that a particular member is detained, or that information about a plot is known, it may accelerate the timing of a planned attack, thus reducing the amount of time the government has to detect and prevent it. If acceleration is impossible, it may still be able to shift the planned activity to a yet-undiscovered cell. *Id.* at 7.

Fifth, a public hearing involving evidence about terrorist links could allow terrorist organizations to interfere with the pending proceedings by creating false or misleading evidence. Even more likely, a terrorist might destroy existing evidence or make it more difficult to obtain, such as by threatening or tampering with potential witnesses. Should potential informants not feel secure in coming forward, that would greatly impair the ongoing investigation. *Id.* . . .

Finally, Watson represents that "the government cannot proceed to close hearings on a case-by-case basis, as the identification of certain cases for closure, and the introduction of evidence to support that closure, could itself expose critical information about which activities and patterns of behavior merit such closure." (Watson Dec. at 8-9.) Moreover, he explains, given judges' relative lack of expertise regarding national security and their inability to see the mosaic, we should not entrust to them the decision whether an isolated fact is sensitive enough to warrant closure.

The Newspapers are undoubtedly correct that the representations of the Watson Declaration are to some degree speculative, at least insofar as there is no concrete evidence that closed deportation hearings have prevented, or will prevent, terrorist attacks.[14] But the *Richmond Newspapers* logic prong is unavoidably speculative, for it is impossible to weigh objectively, for example, the community benefit of emotional catharsis against the security risk of disclosing the United States' methods of investigation and the extent

---

14. The Newspapers contend that speculative evidence is insufficient to withstand strict scrutiny. *See Press-Enterprise II,* 478 U.S. at 13 (requiring "specific, on the record findings"); *Globe Newspaper,* 457 U.S. 596, 609 (1982) (finding government interest insufficient to merit closure without accompanying empirical support). While we acknowledge the force of this contention, strict scrutiny is appropriate only after finding a First Amendment right. Because we find no such right to attend deportation hearings, the speculative nature is not fatal.

of its knowledge. We are quite hesitant to conduct a judicial inquiry into the credibility of these security concerns, as national security is an area where courts have traditionally extended great deference to Executive expertise. *See, e.g., Zadvydas v. Davis,* 533 U.S. 678, 696 (2001) (noting that "terrorism or other special circumstances" might warrant "heightened deference to the judgments of the political branches with respect to matters of national security"). *See also Dep't of the Navy v. Egan,* 484 U.S. 518, 530 (1988) (noting that "courts traditionally have been reluctant to intrude upon the authority of the Executive in military and national security affairs"). The assessments before us have been made by senior government officials responsible for investigating the events of September 11th and for preventing future attacks. These officials believe that closure of special interest hearings is necessary to advance these goals, and their concerns, as expressed in the Watson Declaration, have gone unrebutted. To the extent that the Attorney General's national security concerns seem credible, we will not lightly second-guess them.

We are keenly aware of the dangers presented by deference to the executive branch when constitutional liberties are at stake, especially in times of national crisis, when those liberties are likely in greatest jeopardy. On balance, however, we are unable to conclude that openness plays a positive role in special interest deportation hearings at a time when our nation is faced with threats of such profound and unknown dimension.

V. CONCLUSION

Whatever the outer bounds of *Richmond Newspapers* might be, they do not envelop us here. Deportation proceedings' history of openness is quite limited, and their presumption of openness quite weak. They plainly do not present the type of "unbroken, uncontradicted history" that *Richmond Newspapers* and its progeny require to establish a First Amendment right of access. We do not decide that there is no right to attend administrative proceedings, or even that there is no right to attend any immigration proceeding. Our judgment is confined to the extremely narrow class of deportation cases that are determined by the Attorney General to present significant national security concerns. In recognition [of] his experience (and our lack of experience) in this field, we will defer to his judgment. We note that although there may be no judicial remedy for these closures, there is, as always, the powerful check of political accountability on Executive discretion....

Because we find that open deportation hearings do not pass the two-part *Richmond Newspapers* test, we hold that the press and public possess no First Amendment right of access. In the absence of such a right, we need

Chapter 15. Public Access to National Security Information

not reach the subsequent questions whether the Creppy Directive's closures would pass a strict scrutiny analysis and whether the District Court's "national in scope" injunction was too broad.

The judgment of the District Court will be reversed.

[The opinion of SCIRICA, Circuit Judge, dissenting, is omitted.]

NOTES AND QUESTIONS

1. *Closing the Door on Democracy?* How would you compare the general attitudes of the Third and Sixth Circuit courts about their roles in cases implicating the national security? What specifically do you see in the two opinions that reveals a difference in attitudes?

Which court do you think struck the better balance between the public's interest in openness and the risk to national security, and why?

How much importance do you think the *North Jersey Media* court attached to government assertions that some "special interest" cases involved aliens associated with al Qaeda or with the September 11 hijackers? Should the court have demanded proof of these assertions?

Because of the importance of these cases, as well as the sharp split between the circuits, many were surprised by the Supreme Court's decision to deny certiorari in the *North Jersey Media* case. What, if anything, do you think this portends for First Amendment-based access to government activities and information in the future?

A spate of law review articles analyzing the two principal cases includes Lauren Gilbert, *When Democracy Dies Behind Closed Doors: The First Amendment and "Special Interest" Hearings*, 55 Rutgers L. Rev. 741 (2003); Heidi Kitrosser, *Secrecy in the Immigration Courts and Beyond: Considering the Right to Know in the Administrative State*, 39 Harv. C.R.- C.L. L. Rev. 95 (2004); Kathleen K. Miller, Note, *Do Democracies Die Behind Closed Doors? Finding a First Amendment Right of Access to Deportation Hearings by Reevaluating the Richmond Newspapers Test*, 72 Geo. Wash. L. Rev. 646 (2004); Shirley C. Rivadeneira, Comment, *The Closure of Removal Proceedings of September 11th Detainees: An Analysis of Detroit Free Press, North Jersey Media Group and the Creppy Directive*, 55 Admin. L. Rev. 843 (2003).

2. *The Detainees Redux.* In a suit seeking information about more than 700 persons detained inside the United States in the wake of the September 11 attacks (the detentions are addressed in the casebook at pp. 728-736), the court considered and rejected First Amendment grounds for releasing

the names of the detainees. Center for National Security Studies v. United States Dept. of Justice, 331 F.3d 918 (D.C. Cir. 2003). *Richmond Newspapers* was central to the First Amendment portion of the decision, and the court sought to distinguish the *Detroit Free Press* case:

> Plaintiffs characterize the information they seek as "arrest records," and contend that the public has a right of access to arrest records under the First Amendment, as interpreted in *Richmond Newspapers*. We disagree. Plaintiffs seek not individual arrest records, but a comprehensive listing of the individuals detained in connection with a specified law enforcement investigation as well as investigatory information about where and when each individual was arrested, held, and released. The narrow First Amendment right of access to information recognized in *Richmond Newspapers* does not extend to non-judicial documents that are not part of a criminal trial, such as the investigatory documents at issue here. . . .
>
> Neither the Supreme Court nor this Court has applied the *Richmond Newspapers* test outside the context of criminal judicial proceedings or the transcripts of such proceedings. When the "experience and logic" test has been applied beyond the trial itself, as in *Press-Enterprise II*, it has been limited to judicial proceedings that are part of the criminal trial process. . . .
>
> We will not convert the First Amendment right of access to criminal judicial proceedings into a requirement that the government disclose information compiled during the exercise of a quintessential executive power – the investigation and prevention of terrorism. The dangers which we have catalogued above of making such release in this case provide ample evidence of the need to follow this course. To be sure, the Sixth Circuit recently held that the public has a constitutional right of access to INS deportation hearings involving the same INS detainees at issue in this case. *See Detroit Free Press; but see North Jersey Media Group* (finding no right of access). However, the Sixth Circuit applied *Richmond Newspapers* only after extensively examining the similarity between deportation proceedings and criminal trials, *Detroit Free Press*, 303 F.3d at 696-99, and noting the crucial distinction between "*investigatory* information" and "access to information relating to a governmental *adjudicative* process," *id.* at 699. Inasmuch as plaintiffs here request investigatory – not adjudicative – information, we find *Detroit Free Press* distinguishable. We therefore will not expand the First Amendment right of public access to require disclosure of information compiled during the government's investigation of terrorist acts. [331 F.3d at 933-934.]

Are you persuaded by the court's application of *Richmond Newspapers*? By its distinction between investigatory and adjudicative information in *Detroit Free Press*?

3. *Media Access to Terrorism Trials.* During the criminal prosecution of Zacarias Moussaoui for his alleged involvement in the September 11 terrorist attacks (see p. 315 in this Supplement), a consortium of media companies asserted common law and First Amendment rights of access to sealed records of pleadings, discovery materials, and oral arguments that included some information classified top secret. The court rejected the government's argument that the Classified Information Procedures Act (CIPA), 18 U.S.C. App. 3 §§1-16 (2000) (described at casebook pp. 880-888), could alone override a constitutional right of access. United States v. Moussaoui, 65 Fed. Appx. 881 (4th 2003), at 887-888. Instead, the court determined that the "interest of the public in the flow of information is protected by our exercising independent judgment concerning redactions" of materials from the records. *Id.* at 888. As for access to appellate proceedings, the court ordered bifurcated hearings. Arguments not involving the discussion of classified information would be open to the public, while others would be conducted in a sealed courtroom, followed by the prompt release of a redacted transcript. *Id.* at 890. The litigation is analyzed in Cameron Stracher, *Eyes Tied Shut: Litigating for Access Under CIPA in the Government's "War on Terror,"* 48 N.Y.L. Sch. L. Rev. 173 (2003).

In civil litigation growing out of the terrorist attacks on the World Trade Center in 2001, a court refused to order service of process on several individuals alleged to be in U.S. custody. Federal Insurance Co. v. Al Qaida, No. 03-Civ.-6978, 2004 U.S. Dist. LEXIS 10944 (S.D.N.Y , May 28, 2004). Responding to government concerns that returns of the service in court records would publically reveal the identity of the individuals, the court declared that it "defers to the judgment of the executive branch with respect to issues of national security . . . ." *Id.* at *5.

4. *The Case That Didn't Exist.* In what may (or may not) be an unprecedented development, a federal district court and court of appeals conducted secret hearings and issued secret rulings in a habeas corpus case that appeared on no public record. M.K.B. v. Warden, 540 U.S. 1213 (2004), concerned an Algerian waiter in south Florida who was detained by immigration authorities and questioned by the FBI. The case was discovered by a reporter only because of an appeals court clerk's docketing error. Despite arguments by news organizations that the First Amendment and a common law right of access required unsealing the records, the Supreme Court refused, without comment, to grant certiorari, following submission of a sealed brief by the Solicitor General. Thus, the government's theory of the case, like the fate of the detainee, is completely unknown, although we might assume that it included the arguments made

earlier in *North Jersey Media.* The story is reported in Linda Greenhouse, *News Groups Seek to Open Secret Case,* N.Y. Times, Jan. 4, 2004; Dan Christensen, *Plea for Openness,* Miami Daily Bus. Rev., Nov. 5, 2003.

F. PROTECTING "STATE SECRETS" IN CIVIL LITIGATION

Page 977. Add this material to Note 5.

The Supreme Court's landmark 1953 decision in United States v. Reynolds grew out of the crash in 1948 of a B-29 bomber. Surviving family members of three civilian engineers who perished brought suit for damages under the Federal Tort Claims Act. When they sought access through discovery to the official accident report, the Supreme Court accepted without question the Air Force's assertion that disclosure of the report would "seriously hamper[] national security." 345 U.S. at 5. The Court refused even to order in camera review of the report. When the report was declassified many years later, it was found to contain nothing that could apparently have been helpful to the nation's enemies, but instead to show pilot error, a failure to carry out special safety orders, and a history of maintenance problems with the B-29. In early 2003, surviving *Reynolds* plaintiffs and their heirs asked the Supreme Court to set aside its half-century-old ruling on grounds that the Court was defrauded by government misrepresentation of the contents of the report. *See* Petition for a Writ of Error *Coram Nobis* to Remedy Fraud Upon This Court, In re Herring, No. ___ (U.S. filed Feb. 26, 2003), *available at http://www.fas.org/sgp/jud/ reynoldspet.pdf* and *http://www.fas.org/sgp/jud/reynoldspetapp.pdf. See also* Timothy Lynch, *An Injustice Wrapped In a Pretense,* Wash. Post, June 22, 2003; David A. Churchill & Elaine J. Goldenberg, *Who Will Guard the Guardians? Revisiting the State Secrets Privilege of United States v. Reynolds,* 72 U.S.L.W. 2227 (2003). However, the Court denied without comment a motion for leave to file the petition for a writ of error *coram nobis* on June 23, 2003. In re Herring, 539 U.S. 940 (2003). Can you guess why the Court refused to reopen the case? Do you think the Court would have reacted differently to an effort to reopen its 1944 decision in Korematsu v. United States, 323 U.S. 214 (1944) (casebook p. 796), in light of the revelations of government fraud in that case 40 years after it was decided? See Korematsu v. United States, 584 F. Supp. 1406 (N.D. Cal. 1984) (excerpted at casebook pp. 805-807).

The *Reynolds* survivors subsequently filed a new action in the federal district court where the case had been heard 54 years earlier, asking for a ruling that the government had perpetrated a fraud on the court, and for damages. *See* Herring v. United States, No. 03-CV-5500-LDD, 2004 WL 2040272 (D. Pa. Sept. 10, 2004). The court found that the Air Force did not intend to "deliberately misrepresent the truth or commit a fraud on the court." *Id.* at *5. "[I]t is proper," the court said, "to defer on some level to governmental claims of privilege even for 'information that standing alone may seem harmless, but that together with other information poses a reasonable danger of divulging too much . . . .'" *Id.* (citations omitted). The court also declined to "draw firm conclusions as to military intelligence concerns in existence some fifty years ago." *Id.* at *9.

Do you think these developments will have any bearing on the way courts consider state secrets privilege claims in the future?

Page 977. Substitute the following material for Note 9.

Tenet v. Doe
United States Supreme Court, 2005
125 S. Ct. 1230

Chief Justice REHNQUIST delivered the opinion of the Court. . . . Respondents, a husband and wife who use the fictitious names John and Jane Doe, brought suit in the United States District Court for the Western District of Washington.[15] According to respondents, they were formerly citizens of a foreign country that at the time was considered to be an enemy of the United States, and John Doe was a high-ranking diplomat for the country. After respondents expressed interest in defecting to the United States, CIA agents persuaded them to remain at their posts and conduct espionage for the United States for a specified period of time, promising in return that the Government "would arrange for travel to the United States and ensure financial and personal security for life." After "carrying out their end of the bargain" by completing years of purportedly high-risk, valuable espionage services, respondents defected (under new names and false backgrounds) and became United States citizens, with the Government's help. The CIA . . . began providing financial assistance and personal security.

With the CIA's help, respondent John Doe obtained employment in the State of Washington. As his salary increased, the CIA decreased his living

---

15. The Government has neither confirmed nor denied any of respondents' allegations. We therefore describe the facts as asserted in respondents' second amended complaint. They are, of course, no more than allegations.

stipend until, at some point, he agreed to a discontinuation of benefits while he was working. Years later, in 1997, John Doe was laid off after a corporate merger. Because John Doe was unable to find new employment as a result of CIA restrictions on the type of jobs he could hold, respondents contacted the CIA for financial assistance. Denied such assistance by the CIA, they claim they are unable to properly provide for themselves. Thus, they are faced with the prospect of either returning to their home country (where they say they face extreme sanctions), or remaining in the United States in their present circumstances.

Respondents assert, among other things, that the CIA violated their procedural and substantive due process rights by denying them support and by failing to provide them with a fair internal process for reviewing their claims. They seek injunctive relief ordering the CIA to resume monthly financial support pending further agency review. They also request a declaratory judgment stating that the CIA failed to provide a constitutionally adequate review process, and detailing the minimal process the agency must provide. Finally, respondents seek a mandamus order requiring the CIA to adopt agency procedures, to give them fair review, and to provide them with security and financial assistance. . . .

A divided panel of the Court of Appeals for the Ninth Circuit . . . reasoned that *Totten* [v. United States, 92 U.S. 105 (1876)] posed no bar to reviewing some of respondents' claims and thus that the case could proceed to trial, subject to the Government's asserting the evidentiary state secrets privilege and the District Court's resolving that issue. 329 F.3d [1135 (2003)], at 1145-1155. . . . The Government sought review, and we granted certiorari.[4]

---

4. Preliminarily, we must address whether *Steel Co. v. Citizens for Better Environment*, 523 U.S. 83 (1998), prevents us from resolving this case based on the *Totten* issue. In *Steel Co.*, we adhered to the requirement that a court address questions pertaining to its or a lower court's jurisdiction before proceeding to the merits. 523 U.S., at 94-95. In the lower courts, in addition to relying on *Totten,* the Government argued that the Tucker Act, 28 U.S.C. §1491(a)(1), required that respondents' claims be brought in the Court of Federal Claims, rather than in the District Court. The District Court and the Court of Appeals rejected this argument, and the Government did not seek review on this question in its petition for certiorari.

We may assume for purposes of argument that this Tucker Act question is the kind of jurisdictional issue that *Steel Co.* directs must be resolved before addressing the merits of a claim. Nevertheless, application of the *Totten* rule of dismissal, like the abstention doctrine of *Younger v. Harris,* 401 U.S. 37 (1971), or the prudential standing doctrine, represents the sort of "threshold question" we have recognized

In *Totten,* the administrator of William A. Lloyd's estate brought suit against the United States to recover compensation for services that Lloyd allegedly rendered as a spy during the Civil War. Lloyd purportedly entered into a contract with President Lincoln in July 1861 to spy behind Confederate lines on troop placement and fort plans, for which he was to be paid $200 a month. The lower court had found that Lloyd performed on the contract but did not receive full compensation. After concluding with "no difficulty" that the President had the authority to bind the United States to contracts with secret agents, we observed that the very essence of the alleged contract between Lloyd and the Government was that it was secret, and had to remain so:

> "The service stipulated by the contract was a secret service; the information sought was to be obtained clandestinely, and was to be communicated privately; the employment and the service were to be equally concealed. Both employer and agent must have understood that the lips of the other were to be for ever sealed respecting the relation of either to the matter. This condition of the engagement was implied from the nature of the employment, and is implied in all secret employments of the government in time of war, or upon matters affecting our foreign relations, where a disclosure of the service might compromise or embarrass our government in its public duties, or endanger the person or injure the character of the agent." [92 U.S. at 106.]

Thus, we thought it entirely incompatible with the nature of such a contract that a former spy could bring suit to enforce it.

We think the Court of Appeals was quite wrong in holding that *Totten* does not require dismissal of respondents' claims. That court, and respondents here, reasoned first that *Totten* developed merely a contract rule, prohibiting breach-of-contract claims seeking to enforce the terms of espionage agreements but not barring claims based on due process or estoppel theories. In fact, *Totten* was not so limited: "[P]ublic policy forbids the maintenance of *any suit* in a court of justice, the trial of which

---

may be resolved before addressing jurisdiction. See *Ruhrgas AG v. Marathon Oil Co.,* 526 U.S. 574, 585 (1999) ("It is hardly novel for a federal court to choose among threshold grounds for denying audience to a case on the merits"). It would be inconsistent with the unique and categorical nature of the *Totten* bar – a rule designed not merely to defeat the asserted claims, but to preclude judicial inquiry – to first allow discovery or other proceedings in order to resolve the jurisdictional question. Thus, whether or not the Government was permitted to waive the Tucker Act question, we may dismiss respondents' cause of action on the ground that it is barred by *Totten.*

would inevitably lead to the disclosure of matters which the law itself regards as confidential." *Id.*, at 107 (emphasis added); see also *ibid.* ("The secrecy which such contracts impose precludes *any action* for their enforcement" (emphasis added).) No matter the clothing in which alleged spies dress their claims, *Totten* precludes judicial review in cases such as respondents' where success depends upon the existence of their secret espionage relationship with the Government.

Relying mainly on *United States v. Reynolds,* 345 U.S. 1 (1953), the Court of Appeals also claimed that *Totten* has been recast simply as an early expression of the evidentiary "state secrets" privilege, rather than a categorical bar to their claims. . . .

When invoking the "well established" state secrets privilege, we indeed looked to *Totten. Reynolds, supra,* at 7, n.11 (citing *Totten, supra,* at 107). But that in no way signaled our retreat from *Totten's* broader holding that lawsuits premised on alleged espionage agreements are altogether forbidden. Indeed, our opinion in *Reynolds* refutes this very suggestion: Citing *Totten* as a case "where the very subject matter of the action, a contract to perform espionage, was a matter of state secret," we declared that such a case was to be "dismissed *on the pleadings without ever reaching the question of evidence,* since it was so obvious that the action should never prevail over the privilege." 345 U.S., at 11, n.26 (emphasis added). . . .

Nor does *Webster v. Doe,* 486 U.S. 592 (1988), support respondents' claim. There, we held that §102(c) of the National Security Act of 1947, 61 Stat. 498, 50 U.S.C. §403(c), may not be read to exclude judicial review of the constitutional claims made by a former CIA employee for alleged discrimination. In reaching that conclusion, we noted the "'serious constitutional question' that would arise if a federal statute were construed to deny any judicial forum for a colorable constitutional claim." But there is an obvious difference, for purposes of *Totten,* between a suit brought by an acknowledged (though covert) employee of the CIA and one filed by an alleged former spy. Only in the latter scenario is *Totten's* core concern implicated: preventing the existence of the plaintiff's relationship with the Government from being revealed. That is why the CIA regularly entertains Title VII claims concerning the hiring and promotion of its employees, as we noted in *Webster,* yet *Totten* has long barred suits such as respondents'.

There is, in short, no basis for respondents' and the Court of Appeals' view that the *Totten* bar has been reduced to an example of the state secrets privilege. . . .

We adhere to *Totten.* The state secrets privilege and the more frequent use of *in camera* judicial proceedings simply cannot provide the absolute protection we found necessary in enunciating the *Totten* rule. The possibility that a suit may proceed and an espionage relationship may be revealed, if the state secrets privilege is found not to apply, is unacceptable: "Even a small chance that some court will order disclosure of a source's identity could well impair intelligence gathering and cause sources to 'close up like a clam.'" *CIA v. Sims,* 471 U.S. 159, 175 (1985). Forcing the Government to litigate these claims would also make it vulnerable to "graymail," *i.e.,* individual lawsuits brought to induce the CIA to settle a case (or prevent its filing) out of fear that any effort to litigate the action would reveal classified information that may undermine ongoing covert operations. And requiring the Government to invoke the privilege on a case-by-case basis risks the perception that it is either confirming or denying relationships with individual plaintiffs.

The judgment of the Court of Appeals is reversed.

It is so ordered.

[The concurring opinions of STEVENS, J., joined by GINSBURG, J., and of SCALIA, J., are omitted.]

NOTES AND QUESTIONS

1. *In re Totten and Its Progeny.* An increasing number of lower courts in recent years have invoked In re Totten to dismiss claims without trial. In 1987, for example, during the Iran-Iraq War, an Iraqi Mirage fighter fired two Exocet missiles at the U.S. frigate *Stark* in the Persian Gulf, killing 37 American sailors. Surviving family members filed suit for damages against several defense contractors, alleging that the Phalanx missile defense system on the ill-fated ship was defectively designed and manufactured. The court refused to allow the case to go forward, fearing that, discovery aside, a trial on the merits might lead to the inadvertent disclosure of state secrets.

> [T]he danger that witnesses might divulge some privileged material during cross-examination is great because the privileged and non-privileged material are inextricably linked. We are compelled to conclude that the trial of this case would inevitably lead to a significant risk that highly sensitive information concerning this defense system would be disclosed. [Bareford v. General Dynamics Corp., 973 F.2d 1138, 1144 (5th Cir. 1992).]

Other cases dismissed on the same grounds include Edmonds v. United States Dept. of Justice, 323 F. Supp. 2d 65 (D.D.C. 2004), *aff'd,* 2005 U.S.

App. LEXIS 8116 (D.C. Cir. May 6, 2005) (fired FBI whistleblower's suit for damages); Burnett v. Al Baraka Investment & Development Corp., 323 F. Supp. 2d 82 (D.D.C. 2004) (deposition in damage suit by 9/11 victims); Trulock v. Lee, 66 Fed. Appx. 472 (4th Cir. 2003) (defamation suit growing out of the Wen Ho Lee case); McDonnell Douglas Corp. v. United States, 323 F.3d 1006 (Fed. Cir. 2003) (defense contract dispute); Tilden v. Tenet, 140 F. Supp. 2d 623 (E.D. Va. 2000) (alleged gender discrimination by CIA); Guong v. United States, 860 F.2d 1063 (Fed. Cir. 1988) (employment contract with CIA); Fitzgerald v. Penthouse International, Ltd., 776 F.2d 1236 (4th Cir. 1985) (alleged Navy and CIA use of dolphins for military and intelligence purposes); Salisbury v. United States, 690 F.2d 966 (D.C. Cir. 1982) (NSA intercepts of electronic communications); Weinberger v. Catholic Action of Hawaii, 454 U.S. 139 (1981) (possible storage of nuclear weapons on Oahu); and Farnsworth Cannon, Inc. v. Grimes, 635 F.2d 268 (4th Cir. 1980) (Navy cancellation of a defense contract). Some of these cases and their significance are analyzed in Sean C. Flynn, Note, *The Totten Doctrine and Its Poisoned Progeny*, 25 Vt. L. Rev. 793 (2001).

2. *Grounds for Abstention?* Did the Tenet v. Doe Court refuse to hear the case because it lacked jurisdiction to decide it, or was its ruling based instead on prudential considerations? If the latter, can you say what those considerations were? Do you think it matters which theory the Court adopted?

3. *The State Secrets Alternative.* In In re United States, 872 F.2d 472, 477 (D.C. Cir. 1989), the court declared, "Dismissal of a suit, and the consequent denial of a forum without giving the plaintiff her day in court . . . is indeed draconian." It avoided outright dismissal, concluding that "an item-by-item determination of privilege will amply accommodate the Government's concerns. First, the information remains in the Government's custody. . . . Thirdly, the case will be tried to the bench, a circumstance that will reduce the threat of unauthorized disclosure of confidential material." *Id.* at 478.

In Tenet v. Doe, a Ninth Circuit panel ruled that "because the net result of refusing to adjudicate the Does' claims is to sacrifice their asserted constitutional interests to the security of the nation as a whole, both the government and the courts need to consider discretely, rather than by formula, whether this is a case in which there is simply no acceptable alternative to that sacrifice." Doe v. Tenet, 329 F.3d 1135, 1146 (9th Cir. 2003), *reh'g and reh'g en banc denied,* 353 F.3d 1141 (9th Cir. 2004). "*Totten* permits dismissal of cases in which it is asserted that the very subject matter is a state secret only *after* complying with the formalities and

Chapter 15. Public Access to National Security Information 389

court investigation requirements that have developed since *Totten* within the framework of the state secrets doctrine." *Id.* at 1149. Thus, the court directed the government to formally assert its state secrets privilege, leaving the court to test that assertion by conducting in camera and ex parte review of documents.

Why do you suppose the government in the principal case was so determined to avoid application of the procedures associated with the state secrets privilege? What did the Supreme Court have to say about the sacrifices of the plaintiffs in the name of national security?

4. *Secure Adjudication?* The Court of Appeals in the principal case said it would make "every effort" to find ways to adjudicate the plaintiffs' claims while protecting the national security, including in camera proceedings, sealing or redaction of records, requiring security clearances for court personnel and attorneys, protective orders, and a bench trial. *Id.* at 1148-1149, 1153. A number of courts have adopted similar protective tactics in cases involving sensitive information. *See, e.g.,* Loral Corp. v. McDonnell Douglas Corp., 558 F.2d 1130 (2d Cir. 1977) (special master); In re Under Seal, 945 F.2d 1285 (4th Cir. 1992) (protective orders); Halpern v. United States, 258 F.2d 36 (2d Cir. 1958) (secret trial). *See generally* Frank Askin, *Secret Justice and the Adversary System*, 18 Hastings Const. L.Q. 745 (1991); Stephen Dycus, *NEPA Secrets*, 2 N.Y.U. Envtl. L.J. 300 (1993). A special court, organized along the lines of the Foreign Intelligence Surveillance Court (casebook p. 682), might be created to deal with these difficult cases. Can you think of other ways to try such cases without undue risk? Would any of these resolutions raise separation of powers concerns?

5. *Scope of the Totten Doctrine?* The trial court in the principal case distinguished "purely contractual" claims, trial of which would be precluded by *Totten,* from constitutional claims based on procedural and substantive due process violations, which would not. Doe v. Tenet, 99 F. Supp. 2d 1284, 1289-1290 (W.D. Wash. 2000). *But see* Kielczynski v. United States Central Intelligence Agency, 128 F. Supp. 2d 151, 161-164 (E.D.N.Y. 2001), *aff'd sub nom.* Kielczynski v. Does 1-2, 56 Fed. Appx. 540 (2d Cir. 2003) (on similar facts, due process claim "cannot arise independent of plaintiff's contractual claims"). What importance, if any, did the Supreme Court attach to the distinction?

Will the precedential value of Tenet v. Doe be confined to factually similar disputes, that is, to those involving alleged "covert espionage agreements"? Or will the *Totten* doctrine of nonjusticiability be extended – even without the showing of state secrets required by *Reynolds* – to a wider range of cases involving allegedly sensitive information, as we have witnessed recently in lower court decisions? If so, what do you think remains of the state secrets privilege?